Image Brokers

Image Brokers

Visualizing World News
in the Age of Digital Circulation

Zeynep Devrim Gürsel

UNIVERSITY OF CALIFORNIA PRESS

University of California Press, one of the most distin-
guished university presses in the United States, enriches
lives around the world by advancing scholarship in the
humanities, social sciences, and natural sciences. Its
activities are supported by the UC Press Foundation and
by philanthropic contributions from individuals and
institutions. For more information, visit
www.ucpress.edu.

University of California Press
Oakland, California

Library of Congress Cataloging-in-Publication Data

Names: Gürsel, Zeynep Devrim, author.
Title: Image brokers : visualizing world news in the age
    of digital circulation / Zeynep Devrim Gürsel.
Description: Oakland, California : University of
    California Press, [2016] |
"2016 | Includes bibliographical references and index.
Identifiers: LCCN 2015047427| ISBN 9780520286368
    (cloth : alk. paper) | ISBN 9780520286375 (pbk. : alk.
    paper) | ISBN 9780520961616 (e)
Subjects: LCSH: Photojournalism—Social aspects. |
    Photographs—Marketing—Social aspects. | News
    agencies—Case studies.
Classification: LCC TR820 .G87 2016 | DDC 770—dc23
LC record available at http://lccn.loc.gov/2015047427

Manufactured in the United States of America

25 24 23 22 21 20 19 18 17 16
10 9 8 7 6 5 4 3 2 1

In keeping with a commitment to support environmen-
tally responsible and sustainable printing practices, UC
Press has printed this book on Natures Natural, a fiber
that contains 30 percent postconsumer waste and meets
the minimum requirements of ANSI/NISO Z39.48–1992
(R 1997) (*Permanence of Paper*).

For my mother, Nuran Gürsel
Anneciğim'e sevgiyle . . .

Contents

Introduction

Formative Fictions
and the Work of News Images

A messenger walked over to Jackie's cubicle and delivered a large envelope. Jackie, a photo editor at Global Views Inc., shoved it to a corner of her desk, not hiding her exasperation: "It's Friday afternoon. The magazines are about to close, and this photographer sends me film!" Jackie worked in the New York office of Global Views Inc. (GVI), a visual content provider. It was March 21, 2003, the day the United States and coalition forces launched a massive aerial assault on Baghdad, what the US military and media referred to as the "shock and awe" campaign. Emphatically Jackie pointed at the envelope full of rolls of film: "*Unprocessed* film!" Though they had arrived by express courier and had been shot only two days earlier, it was clear that these undeveloped rolls of photographs of protests in California against the imminent Iraq war could not keep pace with the digital news cycle. They were historical artifacts, obsolete even before being developed. Jackie wasn't going to call a photo editor at *Time* or *Newsweek* or any other magazine to tell them about these photographs. She wasn't going to try to sell them by making an argument that they provided a fresh angle on the state of a nation on the brink of war or that this photographer's personal vision illuminated something new about antiwar rallies. In fact, the rolls of film didn't even get processed before the following week, when they were digitized and immediately archived and linked to images of Americans protesting wars past, instantly becoming potential historical images for a future date. Before the end of the first day of the 2003 American war in Iraq, one thing was certain: this was a digital war.

Jackie is a professional image broker. Her work and that of other image brokers is the central topic of this book. Image brokers act as intermediaries for images through acts such as commissioning, evaluating, licensing, selling, editing, and negotiating. They may or may not be the producers or authors of images. Rather, image brokers are the people who move images or restrict their movement, thereby enabling or policing their availability to new audiences. For example, by not developing the film sent to her immediately, Jackie kept the images on the rolls of film out of circulation for several days. We can think of many different kinds of image brokers—from art dealers to those uploading videos onto YouTube; however, I focus on those who broker news images professionally. These individuals—the people making the decisions behind the photographs we encounter in the news—and the organizations in which they work, whether agencies, publications, or visual content providers, act as mediators for views of the world. Image brokers collectively frame our ways of seeing.[1]

This is a book about photography and journalism based on fieldwork conducted at a time when the form and the content of both were significantly unsettled. I look back to a period of major technological and professional transformation in the news media, one during which the very infrastructures of representation were changing radically.[2] The shift to digital photography and satellite communication on the cusp of the new millennium occurred with shocking rapidity; it allowed photographs to be transmitted from anywhere in the world and made available online almost instantly. Some news publications had printed digital images considered to have unique journalistic value as early as 1998, during the coverage of the war in Kosovo.[3] By early 2003, having the capability to transmit digitally was essential for a photographer to even get an assignment in Iraq. At least two of the older veteran combat photographers, who didn't yet feel entirely comfortable shooting digital images, had gone to Iraq accompanied by young assistants to provide them technical support. Perhaps the starkest monument marking the material changes in the photojournalism industry was a sign placed on the now-obsolete chute that for decades had been used to send rolls of film down to the photo lab at a major US newsmagazine. The sign read: "RIP (Rest in Peace)."

To observe the international photojournalism industry during this time of uncertainty, I conducted over two years of fieldwork at key nodal points of production, reproduction, distribution, and circulation in the industry's centers of power: New York and Paris. I use the term *nodal point* deliberately, because I sought out points of intersection among various actors and institutions, junctions in a system where choices had to be made such as which images to select, which publications to pitch them to, where to make them available, and what to assign to a specific photographer.[4] From 2003 to 2005 I conducted fieldwork in the newsroom of a large corporate "visual content" provider (chapter 2); the Paris headquarters of Agence France-Presse (chapter 3), a French wire service; and the editorial offices of two mainstream US newsmagazines (chapter 4). I also attended several key photography events, principal among them Barnstorm (chapter 5), a photography workshop for emerging photographers founded and run for many years by Eddie Adams, an American photojournalist who made several iconic images of the Vietnam war;[5] Visa Pour l'Image (chapter 6), the largest annual photojournalism festival, held in Perpignan, France; and several events organized by World Press Photo (chapter 7), an Amsterdam-based international platform for documentary photography that organizes the world's most prestigious annual photography competition and also offers seminars on photojournalism. I began this project because I believed that the manner in which the world was depicted photographically had significant consequences and was an increasingly central part of politics. As I watched what began as a war that had to be covered digitally become a digital war of images, I grew increasingly convinced of the political potential of visual journalism. It is far too important a practice not to be scrutinized and engaged analytically.

A TIME OF RAPID CHANGE

The beginning of the American war in Iraq was a moment when photojournalism as a domain was uncertain.[6] This uncertainty stemmed from digitalization. Whereas *digitization* has been defined as "the material process of converting analogue streams of information into digital bits," *digitalization* refers to the way many domains of social life, including journalism and military operations, are "restructured around digital communication and media infrastructures."[7]

Photojournalism was transformed not only by digital cameras, online distribution, and the digitization of analog archives, but by the significant institutional and cultural changes that digitalization enabled. The war in Iraq was not just a digital war, but also the first war in which visual content providers were important image brokers. For example, Global Views Inc., where Jackie worked as part of the news and editorial team, is not a news organization but rather a visual content provider—a corporation that produces licensable imagery and for whom news is just one of many product lines. Hence, regardless of their personal beliefs and motivations, Jackie and her GVI colleagues were producing and selling visual content, commodities that just happened to begin their lives as representations of news. They were not part of the press. Yet during the year that I observed daily work at GVI, I watched Jackie and the rest of the editorial team broker many of the most significant and widely publicized journalistic images of the early war in Iraq. As Jackie edited them for GVI's digital archive, they were transformed into visual content, available for purchase for a range of editorial and commercial uses. I researched photojournalism as the production and distribution process behind news images increasingly became part of the commodity chain behind visual content.

Another manifestation of digitalization was the change in the very nature of the "photojournalism community." Amateur digital images such as the Abu Ghraib photos and cell-phone pictures of the 2005 London bombings, rather than the work of professional photojournalists, were the key images that shaped public opinion. Moreover, images in the press, from photographs to cartoons, were not just illustrative of current events but often also newsworthy themselves or even factors in causing events, thereby playing a critical and highly controversial part in political and military action.[8]

In other words, I studied a very loose community of people collectively engaged in visual knowledge production at a time when the core technologies of their craft, the status of the images they produced and brokered, and their own professional standing amid a growing pool of amateurs and citizen journalists were all changing rapidly. As a result, the professional identity of image brokers, the very value of their expertise, and the ways in which images entered into journalistic circulation were hotly debated topics worldwide. Conducting fieldwork during tumultuous times yielded informants who were constantly questioning and negotiating what their professional world would look like, endlessly debating where their field of expertise began and ended or could be extended.[9] This was very fortunate for me as an anthropologist. As long as I was in the right places, there was no need to provoke conversations about the state of visual journalism; I could just listen in on conversations that were already taking place regularly.[10]

It was also a time when there was a very dominant news stóry that concerned a great many journalists. This book opened with Jackie at her desk a few hours after television news had shown footage of "shock and awe." However, the dominant news story in question was not just the American war in Iraq, which would in fact go on for almost nine years and was a significant event itself. Rather, the news story that dominated journalism and formed the backdrop of my fieldwork was neither the war in Iraq nor the war in Afghanistan but the "War on Terror." This was a significant journalistic dominant because this was not an actual war but a discursive construct that as an umbrella term provided semantic coherence for a whole range of activities, both within the United States and internationally. The "War on Terror" is not a single event or an actual war, then, but a war that was actualized, made real, in part by news coverage of it. Throughout this book when I refer to the War on Terror (without quotation marks from here on), it is this mediated idea of a military campaign against terrorism activities that I am referencing. The War on Terror is inseparable from its representations; it is always also a war of images.[11]

SEPTEMBER 11–13, 2001

Not only are the War on Terror and its representations inseparable, but September 11, 2001, is a key, if controversial, originary moment for both the United States's military operations in Afghanistan and Iraq, and the professional transition to digital photography. It is common knowledge that there had been terrorist attacks before, even at the same site—the 1993 bombing of the World Trade Center. The 9/11 attacks were events of a different scale. Similarly, the first digital camera system marketed to professional photojournalists was introduced by Kodak in 1991, but even a decade later, many in the professional world of photography still resisted using digital images because of what they perceived as inferior image quality. However, when the Federal Aviation Administration grounded all flights for three days following the attacks of September 11, 2001, the photojournalism industry was obliged to accept digital transmission regardless of whether the photographs being transmitted were analog or digitally produced images; images could *move* only digitally. The pace and scale of the digital circulation of news images changed dramatically. The standard of sending undeveloped rolls of film via air, and consequently predigital technologies and scales of circulation, were grounded along with the US airline industry. Only a year and a half later Jackie was astounded that a photographer shooting a time-sensitive topic such as antiwar protests could possibly send images he had shot in California to New York as film, let alone unprocessed film.

The inseparability of the War on Terror and its representations can also be attributed to the fact that the hijackers who crashed two planes into the World Trade Center launched an attack in the realm of the image world at the same time as their attack on the physical towers and the Pentagon. As has been noted at length elsewhere, this was an act of spectacular terrorism not just because of the images of fireballs and gaping buildings but also because, due to the delay between the two crashes, millions of spectators drawn to their screens to view the aftermath of one attack witnessed the second attack and eventually the crumbling of the towers on live television. Hence, the events inaugurated a new type of spectacular terrorism where a visual assault on spectators magnified the symbolic impact of the physical attack and prepared the way for visual revenge.[12] The intertwining of the War on Terror and the worldwide circulation of digital images was perhaps nowhere more evident than in the notorious photographs of American torture in Abu Ghraib prison. However, rather than approach these images as *the* images of the war, *Image Brokers* provides the context of a visual and political economy of images in which the Abu Ghraib images were merely some of the most controversial and widely circulated.[13]

Yet for all the claims about the future of visual news being radically transformed by digitalization and forever changed by the FAA ban, much of the work of the image brokers I observed was structured by ideologies about photojournalism and institutional protocols that had long histories. If I wanted to understand how news images functioned by analyzing image brokers, their work, and the contexts in which this work was performed, I couldn't simply begin with digital photojournalism. Therefore, this book is on one level an institutional narrative telling the story of technological innovation, a now-historical account focusing on a thin slice of time: the early twenty-first century and the beginning of the War on Terror. Yet on another level it is an attempt to address, through the work of contemporary image brokers, some questions about documentary images and their relationship to political imaginations that long predate digital journalism. Moreover, although this book builds on scholarship about images of suffering and atrocity, I did long-term fieldwork with image brokers to be able to analyze such images alongside frames of everyday life.[14] I agree with the critical importance of analyzing what philosopher Judith Butler calls "frames of war." Yet each time we focus our scholarship exclusively on conflict photography we risk narrowing our investigation in ways similar to how the US military manages visual access through embed positions. By not focusing exclusively on the coverage of war or of atrocities but rather on the everyday work of images brokers, I hope to render visible how framing mechanisms are always at work—with significant political ramifications—before, during, after, and alongside military action.[15]

I could not hope to understand how photographs moved and accrued value through their international circulation by studying any one institution or subject matter. So rather than analyze a single object of mass media in a bounded geographical setting—news images *of* Afghanistan or photographs *in* the French press—this book focuses on the networks through which international news images move. It highlights the structural limitations and possibilities that shape decisions about news images as well as their use in contemporary ways of worldmaking.

Not all photographs are news images. Certain photographs become news images through their circulation.[16] For example, a family photograph of former president of Iraq Saddam Hussein became a news image once it was removed from the album in his palace and circulated as a visual document of an opulent lifestyle, one that interested news publications could purchase for use.[17] To understand news images, we need to attend not only to the specific frame in question, with its particular aesthetic and material qualities, whether film or digital, but also to the context in which any particular photograph is produced and the route it travels to become news.[18] Though credited to a single individual when credit information is provided at all, a news image is produced by a network. After the photographer's initial framing of the shot, the final image encountered in a publication has passed in front of the eyes—and, until recently, through the hands—of several decision makers: image brokers and their institutions. The business of news images can be seen as a global industry: the raw material comes from many different locations, the labor is often mobile, and once packaged, the products can travel around the world as complete packages or as material to be repackaged as part of new assemblages. Although on some level this is a commodity chain similar to others, manufacturing news as a product line (journalistic "content"), it is also a genre of knowledge production, a mode of worldmaking through which we understand the times and places in which we live. Hence, news images are very particular products.

LOOKING AT THE WORLD PICTURE

When the photograph shown in figure 1 appeared in the *New York Times* on October 31, 2005, the caption read, "Taj Mian looked at his village, Gantar, from a Pakistani Army helicopter as he and about 50 of his neighbors were evacuated last week. He had never before left Gantar, which lies in the Allai Valley, one of the areas hit hardest by the earthquake on Oct. 8." The photograph, taken by American photographer Kate Brooks, is beautifully composed, highly evocative, and what photo editors would call a "very quiet" photograph, one that does not shout death or devastation. It is the type of image that rarely gets chosen for a daily news publication because it does not directly depict an event. It appeared in black and white on page 4 of the *New York Times* more than three weeks after other images accompanied the news of the earthquake on the front page. By then, the earthquake in Pakistan had become visually recognizable to news followers.

It is a remarkable photograph for being a news image about looking. What it shows is the act of someone looking at a landscape. It is a photograph that allows the viewer to look together with a villager named Taj Mian down at his village a few weeks after it had been destroyed by an earthquake. The image invites the viewer to put herself in the position of Taj Mian, to peek over his shoulder and see what he sees, to imagine how horrific it must be to look down on one's home and see it in ruins. And yet, if the information reported in the caption is accurate—that Taj Mian had never before left Gantar and therefore presumably never before been on a helicopter—then the blurred image of devastation outside the helicopter window is much more recognizable to the average *New York Times* reader than to the man in the photograph whose vantage point we are invited to share. The viewer is familiar with aerial shots of rubble if only from prior readings of newspapers, whereas Taj Mian is presumably adjusting his visual repertoire to comprehend a bird's-eye perspective. Perhaps he is comparing it with views he has seen from hills or mountains he has climbed.

If we read this news image with a critical eye, there can be no pretense that we are seeing *through* Taj Mian's eyes. We cannot see as he sees. Rather, the stark frame of the helicopter window underscores that, like Taj Mian, we are looking from a particular place. This photograph about looking shows how what we see is framed.[19] The camera is in a particular place. The photographer has found a way of getting herself on a particular helicopter. Her agent in New York has circulated the

FIGURE 1. A villager being evacuated after the October 8, 2005, earthquake in Pakistan. *New York Times*, October 31, 2005. Photograph by Kate Brooks/Polaris. Used by the kind permission of the photographer.

resulting images, and some have crossed the desk of a photo editor at the *New York Times*. The photo editor has, perhaps alone, likely in discussion with others, selected this frame to accompany the article alongside which the readers of the newspaper encountered it. Someone has made decisions about its layout and caption. The technologies of image production and transportation, questions of access, and all of the procedures of getting in place to take the photograph in the first place—critical issues left out of the frames of most journalistic images—are hinted at, if not represented, in this photograph.

I draw attention to the mythology of seeing through another's eyes and all it obscures to emphasize that the act of looking is itself a cultural construction. The ability to see, and to interpret what one sees, as someone else is a powerful fantasy. In 1974 anthropologist Clifford Geertz famously claimed that "the culture of a people is an ensemble of texts, themselves ensembles, which the anthropologist strains to read over the shoulders of those to whom they properly belong."[20] Geertz suggested that societies told themselves stories about themselves and that the anthropologist, too, could learn to read these stories or texts from the perspective of the native over whose shoulder he or she was reading. A little over a decade later another anthropologist, Vincent Crapanzano, convincingly argued that there is no understanding of the native from the native's point of view: "There is only the constructed understanding of the constructed native's constructed point of view."[21] In other words, Geertz's metaphor is a layering of fictions, and, in Crapanzano's reading of the text that can be read over the native's shoulder, it is a particularly problematic layering of fictions in which hierarchy and power relations are disturbingly occluded.[22]

It is precisely such power relations that Brooks's photograph offers us an opportunity to grasp. I am not claiming that this particular image was taken, brokered, or published with this particular interpretation or intention in mind. Rather, my reading of this digital image underscores the need to remain aware of the layering of decisions, and the complex layering of attitudes and differences that are behind news images. News images have limited journalistic and analytic value if they serve merely to reinforce stereotypes and provoke knee-jerk expressions of pity.[23] But if they provoke questions and provide an opening for acknowledging the possibility of difference without assuming a facile understanding of the other, then they can contribute to a nuanced type of knowledge production.

In the last chapter of his book *What Do Pictures Want?*, entitled "Showing Seeing," art historian W. J. T. Mitchell draws attention to "a paradox that can be formulated in a number of ways: that vision is itself invisible; that we cannot see what seeing is."[24] Mitchell then describes an assignment for his students that requires them to *show* seeing in some way, as if they were ethnographers "who come from, and are reporting back to, a society that has no concept of visual culture."[25] One might read *Image Brokers* as a manner of taking up the challenge posed by Mitchell's assignment. This book is about making visible the infrastructures of representation behind the work of image brokers: the institutions, processes, networks, and social relations behind news images. *Image Brokers* shows how decisions are made about what news audiences see.

News images are an important component of contemporary visual culture. They are complex cultural products. They circulate as representations of reality—photographs of the world as it is—but they are also aesthetic interpretations and commodities.[26] They are concrete, fixed things even when digital, yet they also mediate abstract ideas about people, places, and their identities.[27] News images perform political and cultural work in the world precisely because they are perceived as truthful, visual facts—facts both in the original sense of things that are made and in the sense of things that provide objective information about the world.[28] As I will explain at length, news images are "formative fictions," constructed representations that reflect current events yet simultaneously shape ways of imagining the world and political possibilities within it. As formative fictions, news images have consequences and play a role in worldmaking. For the large numbers who see them, news images are part of how we construct not just our points of view, but also our very understanding of the world at large in which we formulate our points of view. They influence us today and also have an impact on the way we will assimilate that which we have not yet seen but might see tomorrow.

The very first paragraph of Susan Sontag's 1977 book *On Photography* ends with her claiming that "[f]inally, the most grandiose result of the photographic enterprise is to give us the sense that we can hold the whole world in our heads—as an anthology of images."[29] The next paragraph begins, "To collect photographs is to collect the world." Sontag was specifically addressing material collections of photographs and the ramifications of photographs being tangible physical objects—unlike films and television images, which flicker ephemerally. Over twenty years before Sontag published what remains one of the most widely read texts on photography, philosopher Martin Heidegger claimed that "the fact that the world becomes picture at all is what distinguishes the essence of the modern age." He clarified precisely what he meant: "[W]orld picture, when understood essentially, does not mean a picture of the world but the world conceived and grasped as picture."[30] Heidegger is not speaking of photography or of specific pictures of the world but rather of the very idea that the world can be knowable as an object, grasped as a picture. Yet in highlighting the greatest possible stakes for photography—holding the whole world in our heads as an anthology of images—Sontag might as well be picking up Heidegger's idea of a world picture and asking how photographic technologies contributed to its development and shaped its contemporary forms. It is precisely this kind of a collecting the world in our heads to which news images contribute.

If we return to the image of Taj Mian looking out the helicopter window, it is fairly easy to reflect on the photographer's physical presence: she must have been somewhere behind him in the helicopter to make such an image. But to reflect on the photograph and its circulation as a news image, one would need to understand the work of the image brokers whose desks it had crossed and the editing practices of the specific institutions involved. One might begin by turning to a photograph like that on the cover of this book, titled "The World on a Wire," which also offers us the fiction of seeing through the eyes of someone—in this case, a photo editor at a wire service. Before her are hundreds of photographs of news events that she must edit and push out to subscribers around the world, each of whom is in turn making news for some kind of publication. My aim in what follows is not to present a Geertzian reading of the cultural texts before her in an effort to capture her point of view as a native in the photojournalism world, but rather to render visible precisely the processes by which international news images are constructed as cultural texts that shape journalists' and news consumers' own points of view. Visualizing world news is not merely about specific representations of particular news events but also about how events are made visible to the mind, how they are imagined by readers.

In the fall of 2001, I conducted research on American news readers' reactions to images of the attacks of September 11. Many people I interviewed conveyed their difficulty in recognizing the place captioned "ground zero" in news images as a location in New York City or even within the United States. They made comments such as "That looks like Bosnia," or Lebanon or, forebodingly, Iraq. News images they had seen in the past served as formative fictions, shaping their ideas of these distant places and producing a distance from the events in New York.[31] These readers' reactions convinced me that how a place or population is imaged affects what one can imagine happening in that place or to that people, hence shaping the sphere of political possibility. Put simply, news images matter.[32]

Professional image making is central to processes of worldmaking, a term I borrow from philosopher Nelson Goodman. Goodman emphasizes that representations are central to worldmaking and contribute to the *understanding* but also the *building* of realities in which we live.[33] Moreover, worldmaking involves both ideological and material structures, and it was both of these that I investigated in my research on the international community responsible for providing us with daily visual knowledge of the world beyond our immediate experience. My approach parallels that of journalism scholar Pablo Boczkowski, who underscores that "media innovation unfolds through the interrelated mutations in technology, in communication and in organization."[34] I concur entirely with his insistence that materiality matters in newsrooms.

This project began from a curiosity about photography as a form of journalism. It follows in the tradition of newsroom ethnographies, though my focus was always on images—specifically, ones visualizing international news.[35] Walter Lippman's 1922 classic *Public Opinion* begins with a chapter titled "The World Outside and the Pictures in Our Head," and this project began quite simply from a desire to think about how literal pictures of world news were constructed and how they got into the heads of journalists and readers.[36] I wanted to understand how news images were mobilized for various publics and the repercussions for both those photographed and the consumers of images. However, I began by asking who was behind the production of news images and soon discovered how little I knew.

One way to research documentary photography has been to consider the individuals involved in a photographic encounter. For example, an investigation might center on the subject or subjects in an image.[37] Another way it has been studied is by focusing on the photographers who take these images.[38] Yet another approach focuses on audiences' interpretations, how images affect viewers, often focusing on specific iconic photographs and their uptake by various publics.[39] Much compelling work in the field considers photography from several of these perspectives.[40] Visual studies scholar Ariella Azoulay has proposed "a new ontological political understanding of photography [which] takes into account all the participants in photographic acts—camera, photographer, subject and spectator—approaching the photograph (and its meaning) as an unintentional effect of the encounter between all of these."[41] And yet, at least in regards to news images, this list—camera, photographer, subject, and spectator—is not exhaustive. Those left out are the image brokers. In the end, although this book germinated from research on what work news images did in the world, it developed instead to address the work of image brokers behind these images' production and circulation—work that is typically invisible.

NEWS IMAGES AS FICTIONS

Documentary photographic representations were long believed to be beyond forgery. Soon after photography's invention and dizzying diffusion in the mid–nineteenth century, photographic realism and the expanding institution of journalism became integrally linked. The term *daguerreotype,* the name of one of the first photographic processes, came to mean any study that claimed absolute honesty. In the United States, there was widespread "typification of the newspaper as a daguerreotype of the social and natural world." In fact, the *New York Herald* newspaper was described in 1848 as "the daily daguerreotype of the heart and soul of the model republic."[42]

As my argument will make clear, I consider news images to be particularly rich *fictions* in the original sense of things that are fashioned or formed. Hence, the key issue for me is not whether news images are honest or manipulated: I begin from the premise that all representations are fictions in the sense that they are constructed.[43] The central question I am interested in is how certain fictions circulate with evidentiary or truth value while others do not.

In his book *Keywords,* cultural critic Raymond Williams informs us that the same Latin root *(fingere)* that produced the word *fiction* in the sense of "to fashion or form" also produced *feign,* underlining the ties between fiction, novels, and news.[44] It is precisely this persistence of the threat of deception that makes fiction an interesting category. According to Williams, the word *fiction* took on particular literary significance in the eighteenth century and became almost synonymous with *novel* in the nineteenth century as the genre flourished. Terms often beget their opposites, and it was the popularity of novels that led to the invention in the twentieth century of a category of *nonfiction,* initially used by libraries and those in the book trade. Against the rising tide of novels, Williams explains, this new category of nonfiction was "at times made equivalent to 'serious' reading; some public libraries will reserve or pay postage on any non-fiction but refuse these facilities for fiction."

In other words nonfiction, "serious reading," is institutionally subsidized and aided in its circulation in ways not extended to novels. Williams, moreover, discusses categories within fiction and highlights a distinction that was made between bad novels, which are *pure fictions,* and those that are *serious fictions,* earning this description by telling us *about real life.*[45]

What might such different kinds of fictions look like in journalism? A curious six-paragraph editor's note appeared in the *New York Times* on February 21, 2002, announcing that Michael Finkel, a freelancer under contract as a contributing writer to the newspaper's magazine, would not receive further assignments from the paper.[46] A year later Finkel's trespass was completely overshadowed by writer Jayson Blair's resignation from the same paper for falsifying information, and the following years brought so many examples that one might claim that this form of public acknowledgment of compromised journalism became a subgenre of the news.[47] However, at the time of its publication, the editor's note regarding Finkel's article "Is Youssouf Malé a Slave?" was still remarkable. What exactly had Finkel done to be so publicly chastised and fired?

Figure 2 shows the first two pages of the original article as they appeared in the *New York Times Magazine* on November 18, 2001. Below is an excerpt from the February 21, 2002, editor's note describing Finkel's use of fiction:

> The article was illustrated with photographs, including one taken by the writer, an uncaptioned full-page image of a youth. On Feb. 13, the writer, Michael Finkel, informed *The Times* that an official of Save the Children had contacted him to say that in investigating the case, the agency had located the boy in the picture, and that he was not Youssouf Malé [the boy supposedly described in the article]. The editors then questioned the writer and began to make their own inquiries to verify the article's account. The writer, a freelancer, then acknowledged that the boy in the article was a composite, a blend of several boys he interviewed, including one named Youssouf Malé and another, the boy in the picture, identified by Save the Children as Madou Traoré. Though the account was drawn from his reporting on the scene and from interviews with human rights workers, Mr. Finkel acknowledges, many facts were extrapolated from what he learned was *typical* of boys on such journeys, and *did not apply specifically to any single individual.*[48]

Had he not submitted the photograph for publication, Finkel might very well not have been caught. The rest of Finkel's article might have been read as "a serious fiction that tells us about real life" in Raymond Williams's formulation discussed above. Whereas the identification of

FIGURE 2. Opening two pages of an article by freelance journalist Michael Finkel. *New York Times Magazine*, November 18, 2001. Photograph by Michael Finkel.

Is Youssouf Malé A Slave?

The ambiguous journey of a
15-year-old from Mali who sold himself
into bondage. **By Michael Finkel**

The man came to the village on a moped. Youssouf Malé watched him. A man on a moped was unusual. When visitors did come to Nimbougou, deep in the hill country of southern Mali, they were almost always on foot, or on bicycle. The man on the moped had come to sell fabrics, the flower-patterned kind from which the women in Youssouf's village liked to sew dresses. Youssouf sat beneath a palm tree and watched.

He saw that the man was wearing blue jeans. The man was not that much older than Youssouf, and already he owned a pair of genuine blue jeans. Maybe three people in Youssouf's whole village owned blue jeans. And on this man's feet — my goodness. On this man's feet was something that Youssouf had never before seen. In Nimbougou, people either wore flip-flops or plastic sandals or nothing. What this man wore on his feet looked to Youssouf like a type of house. Like a miniature house, one for each foot. Two perfect, miniature houses, painted white, with curved walls that rose to the man's ankles, with a fence up the front of each one made of thin rope.

Youssouf asked the man about his shoes. He asked how he might be able to get money to have a pair of shoes like that — shoes that made you look important. The man asked Youssouf how old he was, and Youssouf said that he was 14 or 15, though he didn't know for sure. People in Nimbougou didn't keep track of such things. The man told Youssouf that he was old enough to get money. He said it was easy. All Youssouf had to do was leave Mali, where everybody was poor, and cross the southern border to the Ivory Coast, where everybody was rich. In the Ivory Coast, the man said, there were jobs and there was money, and Youssouf could find one of these jobs and earn some of this money, and then he could buy a pair of shoes.

The man said he knew many people who had done this. He said that he himself had gone to the Ivory Coast when he was younger and had started his own business with the money he'd brought home. What the man did not say, but what he surely knew, was that many people come home from the Ivory Coast with nothing. Less than nothing, actually. They come home broken from labor; they come home unable to afford even a loaf of bread; they come home with machete wounds that have turned the specific boy in the image by the wrong name was undeniably a false-hood. Due to its indexical nature, a photograph of a person is always a fact that applies "specifically to [a] single individual." For the *New York Times*, Finkel's portrait of Malé was pure fiction.

Finkel's trespass, as the editors explained in their lengthy note, lay in his "improper narrative techniques." The editor's note ended with this major national newspaper spelling out to its readers: "*The Times'* policies prohibit falsifying a news account or using fictional devices in factual material." The specific narrative technique that was considered a fictional device was the use of a composite character and the falsification of time sequences that it necessitated.

Were it not for the fact that both youths are part of a larger group that might be considered child slaves, the *New York Times* would not be interested in the particular stories of either Youssouf Malé or Madou Traoré. The story gets assigned because there is some indication that a particular condition may apply to a collective. Individuals are sought out for interviews as representatives of this collective, and, in fact, there is little room in traditional journalistic representations for particular facts about any noncelebrity individual that do not apply to a collective. The story is what is typical of boys on such journeys. However, at the moment of crafting a photographic representation, and perhaps only at this moment, the journalist must acknowledge the individual as a unique individual and not part of a composite.

Photographic representation pushes journalistic limits in a critical manner, and differently from writing. Susan Sontag draws attention to one peculiarity of authenticity in photographic representation: "A painting or drawing is judged a fake when it turns out not to be by the artist to whom it had been attributed. A photograph . . . is judged a fake when it turns out to be deceiving the viewer about the scene it purports to depict."[49] The particular form of authenticity in news images is due to a specific characteristic of photography: each body in a photograph is highly singular and indexed to a particular individual, and yet many of the bodies in news images—almost all except images of celebrities—circulate as stand-ins for large numbers of bodies sharing the same condition, bodies that are metonyms for social bodies. [50] News images offer points of departure for imagining collectives that are represented but not present in the frame itself. We read about "Iraqis" or "women" or "Brazilians" as composite subjects in journalism every day when clearly the information is extrapolated from specific individuals. These texts can be accompanied by images of identified or unidentified individuals, yet this practice seems ethically questionable only when a photographic image is explicitly incorrectly identified. Hence, news images circulate based on their ability to contribute to the visual construction of a social body. This is how they function as formative fictions. Yet, as the Finkel case demonstrates, we demand different levels of accuracy in the identification of indexed bodies.

INDEXED BODIES, REPRESENTED SOCIAL BODIES

At times a single face can come to represent an entire country's population. Perhaps the best-known example of this is Steve McCurry's famous "Afghan Girl" image that appeared on a 1985 cover of *National Geographic* (figure 3).

Figure 3 is an indexical representation of Sharbat Gula, an Afghan girl who moved to Pakistan as a refugee. Her image initially appeared with no identifying name; she was merely one of 2.4 million Afghan refugees, and one of 350 female students at a school mentioned in the article, as her persistent pseudonym—Afghan girl—reminds us. That particular photograph indexed only her, and yet it also represented Afghan refugees in general.

In April 2002, a year after the War on Terror had commenced and Afghanistan was once again in the news, Sharbat Gula once again appeared on the cover of *National Geographic.* Cutting-edge biometric technology was used to identify Gula's irises, and a particular thirty-year-old woman was confirmed to be *the* girl in the famous *National Geographic* photograph. This time Gula was clad in a burqa and held a copy of the portrait of her younger self (figure 4).

A caption tells us, "She had not been photographed since Steve McCurry made her portrait in 1984, and she only agreed to be photographed again—to appear unveiled, without her burqa—because her husband told her it would be proper." In this cover photograph, she serves as a human easel for the iconic image made of her eighteen years earlier.[51] The only visual individuality allowed to her by *National Geographic,* an entity stricter even than Gula's husband, is a reference back to their photographer's encounter with her. Hence, even when she is again on the cover of *National Geographic* for being *the specific individual* indexed in the earlier photograph, in the political climate of 2002 when liberating Afghan women was one of the alleged goals of the military operation in Afghanistan, she once again represents the category of Afghan women in general. To return to the language of the *New York Times*'s editor's note, her portrait is a representation of what is *typical* of

FIGURE 3. June 1985 cover of *National Geographic* magazine. Photograph by Steve McCurry.

Afghan women. Though the 2002 article rejoices that "[n]ow we can tell her story," we get only the bare details about her, and the writer underscores repeatedly that many share her story. McCurry's portrait of Sharbat Gula is merely an aggregate of what is portrayed as Afghanistan's timeless, almost naturalized, plight of despair and poverty. US military operations in Afghanistan that began in October 2001 are not mentioned in the story at all, even though it took the US invasion to render Afghanistan a cover-worthy topic once again.[52] Through such images, viewers learn to associate certain places and certain peoples with a certain "look." Formative fictions are not just aesthetic constructions;

FIGURE 4. April 2002 cover of *National Geographic* magazine. Photograph by Steve McCurry.

they also shape how viewers imagine certain categories of people and their political horizons.

I am interested in the conditions of the production and circulation by which photographs become news images; these are critical to understanding their meaning and force.[53] In fact, what makes news images particularly interesting as objects of study is that they are photographs that circulate as truths but can also accumulate value or jeopardize their credibility through their circulation. Unlike in the mid–nineteenth century, when the very word *daguerreotype* denoted an *honest* representation, today, at a time when digital image creation and editing tools are widely available and used by many different populations outside the press, photographic technologies are not assumed to guarantee veracity. Rather, it is the appearance of a photograph in a news publication of note, or its distribution by a well-known wire service, or its having been taken by a veteran photographer who has been recognized for his journalistic integrity that lends a photograph authority. This is not to say that reputable news publications, wire services, and photographers never have difficulties upholding journalistic ethics. [54] (Think back to the example of Michael Finkel's photograph.) Rather, the stakes are so high precisely because it is only by circulating through established circuits of news organizations that a digital photograph is conferred legitimacy. Photographs that become news images by circulating in journalistic institutions acquire truth value and become part of the practices of public worldmaking. These news images are formative fictions because they not only illustrate the world as it is but also powerfully influence political possibilities within it and establish parameters for how future events are imaged.

THE TEMPORALITY OF NEWS IMAGES

Much has been written about the peculiar temporality of photographic technologies and their complex relationships to notions of the past, present, and future.[55] The time of a photograph always exceeds the moment of its production. However, critical for the work of professional image brokers is the fact that photographs can be produced only now, yet their journalistic importance may very well not emerge until some time in the future. News images can accumulate force through repetition or circulation. They can accrue value because the context in which they are being reproduced has changed. The tremendous challenge facing image brokers as they make decisions today is accurately imagining themselves into the future and making sure that what the world will want to see tomorrow has been anticipated and captured visually today. As many individuals will remind us in the chapters to come, physically being there in time is critical to visual journalism. Image brokers need to ensure not only that they have covered the here and now, but that they will also have covered the *futurepast*.

News images move differently than other elements of journalism. When a photo editor at a wire service in Hong Kong validates an image, it can be pushed out to subscribers globally and used in publications from Argentina to Zimbabwe, with accompanying captions in dozens of different languages that can vary significantly. A photo agent might sell a freelancer's photographs to be published alongside articles on a variety of topics in a range of publications. Or a visual content provider will regularly sell historical images, highlighting the fact that news images can have complex temporalities. It is the visuality of news images that shapes the work of image brokers. This work happens in time, and time is often of the essence. In the chapters to come, we will encounter many moments when speed is critical and a key element in why one photograph circulates and another doesn't. Therefore, the pace of work is quick. Until very recently, the time it took to move a photograph from one part of the world to another, whether by plane or over telephone wires, was a key factor in determining what kind of a news image it could become and the types of news it might visualize. It is only since the digital circulation of photographs that their transmission is, at least potentially, instantaneous.

These temporal peculiarities of news images pose a methodological challenge to any researcher attempting to study the force of photographs, for it is hard to predict when a particular image might become formative, let alone trying to find ways to observe its influence.[56] Yet because image brokers need to plan for the futurepast, their decision processes often involve explicitly anticipating how a photograph might accrue value in the future. Which is to say, I didn't ask people which images they thought had been important but instead listened to how they imagined a photograph might become significant in the future. My fieldwork was shaped around sites where image brokers regularly made and remade decisions against the background of an uncertain future. Importantly, I was able to find sites where image brokers had to verbalize the rationale for their decisions to others. Therefore, at the nodal points of photojournalism where I worked, brokers' communicating their decisions and selections during the brokering of news images rendered acts of imagination observable to an anthropologist.[57] This also allowed me to study image brokering in real time and within the intense time pressures of the newsroom rather than relying on retrospective interviews. This was particularly important as I studied image brokers trying to visualize a war that everyone said would soon be over before it began and yet continues in many ways as this book goes to print over a decade later. *Image Brokers* is a study of visual worldmaking at a particularly tumultuous time in newsrooms and the world beyond them.

AN ANTHROPOLOGY OF WORLDMAKING

I was drawn to international photojournalism partly because I entered the discipline of anthropology at the cusp of the twenty-first century, a moment when much intellectual energy was focused on investigating emerging forms of globalization. Photojournalism provided the opportunity to study an industry that had always been built on global interconnections. Moreover, I was interested in systems of description—such as journalism, photography, and the discipline of anthropology—that provide views of the world and make the world knowable.[58] No doubt part of this interest stemmed from my daily consumption of news at a time when geographies that had seem bounded and discrete were becoming visibly porous—most dramatically perhaps with the 1989 tearing down of the wall in Berlin. It was also a time when there was much discussion of globalization and transnational flows, as well as migration.

By the time I began my training, anthropologists had for some time been critiquing the reductionist approach of mapping certain cultures onto bounded places inhabited by essentialized peoples.[59] Many anthropologists, influenced by critical work in the field of geography, turned to space as a juncture of analysis hitherto more or less taken for granted.[60] In other words, when anthropologists designed projects, the typical question asked had always been, and to some extent remains, "*Where* will you do this research?"—presuming that the answer to the question "Would a particular *place* be the best way to organize research on this particular problem?" is always yes. Yet this was a time of significant movements—of people, goods, and capital—and anthropologists were grappling with how best to do research at different scales in a world in flux. Because ethnographic fieldwork is cultural anthropology's primary method, shifting how the discipline thought of objects of study also meant reevaluating the changing contours of the "field" in which anthropological investigation was conducted and the political stakes in the boundaries used to delimit field sites. The power relations inherent in anthropological research that had been discussed in relation to the politics of representation were also discussed in relation to conceptually and practically locating fieldwork itself. Anthropologists Akhil Gupta and James Ferguson argued for foregrounding "the spatial distribution of hierarchical power relations . . . to better understand the processes whereby a space achieves a distinctive *identity* as a place."[61] They predicted that an anthropology that no longer took for granted that its objects of study were anchored in space would need "to pay particular attention to the way spaces and places are made, imagined, contested, and enforced."[62] Studying the practices of image brokers and networks traveled by news images seemed one way to answer the challenge raised by Gupta and Ferguson. After all, news images produce knowledge about specific places and have the potential to circulate widely.

Gupta and Ferguson mentioned mass media as "the clearest challenge to orthodox notions of culture"—the traditional assumed isomorphism of culture, territory, and a people—and the following years did see greater attention to ethnographies of media as exemplified by the 2002 publication of two important anthologies, *The Anthropology of Media* and *Media Worlds: Anthropology on New Terrain.*[63] Yet there was still little in the way of anthropological work on mass-media representations responsible for global-scale place-making. Anthropological research on news and journalism was still relatively novel.[64] Today, anthropologists are certainly more critical of place as a stable self-explanatory concept, but few have taken on place-making itself as a primary object of analysis. How certain places get identified as violent, repressed, exotic while others are perceived as peaceful, democratic, or belonging to the heartland remains an important question for the discipline and is relevant to those interested not just in journalism but also in international politics, humanitarian aid, and tourism—to name just a few domains in which how places are made is directly linked to what types of resources and people circulate through them. We might think of this as an anthropology of worldmaking at both global and more local scales.

Ferguson cautions us against becoming too enamored of novelty and moving too quickly to adapt new methodological approaches to new objects of study. Instead, he suggests we think not of objects of study but rather of relations as constitutive of objects or of objects as a set of practices. Ferguson's own example of this is his book of essays that addresses "Africa" not as a vast empirical territory, historical civilization, or culture region, but rather as a category "through which a world is structured."[65] Or, as he puts it eloquently elsewhere, "to grasp the work that is done by this category 'Africa,' we must understand it as a position within an encompassing set of relations—what I have called a 'place-in-the-world.'"[66] My own work on image brokers is precisely about how such "places in the world" come to exist, partly through the production and circulation of images of certain places that get validated as real. It is not merely that representations feed preconceptions, which in turn shape social realities, but that when images of "Africa" appear in a journalistic context and are captioned as such, they endorse "Africa" as a category that really exists in the world and reify certain sets of relations while making others seem implausible or less significant.

Image Brokers is an attempt to understand the mechanics, infrastructures, and ideologies of worldmaking by which categories such as "Africa" and "the Middle East," "refugee camps" and "the Muslim world," are constructed, validated, and circulated. Ferguson defines *the world* as "a more encompassing categorical system within which countries and geographical regions have their 'places,' with 'place' understood as both a location in space and a rank in a system of social categories (as in the expression 'knowing your place')."[67] Photojournalism, then, is a form of worldmaking that involves making the places (in both senses of the term) of various categories of people visible.

A MATERIALIST ACCOUNT OF REPRESENTATION

In the course of designing this research I benefited from the intellectually rigorous conversations that accompany moments of disciplinary turmoil not only in anthropology but also among scholars of visual art and film. While some anthropologists were grappling with how to move the discipline from one that studied cultures in place to one that could investigate cultures of place making, art historians and film scholars were trying to take a more cultural approach to studying visual objects and practices. This book was written during a time when there was a flurry of name changes in academic departments that had hitherto been called "Art History" or "Film Studies" as many scholars debated concepts like visual studies and visual culture. All of which is to say that I found myself in the sometimes terrifying but also tremendously liberating position of studying the upheaval of the photojournalism industry from academic fields that were themselves in transition. Hence, from the beginning this research not only was influenced by interdisciplinary scholarship but also benefited from heated debates about shifting methodologies, "indisciplined" scholarship, and new objects of study both in anthropology and in visual fields.[68]

In fact, once I had decided to study practices of visualizing world news through the brokering of news images, the most concrete methodological advice I found was in art historian John Tagg's call for a materialist account of representation:

We must not allow ourselves the expedient of imagining something existing before representation by which we may conveniently explain the representation away. Where we must start is with concrete material activity and what it produces. We must begin to analyze the real representational practices that go on in a society and the concrete institutions and apparatuses within which they take place. We must plot the network of material, political and ideological constraints which bear on these institutions and constitute their conditions of existence and operation. We must describe the function of specific individuals within them and their production of operatives to staff them. We must establish the material social and symbolic contexts in which they are sited, in which they operate and in which they intervene.[69]

How does a network made up of image brokers and their work processes constitute a field of research? If my informants were engaged in visual worldmaking, by which I mean the production of visual knowledge about elsewheres, I, whom they liked to call "our anthropologist," was engaged in fieldmaking.

In an excellent article on journalism as fieldwork, Jennifer Hasty suggests that perhaps one reason that the practices of news media have been relatively understudied by anthropologists is that "for an anthropologist schooled in controversies over the politics of ethnographic representation, there is something profoundly uncomfortable about the practices of news media, something vaguely reflective of our own discursive practices, more purely politicized but also more politically compromised than anthropology."[70] Hasty goes on provocatively to investigate how journalistic practices "disrupt and undermine anthropological notions of fieldwork, political engagement and professional ethics." Said differently, it can be awkward as an anthropologist who will ultimately be crafting a representation to ask informants in journalistic contexts to explain the choices behind their daily work of producing and circulating representations.

My experience has been that such conversations tend to make people very self-conscious and moreover, when conducted outside the fast-paced environment of the newsroom, yield information that isn't always accurately descriptive. I conducted formal interviews only toward the end of my stint at each field site once I observed that I could learn a lot more by watching image brokers in action for extended periods of time rather than asking them to articulate why they made certain choices. Much of the talk around news images in editorial rooms, at agencies, or at festivals is precisely about verbalizing what is represented and specifying why a particular representation is significant, troubling, valuable, sellable or not. By observing image brokers in moments of selection at critical sites, I could regularly observe the discourses of image brokering and its decision processes without having to awkwardly intervene and ask informants to translate visual practices into verbal ones for me, the anthropologist. The visual dimension of news images meant that the politics of representation was not just something that I as the anthropologist was thinking about when writing these chapters back at home, but very much part of what I was observing and hearing during my daily fieldwork. Furthermore, these were not abstract ideas or debates but conversations about very concrete, specific images. In fact, in many of my field sites people would discuss a particular photograph with a hard copy of it in their hands even when, as it almost always was, the photograph was a printout of a digital original.[71]

As the following chapters will make clear, image brokers share a large professional purpose having to do with producing, circulating, preserving, and evaluating news images. Many share beliefs about the power of the news image to incite political change. Yet they also have diverse biographical backgrounds, artistic and journalistic identities, and myriad professional roles in a wide array of sites, many with their own very different institutional cultures, such as those of Global Views Inc. (GVI) and Agence France-Presse (AFP), respectively. Some brokers were known to each other; others were not. There was no single culture, certainly not one bound by place; instead one might speak of a dispersed community and shared cultures.[72] News images are produced and brokered in multiple ways and travel all sort of circuits, some sequentially, others simultaneously. This was not a neat exchange network where a photographer's image would get filtered through a wire service to a magazine, win an award, and then be used to train a younger generation of photographers. Sometimes this happened, but more often it did not. Rather, images and image brokers of all kinds—photographers, editors, and agents—circulate and influence each other and yet remain geographically, institutionally, and culturally situated. In order to comprehend how news images were produced and circulated, I had to study many institutions and sites; there was no predetermined field.

The fieldwork behind *Image Brokers* was multi-sited, but not because it required that I live in two different cities—New York and Paris—or because there were several side trips of consequence to upstate New York, Perpignan, Istanbul, and Amsterdam. Perhaps precisely because the term *multi-sited ethnography* emerged at the same moment that anthropologists were challenged by the global scale of certain research topics, it was most often taken to mean "ethnography conducted in more than one geographical place." However, this is a narrow interpretation of George Marcus's proposal for multi-sited ethnography, one that ignores the need to think theoretically about anthropological locations as argued for so cogently by Gupta and Ferguson. Rather, the research behind *Image Brokers* at nodal points in the photojournalism industry is multi-sited according to Marcus's definition that multi-sited research be "designed around chains, paths, threads, conjunctions, or juxtapositions of locations in which the ethnographer establishes some form of literal, physical presence, with an explicit, posited logic of association or connection among sites that in fact defines the argument of the ethnography."[73]

That I was engaged in fieldmaking meant that I was designing research so that I might see the myriad ways in which a news image might get produced or circulated. I developed a sense of what the larger network might look like by watching how image brokers worked within and across different sorts of institutions. A core element of fieldmaking was constantly renegotiating where to be situated and whom to follow but also understanding the significance of the holes in the emerging fieldwork. For example, I never did extensive fieldwork at a major daily publication, but at several of my sites they were constantly evoked as clients or influences and hence played a role in how brokers evaluated images. A key task of fieldmaking, then, was keeping track of such holes in fieldwork and also continually paying attention to what unified the field if not an ethnos, institution, or geography. One decision I made very intentionally was to study powerful players in the world of photojournalism: one of the major wire services, distributing, at the time, over a thousand images every day to global subscribers; the newsmagazines mentioned to me by photographers around the world as where they looked for a sense of how the photographers they aspired to emulate were covering world events; World Press Photo, an institution that explicitly aims to play a global role in the world of press photography. I also chose to study photojournalism's geographic centers of power—which, at the time, meant New York and Paris—because one of the promises of digitalization was that it would render such geographic centers obsolete. To a certain extent, it has. However, in other respects, certain ways of framing the world still dominate over others.[74] I wanted to understand how certain news images became dominant visual narratives about particular places.

THE QUESTION OF ACCESS

The question of access is central to both journalism and anthropology. In a seminal 1969 article, Laura Nader urged anthropologists to "study up" in their own society, which in Nader's case was the United States. Nader was arguing that the colonizer be investigated as well as the colonized. Yet, although a citation of her article has become shorthand for studies of elites or the workings of power, she herself insists, "We aren't dealing with an either/or proposition; we need to simply realize when it is useful or crucial in terms of the problem to extend the domain of study up, down or sideways."[75] When Nader's original article was published, many worried that getting access as a participant observer would be impossible. Nader soberly replied that "anthropologists have had problems of access everywhere they have gone; solving such problems of access is part of what constitutes 'making rapport.'"[76]

Indeed, my first access obstacle had precisely to do with how a potential informant conceived of anthropology. Initially I planned to gain entry into the world of photojournalism by applying for a summer internship with a very well known documentary photographer. The obvious advantage of this plan was that he was visiting my academic institution and had been a longtime collaborator with the director of the Human Rights Center on my campus. Compared with the chances of getting a photo editor in New York to answer my cold call or reply to an email, I thought the chances of being selected for an unpaid summer internship were fairly good. Not so. I needn't even bother applying, I was told. As soon as I approached him and introduced myself as a cultural anthropologist interested in the world of photojournalism, he voiced his displeasure with such philosophical approaches and said he was only interested in working with forensic anthropologists who were interested in actually doing something about human rights violations in the world, not just talking. In other words, I think, for him, any project that did not take the truth claims of photography as a given or had any interest in investigating photography itself as a practice of knowledge production as well as documentation was merely a solipsistic engagement in pointless debates around crises of representation. He denied me access not because he didn't want me to have access to the world of image brokers but because his foregone conclusion was that my research was pointless since I was powerless to intervene in the human rights violations he was documenting.

He was right about my powerlessness, though it was precisely because of researchers' power over research subjects in the past that my research had to be authorized by my institution's institutional review board (IRB). During my fieldwork I had to use two different types of tools—an IRB-approved consent form and a corporate nondisclosure agreement (NDA)—intended to protect against the vulnerabilities created by the relationship between someone granted access and the person or entity giving the access. An NDA is a legal contract that creates a confidential agreement between two parties to protect against non-public business information being released to any third parties. Like all anthropology projects that receive funding from a university or external research-funding agency, my fieldwork had to be approved by an IRB, and I had to get each of my subjects to sign an informed consent form. The IRB process was intended to protect my "human subjects" from any harm my research might cause them.[77]

However, Global Views Inc., a corporation, also thought it needed protection against me. One Saturday when I was watching the photo editor on duty, as I had on many other Saturdays, Portia Friedman, the vice president of global marketing at GVI, arrived to see Michael Strong, the vice president of the news and editorial division, who was the person who had authorized my access to GVI, and who was also in that Saturday. While walking around the floor before their meeting, Michael briefly introduced me to Portia, a decidedly more corporate personality than anyone on the news and editorial team. After Portia left, Michael came over and sheepishly asked me to leave, saying that Portia had insisted I needed to sign an NDA in order to continue my research. To the best of my knowledge this is not standard practice in anthropology.[78] I was bewildered.

Part of the problem was that I was only a few months into fieldwork and didn't know what information I would need and therefore had no way of knowing whether I could commit to not disclosing it. GVI's NDA contained the following text:

> In connection with granting permission to you to observe activities at GVI in connection to your academic work, GVI has disclosed or may disclose to you business information, technical information and/or ideas (including, without limitation, computer programs, technical drawings, algorithms, know-how, formulas, processes, ideas, inventions (whether patentable or not), schematics and other technical, business, financial, customer and product development plans, forecasts, strategies and information identified to you by GVI to be confidential or proprietary in nature) ("Proprietary Information").

It was this expansive type of proprietary information that the NDA would have me hold in confidence and not use. How could I possibly write a book? I emailed the template NDA from GVI to the legal counsel for the regents of my university. Eventually it was a senior administrative analyst for the Office of Sponsored Projects who wrote back. She had gone through the NDA and translated it into understandable English for me. Her primary concern was that I not give GVI the impression that it had any influence over my results. Second, she had a very concrete suggestion for how to narrow what was covered by "proprietary information":

> "Proprietary Information" should be so identified in writing, either by marking such material, or if given orally or visually, the material should be reduced to writing and identified as "Proprietary Information" within 30 days and provided to you. This is a protection for you, because you will know what material cannot be included in any dissertation, presentation, publication or other form of public dissemination.

While I appreciated this administrator's taking the time and writing to me with detailed suggestions, I could not imagine how I would ever get any meaningful fieldwork done if I was constantly asking the photo editors to "reduce to writing" all the information they were giving me. I also imagined Portia Friedman stamping every page of my field notebook "proprietary information." The administrator had also advised me to show the agreement to a lawyer before signing it.

I found a group in New York called Volunteer Lawyers for the Arts to help. They had never worked with an anthropologist before, but since I intended to write a book, for their purposes I could be thought of as a nonfiction writer. Luckily, the university administrator had also suggested limiting the NDA to a number of years. Together with the volunteer lawyer I redrafted the NDA to include a single sentence that proved to be key to solving my issue of access: "The terms of this Agreement will remain in effect for a period of three years from the date hereof." I took the NDA back to Michael Strong, who was happy to sign, was disappointed at the very thought that it might take me so long to produce publishable material, and added that none of what I had learned would have any novelty value by then.[79]

The IRB was concerned about the safety of my human subjects but didn't care about my corporate subjects. The university was concerned that my scholarship remain independent and free of corporate influence, and GVI was concerned that I not trade the information I gathered at GVI for profit elsewhere. Yet for GVI, information was valuable only so long as it had novelty value, but unlike in anthropology, the shelf life of information in the corporate world is very short. So it was through the negotiations over GVI's NDA that I learned the strategic value of slow ethnography. Furthermore, the NDA helped spread my reputation as someone trustworthy with information, or at least contractually bound by multiple entities to anonymity—a reputation that proved very useful in eventually helping me secure access to the editorial offices of competing newsmagazines. If, as Nader claims, all anthropological fieldwork, from the Pacific Islands to the Arctic, involves getting access and building rapport, perhaps nondisclosure agreements don't necessarily introduce anything new to anthropology (other than a need for more legal expertise or assistance) but rather are merely one more ritual or practice of boundary setting that the anthropologist has to negotiate.

Eventually, I got access to one of the largest visual content providers, a wire service, several news publications, and my other field sites by circulating with image brokers. Some took me along to private parties during photography festivals; others got busy executives to return my calls and hear out my request to observe their editorial process; yet others allowed me to join their circle of friends, who were often also part of the professional world behind news images. Sherry Ortner talks about the possibility of gathering data at "ethnographic supplements" while trying to get more direct access to her desired object of study, Hollywood. In her case such supplements included screening Q&As, festivals, expositions, and similar events. I also attended festivals and training sessions. Among the many I could have gone to I chose those that were mentioned as sites where images and photographers accrued most value. I asked photographers which photo festivals were most prestigious or inspirational or where they had met people who had had significant influence on their own work, where showing their portfolio had led to a breakthrough for them; and then I, too, circulated in those spaces, always with informants.

As all anthropologists do, I also tried to understand how various individuals and institutions were viewed so that I could evaluate how my associating with one person or institution would be viewed by another. For example, GVI was powerful but despised by many veterans of photojournalism, both photographers and editors, because the company was seen as one of the wealthy newcomers who had bought up many smaller players and corporatized the culture of the industry. Yet GVI had also managed to hire several respected editors. Hanging around the GVI booth at Visa Pour L'Image was good for helping me understand how new photographers tried to show their work to editors at GVI because it was the glossiest booth, and it got me lots of introductions to young photographers who might then feel comfortable letting me watch as they showed their portfolio to a magazine or newspaper editor in a different context. Yet more-established editors and photographers were wary of my association with GVI until it became clear that I had the trust of the individuals at GVI who were respected despite their corporate affiliation. I needed to get along with the corporate types at GVI well enough to keep my access, but it was important that I highlight my distance publicly so as not to fuel rumors that I was some sort of corporate spy for GVI. I tried contacting an editor at *Newsworld* for months in vain. However, when one saw me at a show for a new photographer represented by GVI and both the photographer and a respected editor at GVI introduced me to her, she was finally willing to meet with me. In short, the fundamentals of how I got access were possibly quite similar to methods used by other anthropologists studying very different kinds of sites; they were certainly very familiar to documentary photographers working on long-term projects.

"YOU GUYS ARE A LOT LIKE US"

A young photographer flatly pointed out to me one evening, "You guys [i.e., anthropologists] are a lot like us." Staying at work with people until midnight; sitting with them through hours of waiting for an editor higher up to make a decision, of waiting to hear from a photographer in a conflict zone, or of waiting for something to happen on a Saturday morning with "no news"; traveling with people to photo festivals and awards ceremonies about which they may have conflicting emotions—all of these activities brought me closer to my counterparts: the image brokers and photojournalists of global news. The friendships were perhaps lopsided—I was writing a book about them—but interestingly, many of my counterparts were themselves well versed in such relationships.

At Barnstorm, a photography workshop for young photographers, the parallels between photojournalism and fieldwork were particularly apparent as I took notes during a group conversation during which the young photographers reported back on how their work had gone that day. One young photographer tried to explain her disappointment with the group of male buddies she had been assigned to shoot: "They were trying to hit on me. They were trying to impress me more than they were trying to relax and be subjects. It was pretty awkward." Another confessed that he had really hit it off with his subject, which had made it much harder to photograph him. The team leader for the blue team, which I had joined, seemed to address participant observation explicitly: "You cannot be completely innocent. Anytime you show up with a camera, you affect the situation." No, the young photographer shouldn't have been in the car when the thirteen-year-old she was profiling drove it, even if she thought it built rapport. "Put some emotional distance between you and the subject," the team leader advised. An experienced photographer and senior photo editor at a major daily publication, the team leader reminded the photographers of the debates over Ross Baughman's 1977 photos of Rhodesian security forces brutalizing antigovernment forces they had captured. Baughman had ridden with a cavalry unit, Grey's Scouts, fighting against the country's transition to black majority rule. He went on to win a Pulitzer Prize for the images, leading some to apologize for his not having been awarded the Robert Capa Gold Medal Award upon speculation that the images may have been staged. However, the team leader at Barnstorm, when telling his group about the images almost thirty years later, neither defended nor condemned Baughman but rather used the reference to couch a discussion about the ethics of distance and to pass on a touchstone from the professional canon to a new generation.

Some were chastised for not getting to know their subject well enough, others reprimanded for not having any distance: "Ask them, 'What would you do if I wasn't here?'"; "When you see interaction, you have to watch it, and watch it through the viewfinder so that the moment's not gone by the time you shoot. You need to *really* watch people to know what he's going to do. Tune your radar. That happens by watching over time." The team leader reminded them that their job was to not let any details skip by them: "Ask about his tattoo." He might as well have been coaching my multi-sited ethnography of image brokers when he stressed, "Try to anticipate moments so that you're in the right position for it when it happens." I use the term *informant* to describe my subjects in this project precisely because inadvertently they often coached me methodologically while also informing me about the worlds of visual knowledge production.

RENDERING WORK VISIBLE

One could very well ask what was at stake for my informants. Why did they put up with my presence in their workplace for days, weeks, or even months, particularly at a time when their own job security was increasingly precarious? One indication of the tumultuous times in contemporary journalism is that almost none of the people I write about in this book have the jobs they had when we met. Moreover, many of the publications mentioned are either exclusively or predominantly digital or have ceased to exist altogether. Visual knowledge production is often dismissed as an auxiliary or less critical form of journalism. As I will discuss in the following chapter, Barbie Zelizer has cogently documented that this has also been true historically.[80] Today, images are everywhere and powerful, and yet the actual work of image brokers is often overlooked within both journalism and scholarship about news practices.[81] I believe my informants collaborated with me in part out of frustration with the press's own textual bias and the regular erasure of their labor. In several of my field sites I overheard an informant proudly (and occasionally jokingly) brag to a colleague from the text side or the sales side, "We have our own anthropologist."

Ironically, per my IRB protocol, in order to protect them as human subjects, I'm barred from crediting their ideas by name in this study of their often invisible labor. Many of their opinions appear in the pages to follow, but with the exception of a few public institutions or comments made in publicly available documents or recordings, I have used pseudonyms throughout the book. I did not attempt to mask Agence France-Presse since it is the only global wire service headquartered in Paris, but I did use pseudonyms for individual image brokers. In the chapters on Barnstorm, Visa Pour l'Image, and World Press Photo, I used pseudonyms for informants I'd followed there, informants I'd mentioned in other chapters, or groups of photographers I met in workshops. I used the real names of people who spoke publicly. Using pseudonyms was a precondition for my fieldwork to comply with protocols of the IRB that approved this research. However, perhaps it has also served this research. In the chapters that follow, the focus is on the types of decisions made by many different image brokers rather than on the idiosyncrasies of particular individuals. Many of the image brokers I learned from were powerful personalities, and I have attempted to give readers a sense of them as individuals. In the end, however, the goal is not to vilify or glorify specific individuals but rather to get us to think about the practices of image brokering in the age of digital circulation.

One significant consequence of maintaining my informants' anonymity is that there are almost no photographs in the fieldwork chapters that follow, despite this being a book about the labor behind images. In order to publish a photograph I would need to credit it, and that would then disclose not just the photographer but also the news publication, visual content provider, or wire service and the specific image brokers involved. Moreover, much of what I discuss concerns photographs that get edited out and therefore never get published. I regret the lack of photographs, since it was the affective, political, and aesthetic power of news images that drew me to photojournalism in the first place, and I would have liked to feature some of the work I encountered during my fieldwork that I admired or that shaped my sense of the potential of photojournalism. Images can also be seductive, and I have found that it is easier to keep the focus on framing mechanisms and thus on the work of image brokers when readers are not looking at a particular frame. Luckily, today there are many venues, both online and offline, from books to exhibits to blogs, in which interested readers can encounter the work of talented contemporary documentary photographers.

Finally, a word about how this book is written. Much of this book is about the talk around and about news images. Hence, there are many conversation fragments and direct quotes in the chapters that follow. I recorded most of my formal interviews on tape and also recorded much of what I overheard in real time in a notebook as I shadowed various image brokers at work. I have attempted to give thick descriptions of each of my field sites. Partly, I have done this because I recognize that I had access to these sites at a critical historical moment both in terms of world events and in the photojournalism industry. These descriptions may be of interest to some readers even if my analysis in this book can touch only on certain aspects. I have tried to write this book for a few different audiences. Readers who want to see the intellectual architecture of the book and learn more about the scholarly conversations of which I see this work as part can find them laid out in the endnotes.

WHAT'S AHEAD

The fieldwork chapters that follow are separated into two parts that attempt to answer two different yet related questions: How are news images produced and circulated? What else is produced in the production of news images?[82]

Part One: Image-Making

How Are News Images Produced and Circulated?

Behind every iconic photograph is a rarely told story of circulation.[83] For news images to have the tremendous affective and political impact that scholars often highlight and analyze, they first need to get to one or several publications. Chapter 1, "What Precedes the Digital News Image?" traces the history of photographs on the move and the development of an international community whose business it is to broker the images that document the news. There are two important stories here: the well-known one about the rise of photojournalism, and the less-known one about the rise of distribution networks and changes in infrastructures of representation. This history of the business of image brokering focuses specifically on the significant restructuring of the industry as a result of digitalization—most importantly, the rise of the visual content provider. The chapter ends with a sales meeting and conversations about merchandising strategy in which I analyze the challenges of news images as a product line.

The following three chapters show the ways news images are produced and circulated, beginning from a site farthest from the news viewer and ending in the newsroom of a major American news publication that also has an important global presence. Chapter 2, "Global Views Inc.: Visualizing Politics, from Shock and Awe to the Fall of Saddam Hussein," takes the reader into the news and editorial division of GVI, one of the largest corporate visual content providers, on the brink of the US invasion of Iraq in 2003. The chapter follows the fast-paced work of Jackie and other image brokers as they negotiate with photographers and publications. News images represent a mere fraction of the profits generated by selling visual content such as celebrity portraiture and stock photos. GVI produces no journalistic text and is not a news organization; hence this chapter looks at image brokers working to produce and circulate images as content for other professionals.

Agence France-Presse (AFP), the subject of chapter 3, "Agence France-Presse: What Is the Dominant?" is on the other hand one of the three largest global news agencies and produces original reportage—both text and photographs and video—for news publications worldwide that subscribe to what is often still referred to as its "wire feed" despite the obsolescence of this medium. Prior to digitalization, AFP would rarely compete with a photo agency because its job was defined as producing fast photographs that summarized an event in a single shot.

This chapter analyzes the politics of visualizing world news in the daily practices of image brokers at AFP's Paris headquarters shortly after the circulation of the infamous photographs of Abu Ghraib prison and amid the first wave of beheading images as Iraq was once again declared a sovereign nation. Specifically, it addresses crises of visualization amid the emergence of new kinds of image brokers who digitally circulate their own representations.

Chapter 4, "Newsworld: Everyday Practices of Editing the World," turns to editorial decisions concerning photography at major US newsmagazines at a moment when the magazines still had sizable print subscribers and robust newsstand sales while online versions were just beginning to emerge. Everyday work at *Newsworld* is about brokering images and reproducing worldviews. This chapter tracks the role played by the imagined reader in how the world section of the magazine is illustrated. Image brokers at *Newsworld* have to negotiate not only with their colleagues, who are writers and text editors, but also with those in the art department, who negotiate presentation issues such as layout and design. This chapter follows the many layers of negotiation behind a finished issue and highlights the rule of text even in news publications known for visual journalism that serve as points of references for photographers all over the world. Moreover, it discusses the challenges of visualizing a war when that war is no longer new.

Part Two: Worldmaking

What Else Is Produced in the Production of News Images?

The second part of this book attends to the ideologies that inform the practices of image brokers and the community of photojournalism. I look at three different platforms that celebrate photojournalism: Barnstorm, Visa Pour l'Image, and World Press Photo. Specifically, I am interested in how ideologies are being reproduced for new generations at a time of great uncertainty about the future.

Chapter 5, "Barnstorm: An American Rite of Passage," takes the reader to Barnstorm, an annual workshop in upstate New York that brings together a hundred young photographers and many of the US image industry's "heavies." Barnstorm 2003 was the last led by its charismatic founder, photojournalist Eddie Adams, before his death. It was also the first Barnstorm after the beginning of the American war in Iraq and brought together many photographers who had taken iconic war photographs—from Joe Rosenthal and his *Flag Raising at Iwo Jima* to Nick Ut and his image of a young Kim Phuc and her napalm burns. We listen in as the next generation of the profession is initiated, is taught to honor its ancestors, and celebrates "the best job in the world."

Chapter 6, "Visa Pour l'Image: Personal Visions and Amateur Documents," takes the reader to Perpignan, the world's largest celebration of photojournalism, held in southern France in early autumn. Visa Pour l'Image celebrates artistic and subjective vision simultaneously with the belief in an indisputable visual truth-telling. Importantly, it is also a celebration of mobility, both of images and of photographers. Based on Visa 2003 and 2004, this chapter looks at photojournalism's confrontation with the amateur threat posed by the rise of citizen journalism and the abuse photographs taken by US soldiers at Abu Ghraib, which are considered by many to be the definitive images of the war in Iraq. I focus on the production of ideals of authorship and individual ways of seeing, "personal vision," alongside the differentiation between local photographers who document specific news events and cosmopolitan photojournalists praised for their masterful storytelling.

Chapter 7, "World Press Photo: Developing World Photography," turns to World Press Photo, an international platform for photography that runs the world's most international and prestigious annual competition in photojournalism. In addition to fieldwork conducted at World Press Photo's Awards Days 2004 and the fiftieth anniversary in 2005, this chapter is based on my experience at the Masterclass, offered in Amsterdam for a highly selective group of a dozen international photographers, and at a seminar for young photojournalists in a developing country held over the course of three years. World Press Photo contributes to a discourse of photography as a universal storytelling medium while also offering seminars in "developing" countries aimed at training promising photographers in how to see in very particular ways. The world in World Press Photo is not one that is given but one that can be developed through photography.

I end by looking at the landscape of photojournalism today. The possible futures of journalism worldwide are even less certain now than they were at the beginning of this research. What happens to image brokering and photojournalism in the age of social media and increased digitalization? The conclusion addresses the paradox that while there has been an increasing demand for imagery, the work of photojournalists and professional image brokers has been significantly devalued. I look at visual worldmaking practices through four recent news events—the 2013 Gezi protests in Turkey, the January 2015 attacks on the French satirical magazine *Charlie Hebdo,* World Press Photo's decision to revoke a prize in its 2015 Contemporary Issues category, and the earthquake in Nepal in April 2015. Only one thing about the future of journalism is clear: it must be visual.

PART ONE

Image-Making

How Are News Images Produced and Circulated?

What kind of a product is a news image? How are news images sold and distributed? Who determines their value? The chapters in part 1 address image-making and provide thick descriptions of visual knowledge production, showing the institutions and brokers that lie behind the two-dimensional images of the world that appear before news followers every day.[1] At the turn of the twenty-first century, digital technologies radically changed the photojournalism industry, affecting both the labor practices behind images and the players involved. I begin, therefore, by situating the photojournalism industry historically to understand how news images came to be the commodities they are today. Then I turn to three nodal points of production and distribution to track how value is created as news images are brokered. News images are sold at all three institutions—GVI, AFP, and *Newsworld*—whether as visual content, as part of a news feed to which publications can subscribe, or as part of a news publication sold directly to readers. Like moments in any production process, acts of image brokering are necessarily simultaneously moments of cultural and political interpretations.[2]

However, news images are not just commodities.[3] Stuart Hall contends that "[t]hose people who work in the media are producing, reproducing and transforming the field of ideological representation itself. They stand in a different relationship to ideology in general from others who are producing and reproducing the world of material commodities—which are, nevertheless, also inscribed by ideology."[4] In my fieldwork among image brokers, reception was not just an activity occurring once a finished product was available to be consumed by a public. Rather, there were many moments of reception by various subjects at each of the nodal points of decision making prior to the publication of the image for a reader of news. Moments of selection within production processes are necessarily simultaneously moments of reception and production—moments in which, in Hall's terms, the field of ideological representation is being reproduced and transformed. Paying attention to moments of selection renders visible the way in which the production and distribution of news images are simultaneous processes of producing representations and reproducing particular worldviews.

In photography circles, the term *decisive moment* is associated with French photographer Henri Cartier-Bresson, whose 1951 book *Images à la sauvette* had the title *The Decisive Moment* when it appeared in English in 1952. Bresson claimed that in photography there is a single fraction of a second that is the creative moment. The photographer's craft, according to Bresson, lies in recognizing a visually stunning moment and releasing the shutter to capture it. A close look at the production and circulation of news images demonstrates that in the process of some photographs becoming news images, there are many decisive moments—only some of which have to do with the instincts of the photographer. I am mainly concerned with these other decisive moments, and throughout *Image Brokers* I aim to extend the temporality of the decisive moment to include the many moments of selection that both precede and follow the act of releasing the shutter button.

At the moment when a photo editor is consuming dozens of photographs to choose one to accompany an article, she is imagining not only the event or population being represented, but also the reaction of the viewer, the collective identity of her publication, and how competitors will visualize the event. Put differently, the work of image brokers comprises everyday practices of imagination. Image brokers' decisions at each stage of the production and circulation of news images are informed by how they imagine various communities—both those represented in the photographs and those in which the photographs will circulate, which may be the same community but often are not. Images and imagined communities, then, are produced, are reproduced, and circulate together.[5]

The historical backdrop of the research presented here is critical. Not only do these chapters look at production processes at a moment of transition in the photojournalism industry, but what is being visualized in many of the images being brokered is world news dominated by the War on Terror.[6] Especially in the early years of the War on Terror, brokers were faced with multiple crises of visualization. They struggled to keep readers interested in a war that lasted much longer than anticipated. Moreover, they had to illustrate a war in which the imagery that would justify the war or visualize some form of resolution—whether weapons of mass destruction in Iraq or the corpse of Osama bin Laden—never materialized. Against the backdrop of the War on Terror, this investigation of image-making renders visible both the processes of producing news images and the practices of worldmaking that are intertwined with them.

1

What Precedes the Digital News Image?

Not all photographs are news images. How, then, do certain photographs become news images? Through circulating in particular types of networks.[1] Another way of asking this question is, What precedes the news image?[2] This chapter provides a particular history of news photography, focusing on how images move and acquire value.[3] The objective is not to repeat the already well-told story of what preceded the news image historically, not what illustrated the news *before* photography, but rather to highlight the infrastructures that enable the production and circulation of news images as a form of visual worldmaking. This chapter lays out the professional history against which my fieldwork was conducted. In the second half of the chapter I describe, especially for readers not familiar with the photojournalism industry, the processes by which a photograph can generate revenue as a news image and the different attitudes toward profit that I encountered.[4]

In the summer of 1839, at a meeting of the French Academy of Sciences in Paris, the process behind daguerreotypes, named after their inventor, Louise Daguerre, was declared "a free gift to the world."[5] As visual culture theorist Ariella Azoulay reminds us, "the same country that bestowed the Declaration of the Rights of Man and the Citizen, France, also nationalized the invention of photography in order to bequeath it, without delay, to all of humanity."[6] That the invention was a free gift to the world is significant because the French government gave Daguerre an annuity in exchange for the patent, thereby acknowledging the commercial value of photography. Mathematician, physician, and Deputy of the Pyrénées-Orientales François Arago details this arrangement in his report to the French Chamber of Deputies, stressing that Daguerre himself had not wanted a lump sum "which might give the contract the character of a sale." Arago continued, "It would not be the same with a pension. It is with a pension that you reward the soldier, crippled on the field of honor, the official, grown gray at his post," and thus, he reminded the deputies, they had honored the families of major scholars after their deaths.[7] From the beginning, then, photographic technology was considered to be a discovery of global interest and something whose significance lay beyond its financial profitability.

Despite the attention attracted by daguerreotypes for accurately capturing the world in unprecedented detail, these photographs were singular material objects. As such, they had limited circulation, and this kept daguerreotypes from reaching large audiences and becoming news images. The excitement generated was about the process and promise of photography, not about any one particularly significant photograph. Almost as soon as the process was made public, photography studios were established in urban centers worldwide. Soon both studios and peripatetic photographers began producing and circulating images of distant elsewheres. By the 1850s a new feverish excitement accompanied the first reproduction of photographs. As historian Rebecca Solnit puts it, "Photographic reproduction would make the world's images and experiences as available as the Manchester mills made cotton."[8] Through the development of photographic reproduction a new, though long anticipated, object emerged: the photograph as commodity. Views of the world could be mass-produced and sold. For larger and larger audiences, the world became a visually knowable object, and photography emerged as a visual medium of worldmaking.

Photographic history can and has been told as a series of technological innovations or a collection of great names or iconic images.[9] Yet each technological innovation had to be preceded by a shift in imagination, and each great photographer rose to eminence in a particular sociohistorical context in which certain images could be deemed iconic. The telling of what precedes the digital news image in this chapter underscores the entangled political, technological, and commercial histories behind changes in visual worldmaking. What follows is a very brief history of photojournalism from its beginning to the early twenty-first century and the years immediately preceding my fieldwork, which saw the transition from analog to digital technologies. Just as significant as the invention of photographic reproduction technologies in the 1850s, the transition to digital reproductions allowed images to circulate in completely new ways and through a whole new range of networks, giving rise to new kinds of image brokers. Digital technologies changed the photojournalism industry radically, yet the elements central to a genealogy of digital news images—contingencies and confluences of capital, technology, transportation, political power, and military campaigns—are the same ones that were central to many other moments of innovation in the history of photographic representation. We are still witnessing radical shifts in the use of new visual forms in journalism and debating their respective commercial and journalistic value. I anticipate that these same elements will be central to future developments.

A SHORT HISTORY OF PHOTOJOURNALISM

It may be hard for the twenty-first-century reader to imagine journalism without pictures, and yet newspaper photography began only in the early 1880s.[10] By some accounts, the first mechanically reproduced photograph in a newspaper, "A Scene in Shanty Town," appeared in the *New York Daily Graphic* in 1880.[11] The *Leipziger Illustrierte* published photographs using a similar technique in 1882. Because of the excessive costs of halftones, photographs were not used regularly but rather employed for special occasions, such as coronations. It was not until 1896 that the *New York Times* used illustrations regularly in a weekend supplement, indicating that the visual was a key aspect of journalism. Eventually "picture newspapers" began to appear. The first few "picture newspapers," such as the *Illustrated London News* (1890) and the *Daily Mirror* (founded in 1904, the first newspaper to be entirely illustrated by photographs), were published in England. *Excelsior* in Paris and the *Daily Graphic* in New York soon followed.

The story of transportation is central to developments in photojournalism in terms of both how images circulated and the obstacles faced by traveling photographers. After all, photographic negatives, even once they were easily reproducible, were material objects. For news images to have the tremendous affective and political impact that scholars often highlight and analyze, they needed first to get to one or several publications. Hence, from the time news publications began using photographs, photographic agencies played an important role in their distribution. By 1894 a photographic agency, the Illustrated Journals Photographic Supply Company of Ludgate Hill, guaranteed images from any part of the United Kingdom in twenty-four hours, thus tying the visual news cycle to the means of transportation available.[12] Many more photo agencies sprang up between 1904 and the beginning of World War I. Soon, people developed ways of transmitting images over telegraph wires and radio waves so as not to have to wait for trains and ships, substituting communication networks for transportation networks. In 1907 the first picture was sent by telegraph from Paris to the *Daily Mirror* in London. The *New York Times* sponsored a daredevil flight from Albany to New York in 1910, and its crash resulted in the paper's first front-page news photograph. In other words, this story of a first involved a medium of communication, a newspaper, sponsoring a feat of transportation, knowing that whether it succeeded or failed, it would make for a newsworthy photograph. The flight resulted in a representation that then circulated as both news and an implicit advertisement for the publication.

By 1913, pictures were being transmitted across the Atlantic by cable, though costs were practically prohibitive, making few international events worthy of news images.[13] In other words, what had to precede a news image was an intricate distribution network dependent on new kinds of publications, commercial interests, and transportation methods of the day.

The invention of two German portable cameras, the Leica and the Ermanox, and the first flash bulb, both in 1925, changed photojournalism significantly by allowing photographers to master time and space, since they could now shoot around the clock in a far greater range of places. Photographers in the late 1920s could take their cameras to places where older, bulkier cameras had been prohibitive obstacles, such as the front lines of war, and they could cover events that took place outside of daylight hours.

Parallel to these technological developments, politics in Europe prompted many accomplished Jewish photographers (such as Alfred Eisenstaedt and Erich Salomon) to immigrate to America. Other emigrants from Europe brought the picture magazine as a media genre to the United States. These photographers contributed their significant talents to the formation of the popular picture magazines *Life* and *Look* (both founded in 1936). These American magazines were following earlier examples set by European magazines such as the *Münchner Illustrierte Zeitung* (1928), the *Berliner Illustrierte Zeitung* (1928–29), and the

French *Vu* (1928), all of which contributed to the rise of the photo essay and the development of a less posed style of photojournalism. New genres and styles of documentary photography emerged as the range of image-able events expanded and the number of publications for those images grew. On both sides of the Atlantic, the 1930s and 1940s were a golden age of documentary photography. Photography acquired the status of an influential medium in which to tell the most important stories of the day. For example, in the United States the Farm Security Administration established a photography program to document rural poverty, and the Photo League brought together established and novice photographers to document life on the streets in the various working-class neighborhoods of New York City.[14]

Photography's popularity, however, did not mean it was immediately accorded journalistic value. Communications scholar Barbie Zelizer convincingly argues that "[t]he '30s constituted journalism's last stand before photography became an integrated part of the field."[15] In 1933, AT&T sold its picture telegraphy service to Associated Press, which launched AP Wirephoto in 1935, resulting in a far greater distribution network for images.[16] AP Wirephoto had the ability to transmit images across very large distances and thus was able to cover the news across extensive geographies, a capability that became particularly important for covering a war that took place on four continents and several different fronts. The AP Wirephoto meant images could travel as quickly and as far as text, which in turn could travel at the speed of electricity. By 1938 pictures constituted almost 40 percent of the content in American dailies.[17] Moreover, photography was one way newspapers could compete with radio for the public's attention.

Yet at the same time that the technology of the AP Wirephoto made photographs ubiquitous, there was much resistance to photography on the part of many journalists. Zelizer draws attention to how this resistance was expressed by "denouncing, disembodying, and deflating" photography. Those who were threatened by this alternative language argued that pictures would encroach upon the written word, the source of journalistic dignity. Even if pictures were accepted as a commercial necessity for a publication, many separated the photographer from the photographs, and some argued that any reporter with a camera could produce news images, denying the specific craft of the photojournalist. Finally, photography was embraced for its denotative dimension, which "positioned photography as a craft in need of the intervention of journalists, making it adjunct to that of word-journalism."[18] In other words, photographs were begrudgingly integrated into journalism on the assumption that they needed to be accompanied by text. Zelizer concludes that the way in which the photographic image was accepted—reluctantly and in spite of opposition—affected the way it was understood by journalists. (As the reader will see in the chapters to come, almost a century later the struggle between text and image is still a core element in the culture of many news organizations.)

Susan Sontag argues that it is natural that photojournalism came into its own during wartime in the early 1940s, because "war was and still is the most picturesque and irresistible news."[19] Whether or not one agrees with this argument about the seductive and picturesque nature of war photography, World War II was certainly a global news story and hence promised opportunities for images to gain great journalistic and commercial value. While the portable Leica and flash meant that World War II could be represented in ways that would have been unimaginable during World War I in terms of subject matter, significant changes also took place in the world behind the taking, selling, transmitting, and mobilizing of news images.

As wire services were able to provide the news publications that subscribed to them with images of most major news events all over the globe soon after the event, photographs gained more and more importance as a way of telling a journalistic story. Increasingly, important news stories had to be visualized. As news publications valued photography more, small, independent photography agencies and cooperatives were established that advocated for photographers and their right to greater editorial autonomy. Since wire services would cover all the major news, freelance photographers represented by small agencies could be sent on assignment for more in-depth coverage of stories a publication deemed particularly significant. Visual journalism increasingly became a way for publications to differentiate themselves from competitors. As a result, photography was more valued.

It was in this context that the legendary photo agency Magnum was established in the spring of 1947, with the hopes of granting photographers more agency. From its inception it was to be a cooperative of photographers, with small offices in Paris and New York. Photographer Robert Capa, most famous for his photograph of the Republican soldier being shot in the Spanish Civil War and already a well-known photojournalist at the time, presided over Magnum's creation at a meeting in the restaurant of the Museum of Modern Art in New York. It was to be a cooperative so that photographers would have the freedom to shoot what they wanted rather than being dictated to by magazine editors. Rather than an agency that primarily served publications, this was to be an agency whose priority was its photographer members. The basic idea was that a publication would send a photographer somewhere and pay for the expenses, but after having shot the requisite stories, the photographer could shoot for himself on the side. By keeping in close touch with the agency in Paris and New York, the photographer would know what the magazines were interested in, and the agency offices would know at all times what their photographers were shooting so they could find new assignments or place portions of the photographer's work in multiple publications.[20] The major change would be that photographers rather than the publications that commissioned them would hold the copyright to their work.[21]

Eventually, however, despite the enthusiasm for photography, the picture magazines established in the 1920s and '30s did not survive the appearance of television: *Life* and *Look* both ceased regular weekly publication in the early 1970s, and almost no picture magazines in Europe survived into the 1980s. Ever since there has been chronic talk of the death of photojournalism.[22] Nonetheless photojournalism continued with new firsts such as the appearance of color photographs in dailies in the 1970s and the regular appearance of photographs in newspapers that had hitherto relied mostly on illustrations such as the *Wall Street Journal* and *Le Monde*.

Infrastructures of Representation

The introduction of digital technologies in the production, distribution, and publication of images, however, was not just a new technological advancement. Rather, it completely transformed the industry in many ways. Anthropologist Paul Rabinow draws attention to the fact that "from time to time, and always in time, new forms emerge that catalyze previously existing actors, things, temporalities, or spatialities into a new mode of existence, a new assemblage, one that makes things work in a different manner and produces and instantiates new capacities."[23] The introduction and widespread dissemination of digital imaging technologies was a new form of this sort and restructured the manner in which news photographs are produced and circulated. In other words, this was a change that challenged and eventually restructured the very infrastructure of representation. This infrastructure includes all of the practices, institutions, and technologies that make news images as worldmaking representations possible. Focusing on infrastructures allows one to see beyond individual spectacles and address the particular politics of events that are themselves also about visual representations.[24]

In order fully to appreciate the significant shifts that digital technologies brought about in the infrastructure of photographic representation, it is important to understand what preceded them in a little more depth. While heeding media anthropologist Brian Larkin's call to "pay attention to the technical features of the technologies themselves,"[25] I also want to emphasize the entangled histories behind these technical features. If we take seriously that new forms emerge "always in time," not only were the changes brought by digital technologies changes of a particular historical moment and highly contingent on factors outside of the world of photography, but the new forms that emerged also structured new relationships to time. What changed radically was the temporality of photojournalism. Until the widespread use of digital photography in the mid- to late 1990s, news publications received images from three main types of sources: wire services, photo agencies, and archived collections (containing mainly historical photographs). One of the main differences between these sources for news images was the time it took for these various photographs to circulate.

Wire services were so called because they functioned through wires. This is an obvious point, but one easily forgotten in today's all-digital environment. News agencies—of which the three largest are Associated Press (AP), Agence France-Presse (AFP), and Reuters—relied on a physical telegraphic or telephonic infrastructure that allowed them to distribute information, eventually sending news farther and faster.[26] Wire services were initially formed as collectives or government-subsidized initiatives to share the very significant cost of transmitting dispatches over the wire. Today, wire services are news organizations responsible for gathering news—text as well as still and moving imagery—and distributing it to a very wide subscriber network of global news providers. They disseminate the majority of the international information broadcast in the world every day. Though all three of the main wire services have wide-reaching networks and disseminate information to similar audiences of subscriber news publications worldwide, their diverse histories give a sense of the various stakes in media industries that shape the cultures of institutions.[27] As the very brief histories I've sketched out below will make apparent, the feat of distributing photographic representations across significant distances involved entangled histories of transportation and communication networks, diverse means of raising the necessary capital, and contingencies that often had to do with the content of the information being disseminated across the wires. The formation and spread of wire services repeats the themes of intermingling of commercial value with gestures of global public interest present in the history of photography since the 1839 presentation of Daguerre's invention as a "free gift to the world."

Established in 1835 as Agence Havas, Agence France-Presse (AFP) is the world's oldest news agency. It was initially set up as an agency for the translation of foreign newspapers and became a public company in 1879. The news section was nationalized in 1940 and then renamed Agence France-Presse in 1944, following the liberation of Paris. AFP continues to be a state-subsidized public corporation, and only in 1991 did the state's share fall below 50 percent. Though a photo service was established in 1944 and pictures were transmitted by Belinograph, AFP did not launch a photo service that reached beyond France and French territories until 1985, prompted to do so by the collapse of United Press International (UPI). In 1995 AFP ended a long-standing agreement with Associated Press and began its own news gathering within the United States. Today AFP partners with the US corporation Getty Images to enhance its coverage.

The Associated Press (AP) was formed in 1848 in order to enable six New York City newspapers to gather news via the newly invented telegraph—an effort that was too costly for any single paper. By the following year, AP had a foreign bureau in Halifax, Nova Scotia. Initially AP had to face competition from Havas of France, Reuters of Britain, and Wolff of Germany. These European agencies dominated news distribution until the third decade of the twentieth century, when AP began full-scale service to Latin America and Japan. Only in 1927 did the company start a fledgling news picture service that delivered pictures by a combined air-sea-rail network. The AP Wirephoto network was born in 1935. By the 1960s, AP owned a picture network that was linked solidly from Tokyo to Moscow. Today AP is a not-for-profit cooperative, owned by its 1,550 US daily newspaper members. One thousand new photographs are transmitted every day by AP alone. AP serves more than fifteen thousand news organizations worldwide and claims that "there is no place on earth too remote for same-day news picture transmission."[28] If this claim feels dated, it is because the shift to digital image circulation via the Internet was meant to render transmission an instant activity that no longer required any time, let alone a day or more.

AP Wirephoto's success prompted the start of Acme, established in 1907 and later known as United Press Newspictures (UP). International News Photos later merged with UP to become United Press International.

UPI was unique in that it allowed anyone to have access to the news off the wire instead of limiting membership to certain publications. However, UPI encountered significant economic difficulties and declared bankruptcy in 1982. Its picture service was eventually purchased by Reuters.

Reuters, nicknamed "the Rolls Royce of the News World," was founded by Paul Julius Reuter in 1851.[29] He had been sending stock prices between Aachen and Brussels using pigeons two years earlier. This linkage with financial services continues today, and Reuters's largest sectors are those related to information about trading and foreign exchange. The company was floated on the London Stock Exchange and NASDAQ in 1984 and is considered the strongest wire service financially.

Fast Photos Versus Good Photos

Prior to digitalization, during a period when it was understood that it took time for a photograph to move from one place to another, there were two types of photographers—wire service photographers and photographers who sold their images to weekly or monthly news publications. Wire services (such as AP and Reuters) would transmit images of a significant news event to their subscriber base of mostly daily publications over the wires. These were "fast" photographs. In contrast, newsmagazines would send freelance or (far fewer) staff/contract photographers on assignment to cover the event and produce a feature story. Freelance photographers were not salaried like those working for wire services, and were referred to as "agency photographers" since they were often represented by an agency. Their income was dependent on whether their agents could get them assignments and sell images they had previously made. Unlike wire service photographers, freelance photographers kept the copyrights to their images. They might get several days or a week on assignment and fly or ship their undeveloped film back either to the photo agency that represented them or to the publication that had sent them on assignment. These images were often published some time after the event had been covered in the dailies, accompanying more in-depth reporting on the event. If a photographer shot an event "on spec" (speculation), most often he or she would have shared the costs with the agency and hoped to sell the images to a magazine after the fact.

Agency photographers were said to take "good" photographs. This is not to say that wire service photos—"fast" photos—were "bad," but that they were perceived as less complex images by editors at news-magazines and others in the photo agencies. The aim for a wire service photographer was to have a visual shot of the event as soon as possible after the event. The photographers' value was in their speed. Since the transmission of a single image took anywhere from four to fifteen minutes and images could be sent only one at a time, wire photographers were trained to take single shots that summed up the event in a single image.[30] Editors would usually try to transmit single images that were a synthesis of the event rather than a series of images that collectively formed a story. When color photographs were sent via wires, each of the three color processes (cyan, magenta, yellow) required seven minutes and then several additional minutes for the photo to be written to tape; hence a single image could take up to half an hour. Therefore, even the unit of representation between the two types of photography was quite different—single shots versus stories.

There was little competition between the two types of images, since they catered to publications with very different production cycles. Because they did not compete, there was much camaraderie and collaboration between the two groups of photographers, who would often travel together and pool resources such as drivers, cars, and translators. A wire photographer might have more resources, especially if the event was in a location where the wire service had a fixed bureau, but an agency photographer might be able to return a favor at a different event if he was working for a large newsmagazine that was paying his expenses.

The transition to digital imagery and digital distribution caused a dramatic shift in the very infrastructure of representation. The magnitude of the promised technological change—that, at least in theory, all photographs could be transmitted anywhere instantly—paved the way for major institutional changes. The physical wire of wire agencies became obsolete; the wire feed also used the Internet. Digital production and circulation spread at an astonishing rate.[31] All digital photos had to be "good" because they were all "fast" photographs. Photographers who had often traveled together precisely because they were not shooting for similar publications suddenly found themselves in head-to-head competition for all available publication space.

Digitalization

One way to tell the story of digitalization would be to suggest that it was just the latest innovation by wire services to get their photographs to subscribers even faster.[32] AP introduced the first digital camera for photojournalists in 1994, and their photographers shot the 1996 Super Bowl entirely without film, confirming that digital technologies could be relied upon for coverage of the most important news stories. When time is of the essence, the fastest reporting—even by a few seconds or minutes—can yield significant premium value, such as in a sports match. However, digital technologies enabled the rise of a whole new type of institution: large corporate visual content providers.

The two visual content providers most often credited (or cursed, depending on the speaker) with changing the landscape of the image industry—Corbis and Getty Images—were founded by a corporate technology heavyweight and two former investment bankers, respectively. These organizations were built on technical knowledge and capital, not experience in journalism. Corbis is a digital-image provider established in 1989 and privately owned by Bill Gates. In 1999 and 2000, respectively, Corbis bought two of the major news photography agencies, SYGMA and SABA. Getty Images, founded in 1993, also grew by acquiring smaller agencies and established image banks. Similarly, at the turn of the twenty first century, two French photography agencies, Gamma and Rapho, which were legendary for their photographers' coverage of the American war in Vietnam and the time period following, were acquired by Groupe Hachette Filipacchi Photos, part of the media division of the Lagardère conglomerate. Lagardère not only owns the world's largest magazine publisher but is also a distribution giant and key player in the aviation, space, and defense industries.[33] Since Corbis and Getty, both American corporations, amassed the largest collections of images, digitalization also meant that Paris was displaced as the center of photojournalism. Rather, by 2003, the battle for the cultural and journalistic heart of the photojournalistic industry was for some still a matter of dispute (as well as whether or not such a center needed to exist at all if images could be transmitted instantly from anywhere). Most agreed, however, that the financial heart of the industry had shifted to the United States.

Whereas earlier there had been wire services, archives, and small photographic agencies that worked on different enough time schedules that they didn't really compete, suddenly all images could technically be transmitted instantly. The rapid dominance of digital photography meant that Corbis and Getty Images quickly became competitors for the three major wire services—Reuters, Associated Press, and Agence France-Presse—and posed a threat to the remaining small agencies they hadn't already acquired. The images produced and distributed by wire services, small agencies, and the large corporate visual content providers are no longer temporally differentiated. Technically, transmission is instant and happens online. This change in the temporal dimension of images depending on the types of institution by which they were brokered altered the practices of photographers and their relationships with other photographers and those who brokered their images. Moreover, the very category of visual content highlights the further commodification of images by blurring boundaries between editorial and commercial images and fundamentally restructuring how images were selected, archived, and made commercially available through searchable online archives.[34] Visual content was a new form or assemblage in the definition given by Rabinow, in that it "produces and instantiates new capacities"; and, like other new forms, it emerged very much in a particular time.[35]

In the increasingly corporatized journalism landscape of the late twentieth century, photojournalism had still been the domain of wire services and small photo agencies, both of which had profit structures in place but also regularly emphasized their role as providers of journalistic or documentary visual knowledge to the world, as suppliers of a critical public good. Moreover, as became clear in interviews with photographers trying not only to inform fellow citizens but also make a living, it wasn't that they naively believed photojournalism had not been sullied by profit before, but rather that there was a widespread perception that there was a "culture clash," as they put it, between the profit-oriented corporate giants Corbis and Getty and the established agencies they had swallowed.

During an interview in 2002 when much was still in flux, a veteran photographer who also taught photojournalism reflected on the cultural change brought on by the rapid rise of the corporate visual content providers:

> It is not that the older agencies were not profit oriented, but that they seemed to put the ultimate priority on photography, which might explain why so many of them, most notably Magnum, were financially very unstable. To put it vulgarly, it's not that we weren't managed by a pimp before. It's that at least that pimp treated us well. He knew we were high-class escort-service-type prostitutes. Now we are all sharing the same street and are thus being told, "You are all hookers." It's simply about who delivers the goods the fastest.

Evident in this comment is the power of an ideal of an agency that, despite commercial interests, valued photography itself. Given the importance attached to the ideal of journalism as a democratic force above mere financial interest, Getty Images and Corbis, whose founders had no journalistic background, generated much ill will as they quickly dominated the industry through a frenzy of acquisitions. Whereas older photo agencies had been key players known to those in the world of journalism, corporate visual content providers launched significant branding campaigns in which the language of market share was front and center. Getty Images, with the rights to seventy million images, boasted that it was a global company "responsible for shaping so much of what people all over the world see each day," and claimed "ownership of roughly 25 percent of the visual content industry."[36] Meanwhile, as the second largest collection of images, Corbis boasted that it was "a world leader in digital media" and had built "the broadest, deepest collection of imagery" in the world. As the second half of this book will emphasize, image brokers had long mythologized photojournalism as a means of informing the public and bearing witness to injustices and atrocities. This new explicit focus on ownership and market share, and imagery that was described in the language of product lines—broad and deep—was jarring to many photographers and image brokers.

Moreover, the photographer's lament above also exemplifies how complaints about the digital giants interested only in speedy delivery were most commonly phrased to me: a comparison of a romanticized view of the agencies of yesteryear with today's corporations rather than more directed complaints about specific practices. Many disgruntled photojournalists gave me the example of the gentlemen's-handshake agreements they had grown used to with the editors at agencies being replaced with five-page standard corporate contracts. Perhaps partly this nostalgia for the older photo agencies had to do with the fact that many of the "old-style pimps" had cultivated strong personal connections with photographers. In other words, interpersonal and institutional loyalties were highly enmeshed. Despite their legendary business acumen and cutthroat competitiveness, directors of old-school photo agencies were often portrayed to me by photographers as charismatic if paternalistic men of European origins known for taking care of their photographers and clients alike. Whether fact or fiction, the constantly narrated difference between the almost caricaturized paternal European benefactor and the cold American corporate executive had purchase on both veteran photographers and younger professionals who came of age post-digitalization. Nowhere was this difference more visible than at the annual Visa Pour l'Image photo festival in Perpignan, France, to which I'll return in chapter 6. The mostly American executives from the large visual content providers gave slick PowerPoint presentations during the day and invited selected guests to lavishly catered lunches and somewhat stiff, invitation-only formal dinners. The old-school agency folk could often be found seated at restaurant tables abundant with food and drink, surrounded by loquacious newsmagazine editors and photographers, conversations and guests often spilling onto the town's narrow streets. Of course, these are both forms of networking—who got invited to pull up a chair at the seemingly spontaneous dinner was a delicate matter and no less exclusionary than the corporate invite lists. There are many cultures at play here—not just photo agency versus visual content provider, but also European versus American business etiquette, small business versus corporation, emphasis on professionalism versus hospitality, and so forth.

Yet the power of these perceptions was substantial and might explain why for the most part stigma was assigned to corporate institutions but usually not to the former owners of the photo agencies that had been sold to them. During the summer of 2003, I interviewed a veteran agent, a man who had once owned a very successful and trusted photo agency. People in the photojournalism industry had described him to me as one of the hard-core news junkies, the type of photo agent who would have images on an editor's desk before the editor even knew that the event had happened or that he might possibly need to cover it. He had sold his agency to one of the large visual content providers. That sale meant not only that he could no longer sell images from the extensive archive he had amassed but that, at least temporarily, he was not allowed to compete in the industry. And while he might have had a predigital photo agency, because of the rapidity of change in the image industry, he was old-school but not old in age. As everyone had predicted, he founded a new agency as soon as his contractual noncompete embargo ended. I spoke with him within a few weeks of his setting up the new agency, and he explained what he saw as the essence of a photo agency to me. Intense, gregarious, persuasive, and charming, he embodied what had been described to me as the earlier style of photo agencies. Not surprisingly, he was spending much of his time cold-calling the younger editors at news publications—those who might not recognize him by name—to introduce himself. When I asked if he thought there was room for a small photo agency in a world of visual content providers, he replied confidently, "Look, I go to the same butcher. I've been going to him for years. I buy from one butcher. Why? He knows what cut I like; he suggests things because he knows what I like. It's the same with photography. We're in the service industry. It's a personal business."

But personal businesses have limited reach. Today there are very few independently owned photo agencies focusing on documentary images (such as SIPA, Contact Press Photo, Panos Press, Redux, Vu, Polaris Images), though there has been a rise in the creation of small cooperatives and photo collectives that try to market their images through websites.[37] A high-profile photographer-owned agency, named VII, established in September 2001, was "formed in response to the dramatic changes taking place in the ownership, representation and distribution of photojournalism."[38] VII was formed by seven internationally known photographers including megastar James Nachtwey. Initially their wish was to remain small and specialize in conflict photography. Their vision was clearly stated on their website and underlined the promise of digital circulation and the hope that everyone having access to speed would once again create a niche for "good" photographs: "In photojournalism, the use of digital distribution means that small groups can have all the reach and speed of big agencies. When this is the case, competition will concentrate more fully on quality of expression, to the lasting benefit of the work we communicate." Nonetheless, VII's early success did not necessarily mean that the image industry was a truly even playing field open to small players, even if VII claimed to balance "artistic, ethical and business aims."[39] The photographers in VII already had established reputations, so they could hardly be taken as an example of what any small group with access to digital distribution can achieve. Moreover, they were photographers with well-established reputations in the specific niche they want to fill—conflict photography. In other words, when there is a major conflict, they are already part of the group of photographers that come to an editor's mind. Over the years VII grew to about twenty photographers and also established a network through which it distributes the work of nonmember photographers. So even here the model became more akin to a photo agency where part of the profits came in through commissions on distributing others' work. Several other small photo collectives have since emerged, such as Noor, Razon, Prime, Luceo, and Cause Collective.

Indeed, with more and more images online and budget cuts resulting in fewer photo editors, getting editors' attention is a major challenge. It made sense that, having established itself as an agency known for good photography, VII would begin distributing others' photography as well, for a big part of the challenge was getting editors to search for images on a particular agency's website. This was where the massive technical, sales, and publicity resources at the major visual content providers made a huge difference in how much marketing muscle could be put behind images. A photo provider of any size needed to create an attractive "storefront." The giants in the industry were able to lure editors to their sites as destinations where they could find images for all their needs or multiple options for any one topic.

Although largely outside the purview of this book, the historical record is also now available for purchase in a hitherto unimaginable way. Significant portions of the visual content industry are historical archives that were purchased, with the promise that they would be digitized. Perhaps the purchase that resulted in the most publicized controversy was Corbis's 1995 acquisition of the Bettmann Archives, a collection of seventeen million images started when Otto Bettmann sneaked two steamer trunks full of images out of Nazi Germany. Today the collection is housed 220 feet underground in a low-humidity, subzero storage facility run by Iron Mountain National Underground Storage in a limestone mine in Pennsylvania, where it is being digitized.[40] What are the ramifications of such a large part of the visual archive being owned by corporations? What new uses will be made of this historical visual archive as it becomes digitally available to people around the world? Who will be able to afford access to these archives?[41] I raise these questions here because in the following chapters readers will occasionally encounter image brokers making decisions about which historical images to put into circulation. Furthermore, this larger project of digitizing the historical visual record has made establishing robust visual archives an important journalistic and commercial goal in the industry. Again and again during fieldwork, image brokers emphasized the importance of capturing the present for distribution in the future, thinking commercially about that peculiar temporality that photography makes possible: the futurepast. The futurepast mandates that image brokers speculate when working today about which images might be valuable tomorrow. For now, however, let me discuss how profits worked in the image industry at the time of my fieldwork.

ROI IN THE IMAGE INDUSTRY

In the new news economy, characterized by visual content providers, returns on investment (ROIs) need to be carefully monitored and accounted for. Because a vast array of clients can search visual content providers' websites on their own and download images, it is possible to calculate returns on individual images. Although celebrity portraits and paparazzi shots have long been a part of what photo agencies provide to varying degrees, old-school photo agencies' clients were mostly news and entertainment magazines. They might sell images to glossy magazines, but for the most part their images were part of the news or entertainment content rather than integrated into an advertisement. Today, however, a large part of the revenues of visual content providers comes from advertising and the commercial licensing of imagery.

Nonetheless, the news and editorial division remains strategically important for these agencies, since it represents a prestigious public face for the company. When an image represented by a visual content provider appears on the front page of the *New York Times, Libération,* or *Der Spiegel,* the image is usually accompanied by a credit line identifying the photographer and the representing agency's or visual content provider's name (credit reads: "[photographer] / [visual content provider]"), and everyone can see that this particular company has global reach and is a major force in covering world events. Well-placed news images act as advertising for the visual content provider, declaring it a respectable source for news as evidenced by its being used by a reputable news source, but also contributing to its brand recognition as a visual content provider. Remember Getty Images' boast that it is "responsible for shaping so much of what people all over the world see each day."

It is important, then, to understand the major ways in which a news image can generate revenue. Once again temporality is often key in image sales: how recent is the image, has it been published before, or is what is being sold a photograph that has yet to be taken? Another major factors in determining a photograph's value is exclusivity. Is the photograph a rare image? Did other photographers have access to the event? How timely is the image? Is it directly related to a current event? Let me run through the most common ways a news image could generate profit at the time of this research, since examples of all of these types of transactions will appear in the chapters to come.[42]

Assignment for a Publication (First Sales)

A visual content provider or a photo agency got an assignment from a publication for a particular photographer.[43] That photographer's expenses were covered by the publication, and the publication paid the photographer a day rate. The rate was standard and, to the chagrin of photographers, rarely increased; however, certain situations, such as combat, merited an increased day rate.[44] At Global Views Inc., the visual content provider where I did extensive fieldwork, the company got 30 percent of this revenue and the photographer 70 percent. (Credit reads: "[photographer] / [agency or visual content provider] *for* [publication (to signal that this was an exclusive assignment)].")

Second Sales

Once the images appeared in the publication for which it had been an "exclusive" assignment, meaning that no one else could have access to the images for a specified amount of time, and the sales embargo had been lifted, a sales team could then sell those images ("second sales") to other, noncompeting publications. Of course, this is a much more profitable activity in a company with a large, dedicated, and specialized sales team interested in meeting sales quotas. Publication of an image not only served as publicity for the agency or visual content provider but also functioned as a storefront—a place where other clients might see the image. Many smaller publications would call to request an image that had appeared in a certain magazine or newspaper. Revenue from second sales were split fifty–fifty with the photographer. (Credit reads: "[photographer] / [agency or visual content provider].")

Guarantees/Space Rates

A photographer's work might be sent to a photo editor at a publication without the photographer being put on assignment. The photographer would cover his or her own expenses or, in some increasingly rare cases, would share his or her expenses with the agency. (Older photographers told stories of agencies advancing the money to cover the expenses and then splitting profits fifty–fifty once half of expenses had been recuperated.) A publication would buy an image at space rate—a negotiated rate paid according to the amount of physical space on the page that the image occupied: half page, quarter page, head shot, full page, or double truck (a single image spread across two pages). Another consideration in pricing was how much of the imagined world visual space (potential visual mind share of the reader or viewer) the image might occupy based on circulation of the publication, whether this would be additional online use, how many countries the image would appear in, whether the image would appear on the cover or an inside page, and so forth.[45] The larger the potential visualscape of the image, the higher the price. As we'll see in the sales meeting I describe at the end of this chapter, the issue of who gets the profits from this type of sale can be contentious, depending on how long after the event the image is being sold. Anything from the archive of an agency or visual content provider will be sold in the same manner. (Credit reads: "[photographer] / [agency or visual content provider].")

A photo editor sometimes sold a photographer's coverage of an event *before* the event took place. In this case, the photo editor at the publication would offer a guarantee. This is a "guarantee against space rate," meaning the publication would pay even if it ended up not using the images. If the publication used the images, it would then pay at a "space rate" equivalent to or more than the guarantee. At a visual content provider, these were all considered first sales and handled by the photo editors on the news and editorial team rather than by the sales team. Profits were generally divided with the photographer in the same way that assignments would be. This type of preemptive sale was more likely if the photographer had an established reputation, and especially if access to the event was limited. In other words, these types of sales took place when a publication wanted to secure exclusive rights to a set of photographs that only a few photographers, or sometimes one in particular, would be able to shoot.

While the above types of sales were business as usual before the rise of visual content providers, large visual content providers are also able to partner with multiple sources and maximize profits with commission earned from content they did not produce but distribute via their website. The following types of revenue-generating collaborations are made possible by the capital available to visual content providers to establish partnerships or acquire an archive as well as staff who can be assigned to such dedicated functions.

Archival Sales

Visual content providers have enormous image banks with which to cater to clients in all types of communications industries. The profitability of archival sales, particularly at a time when there are fewer generations who can imagine historical events without accompanying photographic imagery, requires that editors constantly anticipate future visual needs. Not just "What did the world look like yesterday or today?" but "What types of images of today might be requested in the future?"

What will the futurepast look like? (Credit reads: "[photographer (if known)] / [archive (if part of a specific collection like the Bettmann Archive or Hulton Archive)]—[visual content provider].")

Partnerships with Wire Services

As mentioned above, wire services mostly sell their images through a subscription model, so they have not traditionally been structured to focus on the sales of individual images. At the time of my fieldwork, they didn't usually sell to publications other than dailies and very large weekly magazines (i.e., publications that could afford to subscribe to the wire feed) and were not equipped to sell for commercial rather than editorial use. A visual content provider might partner with a certain wire service to sell its images to entities the wire service would not normally sell to, as well as to provide a platform for selling images that are more than seventy-two hours old but not yet old enough to be considered historical material. The two entities worked out the financial agreement on a wholesale model rather than per image, and an editor at the visual content provider's office might be responsible for editing the wire feed—all the daily images on the wire. Just as important as the revenue, such symbiotic relationship ensured that wire service images were available for commercial use with permission and that the visual content provider's archive was continually fed daily coverage of world events, making it an advantageous arrangement for both parties. (Credit reads: "[photographer] / [wire service]—[visual content provider].")

Partnerships with Newspapers

In addition to subscribing to wire services, newspapers often had staff photographers who were salaried, as well as freelance photographers contracted for certain assignments. If a photo department had a strong group of photographers and could become a revenue generator for the newspaper rather than a cost center, the department could then gain more autonomy. One way to generate revenue was for the photo department to partner with a visual content provider for coverage of a particular event. This partnership worked particularly well if the visual content provider could sell the newspaper's photographs in a market where the photos might not be seen otherwise, such as selling a regional paper's photographs in a different region of the country or in different national markets. Unlike deals with wire services, partnerships with newspapers or other publications tended to be ad hoc and event-driven. When they work, they generate not only profit but also prestige for both parties involved. (Credit reads: "[photographer] / [newspaper for whom photographer is staff] / [agency or visual content provider].")

THE CATEGORY OF VISUAL CONTENT

All of the above types of sales were possible before the emergence of visual content providers. However, the enormous size of the visual content providers' marketing and sales forces led to clients perceiving of them as one-stop shopping destinations, solution providers for the frantic editor in search of images on several different topics and under intense time pressure. Sales representatives at visual content providers promised to help visualize any story. Easily searchable and user-friendly websites became key as they served increasingly as storefronts. Furthermore, because sales were now digitally recorded, prior sales influenced the order in which results were displayed in this shop window.

As sales were increasingly tracked online, it became possible for industry analysts to speak not just of returns on investment but also of returns on specific images.[46] In some sense, now that all images are potentially transmitted instantaneously, the difference between wire photos and agency photos had to do with whether they could be purchased individually rather than through a subscription model. Wire service photographs were still seen as part of editorial imagery that was not available for commercial licensing, though exceptions were being made. As I've detailed above, images produced for the news and editorial division generated revenue in several ways. Increasingly, large visual content providers were cross-selling images, licensing a news image for use in advertising. This book focuses mainly on the circulation of news images within the international news and editorial context. However, because commercial sales of images are significantly more profitable than editorial use, the potential for a photograph to be used in noneditorial contexts served as a backdrop for the production of news images.

Anthropologists Arthur and Joan Kleinman wrote critically of the commodification of documentary images in the late 1990s: "The existential appeal of human experiences, their potential to mobilize popular sentiment and collective action, and even their capability to witness or offer testimony are now available for gaining market share."[47] To some extent, of course, their availability for gaining market share understood as potential for commercial use is nothing new. News images have long been bound together with selling newspapers and therefore generating profits. The real shift is that today the images themselves have been transformed into commodities that can be sold independently of their relationship to a particular world event. An image produced for editorial purposes can be licensed and put to commercial use.

The category of "visual content" rose to prominence with digitalization and the folding of photojournalism into the much larger image industry, including the burgeoning stock photography industry. What is at stake is photography's ability to survive as an analytic tool if access to distribution networks is dominated by providers of visual *content,* who make the bulk of their profits from advertising and publicity images.[48] The key is to pay attention to the consequences of what communications scholar Paul Frosh insightfully analyzes in his book *The Image Factory:* stock photography's—and, I would add, photojournalism's—"being subsumed within a globalized and digitized 'visual content industry' . . . whose ramifications include, among many other things, the accelerated blurring of boundaries between fine art, news and advertising images, and in a culture glutted with authentic and fabricated 'vintage' images, between historical and contemporary photographs."[49] Frosh gives a detailed history of the institutional dynamics behind the rise of Corbis, Getty Images, and other large visual content providers, concluding that

> the connection between the production and distribution of photographs has been increasingly tenuous since the emergence of photography as a media profession, but these latest trends, with the acquisition of historical archives and exclusive reproduction rights by transnational corporations that specialize in visual content, signify the absolute decontextualization and abstraction of images. Thus not only are the distinctions between media erased, so are the differences in the values and purposes associated with different types of photographs. The visual content industry converts the complex material and symbolic specificity of images into an abstract, universal *"content,"* severing each image from the context of its initial production, circulation, consumption and reinscribing it within the overarching system of commercial exchange.[50]

As I observed at Global Views Inc. (GVI), the potential for "crossover sales" caused some tension between the news team and the sales team because the former, by training and culture, evaluated news images for their geographically and historically specific news value, whereas the latter evaluated an image's representational appeal outside of the particular context in which it was produced or initially circulated.

In August 2003, several months into fieldwork at GVI, I spent two weeks sitting on the sales floor rather than with the news team so that I could better understand the sales team's approach to GVI's offering. After two weeks of watching them sell a wide range of images to a broad range of clientele, I tagged along with the sales team to the first joint sales–editorial meeting. It was specifically set up as a free-form meeting so that everyone, both the sales and the editorial teams, would feel comfortable raising concerns.

"IF YOU'RE ON YOUR WAY TO MONROVIA, SHOOT FEZ"

Michael Strong, vice president of news and editorial at GVI (who will be introduced more fully in chapter 2), asked the sales team if there were areas in which they thought GVI's offering was weak, topics the editorial team could go after, or major topics they felt were missing. One go-getter sales rep answered, with a somewhat ironic tone, "We want to see less weepy, third-world, Pulitzer Prize–winning features. Is our focus these really heavy stories? Ebola, prostitution, child prostitution around the world? We've done that story in twenty-seven countries."

"Sorry, excuse us," grumbled a senior editor. She had come to GVI from the wire service world and a culture of evaluating images according to journalistic significance.

The sales rep continued, "The major markets don't need news features anymore. They're asking for everyday subjects. Travel. Food. Medical science. Beauty. Maybe we could focus a little on editorial stock. Things we could sell over and over again . . ."

A second rep continued, "I understand that photographers want to do stories that have an impact, but our bread and butter is more everyday stuff. Makeovers; food and wine. Those step-by-step beauty images are really boring, but it's really good business. We have to hit the bottom end of the market."

Another sales rep chimed in, "Or travel stories like places with Four Seasons hotels."

Michael Strong tried to bridge the clear divide in the room by being receptive to some of these suggestions: "OK, give me a list of five places."

The rep continued, "Maybe you could suggest it to photographers. You know, 'If you're on your way to Monrovia to shoot war, stop in Fez.'" Monrovia, the capital of Liberia, was in the headlines as rebel groups had intensified their armed campaigns against the president at the time, Charles Taylor, who was eventually ousted and exiled. Fez, the medieval capital of Morocco, a city claiming to have one of the best-preserved old cities in the Arab world, was among the hot travel destinations of the year.

"That's the wrong photographer." Strong used Jacques, a very well known veteran combat photographer, whose photographs from Liberia were being widely published in newsmagazines, as an example. "If we tell Jacques to shoot Four Seasons hotels, he'll shoot us."

Yet another rep commented, "Well, let's try to find things that are a bit more timeless. Things we can sell again and again. That's the filter we should push things through. Can we sell this for an extended period of time, and can we sell it across the world?"

Michael once again attempted to bring the two groups—sales and editorial—together: "We're not going to shoot something that's a one-off. We're in sync philosophically." Michael was referring to the fact that he wanted to do "epic" stories that did not illustrate just one particular news event but rather spoke to larger historical, social, or cultural trends.

The meeting continued in much the same spirit as it became clear that the sales team and the editorial team saw their respective goals quite differently. The underlying tension resulted from the fact that the sales team did not profit from the sales of assignment photographers' images unless they were being purchased after the initial news coverage of the event. The debate centered on when exactly an event was over. Since the sales reps can sell images only after they are no longer first sales but rather second sales, the temporal distinction between first and second sales was quite contentious. The sales force was held accountable for individual sales goals, and they receive commissions on total monthly sales if they exceed their goal.[51] The editorial team had never had sales goals and was disturbed by the fact that recently they had started receiving reports showing how much sales revenue they had generated. They took this accounting statement to be the first step in trying to impose the sales-goal model on the news team. Every time things got tense, Strong would step in and try to mollify the sales team: "You're right. You don't get credit for our assignments, but we don't get credit for your stock sales. But let's collaborate. The caliber of our archive is critical for the sales staff." The implication was that if editorial could produce strong content today, the sales reps would have strong stock to sell in the future.

Of course the question becomes what constitutes strong content. For the news team, strong content means images that capture current events and get published in prestigious news publications. For the sales team, strong content often means having potential for "crossover sales," meaning that an editorial image could be used for commercial purposes. A strong image for sales purposes is one that can be sold over and over again all around the world. The categories that the sales team felt the archive was weakest in (such as yoga, tea, traveling with babies, spas, etc.) were often not high-priority news topics. What is at issue here is *not* that the sales reps didn't care about world events and the editorial team did. In fact, the sales rep who opened the floodgates with her request for fewer weepy images was aware of how the editorial team would perceive her comment, as evidenced by her choice of a somewhat ironic tone when voicing her request. However, she needed to think strategically from a business perspective. Toward the end of the meeting she added another angle for the group to consider: "We really need to think about diversity, especially ethnic. Every time we get a request for a black picnic, we have two images to send clients."

As was evident in this sales meeting and in many other incidents during my fieldwork, there were many different modes of speaking about profit and varied levels of comfort with which it was acknowledged that news images make up some portion—albeit a sliver—of the highly profitable visual content industry. Moreover, this meeting also underscored the instability of the category of news image: the sales representatives desired "timeless" images that could be repurposed for commercial value. Editorial teams were trying to support photographers to produce images that were unique and might become iconic of an event. Paradoxically, photographs, even those that were produced or have circulated as news images, are valuable as visual content if they can be repurposed and published in different contexts.

GALERIES LAFAYETTE

My second illustration of differing modes of addressing profit comes from the management teams of two very different institutions. In mid-2004, both Pierre Martin, the director of the Agence France-Presse (AFP) photography department, and Portia Friedman, the vice president of global marketing at GVI—institutions that have very different cultures—independently used exactly the same metaphor of an upscale department store in order to explain their merchandising strategy to me.

In a very slick PowerPoint presentation to the Paris office of GVI in 2004, as part of an internal "roadshow" attempting to bring the various global offices on board with corporate objectives outlined back at US headquarters, Friedman chose a local example to make her point: GVI wanted to be the Galeries Lafayette of visual content providers. Galeries Lafayette is a classic department store in Paris, a Boulevard Haussmann cornerstone and majestic example of early-twentieth-century Art Nouveau architecture.[52] Friedman emphasized what an exciting time this was in the history of GVI, which had just had its most successful year. The challenge now was to get away from the old stock-company feel. "We want to be edgy, poignant, relevant," she said. The takeaway messages from the presentation were: Less is more. Outside-in. Iconic. Find everything in one place: GVI. She explained, "We are a solution provider. We provide visual solutions for our clients to be able to tell their stories.[53] So we are thinking like a retailer, like Galeries Lafayette. Many different collections in one beautiful place with many windows." The outside-in message meant that drawing customers in through these windows was key, particularly in crossover sales, where GVI was the industry leader, according to Portia.

> What have we been selling? What have others been selling? So we started 'cool hunting,' asking key user groups what they are eating, listening to, etc. . . . We are bringing together selling and content development. . . . We are in the privileged position of representing the most important content in the world. We need to think like Galeries Lafayette. [We need to tell editors,] "Make it simple, and begin every project with us."

In his own section of the presentation, Michael Strong, the vice president of news and editorial, emphasized, "Current events is the engine of our international offering. . . . Our goal is to provide the most relevant and distinctive imagery both current and historical to enable powerful storytelling for editorial and commercial clients. . . . We need to get the client to come to our site every single day." Friedman closed the presentation with a return to the Galeries Lafayette commercial model:

> It has never been a better time to be in this industry. There was 'the stock company' or 'the news company,' but GVI gave me goose bumps. We are a powerful player in this market. We're changing the business and it will not be the same. . . . It's a very sexy piece of business. Image licensing is estimated by analysts to be a two-billion-dollar business worldwide. Assignment photography another four to six billion dollars. Even a very small piece can be a very robust company. . . . We've got to keep moving our sexiest content to the front of the window. . . . We want to be Galeries Lafayette, not Carrefour [a global chain of hypermarkets with warehouse-style merchandising and rock-bottom prices].

When I interviewed Pierre Martin, the AFP director of photography, a few months later, I was prepared to hear him state a much less celebratory approach to profit. Yet he used exactly the same analogy when explaining his vision of AFP Photo to me:

> The people who are dealing with photojournalism should be able to find whatever they want on one platform. I use the analogy of Galeries Lafayette, and I oppose it to Carrefour or the retail shops. [Martin gave me the example of Rue Mouffetard, an old Parisian street known for its small stores and open market.] We used to have very small shops that specialized in certain types of photography, whereas because of digitization now it is possible to offer it all on the same platform. We're not Carrefour. They take a good product and they put their name on it and they sell it at the best price they can because of their power over the people who are making the goods and their ability to bring the price down. I don't want to have a cheap picture business, we're already very cheap. I prefer to go to Galeries Lafayette and enter the first floor and find all those brands all around and the prices are completely different; no one has brought the prices down. It's just much easier to find what you want in Galeries Lafayette than anywhere else. That's what I believe in, in terms of pictures. That's why I want partners on the same platform. That's why I want a platform where people know the environment and can find what they want. All the media clients on one floor of the department store.

When I asked how his department felt about this analogy, Martin answered frankly:

> They hate it. Well, most of them hate it. . . . There are no results [performance indicators] here. The commercial department is outside what we do here; they are merely a side track. The aim of a photographer cannot be commerce. . . . So we cannot put picture business in the same category as L'Oréal for cosmetics. That's why my analogy with Galeries Lafayette is hated here. Because it is a totally commercial environment. Even I don't believe we are in Galeries Lafayette with what we are doing. But it is what I would prefer. To gather people with five pictures to sell and people with two million pictures to sell on one platform. So that at least we are on a shared forum. But this is sheer analogy. But some of the people here don't like to sell; they think we are here to keep, we are here to give away, we are here on a mission. And all this is both true and wrong.

He regularly had to justify how much covering the war in Iraq cost to the rest of AFP. It was harder to quantify how much sales this coverage generated.

> We have a mission. I would like to give away my pictures and have the maximum distribution, but on the other hand I need to make sufficient money so that the system keeps going. I cannot put a price tag on covering Iraq versus selling images from Iraq. . . . Information has no commercial value of its

own. It is just that we are in a totally commercial environment, that we are obliged to sell our images; otherwise, we would give them away. In fact, we nearly are giving it away. When you look at the price of any single AFP image to any newspaper in the world . . . it's so marginal. AFP Photo broke even for the first time in 2003. Before then we were always a cost to AFP. But in 2000–2001 several small agencies got bought up and this was good for AFP.

Though what Friedman and Martin meant to emphasize with this metaphor was different, the senior executives of such different organizations—a privately owned visual content provider and a government-subsidized wire service—took a department store's merchandising practices as a model. In both cases, the need or desire to make a profit shapes how world events are visualized and how those representations are circulated and archived.

Pierre Martin knew his organization well: compared with GVI, there was a lot of unease about profiting from news images at AFP. Martin had told me, "The commercial department is outside what we do here." The sales people sat in a corner of the ground floor, separate from the three editing desks. This spatial distancing was merely the physical manifestation of what the sales reps felt was an ostracizing attitude. In an environment where a senior editor on the international desk defined everyone as journalists—"The correspondents write, the editors edit, the photographers make images, and everybody is a journalist"—the sales department was the only group that did not carry official press cards. Their corner of the department was often where there was greatest activity. Whereas everyone else was strictly digital in 2004, the sales reps would print out hard-copy prints of images for those photo editors at magazines not yet comfortable with viewing images digitally. The sales reps also had motorcycles and several times a day would don their helmets and head out to see clients. Their comings and goings as well as the steady stream of motorcycle couriers sent over by clients meant that the "Service Vente à la Pièce" [Retail Sales Service] section of the photo department was often bustling.

Despite the fact that a senior editor had insisted during a tour to new bureau chiefs about to leave for their postings, "It's *business* (pronounced *biz-nez*).[54] Our profession is also to sell," commercial activity was frowned upon at AFP. Patrick, the head sales rep, who himself had worked on the desks before moving into sales, emphasized to me that though they generated significant revenue for the photo department, the sales reps were not respected. "Look at our name. 'Vente à la Pièce,' as if we are selling carrots. Or they refer to us as the 'Cellule Commerciale

Photo,' as if we are a contamination, a terrorist cell." Indeed, others talked about commercial sales as an activity that could potentially threaten the journalistic integrity of the photo department. Patrick continued, "The desks insist on a deep cleavage between us and them. We have been made to handle *people* because it sells. But it's not because we like it. But we're taken for thugs or punks [*voyous*]. Not only do we make money, but we make money with *people*. This is completely contradictory to their principles."

As in Patrick's comments above, even when the rest of the conversation was in French, certain words were used in English only. There was some effort to use *bureau* for "desk," but *business* was always used in English, as was *people* to mean "celebrity photography." Since many saw the commercialization of journalistic photography as linked to American-style business practices, it is worth noting that the words, often those associated with the least desirable elements of the sales department, such as *people* and *business,* were always said in English.

Whereas the wire service business model was predominantly a subscription model, this little group within AFP sold individual images directly to magazines that did not subscribe to the news service. Over the course of a day, during which he edited several stories, sent them to various magazines, and constantly kept an eye on the feeds of both AFP and Getty Images, Patrick explained at length the purpose and challenges of the sales service. The following is culled from transcripts of the entire day's conversations that took place in front of screens featuring images related to a vast range of stories: from the sales of square-shaped watermelons in Japan to Iraq blast victims, an antiterrorism drill in South Korea, the Malaysian economy, a French pedophilia case, and scuffles along the wall being constructed on the Israeli border.

> The subscribers to the wires are mostly dailies and yet dailies use relatively few images. Magazines have room for stories that use multiple images. Now as for editors at the magazines they don't have time to do the rounds of all the possible photo agencies, you've got to get in there and sell them on your product. Now AFP's photographers aren't used to a story culture; the wire service demands that they take good singles. Rare is a photographer of whom you can ask broader treatment of a subject. On the other hand the dailies serve as advertisements for us. Magazines are going to be looking for images that haven't been seen by the whole world.
>
> But you've got to know your clients very well, which is why each of us works with specific magazines. We're a real team. I used to work on the desk, and it's true that our work [in sales] is not valued, but I prefer working in sales a hundredfold. The desk never interacts with the clients; they are only

aware of the competition [from other wire services]. Whereas I am constantly seeing clients. Plus, there is an artistic side since we are still taking over prints so we've got to work with the lab. The competition is monstrous, yes, but you've got to be fierce and persistent. It's about establishing relationships; that's how you ensure fidelity. Magazines have time to anticipate subjects, and if you can find out what themes they are thinking of working on, you can anticipate their visual needs. And if you want it to be your photo they use, you have to offer them ten. The impression of having choice is very important. If an editor goes to two sources for images and one has two images and the other has thirteen, the editor's going to go with the site with more choices.

Plus, since we're a wire service, we print out the text dispatches and take them along so we can use them to dress the photo ["enrober la photo"]. Getty does not have text dispatches that match their images, and this is a big handicap, because when we're presenting images we have only their photo captions to go on, whereas when we've read the whole story we can make much better informed arguments for various photos. Plus, we're a service for the photographers. The dailies don't really have the space to valorize their work. Magazines are the ones who have the space, and you can really add value to the photographer's production.

At the same time, for us a good photograph is one that has been published. Technically speaking, people is the nadir of photography. What you're looking for when evaluating a people photograph is "Has she changed her hairstyle? Does she have a new outfit? A new boyfriend?" We can sell many images to fashion magazines, for example, by paying attention to what they're wearing. For example, this is excellent: the first photo of Gwyneth Paltrow pregnant. OK, so as a photo it is abysmal [*nullissime*] and of no interest or significance, but we know that it will generate interest because of her pregnancy.

At this point another sales rep overheard Patrick and jumped into the conversation: "People need to dream. It eases their minds. Politics doesn't interest them, wars even less, and suffering least of all." Patrick seemed resigned to his status within the overall photo department. Nonetheless, he often substituted the word *distributing* for *selling*, or emphasized that what the sales team did was make an image available to clients who might not have access to it through the wire. "Fine. So we squabble, we play music, we yell, we're punks, but we're professionals, and our job is distributing images."[55]

UNIVERSAL IMAGES

It is the claim of universality that is truly mystificatory here: for the visual content industry is universal, but mainly in the sense that money is: and money is one of the most potent excluders of all.

—Paul Frosh, *The Image Factory*

Now that we've gone digital, the money comes from all parts of the world, which, of course, will then shape our product. Of course, I'm talking about the part of the world that has money. So, East Asia, Europe, North America. Money is, of course, a key factor.

—head of creative intelligence for GVI

To paraphrase the GVI sales rep, as a commodity the ideal news image can be sold for an extended period of time and can be sold across the world. On some level this is a challenge to the fundamental ontology of photography and its particular relationship to time and space. What is being requested is a timeless and geography-less image that can be mobilized to visualize a wide range of times and spaces: a universal image. Moreover, ideally these images can then be used universally. Media scholar John Hartley cogently states the ramifications of photojournalism thus being nowhere and everywhere. Former news images are "available to illustrate any story anywhere in the world, or to be repurposed as decorative design for greeting cards, nostalgia or mood books, and even coffee mugs. Monetisation and democratization have converged."[56]

In order to illustrate how news images are produced and circulated, the following three chapters look at three separate workplaces, all of which are affected by the changes in the infrastructures of representation outlined in this chapter. These chapters explore the production processes and decision criteria at three different sites at which images get brokered. Collectively they illustrate image-making: how a photograph acquires news value and becomes a news image by being circulated by image brokers. Each time an image is brokered, more brokers' decisions and imaginations become embedded in the image. Although the three sites are all involved in the production and circulation of images, they have different relationships to photographers, readers, and, as has already been hinted at, profit.

Global Views Inc.

Visualizing Politics, from Shock and Awe to the Fall of Saddam Hussein

What does it take to find the perfect shot?
Millions of images,
Hundreds of photographers
Global editors
And a partnership with the QRS photo agency

—multimedia ad on the Global Views Inc. website

Even before the war in Iraq began in March 2003, many anticipated that this was going to be the most photographed war in history. This belief persisted despite the general sentiment in US media that this would be a very short-lived war. Eventually the use of digital cameras by both photographers and troops themselves, as well as the continuation of the war for almost a decade,[1] became the reasons most commonly given for why there were so many photographs of the Iraq war. But in 2003, this perception had to do with an announcement by the US Department of Defense that about eight hundred journalists would be given slots alongside specific units and would remain "embedded" with those units and allowed "minimally restrictive" access for as long as they wished.[2]

A few weeks before the war started, I received minimally restrictive access for as long as I wished to the work of the news and editorial team at Global Views Inc. (GVI), one of the world's largest visual content providers.[3] In a newsroom abuzz with phone calls, emails, and instant messages (IMs), I sat on a stool amid the group of open cubicles that formed GVI's news and editorial team and wheeled from desk to desk. I attended daily meetings, met with the group's bosses regularly, and followed the work of producing, editing, and selling photographs. I read the official letters written by Paul, an editor whose job mostly became communicating with military personnel and other officials to try to get photographers access. As an anthropologist in a corporate setting, I learned not just from observing, but also by accompanying one of the key players when he went out for frequent cigarette breaks, listening to one side of phone conversations as well as conversations held on speakerphone, participating in conversations among team members, and reading emails or IMs that were shared with me or commented on as images "moved" from photographers' cameras to editors' screens, were captioned and color-corrected, and then got "pushed" out to potential clients. I followed people at various levels of authority in the newsroom, in the imaging lab, on the sales floor, and at other photography-related work areas. In other words, I attached myself to the news and editorial team at GVI at about the same time that embedded reporters and photographers attached themselves to various military units. While the US Department of Defense was pitching embed positions as windows onto the front line, from which journalists could send back accounts of the war that was about to start, I watched the work that went into producing photographic accounts of the war for journalism outlets. My work included observing editors arrange and maintain embed positions for photographers, observing them edit images submitted by both unilateral and embedded photographers, and observing the range of activities involved in circulating these images and getting them published.

Although I spent many months at GVI, and continued to visit and talk to the image brokers featured below long after I left, this chapter focuses on GVI's news and editorial division as it prepared to cover the Iraq war. I begin two weeks before the initial bombing of Baghdad, the "Shock and Awe" campaign, through to the fall of the statue of Saddam Hussein in Firdos Square on April 9, 2003. Endings and beginnings are critical moments for thinking through visualizing politics. The coverage of these two moments highlights how the war was packaged as an event despite the anticipated end date receding further and further into the future. Shock and Awe was a spectacular beginning, and the toppling of Saddam's statue was the first spectacle that was visually interpreted as some kind of ending, though of course the war lasted much longer and got much messier than many had initially imagined.[4] In other words, both events were visually recognizable as political turning points. This chapter moves between image brokers and government officials as they comment on the politics of how events are visualized. From the beginning of the war in Iraq, the demand for politics to be visualized meant that visuals also drove politics. By embedding the reader among GVI's news and editorial team, I hope to make visible the daily practices of image brokers in a war of images.

Hindsight, as the saying goes, is twenty–twenty, especially when analyzing always future-oriented news cycles. For it is only in hindsight that it is possible to render visible the practices of anticipation that shaped much of the image brokers' work and were particularly heightened in this case, when a war had been predetermined.[5] The looming Iraq war and how to image it best were only the most spectacular and urgent of many futures being managed by those on GVI's news and editorial team. Along with decisions about which future events would need to be covered and how likely they were to actually occur, there was a daily need to manage relationships with photographers and editors at publications, with an eye to future collaborations. The stakes were particularly high for GVI, a visual content provider who had bought up several small news-focused photo agencies and was still grappling with being a newcomer to photojournalism. News images were a fraction of GVI's revenues but very important for GVI's standing in the world of photography and journalism at large. Covering Iraq was an opportunity for GVI to improve its reputation in various circles—among photographers, among news publications, among other agencies. Moreover, as discussed in the introduction, anticipation is central to the work of many image brokers, but especially those working at a visual content provider since their goal is to build an archive that can be mined by those seeking visual content not only for today's news coverage but also for use far into the future. Much of the work of image brokers consists of capturing the futurepast: anticipating which images might be asked for tomorrow to ensure that they are taken today.

In taking the reader back to the opening of the war in Iraq, my intention is to illustrate a time of transition at GVI. This was a moment when GVI was very uncertain about its role. GVI was not a news publication, and yet the news and editorial team were tasked with covering the war. At stake was the question of whether their website was a storefront or a journalistic front page, and the responsibilities that went with those respective roles. I have structured this chapter as a series of daily logs to highlight the central role of time in GVI's newsroom. As the opening scene of this book made clear, this was a newsroom covering war in digital time, a time of faster circulation and shorter news cycles. Image brokers also knew that the value of a photograph as a news image depended critically on time: its being first to show something or the last taken before the magazines went to press for the week, perfectly timed to coincide with accurately predicted stories, or retrieved from the archive at an opportune moment. In this chapter, I show several examples where brokers grapple with the temporality of news images and are constantly brokering information as well as images in the hopes of accurately judging the value of each photograph.

Many of the individuals I observed had strong opinions and were quite reflective at times about their practices. The dialogue was reconstructed from notes I took as I scribbled constantly throughout the day. If at times some of the dialogue feels stilted, it's because I was overhearing only one side of many phone conversations. On the other hand, the image brokers I observed were constantly juggling many different topics, responding to all sorts of requests, and continually being bombarded with new information. Hence, this chapter also reflects the staccato-like quality of discourse in a newsroom. I cannot know now, nor did I assume to know then, what individuals were thinking. Instead I attempt to represent how they were working together by focusing on what was said. Individual personalities contribute much to everyday practices in any newsroom, a place where an "ordinary" day is hectic and focused on scouting out the extraordinary, the newsworthy.[6]

Yet, despite the ever-changing and often unanticipated subject matter involved, there are normative practices of discussing, requesting, editing, and selling photographs to news publications. In the process of becoming a news image and being worked on by different brokers, each drawing on previously circulated news images, a photograph becomes a surface on which many imaginations are concretized. The image brokers were constantly juggling journalistic concerns with business concerns, historical echoes with up-to-the-minute accuracy, and today's demands with what might be valued in the future. Their goal was to have fresh, original photographs that no one else had while also capturing the events and angles deemed by other media outlets as the most important of the day. The televisions that hung from the ceiling above the news and editorial division were almost always on and kept the team informed of exactly what news was dominant at any given moment. It was also through these televisions that the voices of government officials quoted in this chapter entered the newsroom.

Monday, March 10, 2003

When the receptionist waved me in on my first day of fieldwork at GVI, I proceeded to the office of the vice president of news and editorial photography, Michael Strong. The Monday-morning leadership meeting was to be held around the table in his office. Strong, whom the reader might remember from the sales meeting that I described in chapter 1, had been hired from a popular news website. He was young (early thirties), determined, and had been hired in part for his technical know-how. Many in the industry, particularly younger photographers, found Strong very charismatic, and he exuded an almost evangelical belief in both the power of photography and that of digital innovations. Brimming with confidence, and constantly noting but not answering calls coming in to his cell phone during meetings, Strong was the one who had given me "minimally restrictive" access to GVI because he was excited by the chance to have an observer around. "We as a team are ready to reinvent this place," he told me. Strong seemed convinced I would witness the exhilarating transformation of GVI from distrusted newcomer to the industry to the place where all new talent wanted their work represented. My role as an anthropologist was preordained: I would be there to document his and GVI's success.

An older man walked in, and Michael boomed, "Meet Henry Smith, director of news. He's in charge of a solid news organization." The leaders of the various divisions gave energetic and optimistic updates. Henry Smith announced, "Well, as you know, we're getting ready for a war within about ten days. But apparently Nachtwey decided to leave for Baghdad, and *Newsworld*'s director of photography picked up Alex Levy that very day."[7] Jim Nachtwey is one of the world's best-known contemporary photojournalists, and *Newsworld* had arranged an embed position for him with the US Army's 101st Airborne. Henry was telling the team that when Nachtwey decided to leave his embed, the magazine had given the position to Alex Levy, a fresh-out-of-school photographer who had come to GVI just a few days earlier. Alex was already embedded in Kuwait. With unabashed pride Henry reported *Newsworld*'s rate: "One thousand dollars per day—double day rate for conflict!"[8]

Alex Levy was the Cinderella story of the photojournalism world in the spring of 2003. Recently out of college, he had been so desperate for a job that the day he came to GVI to show his portfolio he had also stopped by the Starbucks across the street to fill in an employment application. At least, that was the story as told by Alex himself and repeated by others. Less than a month later, he was on assignment for *Newsworld,* one of the world's most prominent newsmagazines.

Henry walked me upstairs and introduced me to the small news team sitting in cubicles under four televisions, each tuned to a different channel. Henry oversaw a team that included Ed, the most senior photo editor; Jackie, the assistant photo editor; Liz, a young photo editor who worked on feature stories; and Sophie, a temporary hire who had been there for several weeks and who corrected captions and sent images to the lab for color correction.

Ed was explaining to Jackie why he had to get in touch with Alex Levy: "Apparently, there is a couple in the 101st that are a husband and wife, and *Newsworld* needs a vertical shot of them. 'Couple commanders.' You know, something different from all the 'going to battle' stuff we've seen. They want photos of each separately, working with the troops separately. Sandy background, nice lighting. Alex might have a hard time getting them together because apparently the writer already got them together." Indeed, Ed found out they didn't want to be bothered again for the photograph and were apparently reminding those trying to make the arrangements for the shoot, "Hey, we have a war going on here."

Jackie smiled at Ed's impersonation of the commander. "I just tried to call Alex, but I don't know if I got through."

"Does someone answer and say, 'Hello, Hotel Expensive Kuwait'?" Ed quipped. "Try his cell."

Ed, telling me the story of young Alex's good fortune, confessed, "An embed position is a great opportunity for a photographer, but perhaps it might be a conflict of interest. Cynics would say this makes the US media salivate over military embeds, which we are doing. And then there's the rules: you can't interfere with op-sec (operations security); you can't take photos of dead Americans. Actually, I'm not clear on exactly when or where the censorship will be done."

He swiveled in his chair and called out, "Hey, Jackie, remind me, I have to check with *Newsworld* about selling second rights[9] on Alex's images since [*Newsworld*] may be planning an end-of-war special and they may want special rights for that." Before the war had even begun, Ed was anticipating the financial value of certain images for an end-of-war retrospective. In other words, he wanted to clarify with the magazine that had put Alex on assignment whether they wanted to have exclusive rights to the photographer's images for any potential end-of-war retrospective, something they would have to pay for; or whether GVI's sales division was free to sell them to other publications. *News-world*'s tremendous circulation means that publication in the magazine serves as a storefront for editors seeking images for overseas markets or publications with different timelines than newsweeklies. Ed was not just being a savvy businessman. He was also simultaneously being mindful of maintaining good relations with editors at publications and looking out for Alex Levy's best interest by trying to anticipate how his images could generate the most profit.

Later in the day, Ed tried to negotiate a partnership with the chief photo editor of a respected regional newspaper. GVI is a powerful player in the industry because its platform allows it to partner with all kinds of entities, from wire services to newspapers to individual photographers. In this case Ed was proposing brokering the images of a newspaper that cannot sell its material directly to magazines and doesn't have any sales staff to try to sell to foreign magazines, so they are interested in partnering with GVI, who already has the sales structure in place. This is a clever strategy for the newspaper, since it potentially turns its photo department into a revenue generator rather than just an expense center, strengthening the hand of the newspaper's director of photography to make demands on behalf of his photographers. Since profits from sales are shared, GVI gets added income from images it contributes no resources to producing, but it also gets high-quality images from a reputable news source to add to its portfolio of war coverage, thus linking its name with the names of prize-winning photojournalists.

The newspaper's photo editor was trying to negotiate a guarantee against sales (a minimum twenty-five hundred or three thousand dollars a week), and Ed was trying to negotiate for as short a time limit on the guarantee as possible.[10] In other words, Ed wanted to minimize GVI's risk. Since it was not sharing production costs, GVI would lose money only if it paid a guarantee up front but then could not make enough sales to cover that guarantee. The newspaper's editor confidently stated, "Look, I think it'll be over in two weeks. They're going to go in and bomb the living fuck out of these people. Even 9/11 only ran ten to twelve days. There's only so many pictures of people in the sand you can run. I'm saying this as an experienced photo editor: tops it'll take three weeks."

Tuesday, March 11, 2003

At least for those in the New York office, the daily routine of image brokering begins at the 10 A.M. staff meeting. GVI is a global company, and the news and editorial teams in New York and Paris meet via a phone conference every day, often joined by photo editors in London and Los Angeles. Over the course of my fieldwork, I participated in these meetings at both the New York and Paris offices. Each office's news and editorial team would gather in one of the director's offices for these calls, making the meetings both face-to-face interactions with their local colleagues and phone-based interactions with international GVI colleagues. Sometimes editors also joined the conference call from other locations. Especially when the individuals in separate offices had never met face-to-face, this meant that the people who worked together in the same physical office seemed to understand each other's decisions and motivations better. Cultural differences—not just of the individuals but of the European and American news publications (e.g., different closing dates, different labor laws, different notions of public domain, different styles of conducting business)—were often blamed for the perceived differences between the offices, though these were amplified by the fact that for each news team the suggestions of individuals in other offices came through an often crackly speaker rather than from a colleague sitting across the table. Shortly after I began observing these meetings, Michael Strong took a trip to Paris and called in to a few morning meetings with the French team in an effort to coalesce the two teams.

The day after attending the leadership meeting, I attended the news and editorial team meeting, as did Edith, GVI's global research director, who was in charge of the use of the archive for editorial purposes. She had suggestions: "I've pulled together a loose retro of the Iran/Iraq war and chemical weapons. There's quite a lot of ancient Iraqi art in the archive. Does that have a place at all in our coverage? We've pulled the pre-1980 analog files on the Iran/Iraq war and chemical warfare, but we have to be careful with it because it's very graphic. There's a high probability Saddam'll torch the oil wells again and we have that from before, so we've put those images in as well. There were mostly Kurdish victims at the time. In fact we have photos of the north going back as far as World War I—young sheiks and Lawrence of Arabia period." Edith had looked at the analog negatives as well as digital archives and was detailing what historical visual content GVI had so that the editors could pitch it along with the latest coverage. In other words, she narrated to the group the history of Iraq that GVI had the visuals to tell. Edith didn't work in the reactive mode of the news team but rather tried to anticipate future coverage. She didn't wait for events to happen to think about how to cover them but rather focused on what might need coverage in the future based on what had been covered in the past. Alternately, as was the case that day, she anticipated future needs for the history that GVI owned the visuals to tell. Her job was anticipating the futurepast. "I have to plan ahead, so at any given time I have about one to two hundred topics I'm anticipating requests for," she told me. The team agreed that the Iraq retrospective might be useful and that it should be put up on the website for clients to see.

After the meeting, Ed finally heard from Alex. Ed asked him, "Hey, Alex, did the writer tell you the couple story is a cover story? Are you getting on OK with him [the writer]? Is the relationship OK? You're going to have to be gentle with him because I think you're going to be spending a lot of time with this guy. Are you bumping up against bureaucracy? If bureaucracy's giving you shit, just chill with it a little bit, OK? Be cool, Alex, and check in with me once a day, OK?"

"Well, supposedly he's shooting the couple in the morning," Ed relayed to Jackie. "I imagine the writer must be annoyed because here he thought he was going on assignment with Jim Nachtwey and instead he gets twenty-three-year-old Alex. The troops were apparently wowed by Nachtwey, who probably has more combat experience than all of them put together, and now they have young Alex, who has been in Gaza but has no other real war experience." Turning to me, Ed explained, "I wanted to send Ilan." Ilan was another young, but slightly more established, photographer with more combat experience who had recently signed a representation contract with GVI. "But Ilan's got an Israeli passport, so we couldn't get him a visa."

On the cubicle divider next to Ed's desk was a large map of Afghanistan and a whiteboard with the names of several photographers, followed by the list of countries for which each had a valid visa. "Lydia: Yemen, Oman, Kuwait, Lebanon, UAE, Qatar, Iran. Sean: Iraq, Jordan, . . ." These lists simultaneously mapped both the anticipated geographies of imminent news stories and the bureaucratic limits determining where in that geography each photographer could move. Photographers' abilities to capture that "perfect shot" promised to visitors on GVI's home page often depended as much on mundane realities like their nationality and what visas they held as on their talents. The starkest example was Ilan, who was kept out of Iraq by his Israeli passport.

In fact Alex Levy, who was now shooting a cover for *Newsworld,* might not have gotten picked up by GVI at all, and certainly wouldn't have been the photographer GVI suggested when *Newsworld* asked for a replacement to take Nachtwey's embed position, had Ilan been able to get an Iraqi visa.

Monday, March 17, 2003

All the television screens around the news editors' cubicles reflected various packages of the "possible" war in Iraq. One channel's "Show-down Iraq" faced "Brink of War" on another channel. Almost all the nonembedded photographers represented by GVI had ended up in Baghdad. At the morning meeting Henry voiced his concern: "We have no idea how this will play out. Clustering everyone in Baghdad just seems a poor idea. We need to keep people spread out."

Jackie, on the other hand, inexperienced in war coverage, was con-cerned about the safety of the photographers. "ABC and NBC ordered their correspondents out. Do we want to send more people to a place that is so dangerous that other US news media are pulling people out?" she asked. "Are they all in the same hotel?"

Ed, who had told me earlier that he could only be cautious about not encouraging someone to put himself in danger but wasn't about to tell these professionals when to come out, moved the conversation on to the logistics of receiving images. If the professionals he represented were going to stay to produce them, Ed was committed to getting the photo-graphs out of Iraq: "There is so much traffic that a lot of the satellite phones are jammed and photographers are having a hard time transmit-ting." Later, back at their cubicles, everyone, including Ed, seemed gripped by the same anxious tension. Jackie joked nervously, "I've got to clean my desk before this war starts," and set herself to the task.

Meanwhile, Alex Levy had photographed the commander couple, and the issue of *Newsworld* was already on newsstands. Ed talked to the photo editor at the magazine: "The magazine looks really good. Alex was on IM [instant messenger] earlier today, but I haven't been able to get through on anyone's phones. I think something's up. He's been asking me about what you want him to cover, so tell me if you have any ideas for him. He seemed fine. Finished shooting 'People Writ-ing Letters Home to Loved Ones.' I don't know where he is because I try not to ask him that kind of question. I don't know whether lines are monitored or not." Then, with masterful salesmanship, Ed casually tried to interest the editor in an experienced photographer also represented by GVI who wasn't embedded—"But Sean is in Baghdad"—and swiftly launched into the list of other photographers available that the magazine might also consider putting on assignment.

Tuesday, March 18, 2003

The next morning everyone's morale seemed to have improved. Henry congratulated his team: "I'm grateful for all your work. Everyone has done a great job getting a first-rate team together. We are as well set up as any other news team. Hopefully it's a short war." Jackie raised her safety concerns again, and Michael Strong, calling in to the morning meeting from the Paris office, emphasized that they should be telling the photographers to do whatever they feel is safe but reminded Jackie that "everyone is there of their own volition." The team members ran through the positions of all the photographers even more carefully than they did every other day. When they asked each other whom a photographer was traveling with, it was clear that the photographer's safety was on the editors' minds as much as the well-honed instinct to find out what their competition was doing.

As soon as the meeting let out, Ed got a call from Sean, the photographer whose work he had pitched to *Newsworld* the day before. Sean assured Ed, "I feel comfortable with my decision to be here [in Baghdad]. I think it's a little bit of a panic snowball. I don't feel a threatening atmosphere. The only real change is that suddenly there are no Iraqi minders anywhere." This was a significant change, since several photographers had previously reported being under constant surveillance by Iraqi intelligence officers. Hence, Sean was not embedded with the US military but had until very recently been working under the constant threat of Iraqi government censorship.

The sense that nothing spectacular was happening was echoed in Alex's call later in the morning. He had been told that his unit would not move for several days. They were still twenty kilometers from the Iraqi border, and his colonel had said that when the first planes went into Iraq he planned to sit on a sandbag, have a cigar, and watch them fly overhead. "I told him I'd be right there to photograph him," Alex chuckled—though for most of the conversation on speakerphone with Ed, he sounded bored.

Friday, March 21, 2003

Reports were emerging at the morning meeting that coalition forces had taken control of Safwan, a southern Iraqi town, and a GVI photographer had sent a message saying that he'd be transmitting images. Supposedly there had been no fighting and locals had welcomed the troops. Robert, a cynical French photo editor from the Paris office, snickered over the speakerphone, "What'd they do, raise the American flag?"

Alain, the senior photo editor from Paris, filled the team in on a French photographer who had attached himself to a family in Baghdad: "Philippe's still on assignment today. He's found a family: a couple, grandmother, and two children." *Dateline NBC* was also interested in the story. "Now what we need is more bombing," Alain continued. "They are apparently anti-Saddam since the father was in prison last year, so it's a good story." Another Paris editor added, "They have no bunker. The photographer's trying to get them outside the home, but it's hard for them to agree to being photographed."

Ed ran through the positions of all the photographers. Yet even on what was to be the first day of the war, not all the stories on the table were about Iraq: "Suzanne is leaving for Afghanistan this week. She has several different ideas. Women in prisons. Women getting their driver's licenses."

Alain interrupted: "OK, I just got off the phone with Philippe and asked him to hold the photos of the family till tomorrow. The pictures from the family are very good: they are petrified." Pausing before trying out a new phrase, the editor continued in his thick French accent, "They're scared shitless, you know?"

Ed, in the New York office, laughed and said, "You must be hanging out with [Michael] Strong if you're talking like that! Well, on our end, Alex Levy's company is packing up. He's going to be going in with Black Hawks [military helicopters] so he's really psyched. He's hanging out by the showers because they keep having raid drills and people have to run out naked with their gas masks on." The editors regularly told each other which stories their photographers were covering or had mentioned as ideas so that when anyone spoke to an editor at a publication he or she could pitch multiple photographers and stories. Similarly, these meetings allowed for the editors to collectively pool what they had gathered the publications were interested in so they could guide photographers appropriately when asked.

"Hey, guys, it's Strong," a voice broke in. "Just wanted to check in. Listen, it's important to be thinking about getting some emails from our photographers right now. You know—'What it's really like out there'–type stuff. We should really get some text. There are a lot of outlets that are asking for text. People want to hear from us. Also a note coming from you to the photographers would really be great. You know, just a quick 'Be safe. And in your downtime think about sending us some thoughts.' Since it is so hard to get through on the phone right now, any communication is sunshine to them. Support our people out there. And you guys have been mentioning IMs. Some of those IMs I bet are quite fascinating. This is history that we're a part of. You are a part of history. What is it like to be doing this? We're not just documenting visual history, but we should also be documenting the way in which we're working with the photographers." An ethnographer of sorts, Strong wanted the team not only to broker good images but also to document the production of visual history. He was forever thinking of new ways to package photographs. If such text could get GVI's images into new venues, he wanted to make sure text was gathered along the way.

The meeting ended, and Ed went over to Sophie, the self-described "perma-temp" whose desktop was the place where images arrived in GVI's newsroom. Sophie usually got right to work as soon as she arrived, editing photographs that had come in from the photographers while the others were in the morning meeting. Ed would usually review the selection on her desktop before she sent the photos to the lab for color correction. After reviewing captions and changing them if necessary, Sophie deleted redundant frames and pushed images to the lab. The photos of groups of Iraqis surrendering in Safwan had started coming in, and Sophie clicked through them for Ed's approval before pushing them out to editors at various news publications who might want to purchase them for publication. Ed stopped at one that showed a concerned-looking American medic attending to a wounded Iraqi who was seated on the ground next to a tank with a bright yellow MRE (meal-ready-to-eat) pack in front of him. There was blood on the Iraqi man's face, neck, and green uniform, and the medic was holding the man's head in his blue-gloved hands. To the right of the photo behind the Iraqi man, the barrel of a rifle was visible.

"Wait, let me see the caption of that photo."

Sophie opened the file and went to the caption field as Ed had instructed her. It read: "Navy Corpsmen tend to an Iraqi prisoner wounded as Marines took control of an oil pumping station in southern Iraq."

"Excellent!" exclaimed Ed and immediately went to his phone. "Excellent! I'm calling *Newsworld*. They were looking for Iraqi POW photos." When the editor's secretary answered, Ed had the editor paged. "I've got a POW image. Are you interested?" The deal Ed had negotiated with the newspaper a few days earlier was potentially already paying off since the photograph was from one of their photographers. Ed mentioned this to the magazine editor: "I'll give it to you for a one-thousand-dollar guarantee plus one thousand dollars if you run it."

Once off the phone, he looked a bit disappointed as he told his team, "She said two thousand dollars was way too much. If it were an injured American she'd pay that, but it's too much for [an Iraqi] POW. Or if it were the only image out there. But apparently there are other images." He walked over to Sophie's screen again. "I mean it's a total propaganda shot, isn't it? 'Look how nice we're being to them, etc.'" This was typical of Ed. Like many professional brokers, he knew how to talk about the image to underscore its value for other brokers regardless of his own personal opinion of the image. There are formative fictions at work here. Ed anticipates the story that will move the photograph and get it sold. Nonetheless, he also claims it is propaganda. His commitment, however, is to the photographer in the field and selling his or her photographs.

At 1 P.M., the televisions that hung from the ceilings around the office lit up with special bulletins, and people gathered around as news of the outbreak of war flashed across the screens. Soon there were thirty or so people craning their necks to get a better view of the initial bombing of Baghdad.

"Wow, look at that!" an editor from the commercial representation team exclaimed. "It sounds like the Fourth of July. What a sound and light show! So this is the Shock and Awe campaign."

People from other floors kept coming down to the newsroom—the only area with television screens that were always on—to see what was happening. After about six minutes of relatively quiet and intense viewing, the crowd of forty or so people dispersed as if on cue when the CNN reporter commented, "There you saw it, there you heard it."

Within a half hour the screens were transmitting a Pentagon press briefing. Secretary of Defense Donald Rumsfeld and General Richard Meyers presented the objectives of the strikes on Iraq and summarized the position of coalition troops. General Meyers ended his prepared briefing with the expected "And with that, we'll take your questions," but Rumsfeld jumped in:

> Before we do, let me make one comment. Just before coming down, after the air campaign began in earnest about 1 P.M., I saw some of the images on

television and I heard various commentators expansively comparing what's taking place in Iraq today to some of the more famous bombing campaigns of World War II. There is no comparison. The weapons that are being used today have a degree of precision that no one ever dreamt of in a prior conflict—they didn't exist. . . . The targeting capabilities and the care that goes into targeting to see that the precise targets are struck and that other targets are not struck is as impressive as anything anyone could see. The care that goes into it, the humanity that goes into it, to see that military targets are destroyed, to be sure, but that it's done in a way, and in a manner, and in a direction and with a weapon that is appropriate to that very particularized target. And I think that the comparison is unfortunate and inaccurate. And I think that will be found to be the case when *ground truth* is achieved.[11]

I would add also that I think we're probably watching something that is somewhat historic. We're having a conflict at a time in our history when we have 24-hours-a-day television, radio, media, Internet, and more people in the world have access to what is taking place. You couple that with the hundreds—literally hundreds of people in the free press—the international press, the press of the United States, from every aspect of the media—who have been offered and accepted an opportunity to join and be connected directly with practically every aspect of this campaign. And *what we are seeing is not the war in Iraq*. What we're seeing are slices of the war in Iraq. We're seeing that particularized perspective that that reporter, or that commentator or that television camera, happens to be able to see at that moment. And it is not what's taking place. What you see is taking place, to be sure, but it is one slice. And it is the *totality* of that that is what this war is about and being made up of. And I don't—I doubt that in a conflict of this type there's ever been the degree of free press coverage as you are witnessing in this instance.[12]

Shortly thereafter the White House press secretary, Ari Fleischer, answered questions from the press and echoed the language of getting the "totality" of information "in a totality" rather than relying on the press.

> *Q:* Ari, has the President watched any of this, the unfolding events in Baghdad, do you know?
>
> *Mr. Fleischer:* Obviously, the President, having authorized the mission, was aware of the mission, knew when it would begin, et cetera. And I don't think he needs to watch TV to know what was about to unfold.
>
> *Q:* I was wondering if he had any comment on the impact of it.
>
> *Mr. Fleischer:* No, the President's approach is to gather the information about what is happening *in its totality*. He receives the information from his advisors, people who have a sight on all areas of what is under way. The President is aware, of course, of the American people as they watch these events unfold; but he gets his information in a totality . . .
>
> *Q:* Just to clarify Terry's question. You said the President doesn't need to watch TV to know what's going on in Iraq, but you're telling me—these

are pretty astounding images—he doesn't have a television on somewhere, he's not watching what's going on?

Mr. Fleischer: The President, again, understands the implications of the actions that he has launched to secure the disarmament of the Iraqi regime, to liberate the people.

In this first question-and-answer session of the war in Iraq, the image that emerged was of a president as a sovereign who does not need to be informed by the press. Rumsfeld's comments that the international free press *have been offered and have accepted* the opportunity to join every aspect of this military campaign describes the press as part of the campaign managed by the Bush administration rather than as an independent organ of information.

Q: Right, right, right. The question, though, is, Is he watching TV, or not?

Mr. Fleischer: The President may occasionally turn on the TV, but that's not how he gets his news or his information."[13]

In other words, the president didn't rely on the same sources as the public or the press for information. Furthermore, in the first hours of the war, the implication was that visuals—no matter how astounding the images may be—were not influencing politics. They were mere reflections of the political decisions that had already been made. Moreover, in his comments Rumsfeld at once lauded the visual precision of the military's targeting machinery and the unprecedented degree of free press coverage while insisting that what was shown through the press was not the war.

Liz, one of the young photo editors who was generally fairly calm, walked over to Ed's cubicle with a look of concern: "Are people OK?"

"They've been confined to the hotel, so I'm guessing so."

Liz had just heard from another photographer in the field and added, "Well, Lydia is fine; she's in the north. Is it going to be worse?"

"No, that's it."

Andrew, another photographer, called in to say he'd just driven by a downed helicopter but hadn't been able to photograph it. He was with two other photographers, each distributing through different photo agencies, and an Italian television crew.

"Are the news mags closing tomorrow, or Sunday?" Jackie asked the others. Most newsmagazines close on Friday or Saturday but may push back their close time if they anticipate late-breaking news. However, in France magazines close on Mondays. Jackie was trying to get information that would allow her best to guide photographers who were asking what their coverage priorities should be.

"*Newsworld*'s staying open till six tomorrow." (It was at this point that the courier I described at the beginning of this book brought over an envelope of undeveloped film from a photographer in California who had been covering the protests.)

"Why is the refugees story on our front page?" Liz, who had gone back to her desk, asked Ed, pointing to GVI's news and editorial home page on her screen, where a several-day-old story about refugees was still featured. "All people care about right now is the war."

"Yeah, let's put the bombing on the first page—that's what people want to buy. It's good to sell photos!" Ed had his joking voice on but repeatedly stated that their greatest commitment should be to selling photographers' work. Liz's instinct that the main news story should be featured on the homepage is both journalistic and commercial. GVI is not a news publication, yet its "front page" had to parallel that of the newspapers.

Monday, March 24, 2003

The morning conference call began with the Paris office relaying that Jacques, a very senior photographer, had had all his equipment stolen.[14] The photographer thought it was the work of Iraqi officials who had broken into his apartment, but he had no concrete evidence. Robert, an editor, relayed what he had heard from Jacques: "They're coming down hard trying to expel people. They took his telephone, money, computer—everything. Meanwhile several journalists have been killed, so I'm worried about them getting stuck in a no-man's-land. They need to be together with others. So Andrew is traveling with guys from the other agencies."

Liz nodded in agreement: "Lydia was only twenty to thirty meters away from the car that exploded in the north."

Henry tried to assure his team: "Let's get everyone home safely— that's our first priority." The meeting segued into coverage of the Oscar ceremony of the night before. There was a tone of excitement at the meeting; everyone had been selling well.

"We got two double pages in *Stern*," reported Alain.[15] "In France, though, everyone's waiting for the deadlines to buy photos at the last possible minute."

After the meeting, Henry sat at his desk watching the TV coverage and calling the various magazines his photographers were working for, asking if he could syndicate the images overseas now that the magazines had closed the week.[16] Henry was frustrated by GVI's website. "A lot of editors are telling me, 'I go to your website, but I can't find today's images.' They want wire-service speed," he explained to me. "This has turned out to be a much messier war than anyone expected," he repeated several times on his calls. Looking up at the TV images of Iraqi soldiers being captured, Smith said to me, "Honestly, I don't understand why what we show is not in violation of Geneva Conventions."[17] Similarly to Ed, Henry had not received clear instructions on what the Geneva Conventions actually prohibited, nor had this information been provided by the US military in conjunction with the embed program.[18] The assumption seemed to be that the sheer number of cameras in the field would ensure certain standards of ethical behavior. Henry continued: "This is a huge embed effort, though. I mean, there are hundreds of journalists out there and there's enough action so that someone has someone nearby no matter what's happening. This is going to be the best-documented war ever."[19]

Henry Smith, the director of news, had been alerted the night before that an American soldier with a unit still in camp had lobbed hand grenades into the commanding officers' tent, killing one soldier and wounding fifteen others. Coincidentally, it was the unit that Alex Levy was embedded in, and Levy had sent in a whole series of photos showing both the suspect and the wounded men being evacuated to medical facilities. Jackie and Henry had spent quite a bit of time debating whether they could put the photos up on GVI's website. Did the Geneva Conventions apply to your own soldiers? Would the images cause anguish to the families of the injured? Would this compromise Alex's position within his unit? What would be the political fallout for GVI? Of course, what was so apparent that it need not be spoken was the incredible "luck" that this incident of "friendly" fire—a major news item for that week—had happened just a few tents over from young Alex's cameras. Alex had apparently gotten an OK from the colonel of the unit for the release of the images, but nonetheless Henry was concerned that the soldiers in the photos were identifiable. The solution in the end was to post the images on GVI's website and ask the legal department for advice. This compromise allowed the images to be available to any publications that wanted to purchase rights to use the images, and yet allowed GVI to avoid taking on any responsibility for publishing the images, since GVI was not pushing the images out. In March 2003 at least, GVI's website was seen as a sales tool rather than a publicly accessible conduit of information. However, just a few days earlier, Liz had treated GVI as a news publication when deciding what should be placed on the front page of its website.

Many of the people who had been in the industry for a long time—perhaps especially those who remembered all the speculations that television would be the death of photojournalism—seemed thrilled that television news programs were using still images. Several channels were featuring still photographs and including interviews with photographers. Veterans of the industry seemed to think that TV news's featuring still images in this case was confirmation of their belief that photojournalists produced more informative and more compelling visuals than TV cameramen. The question posed to Henry that day was whether GVI should be billing CNN for using GVI's still images or whether this should be thought of as free advertising because the photos were being run with a "courtesy of GVI" label. While he was in the midst of this quandary, Henry's phone rang. It was a photographer hoping to stop by and show Henry his portfolio. Rolling his eyes, Henry said politely, "I'd be happy to meet any photographer, but during the peak of a war is hard. Call me again when Baghdad's over."

Before lunchtime in New York, Alex had called Ed. Part of the unit was planning a helicopter mission, and Alex was trying to decide whether to stay with the mass of troops or go on the mission, which could be dangerous. The editor at *Newsworld* for whom he was still on assignment had repeatedly told him they didn't want him to put his life in danger. Alex hung up undecided, saying he knew the decision was his to make. The danger was real, and Ed listened intently but did not try to sway Alex one way or the other. Lydia, one of GVI's female photographers, called from the Kurdish area in northern Iraq within moments after Alex's call. As Liz had reported to the group that morning, Lydia had been just a few feet in front of a car bomb that killed three others, including a foreign journalist. Perhaps in an attempt to distract her from the tragedy or to emphasize that she was not putting her life in danger in vain, Ed told her, "*Newsworld* used your photo of them hosing down the blood this week."

"It was bloody awful. I realized a guy injured was a guy I knew from Moscow. I spent the night talking to him and he left this morning," Lydia said. Briefly Ed tried to console her, and then they switched to business.

"What's the situation with my day rate?" she asked.

"You're getting double day [rate] as of Shock and Awe in Baghdad last week."

"They asked if I wanted to go back to Kuwait two weeks ago."[20]

"Do you feel safe? There's been a few journalists killed." They wrapped up the conversation with Ed communicating how glad the team was that she was OK. Lydia was a highly experienced and very professional photographer, as indicated by Ed's caring but professional interaction with her. His long years of experience as a photo editor determined when to express concern, when to switch to business matters, and, perhaps most important, when to inject humor into the conversation. This was the art of image brokering. Each photographer and every situation required a slightly different approach. Ed was careful never to make a judgment call on behalf of the photographer. Even when young Alex called again to say he'd decided to go on the mission with his troop but that a sandstorm was forcing them to drive rather than fly in with helicopters, Ed asked some questions but didn't champion his decision or try to change Alex's mind. Yet Ed was cautious about how to advise the least experienced of his photographers.

"When you move, make sure there's someone on either side of you. There's a lot of you, right?"

"Don't worry, I'm OK."

Once off the phone, Ed voiced additional anxieties: "I'm a bit worried about the fact that he's developing camaraderie with the soldiers. He wants to go with the same people he's been with. I don't want him to put himself in a dangerous situation because he's bonded with these people. If one of them gets shot and everyone runs away, I don't want him trying to save the guy. But I guess I can't control him from making a [human] decision. I'm just worried about him bonding with these guys. He's the same age, he's been pissing in the sand with them for weeks. I don't want him to feel like he's obliged to do an act of bravado. These guys are paid to die, they're soldiers. He's not. He's there to document, and I'm not sure he always recognizes the difference." When they spoke later in the day he made a point of adding, "Hey, Alex, if the shooting starts, don't take pictures, OK? Just keep your head down, OK?"

Tuesday, March 25, 2003

As the action on the ground slowed, the team started struggling to find interesting angles to cover the war. How would they keep the imagery of the war fresh? The Paris office suggested looking at religion during the war.

"We're seeing a lot of images of soldiers praying."

"What about religion on the home front? There's also big prayers [for US soldiers] in Doha, Qatar. We could ask: 'Aren't the Americans going too far?'"

"Shall we suggest to the photographers that they keep an eye out for religion?"

The team decided to tell photographers to send in religious imagery.

Meanwhile, another story had been brewing. Alain from the Paris office asked, "Have you seen photos on this virus in China? Masks seem to be the only things that can be photographed."

Henry Smith urged the Paris office to take leadership of the Asian virus story, adding, "I think if the war weren't around it'd be a big story."

After the meeting, Ed rifled through the morning papers, pointing out an image of Iraqis herding sheep with a military convoy in the background: "That's what war is to most people, trucks going by in the distance as life goes on." Ed's comment on this image taken early in the war implies that despite all the media attention on the war, he conceived of it as an event occurring in the background of daily life for many Iraqis. Yet he was actively engaged in representing it through the images being sent in by the photographers, many of which focused on front lines. Henry walked by, looked at the image, and told Ed to keep an eye on the photographer who'd taken the shot, commenting, "He's going to become important."

Ed read the credit below the photograph. "Damn! He's staff. I'm always looking for good photographers to sign up, always looking for the potential quitting/fired photographer, but if he's staff at the *New York Times,* we won't get him." Staff positions that came with benefits and steady work were very difficult to come by in the industry, and hence Ed knew it was highly unlikely that a staff photographer would give up the security of such a position, especially at a prominent paper, and choose to work as a freelancer.[21]

Later that morning Henry and Ed together called Sean, an experienced photographer who had gotten kicked out of Baghdad by Iraqi officials. The photographer was livid. He'd been in the field for three straight months and had sent in an email outlining a plan to drive back into Iraq immediately. Henry and Ed understood Sean's frustration given the intensity of his investment in the story and the fact that he had been expelled just as he might have started taking images that were journalistically and financially worthwhile. Nonetheless, Henry was a little concerned that Sean's decision might be a hasty one: "Let's talk about a situation where it's house-to-house combat or chemical weapons. Are you equipped with a gas mask in case those types of weapons are deployed? How many American journalists are still in Baghdad? Do you think driving in is safe?" All parties got frustrated as the line kept dropping out. Henry emphasized, "Yes, I read your email, but I just wanted to talk with you and make sure that frustration wasn't pushing you into an emotional decision. You can take a couple of weeks off. There's going to be a rich, long, complex story to cover. There'll be a lot of reporting and photojournalism to be done. Is that a better solution for you, or do you want to get in for the endgame? Don't feel like you owe anybody anything. It's entirely at your discretion."

They promised to wire Sean a five-thousand-dollar advance via Western Union and ended the call. Henry seemed assured that Sean wasn't in danger of burning out anytime soon. Yet a few minutes later, Henry expressed concern to Ed, shifting their focus from this particular photographer's situation to GVI's coverage: "Look, soon the war will be over, and we don't want to be caught flat with nothing else in the pipeline. In fact, I just asked Jackie for a 'best of the war' selection, since I'm sure people will be requesting them soon." Henry wasn't alone in thinking the war was nearing the endgame: less than a week after Shock and Awe, the CNN banner on the overhead television screens read, "Pace of war has slowed."

Thursday, March 27, 2003

The team in New York evaluated multiple factors when considering where to position the photographers: the photographers' wishes, their safety, the comprehensiveness of GVI's coverage of the war, its coverage of other news events—especially given the predicted end of the war. Many of GVI's photographers were in Baghdad. The most experienced of them, Jacques, who had had all his equipment stolen, was incredibly frustrated. He had new equipment now but felt he couldn't photograph anything unless the Iraqi minders wanted him to see it. After discussing how to support each photographer in the field, the team listened to the Los Angeles entertainment editor's lengthy update on coverage of Celine Dion's new show in Las Vegas, which was to run for three years.

Alex Levy, who had not been heard from, finally called; his unit had been traveling nonstop for three days, and he promised to send in what he had that night.

Meanwhile Kelly, an American photographer whose work GVI distributed, called from Doha, angry that she could not get *Newsworld* to give her a guarantee. She was trying to get exclusive coverage with General Tommy Franks.[22] Kelly had connections. She had been introduced personally to Franks by Donald Rumsfeld, whom she had photographed before. But she was still establishing her career and was threatened by the imminent arrival of better-known photographers. Her biggest worry was a well-established photographer who had covered US politics for years and had connections to all these people.

"I asked him straight out: 'Am I going to get stomped on by you?' and he said he didn't have any plans as of now to come here."

Kelly had asked *Newsworld* for a three-week guarantee, but so far they hadn't agreed to it, and she was very concerned because she was currently financing the coverage entirely out of her own pocket. At one hundred dollars a night, her hotel room in Doha was a good deal, but nonetheless the accumulating expenses were making her nervous.

"Look, because of the way the industry has gone, I know money is tight," she said, "but this is the biggest story of our time, and I'm the only one who can cover from the inside. Do you guys think I'm out of line?"

Henry, who had himself come to GVI from *Newsworld,* tried to explain the magazine editor's position: "Look, don't be mad at the editor. She's just maxed out her budget keeping her people in the field. This is a very, very expensive war to cover. Do you have any set times for when you'll be getting behind-the-scenes stuff?"

"I don't know when it's going to happen, but I think it's going to be ongoing throughout. Rumsfeld likes me, Franks likes me, the top guy likes me, and they like my pictures. Even if Nachtwey shows up—I think those guys do great work—but it's about access, and there's a tight situation here. I just want to get paid properly. How about if you guys cover the next three weeks at a day rate?" Kelly was highlighting her relationships with these top officials to persuade Henry and Ed that her access would not get blocked at a critical moment, that she had an in that the top brass would honor even if a more famous photographer appeared.

Henry quickly calculated: "Kelly, that's seventy-five hundred dollars. That's what mags [i.e., magazines] pay. I'm not sure I can do that. We need to think about this from a business perspective, not just a coverage angle. Plus I can't imagine that Tommy Franks's people would allow just one photographer to exclusively cover his arrival in Baghdad. Why don't we both think about it and talk again in a few hours?"

After the conference call, Henry and Ed discussed the issue. "If Kelly rides the chopper with Franks to Baghdad we'd make the money back in a day. Or if she gets a shot of Saddam surrendering to him," Henry figured, confirming that Kelly was not out of line in her estimation of the potential sales value of her access to US military officials.

But Ed cautioned, "I can't even guess at the number of photographers in Baghdad right now. She didn't let us try to make the original deal with *Newsworld,* and so she's coming to us now, once they've turned her down. It's not like we don't see Franks; he's doing press conferences. I just can't see her getting consistently good shots for three weeks straight."

"I'm thinking at most a five-thousand-dollar guarantee. She'd break even that way and then we could split profits from sales fifty–fifty."

Showing confidence in his own ability to strike a better deal with the magazine editor, Ed suggested, "How about if I try to get *Newsworld* interested? Let me call the editor and try to get $350 a day plus expenses from them."

"I think she's feeling vulnerable and is in a bit of a panic. If we guarantee her five thousand dollars, we need to sell ten thousand dollars' worth of Tommy Franks pictures just to not be in the hole," Henry calculated.

In the end they decided to cover Kelly's expenses for three weeks but agreed that the photographs had to sell themselves; they wouldn't guarantee an amount on the work.

Jackie came looking for Ed: "We're showing Iraqi POWs' faces. How in violation of Geneva Conventions are we?"

"I think Henry is going to talk to legal about it. I mean, we just deliver the photos on our website, right?"

Perma-temp Sophie pressed Ed: "Yes, but isn't the Internet public domain? And you were the one who wouldn't let us post the images of the grenade attack by the American soldier."

"But it wasn't a moral decision. It was a business decision: I didn't want to jeopardize Alex's embed position."

Cynical Sophie insisted, "Don't you think we should have some standards to follow? *I* don't want to be making these decisions." In the absence of formal guidelines, Sophie, the most junior member of the team, whose temp status was continually acknowledged by her and others, was the one pushing images out to publications or merely posting them to the website, often without much debate about whether they were troubling.

Henry, their boss, seemed confused as well. "Does the Geneva Convention automatically become law of every citizen of a land that's a signatory of that convention?" he asked. "Until we hear from legal, we're keeping the images up. There's no obvious suffering in these images, and we have no Iraqi market. I am concerned about our market, where we might cause hardship to the families of those in the photos." What is clearly getting blurred in Henry's comments is a distinction between market considerations, responsibility to a particular public that a news publication might serve, and a sense of obligation to a more general ethics of visualizing war. This made sense, since Henry had spent many years at *Newsworld* before his job at GVI, and visual content providers' responsibility, if any, toward a public had not been clearly spelled out by GVI's management. This was, after all, the first major war since the rise of visual content providers. What was still unclear was whether visual content providers were in the business of covering war, or merely selling images. This was the beginning of the digitalization of the industry, signaling the collapse of the historical boundaries between the entities responsible for the production, distribution, and publication of news images.

Friday, March 28, 2003

"Well, the *New York Times* published the image that Sophie censored for us, so I think we can go ahead and load it on the website!" Ed told the group with his usual good-humored sarcasm. In the absence of clear directives on what GVI's management thought the group should or should not distribute, the company's image brokers began looking at what other news organizations were doing. Yet, despite his jab that they might have lost a sales opportunity by listening to the ethical qualms of their temp while the paper of record had found the same image unobjectionable, Ed himself was also often quite concerned about ethics. "Look at this photo," he directed, pointing to an image in a different paper that showed two soldiers approaching a truck with rifles at the ready. Ed read the caption: "Dead occupants were found to be unarmed." Exasperated, he added, "What did they die of? Old age?!" Even without speculating on Ed's opinion of the morality of the killing, one could tell that he found the evasive caption troubling.

An editor from a different division came over to Ed's desk and asked, "Have you spoken with Lydia this morning? Her mother just called. She's worried. So I tried to give her lots of reassurance." Ed hadn't heard from Lydia.

Meanwhile, Henry had heard back from legal: "Apparently the Geneva Convention has no force on us but does have force on the US Army, so embeds are key. But Alex is our only embedded photographer. I'm not going to be everyone's conscience and send out a blanket statement about POWs, because the trend is elsewhere. We'll try to be sensitive in the same way we were to US troops. . . . Geneva Accords do not apply to private organizations. Alex Levy is a guest of the military. . . . With him alone we are going to be sensitive, but otherwise, we just provide a source for material. It's up to the individual papers to decide what to run. We're going to provide unambiguous, unbiased distribution." The answer from legal allowed Henry to pass the responsibility of deciding which images were appropriate to others, whether those others were other publications setting "the trend," or the US military.

Ed called the *Army Times*'s photo editor. The *Army Times* had five photographers who were working in Iraq and sending images. Ed wanted to syndicate their work: "Hi, it's Friday, it's a good day to try to get your images sold." Many newsmagazines close on Friday, meaning that it is a good day to try to sell them images. They will most likely run an image they buy on a Friday because the risk is less that a late-breaking development will mean the image has to be substituted.[23] Fridays were busy sales days for Ed, who put a lot of energy into providing publications with a wide range of options through GVI. He asked Jackie to contact a Turkish newspaper whose photographer's images had appeared in the *New York Times* to see if the paper would like the photographer's work to be sold through GVI's website. He was constantly thinking of how to make more images available through GVI.

Ed's phone rang, and the name of the editor at *Newsworld* appeared on the display. After his conversation, Ed passed on the request to Jackie in a hammed-up voice: "OK, they want a soldier who looks like he's dirty, in combat, full of strength, resolve, and the will to go on!" And then, in his normal voice, he added, "I tried to pitch that photo of the three smoking soldiers, but she said it's shot from too far away."

Later in the day, Ed negotiated with the *Newsworld* editor again, this time about the entire week's coverage from a staff photographer for the regional newspaper whose work GVI was syndicating. He was trying to get the editor to commit to four thousand dollars for using anything the photographer had shot that week rather than just pay three thousand dollars to use the particular photographs she was interested in. This was not about purchasing the use of a single frame, but rather about purchasing exclusive rights to the photographer's weekly output so that none of the magazine's competition could use it—essentially taking a certain set of images off the market.

"Given that it's Friday and some magazines won't close till tomorrow, it's a bit of a gamble, no?" I asked Ed, wanting to know what he would do if he got a truly profitable single image the following day, perhaps an image that he knew no one else had. In other words, if the same photographer happened to send in a key photograph the next day, would Ed really not sell it to anyone else and not demand any more payment for it if the editor agreed to this four-thousand-dollar deal?

"Look, if I got something really great tomorrow I'd say the deal was off. I just listen to people's voices and make a decision on the fly. I try to get the various competitors interested."

It was not that Ed and the editor at the magazine did not hold each other to their agreements; rather, each knew and accepted that each side was constantly in negotiations. What mattered most was the long-term overall relationship rather than each individual deal. Of course, long-term trust was built through a series of successful transactions, but there was room for some juggling. The key was having the experience to know how to protect your own interests while still holding on to your reputation and not losing others' trust. For example, the editor at *Newsworld* was thinking of possibly using one of the regional newspaper staff photographer's images for the magazine's cover and emailed Ed an example of the layout. The magazine wanted to crop the image, and so Ed contacted the editor at the photographer's newspaper with whom he had negotiated the syndication deal. It was not a legal matter of permissions and requirements but rather a process of developing and maintaining goodwill and trust and an attempt to get all of the various stakeholders on board about a decision. Ed got a provisional agreement from the newspaper's photo editor and relayed the details to the editor at *Newsworld,* who promised to send over a layout as soon as it was finalized. None of them were contractually obligated to get each other's approval, but each was being courteous and working toward maintaining a long-term relationship.

Henry told Ed he thought they should make a deal with Kelly, the photographer with access to General Tommy Franks, for similar reasons: "I want her in the fold. I like her, and I think she'll be good in the longer term. I'm more buying a future relationship than I'm buying a set of pictures."

When they called her, Kelly was relieved: "The reason I offered it to you first is that it'd be easier for me to go to CENTCOM [Central

Command] and say I'm releasing it to GVI. . . . I've already been here for a week covering lame press conferences just to be present and show my commitment, but I can't afford to stay out here on my own. But I guess you can't pay the whole shebang?"

"Absolutely not," replied Henry. "But I want to support you in this and in the future. We'll give you a four-thousand-dollar guarantee against a fifty–fifty split. There's an increased risk for us because it's not just about 'Will you get the story?' but also 'Can we sell it?' We're not a magazine. We want to share the risk with you. We can help cover expenses and share revenues. If one of the magazines put you on assignment, then they'd cover expenses and pay you a day rate and we'd take 30 percent of that day rate. Perhaps we can sell the images internationally, but that can only come together when you get the images. An upfront agreement for Tommy Franks coverage would be impossible internationally."

"That wouldn't work for me anyway," admits Kelly. "I can't go to my main contact and say I'm covering this for *Paris Match* because he'd put me on the first plane out." This was a moment of high anti-French sentiment in America, particularly among supporters of the war. It was still a mere two weeks after France had refused to support the US military campaign against Iraq. This had triggered such anger that the cafeteria menus in the three Washington, DC, House office buildings had substituted the name "freedom fries" for "french fries." Ed laughed and agreed fervently, "Over! Do *not* mention *Paris Match*." Once off the phone, he turned to Henry and commented on their negotiation with Kelly: "I feel like it's a big mating dance. We dance around and I say, 'Oh I've got a big chest and I've got feathers on my arms,' and she says, 'Well, I've got . . .'"

"Well, that's exactly what it is!" confirmed Henry.

Back at his desk Ed found the layout for the *Newsworld* cover. "Looks like *Platoon* or something. Looks like a movie poster for a Vietnam film," he commented. Apparently the newspaper editor had given the go-ahead. "The magazine's already paid for rights to this week's coverage from this newspaper, but I want an additional for the cover. Fifteen hundred to two thousand is standard," Ed informed me.

We were interrupted by his phone ringing. It was a salesperson asking him whether GVI could allow a magazine electronic rights to assignment images and inquiring about the price per photograph. The salesperson was allowing the magazine to use stock images at seventy-five dollars an image. Ed answered, "Yes, but we can't bulk-price assignment photos, because the value of the image is very content driven," and rolled his eyes, annoyed at having to explain the need to value news images differently from stock images.[24]

Ed's irritation might also have been due to the fact that articulating the particular attributes that made a specific photograph valuable as a news image was one of his talents. He behaved as if it were easy to sell an image with timely and newsworthy content—as if the visible sold itself—whereas how an editor verbally comments on an image is itself a skill, one that Ed had mastered. Moreover, the real art of photo-agency sales was in creating demand and desire for images that do not yet exist and getting publications to pay money to commit to images they may never use. Ed's true talents were in selling the invisible—creating a demand for the visual futurepast and selling it before it had even been framed in a photographer's viewfinder. This talent was a vestige of the days when analog images often had to be sold literally sight unseen. A generation of editors at publications were still accustomed to an agency editor describing an image to them rather than having the ability to see every image digitally before they committed to it. Ed was a masterful salesman because he expertly played off an editor's anxieties about not having the ever-elusive perfect shot, anxieties that many years of experience allowed him to hear in their voices. I heard him jokingly tell one editor he was cajoling into buying the following day's coverage, "You don't know what they are going to get tomorrow. They could get something really good tomorrow. Just so you know, I'll be in the office tomorrow." A master of well-timed humor, Ed never appeared desperate or lost his cool with clients, even when he was extremely anxious once off the phone.

Sophie called Ed over to look at an image of American soldiers lining up to get on a plane. Ed joked, "This way for death!" Later he told Sophie he'd called the *Newsworld* editor again and told her about the image and how it's "reminiscent of Vietnam." But apparently the editor had seemed uninterested; it wasn't the direction the magazine's coverage was taking. And then Ed looked up and noticed me scribbling in my notebook and added, smiling, "I should remember to say only profound things when I come over here." In a stentorian voice he asked, "Are we merely serving as the propaganda arm of the US military? Are the royalties we receive for these images blood money, or is it just money [that's] helping us feed information to the masses?" I include these comments not because Ed was the only insightful or humorous person on the team, but rather because Ed regularly had multifaceted reactions that were carefully tailored to his audience. He was the ideal broker because he was constantly reframing ideas—and even his humor—for his audience, which changed with every visitor and phone call.

Monday, March 31, 2003

Alain, the senior editor in Paris, was telling the team that the photographers in Baghdad were going out at night to photograph the bombings but that during the day they had to take the bus tours arranged by the Iraqi ministry of information and go see whatever they wanted the journalists to see. "Also," he added "we did an assignment about an Italian bishop still holding Mass in Baghdad which would be a good Easter story since Easter holidays are always good for Catholic religious stories." The assignment had been motivated, then, not necessarily by the fact that the Italian bishop was very influential or that his congregation in Iraq was particularly large or significant, but rather because the photo editors knew that newsmagazines in Europe and the United States would be looking for news stories to tack on to their seasonal coverage of Easter. Ulf Hannerz, in *Foreign News: Exploring the World of Foreign Correspondents,* discusses stories typical of certain places, but there are also story lines at home that news abroad can be made to fit.[25]

Henry passed on what he had heard about the Geneva Conventions from the legal department: "The Geneva Conventions do not specifically mention photography. So we are not going to go to pixelating out the faces of Iraqi prisoners. But we're not going to use anything gratuitous, and the same standard applies as for American soldiers. Tell the story, but not by putting the Iraqi in a compromised situation unless there is a compelling journalistic reason. We are an unbiased conduit for material. What they use is the publication's call."[26] Each time Henry passed on this guideline he was reproducing a conflicting message: image brokers at GVI would take ethics into consideration and not compromise the subjects in their images—unless they decided there was a sufficiently compelling journalistic reason to do so. However, GVI was not a journalistic publication, merely a conduit delivering visual content.

The Asian SARS (severe acute respiratory system) story surfaced again, and everyone agreed it was too important not to cover. One editor got siphoned off of the war and put on covering SARS. Henry warned her, "Remember to tell photographers that this story is very dangerous to cover. Maybe more than Baghdad."

Edith, the archivist, mentioned that the archive group had now pulled together a retrospective on the history of dissent during wartime.

Liz added, "That's great to know. Sam [another GVI photographer] is covering US teenagers' reactions to the war."

Suddenly Michael Strong jumped in: "That's exactly the kind of thing we should be thinking, but we should be doing it as big overarching themes. Think big stories. I've been thinking: What's the big story we want to cover for 2004? I think it's immigration. Or teens around the world reacting to war. Do they care? We need to be doing what no one else is doing." Then, referencing a story one of GVI's photographers had recently shot, he added, "Beauty parlors in Baghdad was a brilliant idea. But instead of doing twenty of these stories, let's pick three." Strong was always pushing his team to think of big overarching themes, what he termed "epic stories" with global reach, rather than small reactive coverage that tried to find fresh angles on stories already being covered.[27]

Tuesday, April 1, 2003

The morning started with an editor mentioning that yet another photographer was in Amman trying to get into Iraq: "I asked him if it was like one big waiting room and he replied, 'Yeah, except there are no good magazines!'"

A manager from the sales department congratulated the news team. It came as no surprise to the news and editorial team that war really did sell. The manager reported, "We're getting a lot of placement. This is a great sales month. News sales are up about 125 percent of goal. It's been an absolutely stellar month."

The mood was more somber among the editorial team after the meeting as photographs began coming in. Alex Levy started transmitting explicit images of the aftermath of house-to-house combat in Iraq, and Ed worried about him: "When Levy comes back he's going to be fucked up like the rest of them. They've seen too much and they can't cope with it." Yet Ed must have decided that this was not the time to share his concern with Alex, for when he called, Ed chose to focus on a temporary competitive advantage instead by relaying a rumor that the satellite phone of the senior photographer working for *Newsworld* had broken down. The implication was that Alex had a greater chance of getting his images into this week's magazine because the senior photographer couldn't transmit his photos due to this technical glitch.

The magazine had asked for a self-portrait of Alex, and he had sent in a selection of images. In one he was holding a large rifle. Ed removed the image before forwarding the others to the magazine editor. "You can't have newsmagazines publishing a picture of a war correspondent brandishing a large gun with a huge grin on his face," he explained to me. Michael Strong, who saw the image later, agreed: "It looks like he's mocking the army." Ed and Michael may not have objected for the same reason, but both felt it important for the photographer to not be visually confused for a soldier.

Meanwhile, other photographers had noticed that young Alex Levy's images were appearing on the cover of major publications like *Newsworld* and that the magazine featured his work on double trucks—two-page spreads in magazines, with minimal or no text. Alex Levy's coverage of the war in Iraq was garnering a lot of attention, and his credit line at high-profile publications, signaling that he was represented by GVI, served as an endorsement for GVI among photographers. Even in a tough market, it seemed, GVI could get photographers good work and support their careers. A frustrated established photographer with another photo agency came in to GVI to show his portfolio. He wanted to know if the company would be willing to take him on as a photographer, and he let it be known that he worked regularly with the *New York Times* as a freelancer. In other words, he could immediately bring revenue to GVI. He commented, "It seems like this is the place that's going to pick up photographers from other agencies. Alex was really excited. You've done fantastically for him." Henry responded modestly, "He's done fantastically for himself," but there was no hiding the pride in his voice. After reviewing the photographer's portfolio, Henry simply said that he wasn't considering sending anyone else to Iraq right now, and the photographer left.

Later in the day Ed managed to get a deal with *Newsworld* for Kelly's potentially exclusive images of Tommy Franks. He was a better broker of Kelly's images than she herself had been. *Newsworld* agreed to cover Kelly's expenses for two weeks, and GVI was no longer sharing any financial risk for Kelly's production. Clearly, visual opportunities don't seal the deal themselves; they need to be expertly brokered.

Thursday, April 3, 2003

The morning meeting focused on Jacques, the photographer whose equipment had been stolen. Alain was concerned that Iraqi officials were preparing another expulsion of journalists, and he was trying to get together tear sheets (examples of published work) that proved that

Jacques was a working journalist whose work got published so that Jacques could make a convincing argument for himself.[28] "Victims would be good," Alain said. "Let's prepare a package he can use to convince the Iraqis that he is showing what the US is doing to the Iraqi population."

Later in the day Ed looked over some images at Sophie's computer and explained to me, "The photographer is the first editor. We're the second editor. We're not making news for people to consume, we're making pictures for people to buy. We're not making fast-breaking news.[29] When I'm sorting stories I focus on how a client would find this rather than which picture tells the story. You want to have as many photos as possible available online for licensing. There are very few out-takes for war photos. Oh, look at that, Jackie," he broke off, pointing to pixelated faces of Iraqi prisoners of war on CNN.

Jackie commented, "I guess CNN is seen as a news outlet, whereas we're a reseller. Strong might change our whole motto and make us a content provider, but for now, we're just resellers," she added, spelling out that she perceived GVI not as a news producer but rather as a visual content provider.

Ed nodded emphatically: "My job is to provide an income for photographers and that's all. I mean, are we a business or are we a news organization? I don't think we are a news service!"

Alex Levy sent in a new batch of images, and Sophie and Ed edited them together. "We couldn't have picked a better guy to send on this stupid embed thing," Ed commented.

Sophie, never one to shy away from controversy, goaded Ed: "I guess it depends what you call a good photograph."

"A good photograph is one that will sell, not necessarily a great photograph. Come on, Sophie, he's got a very good eye. This is excellent photography. I think you're being overly critical. I mean, he's still very young and still developing his eye." Ed looked up and spotted Ilan, the Israeli photographer who should have gotten the embed arranged for Alex, who was visiting the office. "Don't look at these, Ilan," he said to him, "you're going to get uncontrollably jealous."

Ilan went through the images on the screen anyway.

"Pissed you off, right?" asked Ed.

"Yeah, I'm going to kill him when he gets back," Ilan answered, painfully aware of the professional opportunities he was missing because of his nationality.

Friday, April 4, 2003

Robert from the Paris office wanted to know if they should let the Pentagon know about their photographers' locations: "So that if US troops storm Baghdad—" Before he could finish, Paul, responsible for all correspondence with the military, interrupted: "Their official position is that either it's an embed or they can't do anything for the photographers."[30]

Robert switched topics. At least they had been able to get Jacques new equipment—most importantly, cables he needed to transmit his photographs. Known more for cynicism than praise, Robert surprised the team when he brought up French publications' interest in Alex Levy and extolled, "This guy's a revelation. We are all honored. This is excellent stuff."

After the meeting Ed repeated to the others, "'Revelation.' That's a rare compliment from Paris!"

Michael Strong and his right-hand man, his technical collaborator, spent the afternoon on the phone with GVI's core technical team trying to figure out how to redesign the delivery of images to their website and from there to clients' servers. Strong was trying to explain that although news images might be only a small part of GVI's revenues, they were critical to its reputation, and therefore the specific needs of news imagery had to be met.

"News doesn't sleep," Strong said. "GVI is not architected to be a twenty-four/seven operation, but I can't have a photographer slogging in the mud in Iraq and tell him 'Sorry, our FTP [file transfer protocol] server is down and so we can't distribute your image.' Our technical side has to be bulletproof." When someone complimented him on the ubiquitous placement of Alex Levy's photographs, Strong jumped on the opportunity to reiterate why GVI's technical architecture was critical to its being able to compete in the world of photojournalism: "You know, we met Alex through an email Listserv. He's just a kid, and he wasn't selected to go to Iraq. Another photographer, Ilan, was. But Alex ended up going, and this wild-eyed kid who's really green got the cover of *Newsworld* magazine! There's no better example of what GVI can do for a guy. But we need to technically be able to get his stuff out immediately."

After the meeting Strong was frustrated. He wanted to know what was technically possible and felt that others were questioning his business decisions without understanding the demands of news. I asked him the question the team had been struggling with lately: "Is GVI a visual content provider or a news provider?"

"Both," he answered. "Proactively, we are a news provider. This is why we have assignment photographers. But reactively, we are a visual content provider because we need to have images of events that have happened. So we have partnerships with newspapers and other image providers like wire services so that we can syndicate their coverage and sell their images to publications that aren't subscribing to them." In other words, GVI had to be visualizing both the past and the future constantly. Its business was to provide the raw materials for others' use, but Michael was trying to push his team to think and produce like a news publication with the strongest visual journalism.

The GVI photographers in Baghdad managed to get permission to stay for another ten days. Ed, adept at spotting opportunities, immediately wanted to know whether any photographers with other agencies had been expelled so that he could offer GVI's coverage to those publications for which they'd been on assignment. The value of news images is directly tied to their potential exclusivity, so knowing how many other organizations might possibly have the necessary access to produce them is a key piece of information for an image broker trying to pitch a photographer's coverage and gauge its value relative to what else is being produced.

Saturday, April 5, 2003

Despite its being a Saturday, and one during a weekend when he wasn't supposed to be on duty, Ed was in the office in anticipation of US troops entering Baghdad. Someone from the news team was always in the office on a Saturday, but this week, in addition to Michael Strong, who seemed to work practically around the clock, there were two editors. Ed reported that yet another of the photographers affiliated with GVI was in Iraq: "Ahmed went in with an Arab passport and just walked into Iraq with an assignment for the *New York Times*. He hooked up with the writer by himself, not through GVI, but he should have the *New York Times* run the GVI credit for him if he'd like to have us syndicate his images." The photographer was not compelled to share profits with GVI since he had found the assignment independently and GVI was not financing his coverage in any way. However, getting the newspaper to credit GVI beneath his photographs would be good publicity for GVI and a signal to other image brokers who might want to publish his work that it was available on the GVI website.

Then he brought the subject around to his rookie photographer: "Also I'm worried that Alex Levy is doing some translating for the unit he's embedded with when they have prisoners of war. It just gets him deeper in the story and I think he is crossing an editorial line. He's somehow becoming complicit in the treatment of these people."[31]

But as was typical in the pace of the newsroom, before he was able to dwell any further on that thought, his phone rang and he switched into salesman mode: "I just worry that you're missing out on an opportunity here," he told the photo editor at the *Army Times,* whose coverage GVI wanted to syndicate online. The *Army Times* hadn't signed the official partnership agreement, and Ed was pushing them to do so. However, as Ed knew too well, even a conversation that does not result in a sale can be profitable. Ed was always getting information about what other photographers were telling their editors. This often required him to share some information as well: "That's what I heard from my guy, too, that the US took Baghdad airport. Though my embed can't really talk to me on the phone. Listen, if you can get me 'Tanks in Baghdad' I can do a lot with that today." Saturday on a big news day was prime time for the last-minute sales of news images. Ed knew that all newsmagazines that had Saturday closes were holding off on putting the week's issue to bed until the last possible moment to see whether they could get coverage of the US entering Baghdad. 'Tanks in Baghdad' was what everyone was hoping for.

That afternoon Liz, the photo editor officially on duty that day, had to write a caption for an image showing bullet-ridden portraits of Saddam Hussein taken by photographers traveling with US troops. Reading the attached caption, "Redecorating Saddam's portrait," Liz was troubled by what she perceived as a flip tone. Ed responded, "I feel as if we are in collusion with the armed forces. I mean, we're selling these images and moving them." Liz changed the wording of the caption to read: "Bullet holes left as a souvenir by US Marines on a portrait of Saddam Hussein on the road to Baghdad."

Later that day a series of photographs arrived that disturbed her so much that she turned away from the screen. A series of nine images showed women crying and clutching a baby, corpses of children lying in a pool of blood on a bus, the corpse of an alleged Iraqi Republican Guard leader and his driver, the map found in his vehicle, and an American soldier washing stretchers. Liz tried to formulate a title for the image set, struggling with her word choice.

"Aftermath of US incident on Iraqi bus." Then she deleted *incident,* and her title read: "Aftermath of US fire on Iraqi bus." "I was going to say 'Iraqi civilians,' but then it sounds like we meant to do that. The photographer uses the word *attack*. 'Aftermath of . . .' There were seven women and children on the bus. Do we have a word for . . . ?"

"Slaughter?" suggested Ed in macabre jest.

"Ed! We're trying to tone down *attack*." Clearly, she was perturbed by the attempt to find words that were truthful without editorializing. "'Iraqi civilian casualties'? 'Aftermath of US attack on civilian bus'?"

"Have you seen it corroborated in the press?" Ed asked. Liz went on to the website www.yahoo.com to see if the incident had been reported.

She did find other references to the event and typed out a new head-line—"US Marines shooting on bus ends in civilian deaths"—but finally decided on "Bus shooting by US Marines ends in civilian deaths." "Good, that doesn't imply whether there were any Iraqi military on the bus," she mumbled to herself or possibly to me. When a photograph or series such as this one is archived, part of what gets erased is brokers' reactions—in this case, Liz's emotions when captioning the images.

Tuesday, April 8, 2003

Edith, the archivist, told the group that the Saddam retrospective was ready. "But we need another edit because we have too many pictures," she added. Henry Smith was insistent: "Well, let's have it ready. If they announce this afternoon that [Saddam's] in the rubble then we want to have something available."

Edith also mentioned the retrospective on antiwar protests.

"But when we put that out there we attach a disclaimer to it, right?" Ed asked. "GVI is starting to editorialize, isn't it? We don't want to be slapped with 'GVI supports antiwar movements.'"

"We only produced it," explained Edith. "The subject matter is in the news. We're putting out content that's saying this isn't new. It's got history. When I spoke with one magazine they said, 'We can't do any-thing political, but we're interested in this because it is historical.'"

"As long as you have that word in there . . .," Ed responded. Liz agreed, emphasizing the role of the category "historical."

Meanwhile, the Paris office was on to other, non-war-related stories: "We're planning a story on road accidents, which is a real plague in France. We're thinking about recouping images from the family albums of all the people who die in one weekend. Easter weekend is one of the biggest killers of the year."

Henry cautioned, "I'd try to get a little separation between war and killer accidents. I think people need a break, need happy stories.

Something less about death. Anyway let's talk tomorrow. Also let's be ready to talk about ideas for postwar Iraq."

When Ed emerged from the meeting, Sophie was grimacing and quipped, "Ed, your boy Alex Levy didn't send captions." Ed promised to bug him about it. Photographers are supposed to always send in captions with images. At every one of my field sites, editors were constantly reminding photographers that captions mattered. Several times I overheard Michael Strong telling a young photographer that writing great captions was critical to getting a break as a photojournalist.[32]

Ed noticed Strong walking a visitor around the office.

"Hey, Jackie, who's the woman with Strong?" he asked.

"I don't know. The consultant?" she joked, referring to *Office Space*, the team's favorite movie about mind-numbing corporate politics.

"No, she's another anthropologist! The anthropologist to study the anthropologist!" This moment of comic relief was welcomed by all—myself especially. During my initial weeks at GVI, I was constantly reminded that gaining access to an institution did not mean that I now had the trust of everyone who worked there. Michael Strong had given me unfettered access to his team in the GVI newsroom, and Ed couldn't object to this publicly since Michael had framed it as such a good opportunity to have someone document how the team, as a team, were going to turn around GVI's news and editorial division and its standing in the documentary photography world. Yet Ed initially made it clear that he did not want me around. As I mentioned earlier, I observed the workings of the newsroom by sitting on a small stool and moving between the desks of the main editors, and much of my time was spent with Ed. For the first two weeks, I arrived every morning to find that the stool had once again disappeared. Luckily Ed was even more polite than he was shy or adversarial, so the stool would usually turn up after I had stood for a few hours of work. So I, too, could laugh at the joke about the anthropologist being brought in to study me.

Before Ed could finish chuckling, his phone rang. It was Alex Levy saying that he might want to leave his embed. But Ed thought it might be too dangerous for Alex to wander off alone. Alex suggested that he might head to Baghdad.

"Look, Alex, I know you want to be a part of the action, but it's a big country. Baghdad's the endgame, but it's not the only thing to cover. I also don't know that *Newsworld* is going to want to keep four photographers in Baghdad. They're going to start ending some stints." After the call, Ed commented to Jackie, "Now we need to try to continue Alex's growth. Does he want to be a combat photographer? I don't think so, but it's up to him." In addition to scouting talented new photographers, one of Ed's tasks was to imagine future assignments for the photographers, to help them craft a profile to keep them working. The future of GVI depended on the future of its photographers, and Ed was particularly concerned that Alex not be typecast as a combat photographer.

The CNN headline was heard from the TVs hanging above the editorial team's desks in the office: "Journalists under fire." "Well, they're in a war zone!" exclaimed Jackie, who in the last few days had come to worry less, now that she had accepted that the photographers were there of their own volition.

The team was also actively courting respected photographers for GVI and had long been trying to get Yoshi, an up-and-coming photographer who was very well regarded among his peers, to sign a contract. Yoshi told me he had been hesitant to sign a representation contract with GVI partly because of the way older photographers talked about it as the corporate giant that had upended the photojournalism industry. Several members of the editorial team gathered in the evening for drinks with Yoshi to show their enthusiasm for his work. They flattered his unique style and what they perceived as his non-testosterone-driven approach. Yoshi shot film and made his own prints, the quality of which impressed everyone. His choice to not go digital somewhat dictated what he was being asked to shoot: stories that could afford to be slow. For example, although there were photographers in Iraq in April 2003 who typically had shot film, they were all now shooting and transmitting digital images. Yoshi had worked primarily for adventure-focused magazines but wanted to try to do more political photography. One editor was surprised by that information: "Really? If Kosovo were happening today, would you like to go?" Yoshi was a very humble photographer and lacked the swagger common to many of the combat photographers. In fact, slightly embarrassed by being the center of attention, Yoshi deflected the flattery and quipped, "OK, OK. I want a satellite phone and a pony!"

Wednesday, April 9, 2003

By the time the news team came in, close to 10 A.M., all TV screens showed a large group of people at Firdos Square gathered to topple a statue of Saddam Hussein.

"Everybody capable of holding a camera is live on the statue," Ed announced. "Though I'm not sure about the jubilation and sense of liberation the anchors are going on about. I mean we're not sure Saddam is gone." Turning to Jackie, he continued, "There are Eastern European parallels, aren't there?" Then, chuckling, "Oh, look at that, they're going to bring in a tank to help!"

The whole team was gathered under the screens, trying out headlines or sales pitches and discussing the day's coverage.

"It's what we were waiting for!"

"Freedom has come back!"

"We want to avoid bunching up in the same place. Statue toppling is an obligatory cover, but the main thing is how to get a different photo [of it]."

"Where's Jacques?"

"We might see him onscreen." Sure enough, every TV camera angle showed photographers the GVI news team recognized.

Ed asked the Paris office if all the French TV channels were broadcasting live on the statue.

"Yes, of course," came the response. "But we managed to tell one of the photographers about the rumor we heard from the *Newsworld* editor that Saddam Hussein might be at the Russian embassy, so he's over there to investigate."

"Any ideas on stories for the rest of the week?" Henry asked his team. "What will the future look like?" Editors in both New York and Paris brainstormed:

"All these towns haven't fallen. There's all the fedayeen up there. No pictures of arrests yet. Saddam and his minister of information, whereabouts unknown."

"Then we're desperately in need of Saddam's palaces and bunkers."

"Refugees, maybe following a family going home?"

"New government."

"Palaces."

"The mourning of families."

"Daily life returning to normal."

"We could do oil fields. The road from Kuwait to Baghdad. Bring a top photographer to do the symbols of war, maybe in black and white?"

Ed reminded people of the edit of Saddam portraits: "People are going to need covers. When Ceaușescu fell I remember one photographer picked up all the family albums. They're very good for revenue. You know, all the forbidden pics." Then Ed had to leave the meeting to take another call.

Robert, in Paris, told the others, "We have the cover of *Paris Match* this week. But in France magazines are finding out that war doesn't sell."

Henry concurred: "Yeah, today's the first day that the *New York Post* does not have the war as lead story."

Robert interjected, "TV is killing the surprise element of magazines. By the time you get the magazine you've heard so many experts, consultants, and seen endless footage."

The meeting ended with a sense that although the war might be winding down, there were still many angles of the Iraq story to be pursued. It was up to the editors to relay these to their photographers in the hopes of generating photographs. This is how formative fictions are constructed. Photo editors often complain that even their family and friends don't quite understand what they do since the editors are not the ones actually taking the pictures. I asked Ed who had called during the meeting. "My mother," he confessed sheepishly. She had wanted to let him know what was happening on the news. As if unaware of what his work entailed, she had asked: "Ed, are you watching the TV? It's like the Berlin Wall!"

At 10:35 A.M., an American soldier climbed up the statue and covered Saddam's face with a US flag.

"I don't think that's so appropriate," commented one soft-spoken photo editor. "They should let Iraqi people take the lead."

Sophie called out, "Ed! Photos of Jessica Lynch's parents in Ramstein are in!" Private Jessica Lynch had been injured and captured by Iraqi forces on March 23, 2003. Her recovery by US special operation forces on April 1, 2003, had garnered much media attention as the first successful POW rescue mission from Iraq, and Sophie knew that Ed would be interested in these photographs since they were highly likely to sell.[33]

The group watched the statue of Saddam get pulled down.

Jackie started laughing when the statue got stuck midtopple: "He's stuck. This is hilarious. I guess they used special glue on his feet."

"It's a total visual letdown isn't it?" asked Ed. "It was a beautiful image when it was the Iraqi people bringing it down, but now it's just boring."

Alex Levy called and was cautious about revealing his unit's position over the phone. Nonetheless, Ed tried to get information that he could then pass on to editors at the magazine—efforts that resulted in a riddle-like string of questions: "You're heading in the right direction, right? Do you have anything to send? You're heading north but you can't say where? Are you with the writer? Do they have a pretty interesting thing to do when they get wherever they're going?"

Then the team was back to discussing the toppling of the statue.

"It just ruins it visually," Ed lamented

"Yeah," Jackie concurred.

"I want crowds of peasants liberating their own country, not some friggin' tank pulling it down," Ed added.

Cynical Sophie chimed in nonchalantly, "Yeah, but this is reality. When you make the HBO version, you can change it."

"Ed, do I keep charging double day hazard rate?" Jackie asked.

"Always charge double rate till they complain!"

"*Focus* magazine [a German weekly newsmagazine] might be interested in putting someone on for Baghdad after the war. Should I show them photographer portfolios?"

Ed nodded.

"Real ones [i.e., physical portfolio books] or digital?"

"Digital," Ed replied, adding emphatically, "Digital is real!"

"So you're going to be at Saddam International Airport tomorrow?" Ed asked Alex on their next call. In turn, Alex asked Ed for news from Baghdad.[34]

"This morning the press showed up for a regular meeting, and no Iraqi officials showed. Everyone walked out and started reporting freely. There's been looting, pockets of sniping. But there's a general air of jubilation. There was a ridiculous live event. They toppled a Saddam statue for the Iraqis and there was a lot of screaming and jumping. There's a rumor that Saddam's at the Russian embassy trying to escape to Syria." In response, Alex expressed some concern about the futility of going to Baghdad now that it was swarming with photographers.

"There are lots of other stories to do once you get there," Ed assured him. "Just because the bang-bang is finished doesn't mean the story's over. Today's the first day that people reported freely."

Meanwhile, another editor was trying to tell me precisely what was so disappointing about the statue toppling: "Politically and psychologically there is a weight to a people tearing down its own icons. But this toppling an icon doesn't mean much." He was well read and often spent time reading non-American publications' coverage of events. "The Arab press is reporting that not only do Arabs need to stand up to the US but there are a lot of symbolic things happening in the defacing of photos." He felt that all of that was being ignored for the predictable image of the falling statue.

And still another editor complained, "Those were hardly throngs, were they?" The entire team seemed unconvinced by the spectacle of the statue; it fell far short of their visual expectations. Furthermore, the sheer number of photographers in the crowd in Firdos Square and the likelihood of many similar, competing photographs meant that it was unlikely that any of the images produced would be particularly valuable since none were likely to be unique. And yet, even in the midst of expressing disappointment at the weakness of the spectacle produced, none of the team members made a comment that expressed any doubt about the signal that the visual was being tied to by all the news sources around them—that somehow this marked the beginning of the end of the war. Formative fictions are powerful after all. Even in the midst of critiquing the particular construction of a photograph of a toppled statue of a leader, these brokers were not voicing doubts that this could be a moment of regime change. After all, it looked like a regime change.

When Jacques, the experienced photographer, called Ed and told him he'd been in the square, Ed immediately asked which other photographers he'd spotted. He was trying to assess the value of Jacques's photographs in relation to others from the scene. Since it was clear that he wouldn't be able to claim exclusivity, Ed was trying to find other ways he could sell Jacques's coverage. Perhaps Jacques had been the most senior photographer on the scene? "Was Jim Nachtwey there?" Ed asked. If he had been, this would hurt Jacques's chances of getting his images into that week's *Newsworld*.

Afterward, Ed filled Jackie in: "Apparently the mood changed in ten minutes. One minute people were threatening to kill him [Jacques], and the next everyone was cheering. Also, *Newsworld's* editor said they saw Nachtwey and another of their photographers on their TV screen!"

Another senior photographer phoned in from Baghdad. His first question was whether there were a lot of other photographers in Baghdad, and Ed confirmed his fears: "There are a lot. But listen, the story's developing from here on out. If you get into the palaces look for covers. End-of-Saddam-era kind of pictures, smashed-up Saddam portraits. . . . Good luck and take care, there's a lot of looting going on." Ed was always positive on the phone with photographers, coaching them more or less depending on their experience level and how much sense he had of which directions the publications' stories were going in. In keeping with his stated mission of providing photographers with an income, Ed worked with each one to think about unique angles to cover. Yet when taken collectively, his suggestions to his photographers about a range of different stories they might pursue were also about rigorously developing the journalistic investigation. As an image broker, then, Ed served both the photographers and the news story.

Henry Smith, the director of news, looked over Sophie's shoulder at the images she was editing. "I don't need five angles of the statue falling," he told her. "A Shiite in a small town beating up a Sunni is going to be more valuable than another picture of the statue." Henry was already looking for a fresh angle on the story, something that had yet to be visualized. Anticipating how the story might develop, he wanted to have photos that first indicated the direction the struggle might take, the earliest images of the futurepast.

Sean called from the Iraqi border and told Ed the borders were crumbling and a bunch of journalists were going in. He wanted to know if Ed had heard any report of road conditions. "No," Ed told him, "but look, Baghdad is now crawling with photographers. There's a lot of stories in Karbala but there haven't been any journalists there. We're bunching in Baghdad." So the photographer agreed to try to convince the other journalists in his convoy to go to Karbala. Casually managing expectations, Ed warned him before they hung up, "Now that there are so many photographers free to roam there, getting you published may be difficult." The conversation ended with him expressing concern for Sean's welfare: "Are you taking a bulletproof vest and helmet?"

Sean responded coyly, "I shall rely on my winning smile to deflect incoming bullets." As in so many of Ed's conversations with experienced photographers, humor and laughter functioned as an instantly effective bonding tool over the crackling phone lines poorly connecting great distances. Ed and Sean had been working together long enough to afford being ironic.

Three other photographers that day voiced a desire to go to Baghdad. One informed Ed that journalists were being invited in and told, "You can stay as long as you like." But Henry was adamant that GVI was "overcovered" and discouraged anyone else from going to the capital. The disgruntled photographer threatened, "When Mosul starts to happen it's going to spread thin," implying that GVI might regret the decision later.

Ed ended the day by commenting with some concern, "All our photographers are going to be in Iraq within two days!" He would need to find ways to differentiate their coverage. Doggedly persistent, he called the *Newsworld* editor one more time before leaving the office: "We just got some images of looting. Any interest?"

REVIEWING THE VISUAL CONTENT OF WAR

Michael Strong regularly emphasized that "realities are often unforesee-able," and this was precisely the challenge of an industry constantly trying to guess what the future would look like so that its photographers were sure to be in place to *have taken* a relevant image. The irony, of course, is that what the future will literally look like in photojournalism has a lot to do with what the past has already looked like, and what the various brokers of images—photo editors at agencies and publications as well as photographers themselves—imagine the future will look like based on news images that have already circulated and created expectations. In other words, formative fictions structure future frames. Henry, Ed, Liz, Jackie, and their respective interlocutors were constantly speaking of military operations "looking like 'Nam," or the fall of the Saddam statue being reminiscent of events in Eastern Europe in the late 1980s and early 1990s. What does it mean for image brokers to have expectations of what types of images will best capture a dictator's life? When Ed reminds his team of how well images of Ceauşescu's family albums sold in order to encourage them to seek similar images in Saddam's palace, there is a visual conflation between Iraq in 2003 and Romania in 1989, despite very different political contexts.[35] If we fast-forward to the futurepast and look back on today's news coverage as the key component of tomorrow's visual history, we need to consider what characteristics this type of visual history will have ingrained in it because of the conditions of possibility in which it was initially produced and circulated. Throughout this chapter we've seen formative fictions in action in the daily acts of image brokers attempting to visualize politics.

I was struck when the photo editor of a major regional US daily newspaper with whom Ed had sealed a syndication deal emphatically stated, "I'm saying this as an experienced photo editor: tops [the war in Iraq will] take three weeks." Why would experience as a photo editor give him any knowledge or authority by which to speculate confidently on how long a war might last? But perhaps he does have some relevant experience in a military attack where the attacking country's secretary of defense—in his first nonscripted comments to the press and, through them, to the public—talks about photographic representations of the war his country is engaged in. In a war of images, image brokers play a very different role than we, or even they, might suspect. Within three weeks of the war's beginning, the politics of visualizing the war in Iraq meant that the fall of Saddam's statue could temporarily represent a political end to the war and get widespread circulation, even if the images were visually underwhelming and the conclusion they suggested was politically inaccurate.

Furthermore, as the events I've detailed make clear, it is very complicated to delineate the lines between media production and reception, particularly when the military and governments are such active participants in media production. After all, at a time when US–French relations were very tense because France was not supporting the invasion into Iraq, commanders in the field could be swayed to grant a photographer access if she was shooting for *Newsworld* but might not have been had she been on assignment for *Paris Match*. On the other hand, tear sheets were prepared specifically with an eye to selecting images that emphasized a French photographer's documentation of Iraqi victims, with the goal of convincing Iraqi minders and information officials to grant him access and not expel him. Even for unembedded photographers, access was politically policed, framing the coverage before a single image had been made. Can any of the media producers or image brokers structurally claim to be *unbiased conduits* of information in the terms Henry Smith used to describe the work his team produced?

Remember the editor in Paris telling the photographer crossing the Jordanian border to keep an eye out for religious symbols, or the photographer in southern Iraq calling the photo agent in New York to hear news from Baghdad—which the photo agent *himself* had culled from other editors and agents (in turn reporting what their photographers have relayed to them) and what the agent is absorbing from the bombardment of media outlets around him. Where precisely are the grounds upon which any "*ground truth*" can be achieved? Yet what does it mean when the argument that there is no single ground truth and that each image or report is instead but a subjective *slice of the war* has been officially co-opted by the military? From the first press conference of the war in Iraq, the US military claimed that this war could be understood and evaluated only by those who had "a sight on all areas of what is under way"—those like the president and his advisors—thus creating the impression that they themselves, those whose interactions with the public are always mediated, have direct omnipotent vision.

In this construction, there seems to be little role for a free press if the media by nature cannot see in totality and yet only through the media does the public have any access to the leader who allegedly can. Rumsfeld warned that "what we are seeing is *not* the war in Iraq." His simultaneous insistence that the humanity that went into the precision of military targeting would undoubtedly be made clear once ground truth was achieved serves as a parable. The very rhetoric of precision and clarity obscures in its attempt to convince the news-viewing public not only that things are not as they seem but that what the public sees cannot possibly be what it thinks it sees because that which it would need to see in order to understand and intervene meaningfully is unseeable. Abstract state oversight is glorified, while all specific visuals are discredited.

This sleight of hand was indeed successful, and it contributed to the perception that this would be a very short war. Just a few days into the action, as we have seen, it became clear that things were "much messier" than expected. Of course, "Baghdad" was not over until 2011—if it can be said to be over now, five years later on—and the news media struggled with how to report on a war that was never anticipated to last past the fall of Saddam's statue.[36] How did journalists' conviction that this would be a short war affect their reporting? Perhaps media outlets' expectation of instant reporting actually hampered their ability to investigate and report on longer-term events. Or conversely, when news cycles are so short, is there an automatic expectation of short historical cycles, quick events that can be iconically represented by "best of" image sets just a few days or weeks into the event? Perhaps the temporality of war itself was expected to comply with the digital temporality of news coverage, one that leaves no time for events or information gathering to unfold. To better understand how speed and worldwide distribution shape visual worldmaking, I turn to Agence France-Presse and focus on transformations in the very infrastructures of representation and the everyday practices behind wiring news images worldwide in the age of digital distribution.

3

Agence France-Presse

What Is the Dominant?

Every day at around 9:25 A.M., someone would yell, "Shall we go up?" and two representatives from "Photo" at Agence France-Presse (AFP) would ride the small, arthritic elevator up to the morning meeting on the fifth floor of the news agency's Paris headquarters. The joviality of the photo department would follow them onto the elevator but cede its place to the more muted tone of the text services as soon as they entered the meeting room, which was not much larger than the table it contained. There, they would join the editor in chief, flanked by two text editors—one responsible for France and the other for International. The International text editor sat next to the International photo editor, and the respective France editors did the same. Around the table were representatives of the various sections: Economics, Sports, Politics, Arts and Culture, and so forth. Collectively, they reviewed the day's news prospects. The editor in chief routinely began the meeting with *"Qu'est-ce que c'est le dominant?"* ("What is the dominant?")[1]

In the context of the daily high-level meeting at one of the world's largest news services, the question elicited information that would shape the next day's headlines on the front pages of AFP subscribers' publications around the world. The wording of this routine question emphasizes the constant hierarchies being evaluated in the production and circulation of news. At a news service, what is being evaluated is a news story's perceived importance. Wire services, also known as news services, function as journalistic wholesalers, and their subscribers pay not for coverage of individual stories but for access to the wire "feed." One might think of them as the journalistic equivalent of a utility, such as water or electricity. For one story to be dominant—literally, to be the most influential, to exercise authority over others—other stories need to be dominated, given less priority. Whereas individual publications, such as the *Yomiuri Shimbun,* the *Times of India, Time,* and *Bild,* might decide their coverage on the basis of imagined reader interest or market-ability, the debates about which of the many news stories of the day should dominate the wire service's coverage are phrased in terms of global significance.[2] Institutional hierarchies within AFP and between AFP and its competitors, as well as political hierarchies in the world at large, featured prominently in the discussions about which world events should be represented in which manner the following day.

Rapid-fire reports provided by the assembled editors addressed cover-age of planned events (official government visits, the European parlia-mentary vote of 2004), recurring events (G8 summit, NATO summit, European Cup, annual World Refugee Day), and breaking news (active conflict areas, natural disasters, airline crashes). Furthermore, there was always an attempt to anticipate future stories and follow up on events of the recent past. The daily meetings had two purposes. The first was to evaluate AFP's coverage of the previous day's events, particularly in regard to its competitors' coverage: "We were very late compared to AP [Associated Press]"; "We had a huge jump on Reuters";[3] how many pub-lications had chosen to use the AFP image?; had an AFP photo appeared "*à la une*"—that is, on the front page—of any of the major newspapers? The second purpose was to review how the main events of the day ahead would be covered. In other words, the editors at the meeting evaluated both the coverage of the current day's dominant and what they antici-pated would dominate headlines the following day.

Salient in these meetings was "newstime"—that peculiar temporality in which the present is so thin as to be nearly nonexistent yet absolutely critical to capture. Journalists at these meetings conflated events with representations of them; they conceptualized events in terms of how they might be reported on in text and image. Therefore, their focus was either on the recently reported past or on the pressing future demanding immediate attention. Time was palpable.

Every day for a month, I joined the AFP photography department representatives as they rode the rickety elevator up to the meeting, attended the meeting, stopped in with the reps for the obligatory post-meeting debriefing at the second-floor café, and observed them hold a follow-up meeting once back on the ground floor, where the photo department was located. Then I would track Photo activities on various desks for the rest of the day. Conversations on the elevator, in the meeting with the editor in chief, among the senior photo editors in the café, and back in the photography department were slightly different. Whereas the editor in chief was asking every morning what the dominant was in both text and photo, I was trying to understand how a visual dominant was constructed through the labor of those in the photo department. The challenge for Photo was not only to attempt to provide images for each story deemed important by the editors at AFP and its clients, but also to dominate the competition and get AFP images "played" in publications worldwide.

NEWS IMAGES IN A TIME OF CRISIS

The summer of 2004 was politically a particularly eventful time. During my time at AFP, US-led coalition forces that had occupied Iraq since March 2003 transferred sovereignty back to the country. Like the toppling of Saddam Hussein's statue in Fridos Square, this was another event that signaled the beginning of the end of the war that didn't end. In July 2004 Saddam Hussein, who had been caught in December 2003, first stood trial. It was also a visually remarkable summer, a time just after the circulation of the Abu Ghraib images and during which terrorists were widely and regularly disseminating videos of beheadings. News images were not just visualizing world events but were often also factors in causing the events. Which is to say visuals and politics were powerfully intertwined.[4] I do not mean merely that the journalistic representations of events contributed to the worldviews that provided the conditions of possibility for further events.[5] Rather, the circulation of certain visual representations were themselves consequential events, not merely illustrations of events. On the one hand, the Abu Ghraib photos produced by rogue US soldiers and circulated widely in May 2004 were amateur images that dominated headlines. Their transmission was as subversive as their content in that, at least initially, it bypassed the infrastructures that had traditionally circulated news images. On the other hand, terrorists made political demands in the form of direct-address videos and photos promising and delivering severed heads—images that were then validated as they circulated through the reputable news infrastructure.[6] My fieldwork continually revealed to me that the War on Terror was always also being fought in a visual register and was, hence, a war of images.[7]

As this chapter will make clear, the structures and routines that allow a wire service to "dispatch" news about events and to "cover the world" visually for worldwide publications were critical to this war of images. I am interested in the infrastructure of representations—all of the practices, institutions, and technologies that make news images as worldmaking representations possible. I pay particular attention to moments of crisis in the sense of turning points and moments of judgment, for these moments reflect underlying assumptions about what constitutes appropriate ways of imaging the world. Yet crises in the sense of unexpected world events are also precisely what newsroom routines are designed to address.[8] Based on my fieldwork in AFP's Paris headquarters and the routine coverage of crises in the world, I investigate crises of visualization. A crisis of visualization is a moment when routine visualization itself is challenged or disturbed. It is also a crisis of hierarchy within both AFP and the world at large that affects which representations get distributed on the wire. Crises not as the content of news but, rather, in the production and circulation of news are noteworthy because they make the otherwise often invisible infrastructures of representation visible. Such crises both shape and are shaped by the work of image brokers.

This research contributes to and expands on the very productive debates around the politics of representation both within and outside of the discipline of anthropology.[9] However, rather than focusing only on the politics of representation, I continue in a tradition of scholars who also pay attention to the politics of the infrastructures behind visual representations.[10] Conducting fieldwork in the visually incendiary first few years of the War on Terror demanded that I consider how crises of visualization are exacerbated by structures in which images are mandatory, when any dominant must be visualized. A focus on infrastructures allows one to see beyond spectacle and address the particular politics of events that are themselves about visual representations.

REWIRING THE WORLD

As the reader will remember from the history I provided in chapter 1, news agencies—of which the three largest are Associated Press, Agence France-Presse, and Reuters—were after all named *wire services* after *the wire*—the physical telegraphic or telephonic infrastructure that allowed them to distribute information. Moreover, wire services were initially formed to collectively share the cost of transmitting dispatches over the wire, thereby sending news farther and faster. Although the physical wire has been superseded, wire services persist as important news organizations responsible for gathering news—text, photo, and video— and distributing it to a very wide subscriber network of global news providers.

The senior manager of the AFP photo department, always referred to by his last name, Valery, defined a wire service for me in a single word: *speed.* Valery was proud of the work of his photographers, mentioning several awards they had received and reminding me that many established freelance photographers had initially worked for AFP. Yet he was also sober in his evaluation: "We've got a good mold, good production, but it's not Magnum."[11] The implication was that AFP was a great place to start and get trained as a professional photographer even if one was talented enough eventually to leave the wire service and become a sought-out freelancer represented by a top agency and no longer required to cover multiple stories a day.

His comment underscored a predigital ranking in the photojournalism industry described at length in chapter 1. Until the widespread use of digital photography in the late 1990s, news publications received images from three main types of sources: wire services, photo agencies, and archival collections (containing mainly historical photographs). Wire services would transmit images of a significant news event to their subscriber base of mostly daily publications over the wires. These were "fast" photographs. In contrast, news publications would send freelance or staff photographers on assignment to cover the event or produce a feature story. Their images, shipped back to agencies or publications as undeveloped film, were often published some time after the event had been covered as breaking news in the dailies but might accompany more in-depth reporting on the event. These were thought to be "good" photographs. The aim of a wire service was to have a photograph available on the wire as soon as possible after the event.

This aim—speed—has remained, even if the shift to digital transmission over the Internet eventually rendered obsolete the physical infrastructure that had enabled the circulation of images over wires. The Internet also enabled many more image brokers to put images into potentially global circulation. Yet wire services have thus far survived the obsolescence of the wire. They now use the Internet in their operations, and they still disseminate a majority of the international information broadcast every day.[12] This is because of the continued pertinence of the wire's infrastructure, understood not only as the physical wire but also as the totality of organizational structures, protocols, practices, and conditions that allow for and direct the circulation of news by a wire service.

In a speech to the US House Armed Services Committee just a week after the Abu Ghraib scandal broke, Defense Secretary Donald Rumsfeld memorably pronounced: "We are constantly finding that we have procedures and habits that have evolved over the years from the last century that don't really fit the twenty-first century. They don't fit the information age, they don't fit a time when people are running around with digital cameras."[13] It was, of course, not merely that people were running around with digital cameras that caused havoc, but that the images downloaded from soldiers' cameras could spread with unprecedented speed and without any institutional monitoring. Regardless of the politics of the content of the images, the change in the infrastructure of representation through online distribution magnified their impact significantly. During my fieldwork at a major wire service just a few weeks after Rumsfeld's remarks, many professional image brokers were bemoaning the loss of control over powerful images. They, too, were constantly finding that they had "procedures and habits that [had] evolved over the years from the last century that [didn't] really fit the twenty-first century," and what I observed were early attempts to establish new grounds for their authority.[14]

OFFICIAL ENTRANCES AND REVERED IDEOLOGIES

There are two entrances to the AFP building. One is the official entrance, where video screens constantly show the images that are being sent to the wire. Three plaques that line the wall next to the elevators inside the main entrance offer some insights into what AFP understands to be its mission and the sources of its authority. Their inscriptions about the role of the free press span two centuries. The center plaque quotes from the portion of the 1957 statute establishing AFP as an independent entity that concerns the agency's obligations to maintain objectivity and to resist legal or de facto control by any ideological, political, or economic group. This statute is also quoted on the AFP website next to a photograph of the headquarters building. A government-chartered public corporation, AFP is a commercial business that operates independently of the French government, yet several members of its board are government representatives or representatives of government-owned radio and television corporations.[15] The two other plaques link AFP to an ever-broadening discourse of rights. On one, an excerpt from the 1948

Universal Declaration of Human Rights emphasizes "the right to receive and impart information and ideas through any media and regardless of frontiers." On the other, Article 11 of the 1789 Declaration of the Rights of Man and of the Citizen proclaims, "The free communication of ideas and opinions is one of the most precious of the rights of man" yet warns that with this freedom comes responsibility and that abuse of this right should be legally punishable.[16] The main entrance has been renovated since my fieldwork, yet these plaques were considered important enough to incorporate into the renovation unchanged despite significant changes in the way AFP now operates, distributing not just textual information but also images, graphics, video, and prepackaged multimedia for Internet news. In other words, the implication is not only that these ideals are timeless but also that they are not medium specific. Anyone who arrives for an appointment at AFP, in the brief time it takes to hand over an ID to the person who will announce the visit, is reminded of the major challenges of news gathering that persist in the digital age: the age-old dilemmas of freedom of information and its accompanying responsibilities, the promise that AFP is an unbiased conduit of knowledge, and the utopian ideal that information can travel regardless of frontiers and that this is always desirable.

The photo department employees, like those who work on the side of the vast building farthest from the main entrance, use the back door. At the back entrance, there are no screens showing news feeds and no idealistic plaques. No guests enter here. After my first day, I also used only this door.

THREE DESKS COVERING NEWSTIME

The photo department occupied the basement and first floor of the mammoth building. Pierre Martin was technically the "*chef du département photo*," but, as a man who had come from the text world upstairs, he did not get involved in the daily workings of the department. That responsibility belonged to Olivier Valery, the department's senior manager, who had defined a wire service's goal for me as "speed." When in his office, Valery was usually following news coverage either on TV or on the phone, often both. His desk was dominated by telephones: the office phone, his personal cell phone, and two separate wire-service cell phones—all four usually spread in front of him. A large world map covered the wall behind his desk, and an even larger map of Europe covered another wall. Within minutes of my first entering his office,

Valery showed me *Patterns of Global Terrorism,* a report published and distributed by the US State Department he'd recently been given. He said, "I'm supposed to look at it and start developing ideas of how our coverage is adequate for contemporary events. The photos of Abu Ghraib risk becoming *the* photos of the war in Iraq, but they were not taken by professional photographers, they were taken by soldiers. You have to ask, Whose eyes are we seeing through, and does it matter?"

The large room that took up most of the space at AFP's Paris photo headquarters was divided into two banks of computers at which editors were working on images coming in from photographers. One side of the room, the "Desk France" side, covered France, and the other, the "Desk Inter," covered international news. "Newstime" requires around-the-clock coverage, and above the Desk Inter were digital clocks showing Greenwich Mean Time, local Paris time, and the time in Washington, D.C., and Hong Kong. (AFP also has regional bureaus in Nicosia, Cyprus; and Montevideo, Uruguay).

In the middle of the room on a long table were several newspapers, international and French, that people thumbed through all day, both to read the articles and to see how the AFP images had "played." On the same table, all the "play reports"—sheets showing aggregate usage of AFP-supplied images of various events—were arranged neatly on clipboards. The tally next to an event showed how many AFP images of it had played in the major dailies in each regional market compared with how many Reuters or AP images had done the same.[17] The table, covered in newspapers and clipboards with printouts and tangible play reports, was a physical marker of the transition period from analog to digital transmission of information. Although the wire might be a thing of the past and the photo department was completely dominated by the digital in terms of production, distribution, and circulation, the play reports— the only real measurement of whether AFP journalists and editors had correctly anticipated their subscribers' dominant stories—were dutifully printed on paper. As long as their clients were still printing on what Pierre Martin, the director of the photo department, called "good old paper," there would still be plenty of paper in the office. As if to further emphasize this point, there were still a few old-school fax machines printing out the "dispatches" as headlines were reported on AFP's wire. Particularly when things got busy in the office, these machines would be ignored for a while, since people were developing the habit of reading the dispatches on computer screens and using the hard copies just for record keeping. The resulting mounds of rolled paper covered in urgent news stories and corrections served primarily as physical reminders of a time gone by and a change that was still very much under way and under foot.[18]

At the very back of the large room was the "Third Desk." This desk covered not a specific geography but a specific temporality: the future. Pierre had explained this desk's role as anticipatory. Like obituary writers in the text world, those who worked on the Third Desk tried to anticipate and fulfill any potential visual requests that clients might have in the future. And yet, even this desk, a temporal frontier that could afford to be less reactive to world events, shared the wire service's long-ingrained culture of speed. When I asked Janet, an American working on the Third Desk, what it covered, her answer illustrated the institutional focus on speed: "We fill the archive. We do special-interest coverage and produce feature stories. Hey, we're a wire service. No offense to the fancy-schmancy photo agencies who also work with magazines and advertising, but we're trying to get the picture in the paper the next day. The client pays no travel costs, no expenses. We're in every major city in the world, so we're cheaper, we're faster, and we understand a daily."

In contrast to GVI, AFP bore all the risk of production: the client pays no travel costs or expenses. Moreover, it was rare and controversial for AFP to sell its images for advertising purposes. Despite the Third Desk's relative independence from immediate deadlines, Janet answered as if she were imagining herself as a subscriber to the wire—a photo editor at a daily, perhaps—choosing between an agency and AFP's Third Desk.[19] The notion of "filling the archive" highlights the constant need to anticipate and supply images now of events that may require visualizing later so that the archive can best serve subscribers not only in illustrating today's news but also in meeting the visual needs of the futurepast.

Marc, another senior photo department staff member, also emphasized speed as he led a dozen new bureau chiefs through a departmental orientation one day: "The most important thing for us is speed. We must not leave room for AP, Reuters, or Getty."[20] Marc clearly saw competition coming mainly from rival wire services.

"Do you think publications have any sense of loyalty to a particular wire service?" inquired one of the new bureau chiefs.

"Yes, I believe speed creates loyalty."

PRODUCING VISIBILITY AND INVISIBILITY

The first morning I attended the meeting upstairs, I heard the following answer to the question "What is the dominant?": "The G8 summit and

Venus will be dominant. We should also look ahead to the European parliamentary elections."

The June 8, 2004, transit of Venus across the face of the sun as it passed between the earth and the sun had been a dominant event the day before, and the editor in chief inquired about the play reports: "How did the photos of Venus play?"

"Very good," bubbled Marie, the director of the Desk Inter, referring to a group of AFP photographs showing people in various parts of the world observing Venus transiting the sun.[21] "Even the *New York Times* used our images," she crowed, obviously proud of the front-page placement of an AFP photographer's work. The prominent display of the images was praised by all, yet Marie had expressed her concerns to me about the same photographs the day before. She had found one of the photographs' captions, one that highlighted sangomas (traditional healers) in southern Africa dancing around fires during the passage of Venus, sensationalist and had told me without hesitation, "I don't like such things. It's like the caption should say: 'Look at the African barbarians.'" Marie was often frustrated by stereotypical images of African topics. Yet when a newspaper of record like the *New York Times* placed images "*à la une*," its judgment as a client effectively trumped Marie's professional opinion of problematic visualizations of world news.

African news stories were often ignored if they did not have something to do with Europe. As if to prove her point that African visibility depends on a European connection, the next day while she was working on the Desk Inter a dispatch came across her screen and Marie read it out to those in the room:

"Sixteen people died in a plane crash in Gabon."

"How many French?" asked Manoli, one of the eager sales reps.[22]

"Two. Why? We don't care about the Africans?!"

"Only in soccer," Manoli quipped.

Looking ahead to prepare images to be used on International Refugee Day (June 20), Valery suggested finding images from Zimbabwe or Mozambique. When one of the photo editors suggested asking a photographer to shoot Palestinian camps in Lebanon, Valery demurred, saying, "The refugee camps in Lebanon are cities now. They don't even look like camps anymore." This visual logic implied that the Palestinian refugees in Lebanon could no longer represent world refugees because their habitats no longer looked like stereotypical refugee camps.[23] This example shows that how well an image corresponds to a visual expectation on the part of imagined readers carries greater weight than how representative the specific image actually is: an image of a refugee camp with tents is preferable to one of an urban camp in Lebanon, even if the latter has a larger population or has been a refugee camp for much longer.[24] I will take up these debates over representativeness and recognizable representation again when I shift to the editorial offices of *Newsworld* in chapter 4.

Obviously, some events, although anticipated, do not get represented. For example, in the summer of 2003 France had experienced a severe heat wave leading to a large number of fatalities. At almost every morning meeting during the summer of 2004—despite the gray drizzle outside—someone would report on AFP's preparedness to cover that season's heat wave (*"la canicule"*) when it eventually arrived. It never did. This demonstrates that anticipation and journalistic preparation can keep a topic contending for dominance for days or weeks even when there are no events to justify its doing so.

The European parliamentary elections that June provided a challenge for the photo team for different reasons. The elections were, in fact, newsworthy: 342 million people were eligible to vote, the second-largest democratic electorate in the world after India. They were the biggest transnational direct elections in history. At the café after a morning meeting at which the upcoming elections had come up again, one photo editor complained to Valery, "There's no point sending someone to photograph a voting booth, is there?" The concern was twofold: first, images of people voting are tired and cliché and, in fact, communicate very little about what makes a particular election important; and second, the team believed that the primary feature of this particular vote would be absenteeism, which is particularly difficult to express visually, especially by a photographer assigned to cover a voting booth.

Absenteeism was, in fact, the dominant story the day after the elections. The editor in chief began the morning meeting on June 14, 2004, by joking, "Look at this. There are more people around this table than there were at the elections!" Marie, having already studied the play reports, noted that AFP had done well with election imagery. However, the photo that seemed to be the most popular choice to illustrate the elections was a Reuters image. An important feature of the elections had been that the ten new European Union member states had elected representatives to the European Parliament for the first time, and Marie reported that the image that seemed to garner the most attention showed "little Hungarians with their little skirts"

Elections 2004

EU vote turnout a 'wake up call'

Hungarian women in traditional costume vote at a polling station near Budapest in the European parliamentary elections. **Photograph: Laszlo Balogh/Reuters**

FIGURE 5. Hungarian women at the ballot box for European Parliamentary elections. Published in *The Guardian* and many other publications on June 14, 2004. Photograph by Laszlo Balogh/Reuters.

(figure 5). Photo editors may (and, like Marie, often do) roll their eyes at stereotypical shots such as the South African healers looking at Venus through special glasses or the three Hungarian women in folkloric national costume at the ballot box, but these images do get published, and so photographers keep on taking them. If the wire service photo department sees its goal as providing visuals for as many news stories as possible on any given day, and especially for dominants, photographs that use national, ethnic, or other stereotypes are the easiest way to visualize news events that are challenging to represent. Whether these stereotypes get published or not, they circulate on the wires and enter wire service archives. The lightheartedness and stereotypical nature of the images trivialize the dominant somewhat, even though the intention might be to have the image draw a reader into a political story that is difficult to illustrate.

FILLING THE ARCHIVE

At other times, photo editors are less consciously complicit in the construction of stereotypes. Later that summer the German parliament passed a new bill regarding immigration. Legal stories, like elections, pose a visual challenge because often the moment in parliament is neither particularly rich visually nor illustrative of what is at stake in the legal changes. In this case I watched a photo editor on the Desk Inter field images that came in from a photo editor in Germany. A client who had read the text about the bill had called asking for photos. Eventually three photographs were sent in. The photo editor copy-pasted a portion of the text article into the caption box of all three photos:

> The German parliament passed a bill on 01 July 2004 overhauling the country's immigration policy to attract skilled foreigners and drive out extremists. The legislation, approved by the Bundestag lower house, is the product of four years of bitter haggling between Chancellor Gerhard Schroeder's center-left government and the conservative opposition. It opens up the door to more foreigners from outside the European Union with sought-after skills, promotes the integration of newcomers, reforms asylum policy and beefs up security checks for foreigners on German soil.

The above, in addition to a single descriptive sentence at the beginning of the caption, was now attached to the images. This text effectively packaged these three single images from different geographies and days, even years, into potential visuals to use alongside the text story on the new German immigration bill. The first line in the three caption boxes pertained to the respective specifics of each of the three photographs:

> This picture taken 01 June 2004 shows people rowing at the Olympia Park in Munich while a woman with a headscarf and a man look on.

> This picture taken on 27 August 2001 shows two young participants of a German language course at the Institute for Foreign Relations in the southern town of Stuttgart.

> This picture taken on 28 August 2001 shows two Muslim women walking on a street in the southern town of Fuerstenfeldbrück.

The photo showing the two language-course participants with their respective German dictionaries features two young men. Their linguistic efforts might constitute a form of integration of newcomers. However, how the other two images tie in with the story is more ambiguous. Are we to presume that the woman with the headscarf watching the rowers is an immigrant? A newcomer? A skilled foreigner? An asylum seeker?

An extremist? A foreigner on German soil for whom security checks have been beefed up? The image showing the two Muslim women walking on a street in a small German town is particularly open to interpretation, since it shows the women from behind as a young child on a bicycle, facing the photographer, passes them. The little girl's eyes are turned toward the women, fully covered in chadors, and the stroller they are pushing, and she has a somewhat troubled expression on her face. A blond adult woman is clutching the child's shoulder with a worried look. Given the new caption, I may read this image showing a young German girl terrified or at least disturbed by the two foreign Muslim women while her mother tries to steer her out of their way. However, given that photographs show a particular moment in time, perhaps the photo was really taken as a concerned woman tried to prevent her beginner cyclist daughter from crashing into other pedestrians in this peaceful multicultural town. Or even that the mother was merely concerned that the multicolored teddy bear slumped over the bicycle's handlebars might fall. I do not know why the photographer took the image, nor do I have any evidence that he or she spoke with any of the subjects in the image or had other access to information about what the image "really showed," nor do I even know if the photographer communicated any information to his or her editor. Yet the simple copy-pasting of a few sentences from the text article about the new parliamentary bill rendered this three-year-old, not particularly spectacular photograph newsworthy and therefore justified its being circulated as part of the visual news on July 2, 2004. The content of the revised caption suggested that the image showed something more than "two Muslim women walking on a street." Since the bill is meant to attract skilled foreigners and drive out extremists, I as a viewer am urged to look for one or the other in the image.

As she validated the images for circulation, I asked the photo editor what she thought of the captions. Her initial reaction was "I don't think anyone outside of Germany is going to care about this story." All three images had been forwarded by a German partner photo agency, and the copy-pasting of the caption had been done in the Berlin office. All that was left for the photo editor at the Desk Inter to do was send it out onto the wire, which she did, indicating that the images could be used anywhere but Germany, per the protocol of AFP's agreement with the German agency. However, during a conversation the next day, she commented, "I thought about those images and it's downright racist." As it happened, there was a "large dominant" in the following days' newspapers: Saddam

Hussein stood trial for the first time. Therefore, it is unlikely that the images were used anywhere, and they were certainly not widely published. However, the three images did circulate with the caption and were available to AFP clients even if they were never published in connection with this news story. Moreover, they are now connected to the news story about the German immigration bill and can be recalled from the archive in association with the story.[25]

THE INFRASTRUCTURE OF GETTING IN PLACE

AFP Photo was well placed to cover the 2004 G8 summit. Pierre Martin, the director of the photo department, confirmed that an AFP photographer had been credentialed to cover the event, and, with a hint of cynicism in his voice, added "We paid, therefore we have the right to work the event." AFP had had to pay thirty-five hundred dollars for each journalist attending the event. At the coffee stop on the way down from the morning meeting, several members of the photo team expressed their qualms about how such access fees impeded free press coverage. Yet fees to get credentials or fees to cover the cost of traveling on board an official's flight were, nevertheless, accepted as one of the realities of contemporary journalism, part of the infrastructure of getting a photographer to a story. In other words, financial resources are critical to getting in place to cover an event and to circulating the resulting images.

Especially on longer-term and expensive news stories, it is very important that photographs get played to justify the cost of covering the event. A photographer called the desk wanting to accompany a junior French foreign minister, Renaud Muselier, on a visit to Darfur. Similar to the way in which Kelly, the photographer represented by GVI, emphasized her access to General Tommy Franks as an American photographer represented by an American visual content provider trying to get on assignment for American newsmagazines (discussed at length in chapter 2), the AFP photographer underlined the appeal of this story about Africa because it concerned a French official. Christophe, Marie's peer on the Desk Inter, negotiated for the photographer at the morning meeting: "I think Muselier would appreciate a French wire service having exclusive coverage."[26] Moreover, he emphasized AFP's advantage over the competition: "There's a rumor that no one at Reuters and AP has the requisite visa, so our photographer might be the only one with Muselier." (Recall the lists of visas in GVI's newsroom.)

Christophe ended up having several extensive conversations with the photographer during the Muselier visit because the story was difficult to cover and transportation was a constant challenge. Christophe told others on the desk that the photographer had had "a three-hour flight and a three-hour drive to get forty-five minutes with Muselier. But at least tonight Muselier is going to a high-level meeting and taking him along." Clicking through the photographer's images from the day in Darfur, Christophe read Muselier's visit as mainly a propaganda stunt: "A white guy amongst the Africans. Pretty, no? It will do his office good. Good for public relations."

Just as Marie had reservations about the images of voters in Hungarian national costume or of the South Africans dancing around the fire, Christophe was acutely aware of how certain photographs got mobilized for political narratives. Yet both Christophe and Marie, like Ed at GVI and many image brokers I observed, were highly adept at tailoring their opinions of images depending on the audience they were addressing. They verbally captioned according to context. None of the images were doctored or inadmissible by any strict criteria of objectivity; they were all credible photographs. Rather, the principle in the three AFP entrance plaques that they disturbed was that information should travel "regardless of frontiers." For national frontiers are often quite central in photo editors' negotiations for funding or access. Requiring visas is the simplest way by which governments control the circulation of photojournalists. However, national allegiances come up in myriad ways. Despite his skepticism about the politician's sincerity, Christophe underscored that the French foreign minister would appreciate giving exclusive coverage to a French wire service, in the hope that a promise of exclusivity might help Christophe get the resources he needed to get the photographer well positioned to continue his coverage of Darfur.

Furthermore, his skepticism about the motivation for the official's visit did not in any way dampen his pride in the photos themselves when they got prominent placement. He was particularly excited when the British paper the *Independent* featured one of the photographer's images on its front page. This photograph, of a funeral ceremony for a small child, prompted a favorite ritual of photo editors: the telling of the tale behind the photograph, often highlighting serendipity. Before the photo team rode the elevator up to the morning meeting, Christophe told them, "You know, he was only able to make the photos of the funeral because there was a sandstorm and the plane couldn't take off." Not surprisingly, he did not repeat the same story upstairs, where, instead, he proudly held up the newspaper's front page as exemplary placement. Placement, especially on the front page, and most especially on the front page of a major paper such as the *New York Times* or the *Independent,* means visibility for AFP and reflects well on the photo department for knowing how to get people in place at the right time. Serendipity is good for entertaining colleagues in the photo department, but upstairs Christophe wanted valorization of the photo department's good judgment, foresight, and mastery at putting infrastructures in place in anticipation of the dominant. In other words, Christophe knew Photo would not get credit for having had good luck.

The week had started with the editor in chief noting that "there's lots of interest in Darfur. Let's not downplay it." All week Christophe tried hard to get information on the arrangements for UN Secretary-General Kofi Annan's upcoming visit to Darfur. So, on the day when he could draw attention to the front-page placement of the AFP image of the child's funeral, Christophe tried to advocate for his photographer. He indirectly voiced his displeasure that the AFP text editors responsible for coverage of Africa were not keeping him abreast of updates.[27] Instead, he said, he had had to rely on information from competitors: "We have information from AP about Annan's trip but by the time I was able to ask, there were no more places on the plane." Later that day, when the photographer called in to ask whether he should leave Darfur or wait for Annan, Christophe responded with flattery by telling him about the *Independent*'s cover and reporting the praise he had received at the morning meeting. He did not know how to advise the photographer because he had not been able to guarantee him a spot on the plane. Once off the phone, he angrily confided to one of the desk editors, "I'm sick of this story with the Africa desk. It's a UN trip, the NY bureau should have details. I've been asking for days and have gotten nothing at all. The problem is that the people upstairs [in Text] don't care if we get only one spot on that plane because if there's only one spot they'll get it, not us, and they know that. We can't have photos if we're not there!!"

When he received a fax with the list of journalists approved to be on the flight with Annan, Christophe became livid and started typing a message to his counterpart, an editor in text. "Now, this is a war!!" he told another editor on the desk, escalating the constant struggle over limited financial resources at the news agency. "There are lots of photographers on this list but not one AFP person!" In other words, not only was his photographer not on the flight, but AFP had also lost its exclusivity on the story—a key component of value when editors are assessing a photograph's value as a news image. Just when Christophe got Marie, his supervisor, to sign off on his angry email asking if AFP intended to miss the opportunity to cover the Annan trip, the Washington bureau called saying that, regrettably, there was no more room on the flight. "We've known this was coming up for a week now. Are we a team or not?" Christophe said angrily into the phone. "I've got a photographer who has spent weeks on this story, [his photo] gets on the front page of the *Independent*, and I can't even get a correct schedule on the UN trip. We were the only ones in Darfur. We've got our photos everywhere and yet you're not doing anything for us." Once again, he expressed his frustration with what he believed regional editors who had risen out of text and now oversaw budgets routinely forgot: the infrastructure for producing a photograph is different from that of a text dispatch. One cannot take a photograph after the fact. Or as Christophe argued regularly, "Text can always recuperate information, but we need to physically be there!"

VALIDATING A WAR OF IMAGES

For a long time, getting to an event or its aftermath and finding a timely way to transmit an image back to headquarters were the primary challenges for wire service photo departments. Yet today the challenge is no longer simply to offer a visually impressive representation but to offer a validated representation chosen from the overwhelming number available. Knowledgeable and appropriate selection from among the thousands of news images generated every day by AFP and its partners is much of the service AFP provides. First, not all photographs sent in by photographers end up on the wire, even if it now takes only seconds, not minutes or longer, to "transmit" an image onto the wire. In an age when digital cameras allow photographers to take hundreds of images at an event with minimal financial costs per image, unlike when they shot rolls of film, editors on the desk receive several images that are nearly identical and are tasked with picking the better ones. Sometimes, the photographer will do the first edit before transmitting, and the editor will validate a selection of what is transmitted and post them on the wire. Photographers often send in captions that are then edited and validated. Second, even though they expect each news publication to customize its news selection for its particular readers or viewers, wire services "push" different images and stories to different parts of the world. Deciding which part of their worldwide subscriber network would be interested in a particular story or set of images is another one of the services a wire service offers. Hence, despite the stated ideal of universal coverage, understanding the visual tastes and norms of regions and distributing images with careful regard to frontiers is key to the way the AFP photo department operates.

When the new bureau chiefs (almost all of whom had risen up on the text side) were visiting the photo department, one of them asked Marc, the senior photo editor, "What about images that might shock, what do you do with them?" Marc replied, "Well, we've got a variety of clients. If you send it to Germany, they'll hit the ceiling, but in Asia, they might use that same image. There are diverse mentalities on the issues. How do you illustrate a burnt-out church with corpses in an acceptable manner? Clearly, it's sordid. If the event itself is brutal, how do you illustrate it? In *text,* you will write about it, but gruesome events pose a challenge for Photo." Marc had had a long career at AFP and demonstrated expertise in the visual preferences of diverse audiences. This expertise had been acquired over years of considering the different journalistic challenges facing text editors and image brokers and learning from negative reactions to various images sent over the wire to diverse global clients.

Recent changes in the very infrastructure of representation posed new challenges. One of the new bureau chiefs mentioned the video of Nicholas Berg, the American who had been beheaded by Iraqi insurgents a few days after the Abu Ghraib photographs were made public. "They're using images to escalate things, to fuel the war," one new bureau chief had commented.[28] What seemed disturbing to the editor was that the insurgents in Iraq were circulating images for their own purposes. In other words, changing infrastructures of representation have allowed new image brokers not only to produce but also to distribute images widely and quickly. These image brokers are very unlike traditional competitors like AP and Reuters or even other news agencies or government press officials. That images circulated by such image brokers can dominate the news was a major challenge facing AFP. In the face of these changes, the photo department was constantly struggling to assert the value of its particular expertise and the services it provided.

"That's why sourcing images is very important," Marc assured the new bureau chief who raised the issue of images escalating the war. "The source is really fundamental. If I have any doubts about the source, I won't put the image into circulation." The infrastructure of representation was changing, with an ever-increasing number of images being distributed online from a wider variety of sources, and Marc addressed the concerns of the new bureau chiefs by acknowledging a growing need for nodal points where images get examined for their credibility and appropriateness.[29] Below, I discuss three incidents that occurred during the summer of 2004 that underscored the ways in which professional image brokers working within a wire service photo department were struggling with the changes in the infrastructure of representations. Each dominant forced professionals within AFP to struggle to figure out how to maintain their authority as a news service when new kinds of image brokers were dominating visual worldmaking.

DOMINANT 1: THE DECAPITATED AMERICAN

On a Saturday morning (June 19, 2004), when things should have been slightly quieter than on a weekday, the Inter Desk manager was ready for the morning meeting well in advance. The entire management team, even those on vacation, had spent the previous night trying to decide how to respond to the distribution of very graphic images showing the decapitation of a US engineer in Saudi Arabia. Not bothering with the elevator, Marie, and I behind her, climbed four flights of stairs and went directly to the editor in chief's office. Marie showed uncharacteristic trepidation and hesitated at the threshold of his office. The editor in chief was on the phone and visibly angry, and pointed for Marie to go upstairs to the meeting room. For once, when he started the meeting he skipped the dominant question and asked more pointedly, "Who decided to transmit the decapitated man's photo on the wire? . . . Should we have posted the image? Should we recall it? Photo was the problem. It was posted on the Internet on Drudge [the Drudge Report website], but should *we* have posted it?"[30]

The real issue was that the chain of command had broken down. The Nicosia office responsible for distribution to Middle East clients had decided not to post the images at all, but the editor on night duty on the Inter Desk in Paris not only had overridden that decision but also had sent the images to clients in the Middle East, as if directly challenging the Nicosia bureau chief's decision. The worldwide distribution of the image of the severed head risked bringing AFP under attack for disseminating gratuitously gruesome imagery, but also, perhaps even more critically, it illustrated a collapse of hierarchy within AFP. In other words, what was at issue was not merely the politics of representation but multiple crises within the wire service, the industry, and global politics.

By Monday morning, the release of the severed-head photo had been thoroughly debated. Pierre Martin, the director of the photo department, went upstairs with Marie. The routine question had returned: What is the dominant?

The Desk Inter text editor replied, "In a video broadcast yesterday, al-Qaeda threatened to behead the South Korean hostage Kim Sun-il, captured last Thursday, if South Korea does not cancel plans to send three thousand additional troops to Iraq. They've given them twenty-four hours."[31] This is an example of terrorists using the same logic of an indexed body representing a body politics, a strategy common to news images of formative fictions. The threat is to behead the specific body of Christian missionary Kim Sun-il. However, the terrorists are using the threat of producing the image of that particular beheading as a way to negotiate with the South Korean body politic. What I want to underscore is the repercussions of visualizing a hostage crisis on the part of both traditional news outlets and terrorists.[32]

The editor in chief brought the conversation back to the decapitated American, his tone significantly calmer than it had been on Saturday: "Those images were easy to find on the Internet. It's a question about the functioning of the Politics section. The Fallujah images, for example, automatically appeared on websites that get AFP feed. It's one thing if we put it on the wire, another if we distribute them directly to the public. But AP also posted all three images."

Pierre, the photo director, was decidedly nonchalant: "We've distributed so many severed heads on the wire. I mean ever since Louis XVI, we've seen so many men decapitated. This one was part of the news. Our business is B2B [business to business]. It's for our clients to decide whether or not they want to publish the image. For those websites who automatically show our images [such as Yahoo News], the responsibility lies with them."[33]

Finally, the editor in chief once again highlighted the real crisis: "It's up to us to make sure that the hierarchy decides. The editorial chain needs to be respected." In other words, there was debate in the organization about whether AFP had a responsibility to its subscriber network of news outlets, each of which decides what is appropriate for its local market, or directly to news consumers who might encounter the images on a website receiving the raw wire feed. Concurrently, there was debate about the journalistic value of such violent images. Appeased by the knowledge that a competitor had also run the images, the AFP editor in chief underscored what for him was the crux of the matter—an organizational crisis stemming from the violation of AFP's chain of authority; the wire's editorial hierarchy had been bypassed. Another crisis altogether, of course, was that the images were not supplied by a traditional image broker, such as a competing wire service, but that the terrorists, like the soldiers responsible for producing and circulating the Abu Ghraib photos, were amateur image brokers whose images had dominated headlines. Each time terrorists made political demands in the form of direct-address videos and promised and delivered photographs of decapitations—photos that were then validated as they circulated through reputable news infrastructures—they succeeded not only in performing violent acts but in controlling the news images representing the events as well.

Eventually, the editor in chief turned to Marie and asked what other news she had. "Excellent photos of European Cup football that are completely decent," she replied, and the tension was diffused. Photographs of sporting events constitute the majority, if not the most politically significant, of the images produced by wire services.[34] Getting access often relies on finances and reputation, since sports organizations require accreditation of all photographers. Sports photography offers its own challenges, but professional sports is an arena in which professional brokers almost always control the production and distribution of images. An amateur might capture an occasional shot of fans or a ball out of bounds, but accredited photographers who work for wire services or sports magazines are the ones optimally placed to get the best shots.

At the coffee bar that morning before returning downstairs, I asked Marie why she had prepared a folder of photographs of severed heads to take upstairs to the meeting. It was clear that the event had ruffled her. "No one's disturbed if its Arab or black heads that are cut off, but if it's a white man's head, especially an American, look at the uproar," she said. I looked through the images in her folder as she talked. They were all images familiar to me from the press. One was a particularly horrific photograph made in Liberia after government forces had taken back control of the capital, Monrovia. It showed a man holding a severed head by its ears almost up to his eye level. The caption read, "Loyalist fighter holds up severed head in jubilation." The French photographer, Noël Quidu, had won first prize in the Spot News Stories category of the World Press Photo competition earlier that year for his series of photographs from Liberia of which this was one. Marie gestured at the folder in my hands: "It's more and more this all the time. It's a war of images." Marie, like many professional image brokers I met, was more than aware of competing politics of representation. Her statement could serve as a commentary on the terrorists' decision to put the gruesome photograph of the severed head into distribution: the circulation of comparable violent images was forcing professional image brokers to consider reasons other than regional standards to explain why certain images cause shock and alarm and others do not. Hence, the war of images in the world, by circulating through AFP, prompted some within the agency to reflect on the war of images being waged in the name of the free transmission of information. Editors have long made decisions about what to publish on the basis of perceived public impact, carefully weighing shock value or gratuitous violence against perceived political or social significance. Yet here, a new kind of image broker operating in a system entirely outside that of the professional photojournalism industry was prompting those discussions. In other words, this was a different case from that of an amateur image getting picked up by a wire service or of citizens taking photographs on their own cell phones, cameras, or other digital devices and sending them to press outlets. Those amateurs still operate within the logics of witnessing an event and submitting their representation to an established press institution for validation and circulation. They provide alternate visuals for a story already deemed to be dominant by the press.[35]

Terrorists operating as image brokers in a war of images, by contrast, are staging events whose impact depends on the circulation of their representations; the images themselves compete as potential dominants with other events covered by professional press institutions. A gruesome news image of a beheaded US engineer has far more impact than a text dispatch of yet another Westerner being kidnapped and murdered precisely because, as Marie noted, images of decapitated white heads are far scarcer than those of severed nonwhite heads in the visual history of documentary photography. Hence, the terrorists, as image brokers, rely on the same logics at work in the newsroom in terms of leveraging stereotypes. Visualizing world news is politically charged because of the specific challenges and opportunities of photography as a medium—one that always captures something particular but potentially represents something abstract.[36]

When Marie and I came downstairs, the editors on the desk asked if there had been complaints at the meeting upstairs. In responding, Marie revealed a position very different from the one she had voiced on Saturday, when the image initially circulated: "I'm for transmitting everything. Even if it's gory. That way, no one can say they didn't know. We supply images. Even if it's ugly, this is the way the world is." Momentarily, she seemed to have resigned herself to the role of the wire service photo department as a mere supplier of images.

DOMINANT 2: IRAQI SOVEREIGNTY

Another reason it is critical to keep in mind the changing infrastructures of representation and journalism more broadly is that the War on Terror coincided with the decline in subscriptions to publications and advertising revenues. Even if, as communications scholar Pablo Boczkowski makes abundantly clear, the emergence of online news was a lengthy and complex process, eventually this trend led to the disappearance of many journalistic publications.[37] Yet at the same time that news publications of all kinds were experiencing financial challenges brought about by online distribution, the demand for images increased. Decades of journalistic practice meant that a visual representation of an event was required for the event to be registered as significant. Furthermore, whereas limited physical space in a print publication meant that not every article would be accompanied by an image, online versions of publications allegedly had no space concerns, and so, technically, every news story could be accompanied by images. This dual challenge to produce more images with less funding also affected wire services, which were dependent on subscriptions from news publications. Increasingly, publications shut down all but the most essential foreign bureaus. Wire services also felt the financial crunch. They might send a few journalists and an editor or two to an event itself to set up a temporary bureau. Effectively, this increased the significance of anticipated dominants. Since reporting decisions made before the event influenced where there were reporters in place, dominant news was more likely to be that which had been anticipated.

Just a few days after the beheading incident, AFP's anticipated dominant was the NATO summit in Istanbul, Turkey.

"Qu'est-ce que c'est le dominant?"

"Well, today we start with a surprise. Iraq is dominant because the Americans transferred sovereignty two days earlier than anticipated. We didn't get advance notice. Blair, who is in Istanbul for the NATO summit, made an announcement."

Like news teams elsewhere, everyone in the room had expected the US government's discussions with its allies at the NATO summit to dominate the headlines of the day. In other words, the anticipated dominant had been dominated. Producing an alternative dominant was relatively easy because most eyes—in this case, the collective efforts of image brokers—were already focused on the NATO summit, and accredited photographers were in place. However, because Iraq is not a

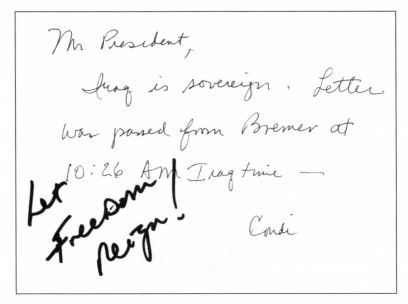

FIGURE 6. White House handout photograph of a note announcing Iraqi sovereignty, June 28, 2004. Courtesy of the George W. Bush Library.

NATO member, Iraqi representatives were not at the event that got worldwide news coverage as the announcement of Iraqi sovereignty.

The photograph that circulated widely as a representation of this event was a strange news image on many levels. (See figure 6.) To begin with, it was a "handout" photograph. Typically, handout photographs are images provided to journalists by the military, a government institution, or a corporation. They are images shared by an interested party and distributed without charge. Throughout my fieldwork, editors saw them as images that needed to be collected in case no other way emerged to visualize a particular news event (such as handout photographs from NASA on space missions), but had dubious journalistic value. Yet the handout photo from the White House the morning Iraq was once again declared a sovereign nation got widely distributed because there was little else at the NATO summit that visually indexed Iraq. The photograph shows a note from the US national security advisor, Condoleezza Rice, to President George W. Bush that was passed to the president by Donald Rumsfeld during the NATO summit. A second note on the same piece of paper, supposedly in the hand of George Bush, reads: "Let Freedom Reign!" This news image is a rather curious visual document that forces viewers to consider the issue of who is being addressed in what looks to be just a personal communication between two individuals. It is a photograph of a seemingly casually penned note confirming the delivery of an official letter in an altogether different geographical location than the NATO event. Even though images were available of Paul Bremer, the director of the Coalition Provisional Authority, formally exchanging documents with Iraqi officials before departing from Iraq, they were not widely published. What was documented and circulated as confirmation of a transfer of sovereignty and national celebration of freedom was a photograph of an informal, handwritten note passed between officials of the occupying nation ceding its authority. Iraq was barely present in this visualization of its newly regained sovereignty. Rather, even on the day when Iraq was the dominant, it was the US handout photo that dominated the visual journalism. US government authorities as image brokers thus trumped the wire services in terms of what got played in the publications. Furthermore, since the photograph showed what appeared to be an informal note serendipitously intercepted by the camera, it created an illusion of free access and transparency.

The Desk Inter was busy with the NATO story all day. An editor had flown to Istanbul and was inside the conference center where the summit was being held. An AFP photographer was outside taking pictures of protestors, another inside photographing officials. Both photographers were sending their photographs to the Desk Inter editors, who were trying to piece the story together and correct captions before they validated the images and pushed them out to subscribers. Watching the image brokers working, I was struck by their meticulous attention to detail and concern for accuracy.

"OK, here the Iraqi flag is misidentified as the Turkish flag," Magda, a Polish photo editor, complained.

"Do you think these are the internationals? You know, the people who go from place to place protesting. Or are they Turks?" Magda asked me as she edited images of protestors. "Look at this picture," she said, pointing to an image showing a man wearing a red bandana and standing behind flames rising from an overturned car. "It's very May 1968 with the car. Very anarchy. 'Turkey falls into chaos, there's no order.'"

Marie read the dispatches on a screen and called the editor on site in Istanbul with a request for a photograph she could use in the future: "Listen, the Czech premier is apparently going to resign, and both he and his likely successor are in Istanbul, though leaving at 2 P.M. Can you get a photo of them?" Later she sat next to an editor at the desk and pointed at two images: "Look at the color difference here. One photographer's image shows NATO Secretary-General Jaap de Hoop Scheffer wearing a cream tie, and in another photographer's photos the tie is yellow. Which is it?" This was part of the agency's attempt to maintain a technically neutral "eye." Every week or so a photo editor would calibrate all the monitors on the desk so that the colors would be uniform on all the screens. The photographer at the summit sent in head shots of the Czech politicians. A lot of energy went into the acquiring of recent head shots of various political figures at AFP. Marie emphasized that a head shot "is not a *belle photo*. This is called a document." Yet journalistically, it was important to have current head shots of all relevant politicians, she explained to me.

This issue of whether something was merely a *document* or a good photograph was brought to my attention by many editors. The editor who had transmitted the photo of the beheaded American and another longtime editor at the Desk Inter explained the difference between "reportage" photos and art photos to me. They defined an art photograph as an image with longevity, one with universal value that could appeal to anyone at any time. "It's not trying to explain anything and is timeless, a photo in its own right," one of them told me. Reportage photos, on the other hand, were illustrative: a photo that synthesizes everything in a single frame. When I asked what an AFP photograph was, they explained it to me in relation to their competitors: "There's a culture of editors over the years. An AFP photographer will send in images that are more *décalé,* more loose in their frame. There is a huge influence from Magnum and art reportage here. So an AFP photo is slightly different, more poetic than other wire photos, different, has the French touch. Whereas the AP has very square lines and a very conservative approach. Here there's a culture of freedom to express how you saw it. AP also passes a lot of images from the [US] military.[38] All the information is there but there's no life in the picture. . . . They're pumping out the official version all the time." I pointed out to them that France is the country where by law each person owns his or her image and just that day I had watched them make an effort to pixelate handcuffs on a photograph of an accused man. They agreed that things in France often made it hard for photographers to work: "In the hearts of everyone here [at AFP] there is a fear of conformity. But things are changing. There are younger and younger editors on the desk, and freedom of photojournalism gets eroded if you don't stand up each time. What happens when you can't really see anything anymore? It's not really a picture, it's just a document." The editor responsible for the circulation of the images of the slain American's head emphatically explained that it was his job to verify the accuracy of the information: "As soon as I see handcuffs blurred I always ask for the original version.[39] It's basic good journalism. Sometimes you don't have the right to show things, but if we have the right to show, we should."

DOMINANT 3: SADDAM HUSSEIN ON TRIAL

Two days later, on July 2, 2004, Iraq dominated again, and this time the dominant was so large that there was little room left on front pages for any other stories. Former Iraqi president Saddam Hussein would make his first appearance in court. The morning meeting at AFP focused on preparing the best coverage possible.

Marie reported, "The event of the day is Saddam's appearance before the Iraqi court. It's going to be pool coverage, both text and photo. A US newsmagazine got the pool slot, but there might be a chance to photograph Saddam later, perhaps at the airport. Let's update our profile of Saddam, see what we have in the archives." In pool coverage, one journalist is given access to an event but shares his or her coverage with multiple media outlets. This allows other professional journalists to have access even when there is not enough physical room for them to be present or when access is limited for other reasons. Typically only one of the three wire services might get pool access to an event and be required to share its coverage immediately. It was slightly unusual for coverage of an event of this importance to be given to a photographer on assignment for a US magazine.

When asked by the editors on the desk Inter, Marie had no idea why a wire photographer had not gotten the pool, and some speculated that the photographer must have had connections to the US military officials in charge of the trial. Christophe suggested that because CNN would also be at the event, perhaps AFP Photo should get TV grabs. Since there would be no AFP photographers at the event, there would be no photographs to put on the wire until the pool photos were released after the event. Christophe decided to get stills of TV coverage to minimize the risk of subscribers looking elsewhere to illustrate a dominant news story. His decision shows how strongly those on the photo desks felt the need to have news images of major events up as soon as possible in order to keep the wire current and relevant for subscribers.[40]

There were constant discussions about the importance of keeping the AFP newsroom a commercial-interest-free environment. Although retail sale of individual photographs was tolerated, it was handled by a few employees seated apart from the others (the Retail Sales Service described in chapter 1) and was seen as a suspect activity that risked contaminating the entire newsroom with profit-making goals. Remember the 1957 statute on one of the entryway plaques demanding that AFP never come under the influence of any ideological, political, or economic group. Yet, due to limited access to the Saddam trial, momentarily AFP was dependent on CNN's news coverage. Until the pool photos of the Saddam trial had been released, AFP could release only screen grabs from CNN. Yet CNN's coverage was itself under the influence of the US military—an entity that had increasing power as a broker in the war of images.

Convinced there was nothing better for an anthropologist to do, Christophe positioned me in front of a screen to watch CNN diligently. "When you see a nice shot of Saddam," he instructed me, "press this key and get us a TV grab we can put online." And so, my hands on the keyboard, I watched CNN with rapt attention. The coverage was bizarre; CNN and Al-Jazeera cameras had been allowed into the courtroom, yet what viewers were being shown was not live coverage from the trial. While news viewers waited for the images to be released, reporter Christiane Amanpour stoked anticipation by narrating what the images would show. The audio recordings of the trial were not released at the same time, and so, in many ways, Amanpour's voice-over preceding the images both created suspense and established her complete authority on the spectacle. The absence of immediate images meant Amanpour, intentionally or not, made the most banal descriptions seem like breaking news. She told audiences that Saddam had been wearing a gray suit jacket, a very starched white shirt, a belt, brown trousers, brown socks, and highly polished black shoes and that he still had a beard, though more neat and tidy than it had been when he was pulled out of a spider hole in December.[41] Amanpour's report began, "Well, I've just rushed back from the courtroom to this convention center, where we're going to get the video distributed. So let me tell you about what we just saw."[42]

What Amanpour *saw* is relevant because, although there was a translator working with her, she made a point of saying in her initial reports later that day, "We're still waiting for the full translation of this because this all was in Arabic."[43] Therefore, her report focused on what the trial looked like. Eventually, the video was distributed, and viewers got to see what Amanpour had told us she had seen.

As instructed, I captured several grabs of Saddam Hussein in the courtroom. Each grab showed the entire screen, complete with the red "Breaking News" banner across the top, "First Images of Saddam Hussein from Today's Proceedings" along the bottom, and the permanent CNN logo with stock quotes below it. The tab on the bottom read "The New Iraq" and included a picture of the newly revised Iraqi flag. After all, just three days earlier, the United States had handed sovereignty back to Iraq. Completely influenced by the narrative Amanpour had given of the images before they had been aired, I focused on the screen to choose the moment that best captured Saddam's attitude. Just then I noticed a text imprinted on the video footage of Saddam that read "Cleared by US military." Christophe was printing out the TV grabs as I made them. Looking over at the printer, I noticed that in one particular grab, the words "Cleared by the US military" appeared directly on Saddam's forehead, as if announcing his acquittal. Others, at CNN or perhaps in the military, must have noticed the odd and emphatic political commentary unintentionally conveyed by the visuals, because less than two minutes later the text had been changed to a more precise message: "Video Cleared by US Military."

Within minutes, Christophe had put several of the grabs on the wire, and the photo editors on the desk began discussing the trial. Immediately Saddam had questioned the legitimacy of the court, asking the judge on what legal basis the court had been formed and jeering, "So you are an Iraqi—you are representing the occupying forces?"[44] The CNN visuals were effectively resonating with Saddam's claim. After all, despite the tab reminding viewers that sovereignty had been handed over to "the New Iraq," it was the US military that had cleared the video of the trial. It was the US military that had censored the trial in the first place: Robert Fisk of the *Independent* reported that a US admiral had told camera crews that the judge had demanded that there be no sound and ordered them to unplug their sound wires.[45] Another criticism was that the one Iraqi journalist present was not allowed to remain in the court for much of the proceedings. White House spokesman Scott McLellan's comment that "what is important is that Saddam Hussein and his band of oppressors are facing justice from the Iraqi people in an Iraqi court" seemed gravely at odds with the coverage of the proceedings. Beyond the act of military censorship, two things are of interest to me: the role of limited access, and the role of the still photographer.

The *Guardian*'s headline the following day deemed the Saddam court coverage "shambolic" because so few members of the press had had access. Furthermore, even though CNN's footage was made available to other broadcasters, Amanpour claimed she was there not as journalist for CNN but in a "unilateral" capacity; Peter Jennings likewise claimed not to be representing ABC. Having access to what some called "the trial of the century" became a feather in veteran star journalists' caps; hence, the limited access and the importance of the news event were mutually constitutive. For years afterward, the *New York Times* website underscored that John Burns was "the only Western print reporter to witness the start of Saddam Hussein's trial." Amanpour claimed the story among the top ten of her career, adding, "There were only a handful of journalists in the cramped quarters, and I was among the exclusive few—one pool reporter, me and one other journalist. There were just a few cameras there from Arab television stations."[46] In this count, the Arab journalists operating the cameras disappear behind their cameras, despite their linguistic advantage. Other journalists had to rely on interviewing those who had been in the courtroom, sources that seem especially problematic given that there was no audio anyone could rely on for reporting and none of the three reporters who briefed the remaining press was fluent in Arabic.

There was, in fact, another journalist in the room, an American, the pool photographer on assignment for a US newsmagazine—chosen by the deputy director for Coalition Operations. Yet in the various tellings of the trial, the photographer is completely erased, even though her images "played" everywhere in the following day's coverage per her pool agreement. Like the cameras of the Arab television stations whose microphones had been unplugged, the photojournalist seems to have been there merely as a visual recording device. Photographers are often forgotten.[47] In this situation, a courtroom spectacle was the anticipated dominant, and because of the linguistic limitations of the foreign reporters in the room, all that could really be reported on was what the trial looked like. And yet the photographer was discounted as a journalist, and with her, part of the labor of knowledge production behind the news was also effaced. Although US coalition forces had just days earlier handed over the nation's sovereignty to its new leaders, they continued to wield sovereignty over the images of the former leader's trial.[48] Eventually the photographer released her photos to the pool, and they were put on the wire.

What all three of these examples—the American engineer's beheading, the 'Iraq is sovereign note,' and Saddam Hussein's trial—emphasize is

AFP's struggle to maintain its authority as a source of credible news amid changing infrastructures of representation. That dominants must be visualized and AFP must have images on the wire to illustrate them as soon as possible meant that, in all three situations, the agency was reduced to circulating images produced and validated by other image brokers, whether terrorists, the US government, or the US military via CNN. Even when the appropriate person at AFP in Nicosia decided, on the basis of his regional expertise, that the decapitation image was too gruesome for Middle East audiences and therefore should not be circulated in the region, an editor at Paris headquarters overrode that decision, reflecting much controversy over what AFP's role was in this changing journalistic landscape. Accreditation and access had become even more critical to news coverage, but even the most exclusive access could be trumped by military censorship. Finally, in all three cases, the labor of professional image brokers was effaced even as the events themselves emphasized the power of imagery. The images produced by these alternate image brokers dominated not because they were better representations than those produced by a wire service, or because the events were too remote for a wire photographer to get to, but because the very infrastructures of representation had been coopted by others.

CRISES OF VISUALIZATION

The uncertainty and flux I observed at AFP in the summer of 2004 and in the broader world of international photojournalism during my fieldwork in 2003–5 reflected anxieties precisely about who dominates not only headlines but also the very infrastructures of media representation.[49] Battles over how news events are visualized were about dominance within the political world that the images supposedly reflected, within the image industry, and also within AFP itself.

As the examples above demonstrate, being the first to get in place and the fastest to deliver no longer guarantees success for a wire service. Valery himself told me that the editor of the future would need training not only in aesthetics but also in methods of determining which amateur or citizen images of an event to use. In other words, new challenges arise from an abundance of images. In 2015, AFP Photo's website claims that they produce up to three thousand new photographs every day.[50] Editors told me that, although getting to the news site first remains important, it is now also important to be the source that has photographers who can take images and editors to evaluate and validate them close to events so that they can understand images in context and gather citizen-produced images, if necessary. Speed is assumed. The competition is over quality, though what constitutes the quality of a news images is shifting as well.

A key question for many in the photo department was how authority and accountability function when digital circulation on the web makes it difficult to gauge who an audience for a particular image might be. Is a wire service merely a B2B provider, or does it directly feed an online public through news aggregators that stream the wire feed with minimal, if any, editing? Many grappled with the challenge of how to provide credible news images that convey important visual knowledge to global news audiences without contributing to an escalating war of images.

I return here to Valery's showing me *Patterns of Global Terrorism* when we first met. What interests me is not so much that, just a few weeks after their circulation, Valery correctly anticipated the historical impact of the Abu Ghraib images or that he was clearly troubled to be seeing the Iraq war through the eyes of US soldiers. Rather, it is that Valery did not seem troubled that he had been told to consider the US State Department's anticipated terrorism hot spots when building his organization's capacity. In other words, Valery assumes that in photographs taken by US soldiers, the viewer can see only through the eyes of the soldier. AFP values a professional, neutral eye—remember the meticulous attention paid to calibrating the color on each of the screens on the desk. Yet Valery did not seem troubled by the suggestion that he put reporters in place based on a US government document. Perhaps it was obvious to him that if news follows terror (as defined by governments), then that define the news.

RETHINKING THE PLAQUES

The plaques in AFP's main entry reminded all of the importance of information traveling freely, knowing no borders, and always being unbiased, its circulation unimpeded by politics, profit seeking, or ideology. Yet clearly there is significant friction involved in information traveling, particularly in the form of images, and frontiers can be ignored only at significant costs. The plaques seem to belong to a simpler model of news distribution, in which wire services had control over the wire and therefore much greater control over the construction of dominants. Yet now, while the infrastructures of journalistic representation, both text and image, are still in flux, is a critical moment to rethink those plaques and grapple with new codes of ethics that can guide knowledge production in the contemporary world. What principles should guide responsible and effective brokering of news images in the age of digital circulation? The photo department employees always used the back door at AFP headquarters. A very modest entrance, it led to the stairs and the rickety elevator. During the summer of 2004, the job of checking IDs at the back door was relegated to a university student majoring in economics. While on duty he spent many weeks reading Samuel Huntington's *The Clash of Civilizations and the Remaking of World Order.*

As it was that summer, world order and disorder continue to be highly visual. Battles over the infrastructures of representation are battles over visual worldmaking. Image brokers have increasingly to ask not only whose eyes one is looking through but who is competing for the very infrastructures of representation. Global millions have access to the means of production and circulation of visual representations and regularly broker information, especially images, by being "i-witnesses," citizen journalists—or, increasingly, simply by being avid social media users. If world order and disorder are highly visual, anthropological fieldwork at sites of visual worldmaking seems a necessary tool to understand how different forces come to clash or become interlaced or interfere with one another through images themselves.

I now turn to the editorial offices of *Newsworld,* a weekly news magazine that regularly uses images from both GVI and AFP to visualize world news. As a publication, *Newsworld* must craft comprehensible text and image stories for specific imagined readers. The tension between text and image, apparent at AFP in the allocation of reporting resources and logistical support, manifests itself as battles over physical space on *Newsworld*'s pages.

4

Newsworld

Everyday Practices of Editing the World

"Our job is to put a human face to a map," Maggie, an experienced photo editor at *Newsworld* magazine, emphasized as she explained her role in the production of the World section. In this chapter I highlight how image brokers like Maggie articulate geography and race or concepts such as modernity and democracy as they select specific faces to represent particular places in their everyday duties editing world news. Whereas I was analytically interested in processes and traditions of visual worldmaking, the image brokers I was following were gathering "world news" for the "World section" of a publication that promised to keep its readers well informed about the world. In other words, for these brokers "the world" as a knowable entity is part of the commodity they are producing.

The World section of *Newsworld* is responsible for international news—as opposed to the Nation section, the Arts section, or Sports, for example. This separation of news into categories of "nation" and "world" is common in news publications around the globe. One consequence of this categorization is that the nation is reified as an organizing principle around which to investigate the world. Yet in day-to-day operations it wasn't always clear-cut which section should be responsible for a given story. For example, when the Mars exploration rover *Spirit,* NASA's robotic geologist, landed on Mars and successfully submitted images to Earth in January 2004, one photo editor responsible for national news coverage asked her boss, Eric, a senior photo editor who oversaw multiple sections, "Is Mars a national or international story?" He laughed and said it was a tough question. After some thought he concluded, "If you take the US perspective, it's a domestic issue." At the morning meeting, it was assigned to the editors in the Nation section of the magazine.

Unlike GVI or AFP, who produce and circulate news images for other media professionals to use in various packages but are not themselves news publications, the image brokers at *Newsworld* produce a weekly newsmagazine spanning a limited number of pages to be sold to a specific public and, increasingly, viewed online.[1] As they performed their weekly duties as image brokers collectively editing the World section of the magazine, image brokers acted as mediators for views of the world. By observing the process of laying out several stories by collaborating teams of art directors, photo editors, and text editors, it became clear to me that worldmaking at *Newsworld* was an everyday practice of imagination: images and imagined communities were produced, reproduced, and circulated together.[2]

The worldmaking at *Newsworld* is particularly influential, for *Newsworld* is a pseudonym that I use in order to discuss in aggregate fieldwork and interviews with image brokers at the three US newsmagazines with the highest circulation: *Time, Newsweek,* and *U.S. News & World Report.* In 2004 these magazines' collective circulation, based on paid copies sold, was about nine million.[3] However, there are multiple viewers of any single copy. Although the circulation figures are lower today and some are no longer in print, there are large numbers of readers online. Furthermore, as will come up in the chapters to follow, many photographers and editors at all kinds of publications around the world look to these magazines, and increasingly to their photo blogs online, to understand trends in photography. The images in them influence other image brokers and have at times set the norms for international photojournalism. In some news publications I visited outside the United States, I saw images from these magazines literally, if illegally, being copy-pasted into local news publications. Moreover, almost all the photographers I interviewed—whether freelancers or wire agency photographers, based in the United States, Europe, or farther from the editorial offices of these magazines—told me they regularly looked through the news images published in these three publications (very few said they read the articles) and took note of each magazine's visual style. One photo editor complained that photographers tone down their imagery to fit what they perceive of as the magazine's style and that this is particularly frustrating in a digital age when the photographers send only those images that they believe the editors will want.[4] In other words, the views of the world published by *Newsworld* have a lot of force in influencing how other image brokers visualize world news.

THE DISCOURSE OF WORLDMAKING

My focus was on the work behind the images in the World section of the magazine.[5] Talk in the form of conversations, both among the self-identified "visual people" and between them and those they referred to as "word people," was central to the everyday practices of imagination that I observed. News images are concretizations of many brokers' work and thus a layering of various individuals' imaginations. Whether the photographs are sourced directly from a photographer on assignment for the publication, a wire service, a historical archive, a photo agency, or a visual content provider, by the time they reach the image brokers at *Newsworld,* they have already been worked on by someone else—often many other people, as the preceding chapters illustrated. The work of image brokers at *Newsworld* often involves explaining their decisions in relation to the imagined reader of the magazine. This practice of worldmaking at *Newsworld* involves much negotiation and many levels of approval, since each edition of the magazine is a highly collaboratively produced object. For the observing anthropologist, it was often the talk about images that rendered visible the process and logics of worldmaking, which is why dialogue once again features heavily in this chapter.

At the daily morning meeting, attended by both word people (writers and editors) and visual people (photo editors, graphic designers, art directors), everyone sat around one large table, although the word people tended to be much more talkative. The word people also often sat closer to the editor in chief than the visual people did. Though the atmosphere was collegial, it was clear that there was a hierarchy of opinion, and most jokes were made by a handful of senior word people. The visual people tended to be very quiet unless spoken to or asked for specific clarification on which photographer was shooting a story or what imagery was available on a particular event. Early in a given week, the meeting functioned by the various sections of the magazine pitching their stories and trying to win pages from the editor in chief. The answer to the often-asked question "What size of a story is it?" was given in either lines or pages—for example, sixty lines or four pages. As the editor in chief doled out favor in the form of pages, it was the text side that dominated the talk, even if some of the talk was about images. Later in the week, the meeting focused on future planning, status updates to stories under way, and debates over whether a breaking story needed to be covered that week and if so what would be displaced to make room for the new dominant.

After the meeting, the senior photo editor communicated what work was needed to each of the photo editors responsible for particular sections, such as World, Nation, Arts, and Health. One photo editor explained, "It's often like a game of telephone because I am often not in the meeting where the editor in chief explains what he wants so I don't hear him express it." Even if sometimes more photo editors attended the meeting, as did happen on occasion, there was still a game of telephone in the presentation of the selected photographs through the various steps in the process. Which is to say, I had many opportunities to hear individuals verbalize visual needs. First the photo editor would either pass along the assignment to a photographer in the field or, if the news to be visualized was already in the past or in a remote area where *Newsworld* was not likely to get a photographer in time, would search various photo agencies for an appropriate image. During conversations with photographers in the field, the photo editor mediated by describing the needs of the staff in the office while simultaneously trying to gather information about the reality in the field and brainstorm about potential shoots. If a photographer had already transmitted his images, this conversation addressed particular images on the photo editor's screen, and the photographer would be asked to describe the context in which the photographs were taken. Occasionally because of time differences or linguistic facility this conversation happened not with the photographer himself or herself but rather with a photo editor at an agency or with a foreign bureau photo editor, who would then communicate with the photographer. This added one more layer to the imaginations concretized in the final news image.

In this chapter I will share examples of photo editors commissioning a specific image from a photographer, trying to persuade the text editor of the story to use a particular image or set of images, working with another photo editor to decide how to visualize a particular story, expressing anger at a particular image not being used, and discussing layout options for a story. In each case, it was ultimately the talk about and around images that determined what got visualized and what did not. Though I am presenting aggregated research, all dialogues presented here are copied from my transcriptions of actual conversations as they happened during my research. Conversations were central, then, to capturing how a photograph became a layering of imaginations in the process of being either selected for publication or dismissed. One of the benefits of my conducting fieldwork at news publications is that it enables me not only to discuss the decision processes leading up to the publication of a certain image but also to address news images that did not get published. Attending closely to the minute details of worldmaking is critical to understanding how categories of people are produced through images that in turn inform how that category is defined and visualized in the future.

BATTLES FOR REAL ESTATE

On a cold January morning in 2004 at the daily 10 A.M. meeting, a usually even-tempered senior text editor at *Newsworld* exclaimed, "We're turning into a picture book! There's no room for my stories anymore. It's a newsmagazine—or at least it's *supposed* to be a newsmagazine. We hardly have any stories. We don't have any *space* for news."

"There are a lot of sacrifices made on the visual side, too. All we do is one-picture stories. We all have to give blood equally!" replied Eric, the senior photo editor. The trigger for this unexpectedly heated exchange was an image that was going to take up more than a page—the implication being that the news for which there was no space was located in the text, and not the image. The issue was not the specific image—which was actually an illustration, not a photograph —but rather a much larger philosophical difference about the role that visuals play in journalism, one that I observed again and again during my fieldwork. As detailed in chapter 3, at AFP there was a constant battle between text and photo over limited resources to cover any particular news event. Editors at *Newsworld* grappled weekly with negotiations over finite space on the pages of their publication. In the end the magazine could go to press only after an actual concrete version had been agreed upon and approved by the editor in chief. Each weekly edition had a mix of photographs, text, and illustrations or other visual elements within a particular format familiar to the reader as a magazine's particular look. Many "word people" saw visuals as merely illustrative of the news story conveyed in the writer's text—necessary, or worse, decorative gimmicks to break up blocks of text and to keep the reader's attention. "Visual people" saw visuals as journalistic contributions in their own right.

One photo editor I shadowed explained, "It's about real estate. Trying to get space." Although later she added, "The ideal situation is a marriage of words and images, *not* a battle for real estate." But during my fieldwork at *Newsworld* in 2003 and 2004, I observed very little marital bliss and many battles for real estate. The particulars of this battle over physical space on the page underscored power relations that shaped the production and circulation of news images as part of world-making.

The physical real estate being fought over was space on "the wall." The wall at *Newsworld* was an actual wall on which a mock-up of the week's magazine was displayed page by page. As Mary, an experienced art director, pointed out to me, "First you start with how many ads have been purchased and where they are [in the layout], so then you can calculate how many singles and spreads [two consecutive pages that will be visible together] you have." On the wall at one magazine I observed, advertisements were marked by bright orange sheets—full page or sized according to the ad—whereas editorial content was printed out in black and white. Over the course of the week the magazine mock-up on the wall would slowly get filled, with several changes along the way. In the battle for real estate, the wall was the scoreboard that was constantly being updated. Furthermore, at a production site where work was divided not only by function, such as writer or photo editor, but also according to corresponding sections of the magazine—Arts, Nation, Science—the wall was a concrete reminder that the final product was an assemblage—a unified, bound news publication. The one person who always thought about the magazine as a package was the editor in chief, essentially the one making decisions about how the pages worked together. For example, in one morning meeting I heard a particularly visually savvy editor in chief ask his staff, "Should we have a male or female in the illustration [for that story]? It seems a very male-image-dominated magazine this week. Is that wise? Is that something we care about?" He wasn't thinking about one particular story, but, rather, the reader's experience of the entire magazine.

LAYOUT LOGICS

Maggie explained to me that the task of laying out a story is about wielding emotions in order to "bring the story closer" and educate the reader.[6] Even with a story the reader might already be assumed to know, photo editors like Maggie believe images can supply an emotional connection that might have been absent in the reader's previous encounters with the same news story. Although much world news goes unvisualized in publications, certain stories, such as ongoing wars, get a lot of exposure, which can make finding such novel emotional angles challenging. So whether the story is new or needs to be portrayed in a new light, the photo editor's task is to determine what is visualizable and then to find ways to photograph it.

One particular story looked at Israeli and Palestinian youth growing up in Hebron and Ramallah, respectively. Watching Sarah, a text editor, and Maggie work with Mary, the art director, and Maggie's boss, the senior photo editor, on this potential photo essay made apparent how the reader's interpretation was anticipated differently by each individual. Sarah, the most senior member of the team, interpreted the images and then articulated suggestions to the others.

> *Mary* (art director): I have this idea about doing pairs, spreads. [In particular she mentioned juxtaposing a photo with balloons in it with another showing a kite.]
>
> *Senior photo editor*: I like that thinking. This [work] has never been published in the US. I like how this photographer made an effort to stay balanced unlike [another photographer working on the topic] who had such an opinion.
>
> *Maggie* (photo editor): These kids are willing to die for their cause. It doesn't have to run this week but we need to make a commitment [to the agency selling the work on behalf of the photographer].
>
> *Sarah* (text editor): I have a concern about pairings because we should try to be fair but that's not always the same as being balanced so I am not sure about having one page on Palestine and then the opposite page show Israel. The Palestinian side will be bad-guy killers and then these [*pointing to the Hebron photographs*] are obviously innocent children. Whereas settlers in Hebron are not innocent. I mean children are always innocent, but these folks have gone into a city and forced themselves into the center. They are colonialists in the worst possible way. They take all the water and make life miserable for these people. So I am uncomfortable with any kind of equivalency.
>
> *Mary*: It wasn't conceived that way.
>
> *Chris* (photo editor who had initially requested the images from the photographer): Through the youth's divided eyes, this shows visually what the problems are. If we don't run this then our competitors will and we'll lose it.
>
> *Sarah*: Plus, the lay reader can't tell a Palestinian from an Israeli.

In the comments above—all of which are part of the work that makes a news image a layering of imaginations and, in the context of *Newsworld,* an act of worldmaking—the content of the images is simultaneously interpreted in terms of politics, aesthetics, news value, and business strategy. Mary's suggestion to pair images is graphically motivated: the balloons in one image and the kite in another form a nice contrapuntal visual. This pairing is interpreted by the senior photo editor as a way of underscoring the photographer's balanced approach, which she finds commendable. Whereas Sarah, the text editor, objects to the pairing because she sees this layout as suggesting equivalence between Palestinian youth and children of settlers in Hebron. Yet at the same time she does not believe that the lay reader will be able to distinguish a Palestinian from an Israeli, in which case presumably the reader would not perceive the layout to suggest equivalence. Moreover, while producing this particular story, the team is aware of producing the magazine's own reputation as an internationally important publication that covers the latest news. That this material has never been published in the United States adds value to the images, and when the text editor seems unconvinced, another photo editor highlights the threat of a competitor running the images, making them more desirable. Hence, what is simultaneously produced is the concrete weekly World section of the magazine, the reputation of the magazine and its ability to bring the reader all the week's most relevant news, and a representation of the world and the political possibilities in it.

THE RULE OF TEXT

Photo editors emphasized again and again that photos are about appealing to the reader on an emotional level. Maggie made this point to me repeatedly: "The purpose of a photo is to intrigue a reader. The photo is going to decide whether or not people read a story. I think that's how I can have impact on a story."[7] Several photo editors complained that while the text people are interested in what illustrates a story, they are not thinking about what will make the reader actually stop to read the story. Sarah was a correspondent before she became the text editor of the World section, and yet she is known as being one of the more visual-friendly word people in her current role. "Photography has to sell the story because the reader perceives the photo first," she told me. "Before, I would have regarded the photo as an intrusion on my space. As a correspondent I am responsible for writing the best story, but I'm not necessarily thinking about what's the best way to tell a story, as I only know one way to do that—in writing! But as an editor I am responsible to my reader, not my story." For Sarah, responsibility toward the reader meant not just thinking about the text but considering the image as well: "Maggie is responsible for thinking only about the photos, and her interest lies with the photographer, not the big picture. Whereas Mary the art director has to marry the words and images."

As Sarah's comments reveal, discussions around photography in newsmagazines highlight the multiple mediations that constitute the everyday practices of editing the world. The editor is mediating between the writer and the other editors; the photo editor is mediating between the photographer and the text editor, and also between the photographer and the writer; the art director is mediating between text and image; and so on. Moreover there is a hierarchy of mediation in which senior editors in each section of the magazine mediate between their section and the editor in chief, and everyone is anticipating the reader's reception of the week's stories.

Perhaps in reaction to the fact that text editors often become the voiceover for the images, silence plays an important role in the everyday practices of photo editors—as if the goal is to keep the editor in chief from pronouncing a negative decision. Any indication that a set of images might be usable even if not immediately, or any reaction other than a direct no, is considered a good sign. Silence is a photo editor's friend; it's a *non-no,* which is a potential yes. One morning Sarah, the text editor, asked Mary and Maggie, "Did you notice how cranky he [the editor in chief] was? I decided within five minutes of the meeting starting that I was not going to say a word." Mary, the art director, replied, "You know, I decided the same thing." The irony was that Mary almost never speaks at the morning meeting unless responding to a question. But this irony was completely lost on Sarah, who seemed not to even register Mary's comment as a joke. Maggie explained the joke to me afterward. The text editor had been silent by choice, whereas the art director had been silent out of habit and well-established protocol. This is not to imply that the image people are not respected, but rather to underscore that there is a protocol that the voices heard in the daily meeting often belong to those who are responsible for producing and editing the words in the magazine.

Art historian W. J. T. Mitchell claims that "the interaction of picture and text is constitutive of representation as such: all media are mixed media, and all representations are heterogeneous; there are no 'purely' visual or verbal arts."[8] My research suggests that at the sites of production of mass mixed-media news publications, however, power relations are not heterogeneous. Said differently, power is not always mixed—

medium-wise. Power may not be inherently textual by nature, but despite constant claims that we live in a world awash with images, and much rhetoric around the power of images, at the sites of production of US newsmagazines, it appears that power is very much textual. I found that within their own publications, photo editors inhabit a very liminal space in which they are constantly mediating between text and image—or between the word people and the visual people. Maggie spent hours reading not just the drafts of news stories as they were being written by the writer, but also any other research she could find on the topic so that she would be in a strong position to guide the photographer if she had one on assignment, and to anticipate the text side's concerns as she crafted a strong argument for the images she selected.

THE IMAGINED READER

Sarah saw photography as a critical teaching tool: "The images get the reader's attention. Which is vital especially with news. . . . Most readers are apt to feel that foreign news is a bit like homework. They are intimidated by it, they don't know the characters, they don't know where these countries are. So we try to make it easier and more appealing. We show you who the characters are so that you can attach a face to a name, and we'll show you where the country is on a map. We try to show people, so readers can attach to a person." Sarah is articulating the logic of indexing a body to represent a body politic. She assumes that if a reader attaches to a person, they will be more interested in that news story.

Maggie, the photo editor, was always trying to see all the images available on a topic even if she had already assigned it to a particular photographer. "You don't want to look like you missed something, yet you want to provide fresh material," she explained to me. Throughout the day she received pitches from photographers, editors at photo agencies, and visual content providers. In the past, it was much more difficult to send copies of negatives to interested editors; therefore, many more images were brokered based on verbal description.[9] In a digital age, Maggie can see the photographs she is being offered. Therefore, even if she didn't want the images for *Newsworld* or was outbid by a competitor, she would know what other newsmagazines might run based on what she had been offered. Asked why she didn't use wire photographs more often, Maggie explained, "The wire photographs appear in local newspapers, so you want something no one has seen before." This concern with finding novel angles to stories is especially a concern in weekly newsmagazines, which routinely risk looking like they are presenting stale news because their production cycle means they cannot cover only breaking news. Eric, another photo editor, concurred: "You can't panic. The whole system is based on panic and the fear that your editor will see what [the competition] had and will say 'Why didn't we have this?'" Eric underscored the importance of being able to anticipate anxiety. Indeed, balancing fresh material with visuals that endorse the view that the reader is really getting the world in one publication is a constant challenge, involving complex choices. For instance, when choosing an image for a story on Shia uprisings in Iraq, Eric compared a tightly cropped portrait of Sistani, the senior Shia cleric in Iraq, with a crowd shot taken at a recent protest: "[The Sistani] photo has been in every publication in the country. The demonstration photo is not as strong but [shows] that we had a photographer there." He then selected the crowd shot. Eric's decision was motivated not merely by providing the reader with new information or visuals she or he might not have seen already, but also by a need to underscore the value of the newsmagazine, its prowess at having people in the right place to capture world news.

All those involved in the production and selection of images anticipated the interpretation of the reader. On my first day of fieldwork at *Newsworld* Eric, an experienced photo editor, drew my attention to the specter of the reader: "They often invoke the name of the reader around here, usually to say he won't understand." Photo editors regularly quipped sarcastically about the "stuff of real substance" they worked on merely to please the reader, such as "Best Things to Buy for Christmas." Yet the reader was also portrayed as discriminating enough to demand a particular *Newsworld* style both aesthetically and journalistically. Though the editor in chief might be dismissive about the readers' popular tastes, such as when quipping, "Putting Clay Aiken on the cover is like printing money," the reader was also imagined as "curious," as proven by the fact that covers focusing on human origin stories had also done well.[10] I often heard comments in which the assumption was that the reader's nationality had to be taken into account: "You need an American soldier because the reader is American [who] will be more interested in a story as she flips through the magazine if there's an American connection."

One text editor insisted, "We have only Iraqis on the first three pages … we should have a US soldier on the fourth spread. … We have to balance the US and Iraq photos." As early as the first anniversary of the

American war in Iraq in 2004, editors had started worrying about how to continue generating interest in a war that had lost its novelty. This anxiety, which only grew with the continuation of the war, was illustrated in a meeting in which editors debated which cover story to run. One group pitched "'Why War?' A story on war throughout human history delving into the motivations behind violence." Another group suggested a story on whether obesity was a matter of personal responsibility or not and the burden the disease placed on health-care insurance providers. A senior editor, worn out by continuously looking for fresh approaches to the war in Iraq, immediately perked up upon hearing the suggestion "I think we should pander to the audience." Imagining the cover, he continued, "Fat? Not your fault!" and chuckled, "We'll sell a million copies!"[11]

CLEAR IMAGES

Eric, the photo editor, had a postcard in his office with a line from Jean-Luc Godard's film *Histoire(s) du cinéma* printed on it: "Il faut confronter des idées vagues avec des images claires [Vague ideas must be confronted by clear images]." Watching the editorial team try to find images for a story on where America went wrong in Iraq was to watch professional image brokers trying to visualize a murky state of affairs. When the group was given the assignment to illustrate the alleged weapons of mass destruction and why they still hadn't been found, Sarah, the senior text editor, commented, "We're trying to illustrate something that doesn't exist, it is going to be hard. . . . How do we illustrate that? At one point they [Iraq] had them, now they don't." Similar difficulties arose with trying to show that infrastructure was not working. Simon, the photo editor in charge of finding images of infrastructural problems in Iraq, explained: "What a photo editor has to figure out is what is visual and can be photographed."

During the time in which I conducted this research, the focus of the World section was almost exclusively on Iraq. One wall in *Newsworld*'s office had three maps on it: Iraq, the Middle East, and the world. It was a moment when the initial support for the administration's decision to go to war was waning and yet before the Abu Ghraib scandal had broken. A lot of the news from Iraq was about what was not going as planned. Yet, journalists at *Newsworld* were hesitant to outright criticize the war. Conversations regularly centered on what could be visualized for the reader and addressed the ethical, aesthetic, and commercial dilemmas behind various visualization strategies.

While working on the story about failed infrastructure in Iraq as an indication of the US mission's shortcomings, Simon called Sergei, a foreign-bureau photo editor in Moscow. Sergei was the primary contact for Alexei, a photographer on assignment for *Newsworld* in Iraq. Alexei had been invited by Iraqi insurgents to watch them setting up mines for American soldiers. "I don't think he should photograph it because when he is out with the American soldiers it is unpredictable, he doesn't know whether or not they will kill anyone," Sergei told Simon. "Here he definitely knows they are going to kill someone and he believes he should not go so he turned down the offer."

"Is he working with the writer?" Simon inquired.

"He's trying to get other possibilities with the resistance. He wants to shoot a training, but not to go on a raid. So he thinks he might shoot them preparing for a raid but then make up a reason not to go. But they just want to use his camera."

"So he feels manipulated?"

"He doesn't want to photograph a planned killing. If he knows about a planned killing, he's obligated to tell someone."

Simon shifted the conversation from Alexei the photographer's reports from the field to the story the writers at the magazine were working on that week: "Something that would be really interesting would be what the inside of an Iraqi police station looks like. I can use that for a story."

"What?"

"In America you'd go to a police station if you had a problem or something was stolen. I'm curious to hear what that's like in Iraq."

"I'd never go [to a police station]," Sergei muttered.

"Well in America that's what you'd do. Alexei shot a police station in Basra a while ago, but I want more routine stuff—or inside a courtroom."

"You want more-official stuff?"

"Yes. Government structures any civilized country would need."

The conversation above began when Sergei, the photo editor in Moscow, who had been talking directly to the photographer, explained what Alexei had been shooting and his rationale behind not shooting the insurgency story. Immediately Simon asked if he had been working with the writer, since any story on which the photographer manages to get the attention of a writer is much more likely to run. Furthermore, the responsibility of the decision not to cover this situation would then be shared between text and visual staff. Then Simon made a request based on information he'd just gotten about the story that would likely run in that week's magazine. The interesting moment here is that at first the foreign-bureau photo editor did not understand the assignment because it was explained in a very American cultural context: if you had a problem, as a routine you'd go to the police. Sergei, in Moscow, translated this request into a request for "official" photography. And once again Simon, the American photo editor, mentioned "government structures *any civilized country* would need"—the implication being that any country without these structures is not yet completely civilized—precisely the argument of the text story being written, which asked if Iraq had the routine infrastructure necessary for democracy. But already at this level there were slight slippages between the various mediators. Notably, the question being asked was not "What do people in Iraq do when something is stolen or they have a complaint" or "What routine infrastructures do Iraqis believe they need for democracy," but rather, "What does this institution that people would turn to *here* look like *there* in Iraq?"

Photographers frequent complained to me about photo editors sitting in a faraway office making ridiculous requests based on story ideas hatched in a meeting rather than on reporting from the field. Yet, most of the photo editors I observed at *Newsworld* were quite sensitive about how to mediate requests from the text editors. In fact Simon, the same photo editor quoted above asking for images of "government structures any civilized country would need," on another day rolled his eyes and complained, "They [the word people] always ask, 'Can we get some US soldiers guarding oil tanks?'" Late on a Thursday night, after she found out that the photographer and writer would be going out on a military raid a few hours later, I witnessed Maggie, the photo editor, cringe as she spoke to the photographer by phone: "I hate to say it, but a soldier with sweat coming down his face on an American patrol would be good." Photo editors did not like to ask for a certain situation to be photographed and tended to respect what the photographer was telling them he or she was seeing in the field. Yet photo editors were less likely to perceive their mediation of the text side's agenda for the week as acts of influencing news images from afar.

Of course the various editors at magazines are not the only ones actively influencing images before they are taken. During a conversation with Sergei, the photo editor in Moscow, Maggie, the photo editor in New York, asked if the photographs from Chechnya that she had seen that morning were dated, and Sergei replied that they had been taken earlier in the month, adding, "But nothing has changed. Tim [another photographer] went [on assignment with a competitor magazine], stayed a week and came back. Apparently he couldn't even lift his camera to his eyes, and he has all kinds of connections." Maggie understood Sergei's hesitation to put anyone on assignment. "I already told another photographer no because they are just going to put him on a dog-and-pony trip," she told me. Upon my asking about dog-and-pony trips, she railed against government officials dictating what could and couldn't be photographed and yet pointed out that publications might still use the images: "North Korea is so difficult to shoot that even if you don't have great images they'll run." Apparently all photographers returned from North Korea with similar images because they had been taken to the same metro station by state minders, the same street, the same school—the rare spots where a photographer was allowed to work.

Certain photo editors even pointed out that *Newsworld*'s own infrastructure reflected certain fixed ways of seeing. After his phone conversation with Sergei, Simon turned to me and explained, "Having a dedicated photo person in Moscow is clearly a leftover from the cold war." Perhaps it was time to shift, he mused. Yet despite the awareness I observed at *Newsworld,* editors still have a reputation among photographers as disconnected from field reporting and hence prone to make stereotypical requests. Furthermore, what disturbed photographers and photo editors most was a demand for a particular image or the sense that photographers' cameras were being manipulated whether by government officials, insurgents, or text editors asking to visualize editorial stories. In the process of producing clear images for readers and performing their duties mediating between word people in the office and visual people in the field, photo editors often trade in stereotypes—ironically, often while looking for novel approaches to a story. I turn now to the preparation of two photo essays—stories where the visual is privileged over text—to highlight the specific processes by which formative fictions get constructed and deployed despite or precisely because of concerns about accuracy and representativeness.

THE PHOTO ESSAY

A photo essay is a story composed primarily of photographs and usually spreads over four to six pages. Photo essays do not appear every week or on any type of regular schedule. Photo essays are initiated by the photo department once it has received either an intriguing proposal from a photographer or a completed project ready to be published. Photo essays appear as stand-alone stories themselves and hence are often the pride and joy of the photo department. They are the antithesis of the *one-picture story* bemoaned by the photo editor in the contentious meeting mentioned at the beginning of this chapter. Multiple images are used, usually from a single photographer, and so photographs are allowed to be the primary vehicle for the story rather than subservient illustrations to the text. Conversely, sometimes they are the bane of the text side. Sarah, a senior text editor at *Newsworld,* explained: "When we're looking at thirty-five or thirty-six pages of editorial material, every page is incredibly valuable. If a photo essay is four pages, that's one-ninth of the magazine—it better be damned relevant!"

Many photo editors I met felt that their contributions were limited by the structure of image brokering in newsmagazines. One emphatically told me, "Magazines are sausage factories. We have no impact on the industry because it's a bunch of text guys!" Precisely because they are not prompted by the decision of the text side to do a story that then needs images to illustrate it, photo essays are a reversal of the usual hierarchy in a newsmagazine. Hence, they are highly valued by photo editors, who express tremendous frustration at being ruled by the text people and being seen as auxiliary. Photo essays are one of the few opportunities photo editors have to initiate a project that tells a story visually and supports the work of photographers working on long-term projects. These are the long-awaited, patiently earned opportunities to display all the photo department's capabilities and the depth that visuals can bring to a story. Photo essays are the reward for finding countless head shots, agreeing to photo illustrations, and watching innumerable favorite photos get left on the editing table week after week, often to be replaced by what are perceived to be lesser images that "the reader will understand." A senior photo editor with more than twenty years' experience editing "the world" for what she perceived as text-driven newsmagazines likened her job to living in a wasteland and explained the critical importance to her of collaborations with photographers that result in photo essays: "I live in a wasteland, but I dream of banks of wildflowers. I live in the desert but dream of the forest." I couldn't help but be reminded of Sarah the text editor's frank aside to me when we were speaking in private: "The visual people see poetry, but we are not a poetry magazine. We're a newsmagazine."

ACCURACY AND METAPHORS

It was in a morning daily editorial meeting that I first heard of the photo essay concerning the separation barrier. The news peg was the United

Nations' October 21, 2003, condemnation of the wall being constructed by Israel in the West Bank and the release of a report detailing the negative implications for Palestinian livelihood.[12] Once the editor in chief agreed that there might potentially be room for a photo essay in that week's issue, Sarah, the text editor who had worked for several years as a correspondent in Jerusalem, Mary the art director, and Maggie the photo editor went to work. Their conversations emphasized how various photographers had approached the task of visualizing the wall—from photographing the actual wall mentioned in the report to visually documenting its impact on those living in areas around it. A very well-respected photographer had sent panoramic black-and-white prints from sites in Gaza and the West Bank to Maggie, who had made an initial selection. She then showed this selection to Mary and Sarah.

> *Mary* (the art director): I like the feel of that one. That one's good for compositional difference.
>
> *Sarah* (the text editor): The dustiness of the background, everyday life. . . . Which of these photos do you like? [*She showed two separate photos of women crossing the wall, pointing to each in turn.*] Here is a traditional woman; here is a working woman, so the empathy factor is higher. [*She then looked closely at an image showing an unveiled pretty young blond woman in jeans.*] I'd be very shocked if that was a Palestinian woman.
>
> *Maggie*: Why?
>
> *Sarah*: She looks so modern.
>
> *Maggie*: According to the caption she's Palestinian, but I'll check.[13]
>
> *Sarah*: [*reaching for another image*] Here you see old women and children, so obviously these are not the elements to cause trouble in the world. So you get the sense that this [wall] is just a total inconvenience. Then I like this one because you have every type of person in it.
>
> *Maggie*: You can see how they are living in this desolate landscape. To me the checkpoint is a more familiar image so it's not surprising.
>
> *Mary*: [*reaching for another photograph*] That one's a bit graphically difficult for me because it's a different shape, but I can practically hear what's going on.

The art director, text editor, and photo editor all act as mediators as they perform their weekly duties in collectively editing the World section of the magazine. The text editor represents the opinion of the writer, whether the writer is down the hall or in the field on the other side of the world. The photo editor represents the photographer or photographers, and the art director mediates between the text editor's desires and the photo editor's desires. In the above example, as in the story on youth in Ramallah and Hebron, Sarah, the text editor, verbally captions the images. She inserts a narrative, and her manner of codifying what she sees then guides how the images are laid out to tell a story. Maggie physically handles the prints, attempts to represent the photographer, and also comments on the images' relation to other imagery on the topic (e.g., "the checkpoint photo is more familiar," implying that the reader has probably seen images like this in comparable publications before).[14] Mary, the art director, voices concerns over the shape of images as well as their compositional elements, which is understandable given that she will be responsible for actually sizing the images and designing the final layout of the photo essay.[15] In the battle for real estate she is ultimately the broker of solutions, finding ways to marry image and text. Furthermore, because real-estate needs are constantly changing—Mary says that trying to understand which cover might run the night before going to press "is like reading tea leaves"—her job as art director is to try to anticipate visual products for all possible decisions.[16]

In the dialogue above, Sarah's anticipation of the imagined reader's interpretation informs her choice in images. What is inferred from her comment comparing the two women climbing over the wall is that the American reader will be more empathetic to the slim, younger woman wearing a loose headscarf and a knee-length skirt shown in one photograph than she or he will be to the older woman with a tighter headscarf and loose dark clothing. Sarah, the text editor, spent many years working in the Jerusalem bureau, so she may be drawing from that experience when she identifies the younger woman as a "working woman," but she anticipates that the average reader will make the same identification. The categories anticipated in the imagination of the reader are "traditional woman" versus "working woman, more like one of us." Yet her very next comment underscores that there is a limit to how much familiarity is possible. In Sarah's mind, the attractive young blond woman in jeans is *too modern* to be Palestinian.[17]

The lay reader is presumed by Sarah to be unable to differentiate between Palestinians and Israelis, but able to distinguish which of the women is a working woman. The reader is then expected to empathize with the woman with whom she can identify. So these image brokers imagine what traditional and modern look like respectively, as they image a particular place for a journalistic publication, and anticipate how their readers will imagine this place and relate (or not) to the people in the images. It is in this manner that news images serve as formative fictions.

When Joel, Sarah's boss and one of the most senior text editors at the magazine, walked in, Sarah had to verbalize the rationale for the photo essay. Joel suggested using an aerial of the wall, to which Maggie responded, "Much of the wall is in no-man's-land so in that sense the wall alone is boring."

> *Sarah*: To make the best use of this photographer's work you would really need to expand the theme beyond the wall.
>
> *Joel*: The wall is a nice focus, though, because once you get away from the wall it gets fuzzier. One aerial shot that wasn't by him wouldn't steal the thunder or mood too much, would it?
>
> *Maggie*: Well, he really proposed a story on the wall in the sense that a wall is a metaphor for isolation.
>
> *Sarah*: It's a metaphor for the strangulation of Palestine.
>
> *Maggie*: To me it's a metaphor for the end of the peace movement.
>
> *Joel*: I am more inclined to look at what the wall actually is: [a story of] the haves and have-nots.

The team discussed the option of finding aerials to augment the selection of images before them. Sarah was concerned that the photographer was not showing the actual wall being evaluated by the United Nations, the wall as it appeared in the news that week: "Barriers have existed in Israel since the Intifada." Maggie tried to make a case for the scope of the photographer's work: "You can tell a lot about what [living with these walls] will be like." Mary, the art director, drew attention to a particular image taken in Rafah, Gaza, showing residents returning to homes destroyed in an Israeli invasion.

All the images from Rafah and the Gaza Strip were technically disconnected from the segment of the wall that had drawn criticism from the United Nations that week—the wall in the West Bank. The UN report—the news peg that made this story relevant at this particular moment—stated concern that the wall might cause disruption of livelihood and further humanitarian hardship for the Palestinians; hence, the report addressed the impact of the wall on life in the region. The geographical specificity of the report was mentioned by text editors several times to emphasize why the scope of the essay should not extend beyond the West Bank, whereas the fact that the report emphasized the impact of the walls in general on life around them did not get repeated.[18] Mary clearly appreciated an image from Rafah but was convinced by Sarah that it did not fit the story, or at least she voiced her interest in the photo without arguing for it to be included in the selection for the photo essay. "Can we number this photo?" she asked. (This allows it to be entered into the magazine's system and potentially used at another time even if not as part of this photo essay.) "It reminds me of a period movie that shows the nastiness of life in those times."

Joel: Yes, it looks very *pre modern*.

Maggie called the photographer to verify that the blonde actually was Palestinian and during the conversation asked several clarifying questions about how each image fit into the story of the wall the photographer was trying to tell. Maggie, who tries to ensure that photographers' opinions are taken into account, repeatedly asked which of the images he felt were the strongest. This is another example of a nodal point of production as two actors involved in different production processes negotiate selections between all possible images.

Maggie: I'm not very knowledgeable about the area. I have never been there, so I am going to ask again, How do the Rafah pictures relate to the wall?

Photographer: Well, the wall takes many forms. I mean the wall along the Egyptian border has been going on for some time now. . . . [It's] part of a process of walling off a country. . . . Physically it is impossible for the Egypt wall to be connected to the main wall. . . . But I mean the idea is not new. The concept of the wall has been going on for a number of years.

Maggie: I am having a hard time making an argument for the entire selection because [Sarah, the text editor] thinks it gets fuzzy if you go beyond the West Bank issue.

Photographer: [*audibly irritated*] Is it just about illustrating a news peg or is it about good photography and showing the psychology of walls? I am a photographer; I show what something *feels* like, not what it *looks* like! All she has to do is caption them very clearly.

Maggie: Her argument is that the walls are not something new except what's happening in the West Bank.

Photographer: It's a very literal [approach to the topic].

Maggie: She wants to show what is new to the reader.

Photographer: But this *is* new to the reader; I'll bet my life on it. People don't know about these walls, they don't even know what settlements are. . . . Yes, it's a metaphor but it is also a very linear thing: the wall is a part of the expansion of the settlement.

Maggie turned the conversation to the image of the blonde, verbalizing Sarah's question as her own: "Is she an Israeli woman or a Palestinian? She just seems so untypical of a Palestinian woman."

Photographer: Look. As photographers we tend to photograph the exotic—the woman in the burka, et cetera. But Ramallah is a very European town. A lot of international Palestinians go to the Ramallah area. It is very westernized and very modern. . . . I would go for the best picture. Anything that needs to be harmonized or clarified, just clarify it. . . . I know what it's like. [Your editor] is sitting there with an idea in her head that she wants but there's nothing there but a ghost. Basically you want images to speak for themselves. . . . It's a photo essay, so if I were you I wouldn't let it be driven by linear analysis. . . . There's nothing wrong with writing a story to go along with it. Writing a story to say, "This is a way of life we are looking at, a condition of humanity."

Once off the phone Maggie told me she was glad to have had the conversation and repeated to me what she had said to the photographer: "The current peg is this wall, but there's life around the walls we should be looking at." She continued, "What I am trying to do is represent the photographer's opinion as clearly as I can because he's not here. I'm trying to translate." Indeed she had to do a lot of translating between the metaphors of the photographer, who was trying to convey what living with the wall *felt like,* and the literal questions of the text editors concerning what the new parts of the wall being erected in the West Bank and those specifically mentioned in the UN's report *looked like.* What is at stake is not merely which particular images will be selected, but the type of journalistic information that photographs can provide, the work that news images can do.

Once the team had reached a layout they were comfortable with, they collectively walked it over to Joel's office. The hierarchy of office space dictates that the text editor's office is much larger and more central than either the photo editor's or the art director's, so Mary and Maggie usually took the images to Sarah's office first, then to Joel's. Just as Sarah had done, Joel stopped at the photo of the young woman, now confirmed by the photographer to be Palestinian. "She's lovely, but what does she have to do with the wall?" he asked. "She's just passed through a checkpoint," Maggie replied. But the image did not make it into the photo essay. In fact, all of the seven images in the final photo essay showed an actual portion of the physical wall itself—what the wall looks like rather than what life around it, or even what observing life around it, *felt* like at a particular moment.

Eventually all four walked it to the editor in chief's office. "Have you noticed how much we all walk around in this place?" Joel asked me one day. Even though his post is senior enough that most people go to *his* office these days, he has likely clocked in thousands of miles of hall strolls over the years. So, collectively, the photo editor/text editor/art director group walked to the editor in chief and showed the piece. Sarah, the text editor, narrated the photo essay and turned to Maggie, the photo editor, only when further clarification was necessary. Maggie had translated the images for Sarah, a text person, and now a text person gave voice to the images in front of the ultimate decision maker—the editor in chief. Ultimately it is the *talk* about and around images that determines what gets visually represented and what does not.

The editor in chief liked the images, so Sarah asked if he would like to run the photo essay that week. "I just don't think we have the space," the editor in chief said. "But if we change covers tomorrow [the day the magazine closes], then we'll need something else." Though nothing explicit was said, it was understood that he had liked the wall piece *enough* so that it had a good chance of running—even if not that week—and that in any case they should prepare it for publication. The photographer was thrilled that the piece might run. He implored Maggie via email to use only the best pictures, adding, "Don't let the word people rule. Visual people unite!" Later that night Mary posted the tentative pages on "the wall" in the magazine's office alongside the rest of that week's content. She came into Maggie's office near midnight and rejoiced: "The fence is on the wall!"

VISUALIZING MODERNITY

Another week I observed the same editorial team—Sarah, Maggie, and Mary—work on a photo essay about Iran. The photographer had been sent to do a story on youth in Iran. Mary, the art director, was pleased with the story because it was a well-rounded portrait of the country. Sarah, the text editor, explained: "Everything from couples stealing kisses to hundreds of fanatics." There were in fact photographs of large numbers of people praying, a couple kissing on a hilltop, young boys air-dancing in the mountains, girls in school and girls in a market. Mary explained her layout choices: "Here I am contrasting girls in school with girls buying mirrors." She had left in a photo of a theater because she had recently read two different stories on Iran that mentioned the significance of the theater. As we've seen, image brokers don't work in a vacuum: their work is influenced by other's reporting. Continuing in this mode of presenting a balanced story, Mary added, "I think if you spend one whole spread [i.e., two pages] on romance on a hilltop then you need to end with something more conservative. Praying with guys in mosque, for example."[19]

Maggie, the photo editor, was worried that the need for balance—the mandate that "if you have illicit lovers on a hill to show balance you have to have prayer"—would mean that the best photography would get left out. "It will be left, right, left, right," she worried. Maggie was often frustrated by clichés winning over excellent photographs.

Indeed, when the photo essay was shown to a senior editor, the story was laid out in contrasting pairs. Joel, the senior editor, expressed concern about the subjects in the images: "These guys won't go to jail for break dancing?" Maggie reassured him that they had all been photographed knowing it was for *Newsworld*. "So this is a story about Iran loosening up?" he inquired.

Maggie's boss, the senior photo editor, stepped in to explain the value of the images: "The whole thing feels visually fresh: Inside of Iran. Stolen moments of Iran. An intimate look. When you look at it from the context of what you normally see, it's pretty extraordinary in terms of how you see." Sarah, the text editor, then glossed the images: "Bad guys, bad guys, good guys, good guys. Traditional versus modern, traditional versus modern." She drew attention to the classroom image, which she believed highlighted a contrast within a single frame. Pointing to the microscopes in the image, she commented, "Very traditional women, but they're studying anatomy."[20]

Joel had moved on to the image of the young women in the market. "Is it surprising to you that they actually have sunglasses?" he asked.

"It's whimsical."

Later Sarah explained her reasoning to me: "With the Iran story you don't want to give the false impression that Iran is liberalizing, so you need to touch all necessary bases." Once again, the imagined reader hovered as part of the conversation. It is the reader for whose benefit the category of traditional and modern are visualized and then balanced through the particular layout of particular images. So the couple or the anatomy lesson instantly index modernity, whereas the praying collectively is automatically traditional.

Image brokers face the dual challenge of rendering visible that which is not always apparent and also rendering intelligible that which may be visible but does not correspond to powerful preconceived notions. The Palestinian blonde in the selection sent to *Newsworld* was too modern and did not fit Sarah's or Joel's image of a typical Palestinian woman. Yet even the photographer admitted that part of the reason for the proliferation of certain images of Palestinians is photographers' preference for "the exotic," even if it contrasts with their lived experience of a place. So while the lay reader might be presumed to not differentiate between an Israeli and a Palestinian, image brokers perpetuate a certain image of a Palestinian by editing out images that do not match images of Palestinians they have seen before. Effectively these image brokers police the category of Palestinian through mediated representations. This is worldmaking in the sense that these international news images produce a reassuring (if false) visual narrative asserting that the publications that promise to inform do indeed, at least photographically, have the capability to grasp "the world" in its entirety as a picture. The World section of *Newsworld* is an imagined seeing "in totality."

TERRITORIALIZING RACE

About a year after the Iran story that in the end never got published, over lunch one day another photo editor narrated an experience of being frustrated at work. The photograph she had chosen as the lead photograph for a story on the Orange Revolution in Ukraine had been killed—not chosen for publication. The photograph in question was a crowd shot taken during a nighttime rally against an alleged election fraud in Kiev. It showed supporters of the Ukrainian opposition leader, Viktor Yushchenko, chanting slogans. The editor had been drawn to the photograph by the facial expressions of the supporters, all wearing orange scarves. Yet the photo had been killed at the editorial meeting because a text editor had pointed to one of the supporters, a black man, and exclaimed, "There are no black people in Ukraine!" The photo editor was exasperated that they killed the photograph because of what she perceived to be an arbitrary reason. After all, there was no doubt about the validity of the representation. The photograph hadn't been photoshopped or staged or actually taken somewhere other than in Ukraine.

A few days later the photo editor sent me the photograph in question and asked whether I found the black man distracting. Apparently he had been nicknamed "Richard Pryor" (after the African American comedian) by the editors, whose rationale for not using the image was that a photograph showing a crowd including a black man in Ukraine would be too confusing for the reader. Her email to me was short and to the point: "Above are two racial stereotyping pictures."

I opened the second image, also unpublished: an August 2004 photograph showing a five-year old girl in a Sadr City General Hospital bed, recovering from shrapnel wounds to the stomach. Her mother had been killed in the crossfire of a clash between Muqtada al-Sadr's Mahdi Army and US troops. Sarah, the text editor, had characterized the purpose of such photographs for me: "Who doesn't identify with a frightened child?" The photograph, taken at eye level, shows the girl naked from the waist up, with a bandaged hand and dressing on her wounds, looking directly at the photographer. The editor in chief of the magazine had apparently liked the eye contact with the reader that the photograph's angle necessitated. And yet the photograph had not been chosen for the end-of-the-year sequence. The problem had been the child's blond hair. She didn't look like an Iraqi. The reader would be confused.

What these examples highlight is how image brokers articulate geography and race or modernity. The young Palestinian at the checkpoint, the black man in Ukraine, and the wounded Iraqi girl are all perceived by the brokers to be images of race out of place. As illustrated in the conversations above, there are often disagreements between brokers. Yet, in the end, the hierarchy enables the production of a neatly bounded map where modernity and race are put in their place for the benefit of the imagined reader who is presumed to need this simplified cartography in order to take interest in world news.

PART TWO

Worldmaking

What Else Is Produced
in the Production of News Images?

Whereas part 1 looked at the worldmaking of image brokers during their daily activities of image-making, part 2 turns to the ideologies that inform the practices and larger communities of photojournalism via three institutions that celebrate the field and its practitioners. Photographers and image brokers are not just producers and purveyors of images; they are also visual theorists who have opinions about what visual journalism is and should be.

I followed image brokers beyond specific sites of production to better understand what else is produced in the production and circulation of news image. These next three chapters delve into workshops and festivals where photojournalism is taught and celebrated, sites where members of the professional photojournalism community themselves value their work, where the network networks. I chose sites where diverse image brokers, photographers, and editors and promoters of photojournalism gather: specifically, Barnstorm, Visa Pour l'Image and World Press Photo. Often I was educated about the importance of these events by image brokers I met during extended fieldwork at GVI, AFP, and *Newsworld*. I accompanied them or met up with them at these annual events, where they scouted out new talent, reviewed the latest trends in the profession, discussed changes and challenges in the industry, and found inspiration as part of the photojournalism community. In other words, the field sites explored in the next three chapters were significant yet temporary nodal points of professional exchange rather than institutions.[1] While the workshops explicitly focused on training younger photographers, the annual competition and festival modeled the profession's ideals in celebrating the year's best photography, remembering the work of revered photographers, and educating the public about the role of photojournalism. Since all of these sites were important opportunities for professional networking, by circulating with the image brokers, I got to encounter them in several different contexts and watch how they constructed their professional worlds.

Again, the time of this research is paramount. The years 2003 through 2005 were an important period in the world of photojournalism in terms of changes to the very infrastructures of representation. On the one hand, as visual content providers consolidated many agencies and archives, the industry seemed to be dominated by newcomers with technical expertise and capital. On the other, digital circulation and increasing space for photography online meant that many more readers around the world could be exposed to news images and more non-Western photographers could participate in their production and circulation. Nikon is a major sponsor for Barnstorm, and Visa Pour l'Image and World Press Photo both received significant funding from Canon. At all of these events, technical experts and others demonstrated new equipment and shared their digital expertise with photographers. At the time, many were still transitioning from analog film to digital. Reflecting back to this period is generative, for it was a time when these were precisely the spaces where image brokers were taking stock of the industry and trying to navigate its shifting landscape. This was also a time of increasing public skepticism about professional photojournalism fueled by the wide circulation of photographs taken by amateurs and incidents involving doctored images. In short, going to these nodal points allowed me to see a journalistic interpretive community evaluating their professional world as they were challenged by immense changes in their profession. One such challenge was the sheer magnitude of the news stories they were trying to cover, from the multi-sited War on Terror to global infectious diseases and widespread migration.

These are sites where photography is being celebrated, untethered from the rule of text or any specific publication's editorial decisions. The images being celebrated are not being sold, at least not directly, and don't need to fit the space limitations of any publications. There are of course different limitations, but at all three sites photography is clearly in the spotlight, and its journalistic value is not only uncontested but foregrounded. A few key questions animate the following chapters, as they did many of the conversations at the events: Is photography universal? Are photographs artistic constructions or truthful documents? What are the ethics of photographing a subject? Is objectivity possible or desirable? What purpose do photographs serve in the world, and does it justify the sacrifices on the part of so many? Most important, these chapters capture image brokers making pronouncements about the role of photojournalism at a time of tension and focus on photographers' own anxieties about and hopes for the future of digital visual journalism.

5

Barnstorm

An American Rite of Passage

The buses for what many photographers had described to me as a transformative experience left from the old Kodak building on 90 Park Avenue in Manhattan.[1] The excitement among those on board was palpable. We were bound for Jeffersonville, New York, depicted by its chamber of commerce as "[a] charming older village nestled in the Western part of the Sullivan County Catskills." Yet this was hardly the beginning of a quiet country getaway. As described on its website, "The Eddie Adams Workshop is an intense four-day gathering of the top photography professionals, along with 100 carefully selected students . . . [chosen] on the merit of their portfolios."[2] True to its description, it is intense. For the top photography professionals it is a pilgrimage, an annual tradition in American photojournalism. As one photographer told me, it's "where you go to remember why you are a photographer." For the one hundred carefully selected students, Barnstorm, as the workshop is also known, is a rite of passage.[3] They arrive as neophytes in this remote, mythologized space and over the course of four days are initiated into the American family of documentary photography. The workshop is a photographic rite of passage. The event centers on revering certain images and the photographers behind them. Furthermore, looking at photographs, talking about them, and producing them are the central processes of this initiation ritual.

Barnstorm is the creation and legacy of Pulitzer Prize–winning photographer Eddie Adams. Much as he may have wanted it to be otherwise, Adams is best known for his photograph "Saigon Execution," showing police chief General Nguyễn Ngọc Loan executing Nguyễn Văn Lém, an officer of the National Liberation Front for Southern Vietnam, on a Saigon street on February 1, 1968. Every year, half of the students chosen to attend Barnstorm are professional photographers with less than three years of experience and the other half are still in college. In honor of Adams's service as a US Marine in Korea, military photographers can also attend, and up to 10 percent of the students in any given year can be foreign students. The faculty are illustrious photographers and photo editors drawn from organizations such as *Time, National Geographic, Parade, People, Sports Illustrated,* Reuters, Associated Press, the *New York Times,* the *Miami Herald,* the *Detroit Free Press,* the *Washington Post,* and the *Houston Chronicle* as well as Getty Images and Corbis. A subset of these individuals are on the board of directors and help select the students every year. Barnstorm is highly selective: close to a thousand applicants each year vie for one of the hundred slots. Moreover, Barnstorm is so popular that even volunteer staff positions are competitive. The staff, known affectionately as "the black team," are recruited from alumni of the program. All faculty and staff volunteer their time. The workshop is tuition-free for students, who pay only a minimal fee for food and lodging, while sponsors—Nikon most important among them—cover the costs.[4] Adams founded the workshop in 1988 as "a place where he and his heroes could share their work with each other and with the country's most talented young photographers."[5] Barnstorm is about the sharing and cultivation of expertise and heroes.[6]

The verb *barnstorming* has a thoroughly American etymology. It was initially used to describe traveling theatrical groups who brought popular plays to the American frontier in the late nineteenth century, often performing and sleeping in barns. Immediately following World War I, itinerant pilots (also called gypsies) bought up surplus military aircraft and "barnstormed" around the country, giving people at fairs their first airplane ride and impressing spectators with daredevil stunts. Meanwhile, American politicians "barnstormed" regularly as part of their election campaigns, and it is this usage of the term that one occasionally still hears today.

Unlike these barnstorms, however, Adams's Barnstorm does not involve frequently changing locations. The storm gathers annually at his barn atop a hill in upstate New York. Barnstorm is a photography boot camp, aptly named because high theatrics, military pasts, politics, stunts, and variety are central to this gathering. Everyone, both faculty and students, works incredibly hard—almost no one gets any sleep—but it is also loud and fun. While the profession's greats gather with the next generation in an ordinary-looking barn for four long days over the Columbus Day weekend, a parade of photographs transports them all over the newsworthy world. There are surprises and pranks, and for all the suffering and tragedies recorded in some of the images shared, there is an underlying sense of playful mischief.

Barnstorm XVI, in 2003, was a particularly interesting one because it was the first Barnstorm after the United States invaded Iraq, and hence an opportunity to observe revered photographers of the Vietnam era pass on their wisdom to the latest generation of combat photographers. The United States was once again engaged in a war that saw large numbers of American ground troops on the battlefield. As earlier chapters have highlighted, despite the war in Iraq already having lasted longer than expected, in fall 2003 the perception was still that, unlike the war in Vietnam, this war was going to be short-lived. Barnstorm XVI was also the last workshop led by Eddie Adams himself. Eddie, as everyone at the workshop called him, passed away a few weeks before the 2004 workshop, but in 2003 he was an energetic master of ceremonies.

Imbibing the history of Barnstorm began on the buses up to Jeffersonville as students were shown a video from the very first Eddie Adams workshop, full of inspirational sound bites pronounced by famous photographers and editors:

"This is the greatest profession in the world."

"Everyone can read a photograph."

"Photographs are the bricks of history."

"The camera is the most important force in changing the behavior of our time."

This short video introduced many of the themes the students would hear repeatedly over the weekend: That photography was important and didn't just represent but made history. That photographs were universally accessible. And—perhaps the one that would come up most frequently over the weekend—that, as newcomers, they would have to be fiercely competitive in order to succeed in this profession. Later in the day, Adams himself would remind the students in his opening comments, "There is a lot of competition in this business. The most significant competition is with yourself. You are here to get better. There is both 'I' and 'we' in competition."

Many of the photographers in the 1988 video shown on the bus were known to the students as the makers of iconic images, many of them images of wars America had fought in the twentieth century. One legendary editor directly addressed the viewer and remarked, "You as a photographer from a highly developed powerful Western nation, you can make a difference. You take pictures of powerless people." Even before Barnstorm had officially begun, the focus was on the camera in the hands of Western and, even more specifically, American photographers. This American emphasis was also apparent to my seatmate on the bus, one of the few foreign photographers attending Barnstorm that year, a young woman from Germany. After we finished watching the video, I asked what she thought of it. She replied, "As a German I don't have this experience of feeling proud of [one's] country." Her comment underscores another theme that would run throughout the workshop and therefore this chapter: the intertwining of patriotism and professional ideals. This was particularly interesting given that photography was also continually celebrated as a universally accessible medium that transcended national categories.

The excitement levels rose even further when we arrived at the Days Inn hotel where we'd be staying and each photographer got a Nikon bag full of goodies. The workshop is not only a gathering in which expertise is passed from revered elders to new initiates but also one where photographers, young and old, get to test out the latest photo equipment and get tips from some of the best technical experts in the world.[7] Before heading up to the barn on the first day, students were given an orientation session that went over rules ("Be courteous to the community. This is where they live. It's Eddie's home") and coached them in how to make the most of the weekend. The alum running the orientation emphasized, "Most of you right now are pumped beyond belief. Calm down! You are going to meet lots of people, *take advantage of it!* When you see that famous person just go meet them, go ask that question you always wanted to ask. . . . What if you don't get to that editor [for portfolio review]? Don't miss what they say to the person in front of you. You're not competing against any other person here, you're competing against your own bad habits. Just relax. . . . There are all these people around you [and many of them] you'll run into for the next decade. . . . There are lots of opportunities to be the person you want to be. . . . You got here by being good." One young woman confided in me that she had vowed to manage the tension between being competitive and being a part of a community: "It's such an honor to be part of this tradition. Photojournalism helped me find purpose in my photography. I want to be a part of this community, I want to help. I decided before I came, I'm not going to be competitive."[8]

Barnstorm consisted of two types of activities: those that focused on photography as a profession, or even vocation, and those that focused on each student's individual development. The first type of activity consisted of presentations by photographers and the occasional editor. These speakers were referred to in workshop lingo as "the heavies." Though the workshop was focused on documentary photography, the heavies were often selected from diverse genres of photography including fashion, sports, art photography, and celebrity portraiture. The idea was to expose young photographers to a great variety of aesthetic styles and professional approaches.

For the second type of activity, students were assigned teams. Each team consisted of two team leaders—one an editor, the other a photographer—a producer who had scouted out the assignments in advance, and ten students.[9] Every team had a theme that connected the individual students' assignments. Throughout the workshop, the students were working on an assignment, getting coaching on everything from technical details of digital photography to lighting, building rapport with their subjects, stylistically pushing themselves, and capturing images that told a story. For the final awards ceremony and group show, each team submitted a story that included at least one image from each photographer (unlike in the professional world, where shooting in no way guarantees publication), making the event both a celebration of teamwork and a recognition of individual talent.[10] Prizes were handed out in the form of internships or assignments (e.g., a paid assignment at the *Washington Post* or a weeklong internship with the White House photo service working as a photographer to the president). For students, Barnstorm included the nerve-wracking process of getting an assignment with a strict deadline, shooting in an environment they didn't know, submitting their images for editing to team leaders they were trying to impress, and all the while competing for what they perceived as potentially career-changing opportunities. Starting on the bus up to Jeffersonville, rumors circulated about former students who had gotten big professional breaks because of an award they received at Barnstorm. One up-and-coming young photographer had won an assignment for GVI that GVI had then been able to get published in a major magazine. He was now regularly doing freelance work for the *New York Times* and was the envy of many at Barnstorm. Other opportunities came from portfolio reviews that happened at the 11:30 club two nights during the workshop. Students waited in line patiently to show their portfolios to legendary photographers they admired or photo editors at publications they aspired to work for. This was called the 11:30 club because portfolio reviews began back at the Days Inn at 11:30 pm and often continued into the early morning hours.

Teams were identified by color, and everyone wore a bandana showing their team's color. The blue team allowed me to join them. So while I remained an outsider to what was touted throughout the weekend as "the greatest profession in the world," my blue bandana at least tied me to a team. Given the cult of rugged individualism that surrounds photojournalists, I wasn't at all surprised that very few bandanas were worn scout-style around people's necks. Again and again photographers portrayed themselves to me as lone wolves, and while they occasionally complained about being isolated, they also took pride in their individuality. So bandanas were tied on legs, arms, heads, camera straps, and stuffed in back pockets—visual proof that this was a group of individuals doing things their own way. Nonetheless, for the duration of Barnstorm they were part of a team, and team identity became very important.

I shadowed the blue team's activities and attended all team meetings. Although I discuss some of the coaching the students received in the introduction, in this chapter I focus more on the state of the profession and core values being passed on to the students as they were highlighted in formal presentations and panel discussions. The fact that Barnstorm includes both types of activities means that students often felt torn: they were expected to attend all the presentations, and yet many wanted to give their all to their assignments in the hopes of impressing someone to give them that once-in-a-lifetime opportunity. I overheard many team leaders emphasizing to students that part of photojournalism was doggedness; they were told to devote themselves to the assignment and be there "when the pictures are happening."[11] I point this out because, although I do not focus here on the trials and tribulations the students faced while completing their assignments, the stress on the individual photographers to produce the best work possible was considerable and ever-present throughout the weekend.

The two kinds of activities also posed a challenge for me as an anthropologist. Partly to spare the students any further stress, when it was time to work on assignments, rather than going on location with the students, I stayed with the team leaders and watched them instruct the next generation of photographer. This meant that though this is a key element of Barnstorm for many, I did not see as much of the camaraderie developing between students as I might have if I had shadowed students exclusively. I concentrated on the presentations and their reception. This also put me in a bind when it came to writing about Barnstorm. For, as in the chapters that precede this one, I asked those I was explicitly shadowing—all those on the blue team—to sign consent forms and shared the IRB protocols of my research with them. They shared ideas with me under conditions of anonymity; therefore, when quoting from them I use pseudonyms or a mere description of the speaker. However, since the presentations were attended by all, they were semipublic performances. They were often discussed afterward, online and in print. In those cases, with one exception that I have noted, I used photographers' real names because I thought it would be disrespectful to not credit individuals' ideas.[12]

THE FAMILY WELCOME

Barnstorm officially begins with the students arriving at Adams's farmhouse. In October when the workshop is held, the barn is surrounded by hillsides awash in fall colors, a picture-perfect American landscape. The yellow school buses drop students off at the bottom of the hill and the students walk up to the barn on a gravel path flanked by the staff and faculty applauding loudly.

In 2003 when I attended Barnstorm XVI, the J. Geils Band's 1981 song "Freeze Frame" blasted in the background as the students arrived, adding a peculiarly renegade substitute for "Pomp and Circumstance" to this initiation ceremony. Apparently other years have featured the similarly photographically themed Paul Simon song "Kodachrome." Several of the most revered names in photojournalism stood at the entrance to the barn watching the youngest generation of photographers climb toward them. Surrounded by colleagues, Eddie Adams himself shook hands vigorously with each photographer, as if personally welcoming him or her not only to the 2003 workshop but also into the fold, the professional family of photojournalism.

So strong, in fact, is the sense that this is an initiation ceremony that I sheepishly slunk up the hill behind the receiving line so as not to intrude. I shouldn't have been as nervous as the students; I knew many of those attending the 2003 Barnstorm as staff, team leaders, heavies, and portfolio reviewers from other field sites such as GVI and

Newsworld. By the time I attended I had been doing fieldwork for eight months. Yet, I shared the students' jitters. I felt highly self-conscious, as many of them told me later they had. Perhaps it was because I was one of the very few not recording the scene through a viewfinder. At the same time, I couldn't suppress a sense of envy as I watched the rowdy procession up the hill. After all, less than a year into my first fieldwork I, too, was somewhat new to my profession, but I couldn't imagine any professional setting where my or anyone else's arrival into the discipline of anthropology would ever be similarly celebrated. No wonder everyone had been telling me that Barnstorm was where you went to remember why you had become a photographer. Feeling profoundly out of place, I took copious field notes to try to contain my nervousness—the anthropologist equivalent of the shy photographer hiding behind his lens. The very first sketch I made in my notebook shows the path leading up to the barn and a large American flag towering above the scene.

The group standing near the flagpole at the entrance of the barn included several Pulitzer Prize–winning photographers and legendary photo editors—the people behind iconic news images, celebrities in the world of photojournalism though known to the rest of the world usually not by name but by the photographs they had shot. Many of the students seemed understandably awed by the heavies—photographers whose images had been central to their education in photography and had perhaps inspired them pursue photography professionally in the first place.

Many scholars have written about iconic images, such as the *Saigon Execution* image shot by Adams, and their significance for public culture.[13] Although I'll be referring to images that are on almost any list of iconic images, particularly lists of iconic representations of war—the raising of the US flag on Iwo Jima; Adams's *Saigon Execution,* taken during the opening stages of the Tet Offensive; and the young girl running with napalm burns—my concern here is not to analyze any of the photographs themselves. Nor do I provide biographical sketches of the photographers responsible for the images or historical revelations about the moments at which they were produced. Rather, I show how the makers and a subject of these images addressed—or barnstormed—the photojournalism community in 2003, shortly after the beginning of America's "new war in Iraq," which at the time dominated most news coverage.[14] My aim here is to investigate what the iconic image makers of earlier American wars communicated to the professional photojournalism community in a context in which the fact that they had taken

FIGURE 7. Official group portrait taken at Barnstorm (2011 example). Used by the kind permission of the Eddie Adams Workshop.

these images was precisely what gave them the authority to speak. Moreover, how does this profession manage the tension between revering combat photographers as heroes and seeing photography itself as a force for peace?[15]

Eventually everyone was summoned into the barn that first evening. As I walked in, I noticed the framed photographs of photojournalists killed "in Vietnam" on the back wall.[16] At Barnstorm, *Vietnam* does not denote a geographic place in the world or a sovereign nation that once defeated the US military. Rather, *Vietnam* denotes a place in US history, and a very prominent place in the history of American photojournalism, especially as it is celebrated at Barnstorm.[17] As students filed in, some noticed the class photographs from previous Barnstorms (figure 7) displayed on another wall. By the end of the weekend they, too, would pose for the photograph that would visually incorporate them into this hallowed barn.

A member of the blue team passed on a rumor that Joe Rosenthal, the photographer famous for having taken the 1945 photograph of the raising of the American flag on Iwo Jima, was among the audience that night. Upon hearing this rumor, a veteran photographer volunteered, "There are two photos in life people remember: the three firemen raising the flag, and Eddie's picture." There was an interesting slippage here. Rosenthal took the photo of US Marines raising the flag on Iwo Jima. The photograph of three firemen raising the American flag atop the rubble of the World Trade Center on September 11, 2001—the photograph referenced in this photographer's comment—was taken by Thomas Franklin. Essentially the photographer's comment conflates Rosenthal's image with its 2001 remake by Thomas Franklin, who was also in attendance at Barnstorm 2003. Some referred to Franklin as Mr. Joe Rosenthal Jr. Another senior photographer told the students that from now on Franklin's image would be as recognizable as the Iwo Jima image. He reminded them that neither had won a Pulitzer Prize, suggesting that the photojournalism profession itself doesn't always honor the right images immediately but that iconic news images eventually get recognized as such. In fact, a common occurrence at Barnstorm was to express disapproval of the choices made by certain prize committees.

Inside the barn, large round tables were set up in front of the stage area, and people sat with their teams. Though the entire workshop experience was built around teams and the colors of their bandanas, the importance of individuality was constantly highlighted in the opening speeches: "Groups are OK for some things, but creativity is always individual"; "The greatest ideas in history of humankind have always started as a single idea in one person's head"; "You should work together as a team, but see through your own eyes." Yet, the goal of this extreme individuality, the students were told, was always in the service of a larger purpose: "You have the opportunity to communicate for all time. The images that you take matter. . . . Destiny is not something that happens to you, it's not something you wait for, it's a choice. You have chosen to live for a larger, more noble motive, to communicate human experience to other human beings."

THE GRAND MASTER OF CEREMONIES

As Frank Sinatra's voice sang "I want to be a part of it," Eddie Adams walked in, flanked by the black team posing as bodyguards. The crowd applauded enthusiastically and Eddie—a truly larger-than-life character in a signature black fedora—took the stage. "Every year I say the same thing: we have the best editors and the best photographers here," he began. Then as an aside alluding to the stereotypical friction between photographers and editors, he added, "Picture editors we don't care for that much, but we got the best ones." The audience chuckled in appreciation. Perhaps more than at any of my field sites, it was clear that Barnstorm was a celebration of photography for photographers run by photographers. Indeed, in the stories told at Barnstorm, non-photographer image brokers and their labors are largely erased.

Adams opened Barnstorm 2003 by telling the story of going to photograph first-graders on their first day of school and being told by the principal that he should photograph Billy so-and-so because his father was an important man. Instead, Adams told the barn full of photographers, he had looked around and seen a kid in the back row with a torn shirt, a kid as he put it, who came from the wrong side of the tracks. "To me, that was me I was photographing. He was on the front page of the paper, he was someone." The moral, Adams emphasized, was that photographers shouldn't forget where they came from and should show respect for those in front of the camera. The implication is that photographers do not come from economic privilege, which is sometimes true and other times not. On the other hand, the story is one where the photographer had great agency in choosing whom to photograph. Adams was able to ignore the principal's suggestion to photograph Billy the son of the important man, and the story is one where the photographer not only has power but also is able to empower another: Adams's subject became someone by having his picture on the front page. This association of power and agency with the function of the photographer rather than with the photographer's personal status was an undercurrent in many stories about photographers told at Barnstorm. It can also be seen in the statement made in the video I described the students watching at the opening of this chapter: "*You as a photographer* from a highly developed powerful Western nation, you can make a difference. You take pictures of powerless people." The photographer has the power to empower the powerless with his images, and yet his power is not his based on individual privileged status but is merely the power of his profession and of his nationality.

Adams's next comments presented two ideas I heard repeatedly in the photojournalism world that somehow are both presented as ideals to strive for, though they are at times contradictory: objectivity and empathy. In the professional mythology of photography in which the photographer hero is never born into power but earns it through his status as photographer and is then able to distribute it to others by photographing them and making their image public, objectivity and empathy were essential traits for the hero to have. Given the purpose of Adams's speech, which was to pump up the young photographers about a profession that rarely pays well or comes with medical insurance despite requiring significant sacrifices, this mythologizing is not surprising.

For Adams, objectivity and having empathy for a subject did not seem contradictory. "I wouldn't put any personal opinions in photographs," Adams told the students. But he also claimed, "I become the person I'm photographing. I actually feel their pain." "Only once did I make somebody look bad, and that was Tim McVeigh. But I regret it because I am not a judge, I'm a photographer."[18] Adams framed the nobility of photography in the photographer's ability to put himself in the position of his subject. He claimed he felt what his subject felt. In a recording of a similar speech he made for an earlier Barnstorm, Adams elaborated: "I've known in my pictures I can feel the aches and the pains and the wounds of the people that I photograph. I also feel their joy and happiness. . . . I never realized I was doing this subconsciously. Like if I'm photographing a king, I become the king and I know what I want the king to look like, or if it's a president of a country or if someone's dying, I really do feel their pains." For Adams, empathizing with a subject leads to knowing how the subject wants to be represented. As a result, the photographer cannot help but produce an image the subject desires.

Adams also made a point of sharing times when "we don't take pictures." One way to think of such decisions is as moments when a photographer as image broker attempts to protect his subject, and doesn't allow a particular image to circulate, by not creating it in the first place.[19] During Barnstorm 2003 Adams mentioned that there had been two such incidents in his career, but he narrated only one: a story he'd covered in Philadelphia in which a little boy had killed the even younger little girl next door and stuffed her body in the basement. The city desk of the paper he was working for had asked him to go to the houses and collect recent photographs of the children. He went to the victim's house first, and as he was walking toward the house a glassy-eyed man passed him and rang the doorbell. "It was the perpetrator little boy's father, and as soon as a woman opened the door the father said, 'I'm sorry.' 'It's your loss as well as mine,' replied the woman, and the two of them embraced and started crying." Adams had turned around, gone back to the paper, and told them he hadn't been able to get into the house. Though he didn't draw the conclusion for the audience that night, elsewhere he is quoted as saying, "There are times and moments when you just leave them alone."[20]

I don't know why Adams didn't give the second example that evening; perhaps he lost his train of thought, was running out of time, or had other reasons. But at other Barnstorms he had spoken of the second incident he chose not to photograph. It occurred when he was covering the marines in Vietnam. During intense rocketing, Adams found himself taking cover directly across from a very young marine. Adams said he'd never seen fear as he saw it on the face of the blue-eyed blond marine. Though he was thinking of all the famous combat photographs of David Douglas Duncan (an influential combat photographer best known for his photographs of the Korean War collected in the book *This Is War!*), and though he felt certain that the frame he was seeing through his viewfinder could be on front pages around the world, or on the cover of *Life* magazine, he couldn't bring himself to take the photograph, and a few minutes later the opportunity was lost as they moved positions. In the recording Adams insists, "The reason I couldn't, I know to this day . . . the fear on *his* face was exactly like the fear on *my* face and I didn't want *anyone* taking a picture of me."

This narration suggests that Adams felt not only the fear his subject felt but also the shame of his fear that he assumed the subject felt. In Adams's telling, both stories illustrated that empathy can also be a reason for not taking a photograph, just as it can be the motivation to take a photograph, as it was in the story of the first-grader. Yet the consequences of Adams's decision not to take the photograph of the marine are also quite different from those of his decision not to intrude on a private, emotional moment. Unlike the grieving parents in Philadelphia, the soldier was not a civilian in a private space but rather a member of the US military engaged in a battle on foreign soil. Fear on a young soldier's face, particularly in a war fought by young draftees as well as a professional army, tells a journalistically important story.

Fear, after all, is precisely what some say is memorably captured on the face of the young man being shot at close range in the photograph for which Adams is best known. Perhaps what Adams, a former marine who had served in the Korean War, did not want to capture was fear on the face of an American soldier. The recording of the story includes him describing the direness of the particular battle: "*We* had about a 50 percent casualty rate." My intent is not to argue that Adams should or should not have taken the photograph of the fearful young soldier or, for that matter, of General Loan. That he regularly ruminated on the ramifications of the images he made even decades afterward is a testament that Adams, like many photographers, took seriously the consequences of his work. Rather, I want to emphasize that news images do not easily transcend national allegiances. This is true not only on a level of potential interpretation on the part of viewers—the execution photograph is credited with having swayed public opinion against the Vietnam War—but also in the photographer's own affective connection with the subject. Whether intentional or not, both examples that Adams gives of deciding to just leave subjects alone involve American subjects.

Adams had a complicated relationship to the photograph that brought him much fame and recognition. He held himself responsible for the damage the photograph did to General Loan's reputation and life. Adams spent much energy trying to build empathy for the South Vietnamese general.[21] In a eulogy published in *Time* following Loan's death in 1998, Adams wrote, "The general killed the Viet Cong; I killed the general with my camera. Still photographs are the most powerful weapon in the world. People believe them, but photographs do lie, even without manipulation. They are only half-truths. What the photograph didn't say was, 'What would you do if you were the general at that time and place on that hot day, and you caught the so-called bad guy after he blew away one, two or three American soldiers?'"[22] Adams does not speak of empathizing with the young man being executed. He is concerned with contextualizing General Loan's actions in a manner that might give an American audience pause before they indict him.

Adams ended his heartfelt address to the students at Barnstorm that night by referring to the fact that America hadn't been the same since 9/11 and encouraging the students to make happy pictures.[23] This is significant because it marks that the photojournalism community, at least as represented at Barnstorm, was using the same historical framing as the US government at the time, positing the terror attacks as the starting point for a single military engagement continuing since then, despite combat taking place in very different geographies. Through its visual echo of the Rosenthal image, the Franklin photograph of the firemen raising the flag instantly declared Ground Zero a battlefield, labeling the attacks as acts of war, almost before President Bush had had a chance to do so. Put differently, photographers and their images were part of the construction of the War on Terror as a single war with coherent logics, grouping 9/11, invasions in Afghanistan and Iraq, and later military engagements elsewhere (such as drone strikes in Yemen, Somalia, and Pakistan) together as a single multisited combat. Adams as a photographer of the Vietnam War was addressing the 9/11 generation of photographers.

THE DIGITAL GENERATION

The technological opportunities for this new generation formed the central point of the vice president of Nikon, who was next to take the stage: "I look out at you and wonder where the next Pulitzer Prize is going to come from."[24] Speaking on behalf of Nikon, he continued, "I greet you on behalf of more than ten thousand employees around the world. . . . One point we never forget is that we will never reach our fulfillment until our cameras reach your sweaty hands. You are what we expect to be the future of photography." Nikon is a major sponsor for Barnstorm and provides gear and technical advice to students for whom the workshop is an opportunity to try the latest equipment without having to buy it. He introduced the members of the Nikon "family" in attendance to help the students over the weekend and emphasized that the last two to three years had brought some of the biggest changes in photography—professional digital photography and the wireless transmission of images to computers. Referring to Matthew Brady, the nineteenth-century photographer sometimes hailed to as the father of photojournalism, who assembled a team to document the carnage of the Civil War, he continued, "[Brady] would have given his front teeth to transmit satellite images from the battlefield." Perhaps, the speaker mused, "he wouldn't have had to drag bodies to make it look real," suggesting that Brady's forgery was merely a result of poor distribution technology.

Within a few years Barnstorm was completely digital. However, in 2003 two of the ten photographers on the blue team had not yet switched to digital cameras. There was an entire team that shot only film, and their team leaders reviewed their slides on light boxes. Veteran photographers and students alike were still adjusting to the demands of digital cameras. Several times the team leaders reminded their student photographers, "Anytime you see an outlet, plug that [your camera] in!" The Nikon VP's endorsement of digital photography ended the evening, and the students returned to the Days Inn to have team meetings and get their individual assignments. The next morning, most of the blue team students confessed they'd been too excited to sleep.

PART OF THE FAMILY NOW

Barnstorm combines the intensity of a military drill with the irreverent tone of adolescent humor: the next day of the workshop began with a quirky video of a teenager at a sweet-sixteen party jumping on a trampoline, face-planting into a pie. On the back of her T-shirt were the names of Barnstorm XVI's sponsors. As the team leaders were introduced, each of them promised the students that this workshop would change their lives and reiterated in various ways that this was the greatest profession in the world. One photographer assured them, "You would be amazed by all the things that happen in a barn. In this barn, dreams come true. You're here because you are special." The first speaker of the day was Rick Loomis, a *Los Angeles Times* photographer and alumnus of the workshop. "He's been to a lot of places you want to go," the audience was told as Loomis took the stage.

> When I came here [eleven years ago] I was wild-eyed and I had a fire in my belly, I was looking for direction. There's a spirit here. A commitment towards a greater goal. I'm part of a family now, and by coming to this Eddie Adams workshop you are now a part of that family as well. We're all sort of unified by coming here and learning from a great group of people. This is a very special moment in time, it will only exist once. You can't help but be inspired.
>
> When I came here I was almost done with college. Within two years of this workshop I had a job with the LA *Times* and I have been there nine years. Lots of things can happen. I have been on the road since February and I came here straight from Israel, where I experienced some of my lowest lows ever. It took a lot of energy out of me so I couldn't wait to get here to feed off some of the energy here, so I appreciate your giving me some of your energy.

His presentation took the audience through the recognizable career landmarks of a certain generation of war photographer: 9/11, Afghanistan, Iraq, and Israel. Photojournalists' career trajectories are remarkable because they are usually lists of geographic place-names but refer to coverage of specific wars. Photographers are not the only ones who conflate country name and specific battles, of course; in the context of military history one often hears of Korea or Vietnam as shorthand for specific wars in those countries. For the generation whose careers began or took off with the War on Terror, "9/11, Afghanistan, Iraq" is the typical lineup. Israel functions as a timeless referent as the country where one can always be covering conflict. 9/11, on the other hand, refers to a particular event only, and yet never did I hear any photographer say he or she had covered "New York, Afghanistan, Iraq." New York was not subsumed as a photographic subject under the category of 9/11, and yet if these other places had become places of note on the journalistic map, it was the arrival of US military forces that had made them do so.[25]

Loomis emphasized the responsibility of being a photojournalist: "You'll be eyes for other people. Don't underestimate the value of that." He also stressed the importance of individuality in a competitive job market: "Develop a style, develop your eye. At this point you are being bombarded with ways of seeing, but your vision will be unique to you." But immediately afterward he returned to speaking of the profession as a collective and made reference to the Brian Walski scandal at the *Los Angeles Times* mentioned in the introduction: "If you do become a photojournalist, be ethical. A friend of mine altered a photograph during the war and lost his job[26]. He should have. The public is already not trusting of journalism. It's up to you to be very stringent with yourself. Don't set up a shot, don't digitally manipulate; be true to yourself and who you photograph." Loomis's appeal to the students highlighted that whereas each photographer competes for specific shots and prizes individually, the public evaluates the profession collectively.

The next speaker was a photo editor from *Sports Illustrated,* followed by a portrait photographer celebrated for his images of hip-hop musicians and athletes, and two legendary fashion photographers. One of the emphases of the workshop was that photographers can learn not only from the heavies that are combat photographers of prior generations, but also from colleagues who work in very different genres than they do. Many photographers, including Adams, cross genres, sometimes, but not always, leaving combat photography once they've reached a certain age or started a family. However, other genres of photography such as celebrity portraiture, sports, and fashion photography are presented with respect at the workshop, not merely as examples of what a photographer might do once his or her knees give. Perhaps this respect for other genres stemmed from the fact that many photographers both new and established have to be versatile to make a living. Nonetheless, the unspoken hierarchy at Barnstorm and the other workshops and festivals I attended placed documentary photography, and especially war photography at the top.[27]

CELEBRATING HEROES

Midmorning, Adams confirmed the rumor that Joe Rosenthal, the photographer who took the photograph of the flag raising on Iwo Jima, which has since had innumerable reappropriations, was in the audience: "We have a man with us today who I think took the best photo ever and two days ago, it was his birthday."[28] A ninety-two-year-old Joe

Rosenthal rose to blow out the candles on a birthday cake as a multi-generational cluster of illustrious photographers jockeyed to get a good shot of him. This was not just a matter of respect shown for Rosenthal's age. This was an expression of collective pride in honoring one of their profession's heroes.

A short while later Rosenthal addressed the students. He began by telling them how he got the assignment in the first place—in other words, how he came to be in place to take the iconic image. This resonated with my teammates, who had each spent time with the blue team leaders trying to get advice on how to get better assignments. Rosenthal emphasized that he did not see the current War on Terror as "a different kind of war": "War is not good at any time, anywhere. The reason for me being there was to get pictures that would illustrate to people at home what their men were doing. Any photographer worth anything wants to be a part of a big story. They say today we've got a different kind of war going on, but I don't agree."

Rosenthal humbly told the story of how he framed his famous image. It was a story he has had to tell over and over again not only because of the photograph's iconicity and patriotic appeal but also to defend it against allegations that it was staged. The famous image is of a US flag being hoisted on Mount Suribachi the day *after* the battle had been won, because the colonel wanted a bigger flag than the one that had been raised the previous day. Rosenthal told the captive Barnstorm audience, "First I thought about getting both flags—the bigger one the colonel wanted going up and the other one coming down—but that would take a lot of explaining", thus confirming what I had repeatedly heard during fieldwork: if an image relied too heavily on an explanation in the caption, it was not a strong image.[29] Rosenthal then described a group photograph he had had the marines pose for after the flag went up so the individual men could be identified. As if responding to Loomis's emphasis that morning not to alter a photograph in a war, Rosenthal elaborated that it was the group photograph taken *after* the flag raising for which he'd encouraged marines to stand by the flag and wave. He was asked if he had staged the image at the press center in Guam a few days later. Rosenthal assumed the question referred to the gung-ho picture of marines waving, so he replied "Sure"—and hence has spent much of the rest of his career battling allegations of fraud.[30] In the version of the story he delivered at Barnstorm, he even mentioned that when asked to stand around the flag and wave, "Some of the marines said, "Hey, we're not Hollywood marines.'" For the famous image of the flag being hoisted, Rosenthal stressed, "We had no warning and we issued no request."

Quite the contrary. Rosenthal said bemusedly that he and the sergeant shooting the event with a film camera had been so concerned about not getting in each other's way that they "nearly missed the whole thing, in which case I wouldn't be here today." Standing in front of a packed barn full of young people hoping to enter his profession almost sixty years after he had taken the image that enabled him "to be here today," Rosenthal explained what he saw as the strength of his photo.

> I'd covered a lot of football, baseball, action shots, so I had a pretty good sense of timing. When you've got action and you can wait for it, there's an instant. The wind turned and I crossed my fingers and the picture was able to contain this composition. This is what makes it a good picture I think. Men struggling gave the image its energy, and this is not a wooden flagpole, but an iron pole, so six of them had to give all their energy to thrust it up. It was just about noon when the sun is almost directly overhead and casts a sculpting effect on the figures.

Rosenthal both acknowledged the contingency of his being there that day to take that particulate photograph, a matter of luck—the wind turning in an instant—but also talked of the skills honed while shooting sports that enabled him to capture that instant. The only element of Rosenthal's experience that clearly indicated that his experience covering war had been different than that narrated by Rick Loomis in the morning was technical and underscored the Nikon vice president's comment that digital technologies were transforming the profession: "I remember shooting that thing and saying 'Oh I hope I got it, I hope it looked like it looked from the inside of the viewfinder.' Everything was judged by how quickly a photo was received in New York. That photo was radioed to San Francisco by navy radio. In its day it set the record for transmission from point of origin to East Coast."

This record speed was still twenty-four hours—an eternity compared to the 2003 standard of digital transmission. Moreover, the 2003 combat photographer would have only had to look at the LCD display behind his camera to know whether he had gotten the shot. Without using the term, Rosenthal was acknowledging the importance of image brokers: "Each one of us does a part in this chain, it's like a relay race." He highlighted the importance of others in physically getting the image from Iwo Jima to the Associated Press's New York office. As we saw in chapter 4, getting the image to the headquarters of a wire service meant tapping into a complex infrastructure of representation. Although the photographers in the audience had much faster transmission options, they still relied on a chain of brokers to get their image to the public in an effective manner. The former head of Associated Press thanked Rosenthal on behalf of all there "for making that photograph which is part of the American experience. It is the greatest photographic icon," and the Barnstorm attendees gave Rosenthal a standing ovation.

The next speaker was Jock Sturges, a fine-art photographer who began by emphasizing how far his work was from combat photography: "I am so in the wrong place, I'm so different than you guys." But his sentence ended ". . . and so honored to have heard Joe Rosenthal." Sturges, whose work on nudist beaches, often featuring adolescents, has brought him under attack from the US government as well as conservative groups, addressed the group of photojournalists as an art photographer: "My work feels pretty frivolous compared to what you do and Rosenthal's contribution to American culture." Yet after sharing some of his work he spoke of an alternative patriotism, an opinion possibly formed based on his personal experiences defending his art but expressed in a manner that spoke directly to the discussions of war coverage: "What you go out and do and say can and does make a difference. There are an awful lot of dark corners of the world right now; international attitudes toward Americans are at an all-time low right now. The notion that you can't be patriotic and oppose the government is bullshit; opposing the government is what patriotism is all about."

Rosenthal had clearly stated his purpose for being in place to take the Iwo Jima image: "to get pictures that would illustrate to people at home what their men were doing." That can of course mean either that the photographs help to raise support for the troops or that they render the behavior of troops on the front line visible and therefore accountable to those at home. Sontag ended *Regarding the Pain of Others* by adamantly claiming that those of us who have not experienced war for ourselves can't understand or imagine it by looking at a photograph. However, imagining what it is like, trying to put ourselves in the position of the subjects in the image or even in that of the photographer behind the camera, may not be the only function of news images. Powerful images can help one ask better questions about news events or visualize the consequences of political choices that one may be evaluating at a distance.

Sturges's talk also placed the focus back on the photographer rather than the event being photographed: "Photography is always about what you know. It's a record of what the photographer knows or doesn't know. It's incumbent on you to know as much as you can. When a tourist stops and takes a photo, they have no idea what they have done. In foreign countries, people often photograph what is different, not significant. Photography is a symptom of something larger. When it's just about photography its boring. [Photography] is an excuse that the camera gives you to do so much."

THE WAR PANEL: VIETNAM TO NOW

One of the key events of Barnstorm 2003 was a "war panel" moderated by David Kennerly, a photographer who won a Pulitzer for his coverage of the war in Vietnam. The day before, Kennerly had told the audience that the Vietnam War boiled down to two photographs: Eddie Adams's photograph of "the general executing the Viet Cong" and Nick Ut's photograph of "the young girl with napalm burns."[31] This war panel, then, was moderated by a photographer who thought of wars in terms of iconic images. Though wars had been documented photographically since the Crimean War, anthropologist Christina Schwenkel argues, "it wasn't until the Vietnam War that photography was identified as a powerful tool that swayed public opinion in the United States." In her research Schwenkel also encountered the belief voiced by many at Barnstorm that "media coverage and graphic violence fueled the antiwar movement and arguably reversed the public sentiment on the war . . . and many photographs took on a fetishized quality as cultural and political icons, or as symbols of the inhumanity and futility of war."[32] However, because Schwenkel provides a cross-cultural analysis of the role photography played in what in Vietnam is termed "the American War," she makes clear that one need only look at photographs taken by North Vietnamese photographers to see that photography did not have only one function in the war.

Schwenkel's study superbly details the important differences between the experiences of Western photographers and Vietnamese photographers during the conflict: "While western press photographers were generally engaged in temporally and spatially bounded, event-driven coverage, for Vietnamese photojournalists, the war demanded a long-term commitment and everyday immersion in dangerous zones of conflict, where they lived, labored, and sometimes fought alongside their photographic subjects, facing severe hardships and often imminent death."[33] With rare exceptions, such as Nick Ut, Vietnamese photojournalists did not go on to cover news events in other countries.[34] Furthermore, in interviews Vietnamese photojournalists emphasize their relations with the people they photographed, which continue to be important today. "Contrary to western journalist discourse, they did not talk about objectivity, yet like their western counterparts, they emphasized their agency and choice in photographing diverse aspects of people's lives and experiences in wartime," Schwenkel concludes.[35]

The speakers on the first Barnstorm war panel since the US invasion of Iraq were Alex Levy, the young photographer represented by GVI; Ruth Fremson, a veteran war photographer on staff at the *New York Times;* and Rick Loomis, the *Los Angeles Times* photojournalist who had spoken about his experiences covering the War on Terror that morning.[36] Both Levy and Loomis had had multiple positions embedded with the US military. Alex Levy relayed his positive experience as a long-term embed with a unit where he had befriended the lieutenant. As detailed in chapter 2, Levy was the Iraq war's Cinderella story, one of the youngest members of the group of war photographers working around the globe. That Alex was young enough to be a student and yet was sitting onstage at Barnstorm was a testament to his talent but also indicative of what GVI representation could do for a photographer. His break had come when he had taken the embed position arranged for Jim Nachtwey, a veteran photographer who had decided not to take it. Perhaps understandably given his career trajectory, Levy's position was that "'[e]mbed' is just a name for something that has always existed anyways—all these programs are just an official name." Loomis, however, emphasized that embed positions had given him access without mobility, that they limited his mobility between units and kept him traveling with a single unit. Yet he emphasized that the *Los Angeles Times* had multiple journalists covering the war and that it was through their collective reporting— embedded and not—that it had covered the war. A critical difference here is that Loomis works for a publication and therefore thinks in terms of how the war is covered by all the photographers on staff for the paper's particular readership. Levy, on the other hand, is a freelance photographer who might be on assignment for any number of publications at any given moment or whose single images, through GVI, might end up in myriad contexts. Institutionally Levy is not positioned to think of a particular version of the war being offered to a public but rather focuses on his own coverage only.

Ruth Fremson, staff photographer at the *New York Times,* had opted to cover the war without being embedded in a particular military unit. "I had the choice to be independent and I wanted to work with a particular writer," she explained, adding that she was skeptical of the contract all embedded journalists had to sign. Nonetheless, she added, "[t]hose of us who were unilateral [i.e., not embedded] benefited from the embeds because the media was not seen as much of an enemy so it was easier to shoot." In other words, she may appear skeptical about the restrictions imposed on embedded photographers, but she acknowledges that the close ties they had with their units contributed to less-adversarial relations between all working photojournalists and the US military in general. She is thinking beyond her particular publication's coverage to how embedded photographers affected the US military's perception of the profession at large. Insofar as this affects access for unilateral journalists, it shapes what the public will be able to know about those fighting in their name.

Contrary to Rosenthal's sentiment that this war was just like all those he'd seen before it, Kennerly argued that there was little similarity between the Vietnam War and the Iraq War. His main reason sounds crushingly optimistic in retrospect: "That war [i.e., the Vietnam War] for Americans lasted ten years." Kennerly was echoing the belief held by many in the photojournalism world by the fall of 2003 that the Iraq War would not last much longer. In fact, the common perception was still that the war had been ending since the topping of the statue of Saddam Hussein in April. Kennerly told the audience of student photographers, most of them born long after 1973 when US troops left Vietnam, that "in Vietnam we could go anywhere we wanted to, you could go see whatever you wanted to see." This is a claim often also made by Hal Buell, another Barnstorm regular and former head of AP Photo, who goes so far as to state, "In Vietnam, photographers had utter, complete access."[37] Given the many restrictions on travel in North Vietnam and the difficulty of getting into villages controlled by the National Liberation Front detailed by Schwenkel, Kennerly's comments demonstrate a retrospective reimagining of territory and ease of traversing space.[38] Perhaps you *could* "go see whatever you wanted to see"— provided that what you wanted to see was controlled by US forces or the Army of the Republic of Vietnam. Nonetheless, Kennerly's point was that photographers covering US troops in Vietnam had more mobility than their counterparts embedded with troops in Iraq.

The photographers on the panel all agreed that the most significant change in war coverage was in the speed with which photographs could be sent. Fremson, the most experienced photographer on the panel, who had covered "the tail end of Haiti, Bosnia, Kosovo, and the Middle

East," volunteered, "How much has changed in the last few years. In Bosnia I had a sat [i.e., satellite] phone the size of this podium; by Kosovo it was as big as the top of the podium. In Afghanistan we were able to use a high-speed Internet connection, and by Iraq we had the Thuraya, which is basically a big cell phone." Levy had brought solar panels with him on assignment to keep his phone battery charged and also used a car battery, and Loomis had taken a generator to the field. Perhaps we need to think of electricity itself and its transportability as part of the contemporary infrastructure of representation.

The photographers then addressed their relationships with editors. Loomis stated that one of the best things about being away was precisely being far enough away that editors on the foreign desk didn't second-guess his edits. He felt they trusted his judgment because he was under difficult circumstances: "I never got a 'Could we get a vertical?'" Levy, too, stressed his autonomy in the field, though he complained about not receiving any direction except when editors told him about stories various writers were working on to see whether he could perhaps work on a similar story. Again, Loomis's and Levy's significantly different institutional affiliations as well as their differences in experience level are important in understanding their differences in opinion. Levy wished for more direction, whereas Loomis was happy to have the freedom to follow his own journalistic instincts. Fremson encouraged the audience to remember how the editors at home continued to work while the photographers were in the field: "They still have to go to that 10 A.M. meeting. So I make sure to give my editor a call and send in something beforehand so that I gain the trust of the editor as well."

Kennerly asked each of the participants about the emotional stress of covering warfare. Levy talked about being on assignment twenty-four hours a day, about the stress of a schedule that consists of "work, transmit, sleep, work, transmit, sleep." Loomis and Fremson seconded Levy's conclusion that it is very important to have a life away from cameras and the battlefield. Yet their answers also made clear that even experienced photographers Loomis and Fremson were both haunted by some of their recent experiences.

> *Loomis:* We all saw things we'd never want to see. It's an important job and if they're going to offer it to me, I'll never turn it down. Worse thing I saw was an injured child and the convoy didn't stop. I'm screaming to the commander and we kept going by. You see a lot of unnecessary carnage. We put our lives in danger. A lot of journalists didn't come back. I'm really sad those people didn't come home.

Fremson: The day Kirkuk fell [to the Americans], we entered the city amid flag waving. People were celebrating. We stopped at the hospital and the ER was full of people dying. There was a dead kid with shrapnel in his head. I could still hear people celebrating. A woman pulled up and her husband was dead in the backseat. It was an incredible experience and I'm very grateful for that balance.

What both Loomis and Fremson's comments reveal is the emotional stress involved in trying to depict situations that are inherently complex and multifaceted, if not contradictory: seeing civilian victims of a battle while hearing other civilians celebrate its outcome. For all the celebration of photography during Barnstorm as a force that can effect change, Loomis's words soberly reminded the audience of the helpless situations photographers find themselves in. Like Loomis embedded in a convoy that passed by an injured child, there are times when a photographer has access to represent an event without any agency to change it. It is precisely this type of emotional complexity that gets lost as images become iconic, particularly once they come to symbolize a particular historical conclusion. Once a war "boils down" to an image, what is lost is the intense and often contradictory elements of the event being photographed.

In her provocative book *The Civil Contract of Photography* Ariella Azoulay argues that an ethical spectator must reconstruct the photographic event. Particularly "when and where the subject of the photograph is a person who has suffered some form of injury inflicted on others, a viewing of the photograph that reconstructs the photographic situation and allows a reading of the injury inflicted on others becomes a civic skill, not an exercise in aesthetic appreciation."[39] Azoulay defines watching as "fixing the gaze for a period of time in order to allow the visible to unfold like a picture in motion. . . . In the case of stills the gesture of spectatorship requires a special intention from the spectator who seeks to reconstruct the situation of the act of photography from the surface of the photograph."[40] In light of the comments of Fremson and Loomis above, I find Azoulay's notion of "watching photographs as a space of political relations," generative.[41] Indeed if one "watched" the image of the injured boy the convoy was passing, one might begin to unravel the conditions of possibility behind its production and reconstruct "the situation of the act of photography from the surface of the photograph."[42] Yet in order to reconstruct the photographic event, one needs more information than is available on the surface of the image—such as the knowledge that the photographer taking the image is embedded with a military unit the commander of which has decided not to stop for the child.

Listening to Loomis's and Fremson's recollections leads me to believe that no amount of watching alone can lead a spectator to an accurate reconstruction of the photographic event. There is tremendous value no doubt in at least thinking about the conditions of possibility of an image while interpreting it, but in order to truly reconstruct the situation in which Fremson found herself, the unfolding images of her photographing the victims in the emergency room would have to be overlaid with the soundtrack of cheering crowds outside; the photographs of a dead husband driven to the hospital in vain would require multiple exposures, with the image of the child dying of a shrapnel wound and images of flag waving all on the same surface, *as if* one could capture what the photographer had experienced. Loomis ended his recollection by commenting on the very real dangers facing photographers. In order to reconstruct many photographic events involving injury accurately, the spectator would also need to superimpose the conscious or unconscious fear of the photographer onto the image, or at least the presence of a threat whether or not it was perceived, for that, too, influences the conditions of production of the image. Photojournalists are often in peril since they have to be on site to work—or "You can't get the shot from the hotel lobby," as many photographers reminded me when comparing their work to that of text journalists. Furthermore, like television-camera operators, they use equipment that often makes them easy to identify and target.[43] Fittingly, the war panel wrapped up with a focus on the personal sacrifices faced by photojournalists, and the workshop participants were then all enjoined to take part in the annual memorial service.

HONORING THE ANCESTORS

Everyone in the barn slowly exited, passing "the Vietnam Photographer Memorial Wall" with the pictures of several photographers killed while on assignment. Each workshop participant was handed a flute of champagne and a yellow balloon. In the distance a conch shell called the group up a hill to a clearing among the pine trees. Faculty, staff, students, and heavies all formed a circle. What followed was a ceremonial of remembrance for the fallen war photographers created especially for the Eddie Adams Workshop by the Nuyagi Keetowah Society, a Cherokee scholars group in the metropolitan New York area. Ray Evans Harrell, the Didahnvwisgi (medicine priest) for the group, has led the ceremony at Barnstorm since 1991. "The ceremony was built to honor the spirits of the seven war photographers. . . . The purpose of the ceremony is for people to come together both individually and as a group and to meet with their ancestors. It is also a way to place the ideals before the young photographers. They have something very important to achieve. They have to be the eyes of the nation." An Elder and respected historian, Harrell is a professional voice teacher and opera director. In the ceremony, he addresses the four sacred directions, and then leads a ritual chant at the end of which he directly addresses the students. Gesturing at the memorial table on which the seven names are engraved, Harrell tells them: "They were our eyes, now you are our eyes." Harrell told me he believed those at the workshop had a very important mission. "If our eyes are blind, if we don't see what's happening, then we can't be wise about it." One sign of how seriously photography is taken at this ceremony is that it is permitted at all. Harrell explained, "We discussed this in our community. We don't allow cameras around our ceremonies. However, they are not photographing a Cherokee ceremony that they are merely observing, they are photographing something constructed for them: a ceremonial of remembrance for the war photographers based in Native American processes." He continued, "in that environment we feel the cameras are their sacred tools. To see and tell the truth is the reason they are there and the camera is their eye."[44]

In 2003, following the ceremonial, Eddie said a word of tribute to all the photographers who had lost their lives covering the Vietnam War, and all those who had died since. He raised his glass and added, "It's still the greatest job in the world." This is the point in the workshop when those gathered commemorate those who have died the year before. Just a year later, in 2004, Eddie Adams himself was mourned here, his black fedora lain on the table by his son. It is the most solemn moment of the workshop, and according to many regular attendees, most years it is the workshop's emotional climax. Family members of the dead lay a bright sunflower on the memorial table, and then everyone lets go of their yellow balloons at once. As they collectively form a yellow cloud rising in the sky and then slowly disperse, people return to the barn.

PHOTOGRAPHERS OF VIETNAM

George Esper, the bureau chief of the Associated Press in Saigon during the Vietnam War, greeted the group once they had assembled back in the barn: "From Homer to Hemingway there have always been those who report on the heroism of war. Vietnam was the first living-room war. . . . This was a new way of reporting that held the government responsible."[45] This belief that coverage of the Vietnam War was exceptional is widespread. The war is "not only significant in the sociohistorical consciousness of the United States, Vietnam or other nations directly involved in the conflict, but has assumed a unique status in global historical memory, largely on account of global mass media coverage of the war."[46] Accordingly, perhaps Barnstorm has a Vietnam focus not only because Eddie Adams and several of the heavies made their professional names while covering that conflict but also because the conflict has become paradigmatic for global mass-media coverage for any conflict. Nonetheless, as the reader will remember from prior chapters, there is often significant variability in the amount of global mass-media coverage that conflicts receive. Visibility in world news is a function of a country's perceived relevance to certain political centers of power, its "place in the world."[47]

Esper stressed the "courage and determination of combat photography," locating the heroism of war not only with the soldiers on the battlefield but also with those behind the viewfinders reporting on them. The heroes of Barnstorm, after all, are veteran photographers. He added, "More than seventy Western photographers died in the Vietnam War. They focused their lives on the truth." Schwenkel's research on the use of photography in public commemoration of the war in Vietnam draws attention to the relevance of this sort of body count.[48] According to the influential exhibition *Requiem: By the Photographers Who Died in Vietnam and Indochina,* prepared by American photo editors Horst Faas and Tim Page, but also on permanent display in Vietnam, 135 photographers were killed in action, of which 72 were from North Vietnam and 4 from the Republic of Vietnam. In other words, according to this count, Esper's count leaves out more than half the photographers who lost their lives during what in Vietnam is called the American War in Vietnam. Esper qualifies his number with the adjective *Western.* He is not miscounting, then, but rather presenting a view of the war from the American perspective. Moreover, this is his segue to introducing the next speaker, the Vietnamese photographer Nick Ut. Ut won a Pulitzer for the 1972 image of the nine-year-old Kim Phuc running with outstretched hands as napalm burned her body. His brother Huynh Thanh My had been working for AP when he was killed in action, and Nick asked the AP for a job. Only fifteen at the time, he was told to go home to his family. According to Esper, Ut replied that his family had died and that the AP was his family now. He began working in the darkroom and learned how to photograph. Eight years later, he took the photo of Kim Phuc. Nick Ut's story contrasts with and parallels the narrative at Barnstorm: the grieving non-Westerner taken into the family of photojournalism, trained by the most talented photojournalists who had converged in Saigon, who grew up to take one of the most significant photographs of the era. This family narrative is also an ideological one. In the *Requiem* count, Ut's brother and other Vietnamese photographers who worked for the Western press were grouped as "South Vietnam," a country that was listed with foreign countries. Hence, Ut can simultaneously be both "the pick of Vietnam" and a native son of Western photojournalism.

At one point during Barnstorm 2003, Eddie Adams made a comment about the universality of photography. It is one he has made on many occasions: "Not everybody can read a newspaper, magazine, or book. Photography is the most powerful weapon. Cameras in the hands of photographers can capture love, hope, and change lives, and it only take one-five-hundredth of a second." Photographs, Adams argued, are universally accessible. Adams's comment establishes the photographer as hero with absolute agency. Moreover, he is an armed hero: his camera is his weapon. The labor of image brokers that might help the photographer get into place, circulate the photograph, or publish it as a news image is invisible. The heroic act is that which takes place in one-five-hundredth of a second.

As Schwenkel's research on photographs of the conflict in Vietnam makes clear, even supposedly universally accessible photographs may signify very different things to different people. Schwenkel asks: "How can an iconic photograph convey important historical knowledge in one context and propaganda in another?"[49] Her attention to the display of such images in history museums suggests, as does my research in the photojournalism industry, that this is possible only if it is not the photograph itself that conveys meaning but rather the discursive frame in which it circulates and becomes a particular news image. In the Barnstorm family, Vietnam is an important place in the history of photojournalism. Students were told again and again about Vietnam as a time when photographs swayed public opinion. I agree that combat photography, and perhaps all documentary photography, requires great courage, and that powerful news images are significant practices of worldmaking. However, what gets lost in the production of the photographer hero and the reiteration of the story of the iconic photograph that stopped the war is Vietnam as an actual place itself. The photograph acquires mythical powers to seal the fate of a nation. Along with the complexity of war, what is erased are the efforts of Vietnamese civilians and soldiers, many of whom died in the fighting.

THE ICONIC SUBJECT SPEAKS

Nick Ut still works for the Associated Press. He has lived in America since 1973. He was reunited with Kim Phuc in 1993, and in 1995 she attended Barnstorm with Ut during her very first visit to the United States.[50] Since then the Barnstorm family has often included not only photographers and editors but also perhaps the most famous subject of an iconic photograph: Kim Phuc. In a video recording of Phuc's first appearance at Barnstorm, Ut introduces her by showing not only the well-known photograph but then several photographs of her and her family, some with him in the frame as he follows her through the years, as if he is combining his award-winning harrowing image with snapshots from a family photo album. Phuc calls Ut "Uncle." They are the Vietnamese side of the Barnstorm family. Ut and Phuc are framed as both universal subjects—the photojournalist focused on the truth and the child victim of warfare—and ethnic Vietnamese.

Phuc thanked "Uncle Eddie" and addressed the youngest generation of photojournalists. More than thirty years after the famous photograph of her was taken, she spoke as a particular individual whose particular body was first burned and then indexed in a photograph that circulated around the world. As it became a news image, her likeness came to represent the plight of Vietnamese civilians. As discussed in the introduction, in this news image, as in many, there is an indexed body—that of Kim Phuc—and a represented social body: all Vietnamese children or even all Vietnamese civilian casualties of the war. What makes the story of Kim Phuc extraordinary is that the moment in which her body was permanently injured and marked by war is also the moment in which she was photographed. Moreover, Denise Chong's biography of Phuc highlights that it was the result of both the napalm burns and the global circulation of her image that caused Phuc injury as she grew into adulthood. Phuc told a moving tale of how for twenty-four years she had to display her scars for foreign journalists whenever minders from the Vietnamese government asked her to do so. Eventually she got sent to Cuba and married. After a honeymoon in Moscow, as the couple was returning to Cuba, the plane stopped for refueling in Canada, and Phuc and her husband escaped.[51] Her message to the Barnstorm students focused on the importance of forgiveness: "'Love your enemies,' Jesus said," she reminded them.

Phuc then passionately introduced the work of the Kim Foundation, which raises money for children caught in warfare. Phuc began the Kim Foundation in 1997 when she acknowledged that her unique indexical relationship to the girl in the famous photograph that had drawn much unwanted attention from her Vietnamese minders and caused her so much sorrow was also the basis for a certain kind of authority. Narrating the moment when a photographer "discovered" her in Toronto, Phuc stressed, "I learned to control that picture. I wanted a quiet life, a normal life. But then a photographer came and took a picture with a long lens and suddenly I was in the papers again. At first I was very upset. I felt like a victim all over again. [Then] I realized that I couldn't escape that picture and accepted it as a gift instead." She ended her address by telling the audience how to interpret the photograph taken by Nick Ut: "Don't see her as crying out in pain; see her as crying out for peace."

Phuc is in many ways the perfect photographic subject to convey to photographers that their work does matter, that their images can change and even save lives. Ut not only took Phuc's photograph but also transported her to the hospital and used his credentials and connections as a journalist to secure her medical care.[52] Her association with the photograph first brought with it an onerous burden. She was often compelled by Vietnamese officials to bare her scars as visual evidence of the carnage wrought by the United States. The photograph alone would have sufficed for that, but her body, always still marked by the napalm, proved that the destruction was continuous and exceeded the moment of the photograph. It is as if the Vietnamese minders displayed Phuc's body with the logics by which image brokers choose images—picking frames in which an indexed body can represent an entire body politic. Her body came to represent all of the damage inflicted on Vietnam during "the American War."[53]

Yet it is also important to note that by the time Phuc spoke to the students at Barnstorm 2003, she was not speaking as a former enemy or even one who might challenge the US-centric version of the war coverage of Vietnam, the way a North Vietnamese photographer might. Phuc's story allows her to be easily folded into the narrative of war seen from the American perspective. "September 11 is a special day for me because it is my [wedding] anniversary. Now September 11 is a date of hate. When I saw the airplane hit the second tower all my memories of fire came back to me. Suddenly there was a new war. It reminded me of why I choose to raise my children in freedom in the West. We must never take it for granted." Phuc tells her story as someone who has chosen to live in the West. Her honeymoon trip is also what enabled her to defect to Canada. Her talk echoed the discursive framing of the War on Terror as a fight against those who hated freedom. Operation Enduring Freedom is after all the official name used by the US government for the multi-sited War on Terror. It was as if this new war reanimated her personally; she is no longer the agentless subject in the photograph. Rather, she now uses it prominently herself for the Kim Foundation. Her taking charge of this image solves one of the ideological contradictions of Barnstorm: if war images are what is most revered and the photographers that have taken them are bestowed heroic status, how convincingly can one argue for photography as a peacemaking tool? Yet the entire workshop is also framed by the importance of Vietnam as a moment when photography influenced public opinion against supporting a war. As Ut's photograph of a victim of war is reappropriated by its subject as a rallying call for peace, it provides a way that photojournalism can hold on to its self-image as a peacemaking force while at the same time revering its war heroes.

AWAKENING

The audience was very moved by Phuc's speech. Many of the students had tears in their eyes when the lights came up. The last word of the evening, however, went to a photographer. On my way to Barnstorm, many in the industry had told me about the legendary gospel-like inspirational speeches of John White, an African-American photographer working in Chicago and a Barnstorm regular.[54] Indeed, White's closing speech was an almost religious paean to photojournalism. "This Barnstorm XVI could be called 'Photojournalism Love,'" he told his listeners. He spoke of "the soul of photojournalism" and asked the audience how their wings were.

> We're all alike. The camera is the glue that connects us, it is our universal passport. . . . We translate. We're not just servants, we're visual servants. Our responsibility is to make something ordinary extraordinary. . . . We must be doers . . . a lightning bolt for humanity. . . . We have this wonderful privilege to go out and meet people. . . . Barnstorm, you don't leave here like

you came. . . . Good, better, best—never let them rest until your good is better and your better best. The lessons of Barnstorm are lessons beyond Barnstorm. . . . You don't belong to yourself, you are a gift to the world. . . . How many times has one image made a difference? Camera is your mission, life is a gift, use it well.

Given the intense competition in the industry, the dearth of staff jobs, the financial difficulties awaiting most freelance photographers, and the constant reliance on luck and visas, it's easy to understand why Barnstorm is such an unabashed celebration of a profession. This is a profession in which individuals have to be extremely self-motivated, where they are rarely given direction or support; and even when they put their lives in danger and produce an iconic image, few people outside this small community ever come to recognize the individual behind the photograph. Barnstorm provided an annual escape to a place where merely being a photographer was considered noble, where even students who'd been working for only a few years were enthusiastically welcomed as part of a family with a larger mission for all humanity. Young talents who had trepidations about pursuing a precarious profession were assured that the choice was not theirs to make: Their talent came with an agency of its own. They did not belong to themselves and had merely to answer a calling as visual servants. Barnstorm was a place where for a few days no one questioned the power of an image to stop a war or change the world. Despite all the challenges in the industry, many plainly visible in Manhattan, just two hours away, here at Eddie's barn, for one more night, being a photojournalist was still the best job in the world.

That evening the 11:30 club was exceptionally well attended, and people stayed and looked at student portfolios until two in the morning.

RETURNING TO THE PROFANE WORLD

The last day of the workshop began with a job panel. The panel of editors gave concrete advice about how to survive in this fiercely competitive industry, including how to make best use of their new family ties. The job panel was a reminder of all the other people involved in the industry, as if slowly the panel were preparing the workshop participants to return to a world where they couldn't survive on enthusiasm for photography alone. Another Barnstorm ended with celebrations of teamwork. Prizes were given to recognize individual talent. Buses left for the city full of students and faculty finally sleeping. Members of the blue team told me they were leaving with larger dreams than they had when they arrived. Almost all of them are still photographers today. Some have returned to Barnstorm as staff or speakers. Every year the list of Barnstorm alumni who have won Pulitzer Prizes and World Press Photo Awards grows longer.

6

Visa Pour l'Image

Personal Visions and Amateur Documents

"I still regard Paris as the world capital of photojournalism—except for the first week in September, when the scene annually shifts to Perpignan for the world photojournalism festival."[1] This comment, written by legendary American photo editor John Morris in 2002, captures the importance of Visa Pour l'Image, the annual photojournalism festival in Perpignan, France, to which image brokers worldwide flock.[2] Held in late summer when news tends to be slow, Perpignan—or Visa, as the festival is called—brings together new photographers just trying to break into the industry as well as veteran photographers and image brokers of all sorts. Although the last decade has seen an explosion of photography festivals, for a long time, and certainly at the time of my fieldwork, Perpignan was a major event. It was the place where new photography collectives such as VII (2001) and Noor (2007) were announced, books were launched, and the professional altercations and scandals of the year were thoroughly debated. It remains the largest international photojournalism festival. This is the shortest chapter in *Image Brokers* in part because as a public event that draws thousands of visitors, industry professionals, and others, Visa is written about in the press of multiple nations every year and also much discussed on social media. Reading the overviews of the festival every year allows one take the pulse of the industry even at a distance.

Throughout the years I have worked on photojournalism, Visa has been a festival celebrating a profession in transition. I attended Visa

Pour l'Image in 2003 and 2004 and again in 2015. This chapter draws mainly on my fieldwork at Visa 2004, but I will make note of a few major changes since. Visa Pour l'Image 2004 crystallized the period of transition in the photojournalism community described throughout this book. At the most material level, the very technology of the presentations was changing: 2003 was the last year that the evening slide shows used actual slides rather than digital projections. Below I give a brief description of Visa and then look closely at the particular language used to describe the state of the field in 2004—specifically, how the language of documents versus visual stories was used to value different categories of images. Visa is a celebration of mobility, whether of photographers or of news images, and a manifestation of the conviction that photographs can move individuals and shape political will. At the same time, images and photographers have limited circulation. This chapter describes the conditions of passage for certain photographers and their photographs, for even when all photographs move digitally, some have much more freedom of movement than others.

ISSUING VISAS

The festival's title—Visa Pour l'Image—implies that the festival is a celebration of photography's ability to travel and inform far beyond national borders, and it conjures up that ubiquitous myth of the news image that is universally legible to everyone everywhere if it can only get published. Nonetheless, the rhetoric being invoked in this title—Visa Pour l'Image—is also one of controlled, impermeable borders and travel documents, such as passports and visas, that ensure a right to passage to some but not to others. The very first Visa took place just a few months before the fall of the Berlin Wall. What followed was a period in which news headlines celebrated the permeability of borders, when all walls could potentially be demolished no matter how formidable they might have appeared. Yet visas can be denied as well as issued, revoked as well as extended, and walls are once again on the rise.

Photojournalism is an industry that, despite being global, certainly knows firsthand the critical importance of visas and the sometimes seemingly arbitrary political implications of a photographer's nationality. Remember the prominent placement of the whiteboard on which various photographer's visas were listed at GVI, the visual content provider profiled in chapter 2. That whiteboard was key in determining who could be pitched for what assignment when a publication called.

Despite all their worldliness, many Israeli photographers without dual nationality had to sit out the early years of the wars in Afghanistan and Iraq, while other photographers who happened to have official ties to any Arab nation were free to roam at will. Issuing or denying visas is one way governments attempt to control how they are represented. Many veteran photographers have stories of being barred from countries after producing work that was objectionable to a particular government. Much of the day-to-day conversations at a photo agency or news publication begin with the question of travel documents—what passport the photographer will be traveling on, whether the right visas have been procured, whether the photographer is going in on a press or tourist visa, and how long she or he will be able to stay.

Moreover, it is not just actual visas that enable access to certain stories. In chapter 2, American photographer Kelly highlighted her good relations with United States General Tommy Franks when she was trying to get GVI to share expenses with her. Ed, the photo editor, had seconded her instinct that in the context of anti-French sentiment during the weeks leading up to the war, the American generals would be more inclined to give her access if she was on assignment for *Newsworld* instead of for *Paris Match*. In chapter 7, Robert, a veteran Swedish journalist, narrates being sent to Saudi Arabia as a staff photographer for a major Swedish paper during the first Gulf war but having no chance at covering the border because none of the US press officers had heard of his newspaper. Meanwhile, in chapter 3, Christophe at AFP had used the argument that junior French foreign minister Muselier "would appreciate a French wire service having exclusive coverage" when trying to secure resources for a photographer working in Darfur. In other words, nationalities, passports, and visas are central to the daily decisions of image brokers.[3]

NAVIGATING PERPIGNAN

Provided those who need them can get visas to travel to France, every year the opening week of Visa, aimed at professionals, creates a temporal and geographic space of a week for the community of image makers and brokers normally dispersed around the globe to congregate and to develop their social and professional networks. Visa completely takes over the city of Perpignan with a population just over one hundred thousand. Perpignan is a Catalonian border city less than an hour from Spain, and during Visa many of its most stunning architectural sites, including chapels and churches, host documentary photography exhibits. Each year there are more than twenty exhibits, often on very difficult subjects, many of the exhibits testimonies to atrocities. Visa is one of the regular sites for the World Press Photo exhibition.[4] In addition, every night during professional week an audience of twenty-five hundred or more gather at the Campo Santo, a fourteenth-century cloister cemetery, for the screenings that begin shortly after 9 P.M. and often continue past midnight. The crowds are such that the final two evening screenings are also projected onto screens in the town's Place de la République for the hundreds who cannot get in to the Campo Santo. Audiences are shown approximately ten thousand images over the course of the week. These evening slide shows are massive spectacles, each evening a parade of still images set to music and projected on giant screens.

Visa is an entirely different celebration of documentary photography than the sequestered intimate workshop Barnstorm, described in the previous chapter. With its many symposia and "meet the photographer" sessions, Visa is a very much a public festival. Simultaneous translation is offered at almost all the events. Though the professionals go home at the end of the first week, the exhibits are open for another week for photo enthusiasts of all kinds, including a program that partners with schools and brings through thousands of schoolchildren from France and Spain.

Visa has been directed by Jean-François Leroy since it began, and he personally curates each of the photography shows from the more than four thousand submitted annually. Like Eddie Adams, Jean François is known for his intensity and passion for photography, and although the two events look and feel very different, rarely do image brokers get any sleep at either. Jean-François Leroy is perhaps the most visible image broker in photojournalism. He often describes Visa as a news publication put out but once a year, and he makes all the decisions about which images will be included. Leroy explained the mission of Visa to me thus: "Firstly, we want to show emerging talent. Many great photographers . . . had their very first shows in Perpignan. Secondly, we aim to confirm well-known photographers. . . . And thirdly, we want to 'rediscover' the greats." He blames much of the turbulence in the photojournalism industry on the speed of digital transmission and the increasing lack of photo editors. "We need better filters," he complains. The festival is partly his response to his frustration with a celebrity- and sports-obsessed press. "Ninety percent of what I show at Visa has never been published," he adds.

During Visa Pour l'Image, Perpignan's geography centers on a few key sites. In 2004 these were the Campo Santo, where the evening slide shows took place; the Hotel Pams, where everyone registered and editors at publications reviewed photographer's work; the Palais des Congrès, where agencies of all sizes set up booths; and Café de la Poste.

Upon arriving in Perpignan, one registered at Hotel Pams, where in 2004 there was a message board that quickly began to reflect the concerns of the smallest players in the industry: new photographers seeking housing or rides at the end of the festival, a small agency searching for photographers in China, or people looking to reconnect with photographers they had met in years past. Editors and agents looked at portfolios as they sat at tables shaded by sun umbrellas emblazoned with "Kodak Express" arranged around the fountain in the courtyard. Often several photographers waited in line for an editor's attention, sometimes getting a chance to see another photographer show his or her work while they waited. In 2003 there were still plenty of photographers showing actual physical portfolios, bound books, or boxes of prints. This was, after all, just a few months after I had observed Jackie in GVI's newsroom ask Ed whether to send a *real* or digital portfolio to a magazine interested in sending a photographer to Baghdad, to which Ed had replied, with some exasperation, "Digital. Digital is real!" By 2004 laptops were more common. Just over a decade later most photographers show their portfolio on tablets or laptops, though a few arrive with what editors refer to as "traditional printed portfolios."[5] Today photographers need not crisscross between Hotel Pams and the Palais de Congrès since Hotel Pams is now used as an exhibition space. Portfolio reviews have moved to the seventh-floor café at the Palais de Congrès. The Kodak Express umbrellas have disappeared. In 2015, photographers were constantly in search of electrical outlets to charge smartphones and tablets to keep their portfolios viable throughout long days.

Despite the local newspapers headline of "More kisses than business" (*Plus de bises que de business*), many photography agencies had booths at Visa 2004. Here they met photographers and looked at their portfolios, but also tried to woo magazine editors. Especially for the larger agencies, the focus was not so much on seeing the work of young photographers and encouraging them as it was on showing off their search capabilities, archives, and online user interface to clients who might turn to them for images. Photo editors both at agencies and at publications looked at portfolios because they were looking for new talent and hoping to sign the industry's rising stars. I overheard one editor asking a photographer if he could introduce him to another photographer who was getting a lot of attention that year. Meanwhile, at the espresso bar, I was constantly overhearing photographers evaluate their agencies to one another. One photographer grumbled to another: "They do nothing for me and then get pissed when I approach a magazine directly!" In other words, he was complaining that his agency did not adequately push his work to publications but got angry when he secured assignments himself.[6]

Finally, although not on the official map distributed by the festival organizers, Café de la Poste, in the center of town, is the unofficial meeting spot, crowded any time of day. Café de la Poste is a fairly typical brasserie on a relatively calm plaza in Perpignan. However, during the professional week of Visa Pour l'Image, it becomes the default meeting place, especially after the evening slide shows let out close to midnight. It is open twenty-three hours a day, and many claim that it makes the majority of its income for the year during the professional week of the festival. Veteran image brokers—whether photographers, editors, or those working for agencies—catch up with old friends; newcomers to the industry hope to meet the photographers they admire or network with an editor who might ask to see their portfolio the following day. Café de la Poste becomes a hub of convivial activity where politics, photography, and journalism are discussed in loud voices encouraged by wine and tap beer. Often the café does not empty out completely between closing and opening for coffee and croissants.

PROFESSIONAL ANXIETIES

Visa is a place where anxieties run high. This is a highly competitive, creative profession, and over the years many young photographers would tell me how nervous they got as they approached editors with portfolios prepared diligently in anticipation of Visa. Particularly for photographers who don't live in Paris, London, or New York, Perpignan offers a rare opportunity to make connections in person. The intense days of queuing for and receiving critiques of portfolios and constantly being surrounded by competition can be very challenging for some. Moreover, the close proximity of all the different locations means that one is constantly running into people and seeing editors react to other photographers' work or seeing who is circulating with whom. There are many public events, most prominent among them the evening screening, but there are also many that are private—from dinners hosted by large magazines such as *National Geographic* to the private parties in apartments rented out by members of photography collectives. Visa Pour l'Image is a time of intense networking and jockeying for a spot with the in crowd, and hence always also a place where the lines between those in the inner circles of the industry and those on the periphery are visible.[7]

The current cohort of well-known combat photographers who, at least in 2003 and 2004, often sported scarves ranging from Cambodian silks to Palestinian kaffiyehs and Afghan shemaghs despite the balmy late-summer temperatures, were aware of the respect they commanded at Visa and regaled each other with the annual crop of stories: near misses with bullets, insurgents, and government censors. Yet people often told me about the fierce competition they felt. In this fast-paced industry a photographer might get a lot of attention based on his or her coverage of a single event, but the question was always whether she or he could last past that particular news cycle. Different photographers came up with different strategies for continuing to work through slow news cycles or budget cuts at news publications. Some tried to build a reputation around a theme such as aging, mental health, or immigration and establish themselves as visual experts on that theme. Others, even if they were freelancers and hence not associated with a regional bureau, would base themselves in an area that was particularly newsworthy and try to become known for their coverage of that area. This was the strategy of the photographer in chapter 2 who came in to GVI to talk about his work in Colombia, where he was based: he was hoping to be the first person any editor thought of after an event in Colombia. Developing "a personal vision" or "becoming an author" was another strategy and likely the most ambitious approach—because the hope then was that publications would want a particular photographer's view on a topic, regardless of the subject matter or where the story was located. Already in 2004 this luxury was afforded to very few in the industry; now it is afforded to almost no one.

The competitive nature of the industry was visible not only among the photographers, but also among the agencies trying to discover new talent and establish a good reputation in the industry. Many of the smaller agencies felt a need to claim a niche and communicate it. How would they get photo editors at publications to think of them first before visiting the websites of the mammoth visual content providers? The owner of a newly established agency made a point to tell me his plan—perhaps precisely because he had heard I was an anthropologist: "I want to own culture. Not in a braggy way, but it is important as a business to think what you want to do in seven to ten years. I want to be the agency you go to if what you want are pictures of various cultures."

There was pressure on the larger agencies as well. GVI spent a lot of time trying to woo editors and photographers to its booth and generally curry more goodwill in an industry that had been resistant to visual content providers. Industry insiders took notice of the efforts GVI put into its booth, referring to it afterward as the best-looking booth in the press center. Ed, the former GVI photo editor who had left GVI for a competitor by the time we saw each other at Visa 2004, asked me the first day if I had seen the GVI booth. Impressed by its flashy set up, he gave GVI a backhanded compliment: "It looks like they've been here three weeks." And indeed many were suspicious of GVI trying so hard. One year GVI also produced a massive, oversize portfolio of the work of the photographers it represented in order to show its dedication to its photographers' work. At a moment when many industry veterans were talking about reduced budgets, GVI was clearly underscoring that whatever it may lack in experience, it could compensate for with financial resources in an industry not known for deep pockets. GVI was simultaneously trying to improve its reputation among veterans in the industry by demonstrating its reverence for great photography and flaunting all it could do for the top-tier photographers it represented, and trying to impress upon editors at publications that they could fill all their visual content needs at one convenient agency.

Perhaps not surprisingly given the intense competition, each year that I attended Visa Pour l'Image, several informants confessed to feeling inadequate in some way, particularly after the second or third late night. Partly I think this is because many of the conversations and public talks at Visa center on the formidable challenges facing photojournalism and the difficulties that lie ahead for all in the industry. Image brokers and photographers tend to be very committed to their work, and many define themselves through it. Therefore, questions about whether it has a future in addition to questions about its political efficacy proved to be personally discomforting for many. For others it was the flood of images on difficult subjects that they found challenging. As I listened to talks, watched portfolio reviews, went to many of the private parties, and participated in long nights of conversation at Café de la Poste, I realized that, ironically, despite its being a celebration of photography, Visa was where photographers, agents, photo editors, and other image brokers confided to me their doubts about photojournalism's ability to instigate political change or their sense that they were questioning their faith in the industry. However, these were conversations held in private.

THE AMATEUR THREAT

Professional anxieties were particularly acute at Visa 2004. In the world at large, the increasingly widespread availability of digital technology and the cell-phone camera had generated an amateur threat that many addressed over the course of the professional week. Defensively, in his introductory remarks the festival president insisted, "While technological developments have brought digital technology to the fore, replacing conventional silver-based photography, with news traveling ever more freely via sophisticated equipment and available to the general public, there will always be a great need for work done by qualified people." The festival director, Jean-François Leroy, then took the microphone and clearly articulated why 2004 had become the year the amateur threat to photojournalism was felt especially sharply: "The photos of the year were not taken by professional photographers, or even by journalists. I am talking about the photos of the Iraqi prisoners in Abu Ghraib. As photographs they are of no interest, that's clear. But what documentary records they are!"

The dizzying rate of digital-image diffusion that infuriated the US military had put photojournalists on the defensive about the value of their professional expertise. Many were asking what qualifications one really needed to take photographs of newsworthy events. Yet professional photographers were still putting their lives in danger precisely because they still needed to be on location to shoot. Digital news images could circulate in incendiary ways, their points of origin and distribution channels not immediately obvious. Not only was the amateur threat clear, but the dangers associated with being a professional were made extremely present that week in 2004 as the director gave nightly updates on two French journalists (Christian Chesnot and Georges Malbrunot) who had been kidnapped in Iraq the week before the festival began.

On Saturday, the last night of Visa Pour l'Image 2004, the Campo Santo was packed with thousands of people watching the large screens on which photos were projected, often as triptychs. The festival always ends with the presentation of the Visa D'Or prize in the news category. In all the evening screenings at the Campo Santo, there were three different temporailities that organized the images shown. A "daily images" section reviewed the day's news coverage visually, usually organized around the same dominants that had structured world news that day. A year-end review section highlighted the major news events during a three-month segment of the previous year. Both of these press-centered reviews were accompanied by an urgent musical soundtrack akin to what you would hear before a television or radio news broadcast. Many of these images were from the wire services. Almost all the rest of the images were projected as stories told over a dozen images or so, with music curated for each story. This assortment of temporally distinct selections of images signaled the different types of uses for news images: quick daily information, a collective review of the year in pictures, or in-depth coverage of a story that a photographer might have shot over a significant amount of time.[8] The daily news images and year-end review used single images, whereas the stories evolved over multiple images, implicitly celebrating the multiple-image story format as the more prestigious format of the industry. In fact, as detailed in chapter 4, photo essays and stories were increasingly becoming a format celebrated at Visa and by the profession, but less regularly budgeted for in publications. They were, however, prominently displayed in online galleries and slide shows that were financially far less lucrative.[9]

SCREENING IRAQ

The stories that last evening of Visa 2004 contained gripping, often wrenching images: Hebron, Kabul, self-immolation in Afghanistan, the coup d'état in Haiti.[10] The visual horror was interrupted only by a single somewhat more lighthearted story featuring the paper-filled offices of Indian bureaucrats. Finally the show culminated in seven stories on Iraq, the single largest news event from the previous year's press coverage. Much of the talk among professionals in attendance that week had been about how Jean-François Leroy, the festival director, who hand-picks each of the images for the screenings and who made no secret of his displeasure with the Bush regime, would handle the coverage of the war in Iraq.

The very first set of images in this series of seven stories was titled "Iraqi photographers." Leroy spoke of the photographers before the series was screened: "They have an altogether different way of looking. They want to bear witness. We should support them. After all, we can leave, but they do not go in and out of their country, and see it slightly differently. As the circumstances of working in Iraq get more and more difficult, both financially and in terms of security, our vision becomes largely dependent on these photographers." Rather than a body of work by a single photographer, the screens showed a series of single images taken in Iraq by Iraqi photographers.

The selection of photographs from Iraqi photographers was in fact the second series of images outside the "daily news" or "year in review" categories that did not fit the multiple-image story format that evening. The first had featured the work of young Afghan photographers trained at Aina—an NGO founded by renowned photojournalist Reza Deghati to build and develop independent media in Afghanistan. The single-image format itself bracketed the work of both the Afghan photographers and the Iraqis apart from the feature stories being celebrated during the festival.[11] What was highlighted was the collective vision of the local photographers—"They have an altogether different way of looking"—rather than the personal vision of any particular photographer.

Watching the display of images of war-ravaged Iraq, I remembered a conversation earlier in the day with an established photojournalist who had been working in Baghdad. We were talking about Iraqi photographers, and he expressed frustration that "these guys who were hired as drivers" were now doing all this photography because so many of the Western photographers felt too threatened to go out and because the magazines were not committed to supporting continuous coverage of the story. Leroy's comment about the deteriorating circumstances of working in Iraq "both financially and in terms of security" and the increasing dependence of "our vision" on local photographers echoed what the photographer had told me. Local photographers were cheaper, publications didn't have to pay their travel expenses, and, already in the second year of the war in Iraq, publications were feeling that Iraq as a news story had gone over budget. The photographer expressed his frustration by categorizing local photographers as a different kind of amateur threat: they had been hired as drivers and had no experience as photographers. Although Leroy praised their vision and included their work in the coverage of the war in Iraq he had curated for the Visa 2004 audience, the single-image format itself kept the work of these photographers apart from the other photojournalism about Iraq being celebrated that evening.

COSMOPOLITAN STORYTELLERS

Following the Iraqi photographers's images, Leroy segued into his introduction of the next slideshow—a collection of images of Iraq by freelance photojournalist Paolo Woods: "The phenomenon of local photographers is not a recent one. They produce very good documents. But theirs is not a style—*une écriture*—that tells me a story. To understand the life of the people of Iraq, I'll turn to Paolo Woods. Here is a real *écriture*. We should help photographers like him to tell their stories."

The biography on his agency's website tells us Paolo Woods was "born of Canadian and Dutch parentage in 1970. He grew up in Italy and now lives in Paris. Paolo Woods worked as a photographer in advertising and fashion before dedicating himself to photojournalism in 1998. He has shot pictures in Italy, Haiti, Vietnam, Morocco, Egypt, Kosovo and Albania."[12]

Leroy's segue from local document-producing photographers to a cosmopolitan visual storyteller at the much-anticipated climax of the photojournalism industry's annual festival illustrates the rhetoric of praise in contemporary photojournalism. The cosmopolitan storyteller gets to tell stories; it is through him that one can understand the life of the people of Iraq rather than just see their existence documented. These comments are of course not particular to Paolo Woods. Even Leroy quickly shifted to "photographers like him" in his introduction. Woods's particular biography is pertinent only in that it underscores that photographers can accrue professional capital in the circulation of their news images, and that photojournalists acquire their ability to tell stories by circulating worldwide, or that at least they can increase their currency and reputation as storytellers by circulating.[13] Not only is Woods being praised for an *écriture* that allows him to convey the lives of Iraqis in a unique manner, but furthermore, the story that emerges is viewed as his story: "We should help photographers like him to tell their stories."

Écriture means a system of visible signs and traces representing spoken language, someone's personal handwriting, and the manner of writing or style of an individual or period. This textual reference at the apex of a celebration of photography, a medium forever battling for its freedom from text and defensively arguing for the universality of images as truths that do not need translation but can be used across cultural contexts, is odd but indicative of the power of textual metaphor even in a context where what is being celebrated is visual journalism. What interests me in the invocation of *écriture* and authorship is that in 2004 it signaled a desire not for an automatic tracing of the real, but rather for carefully constructed photographs and the visibility of a legible and indentifiable hand.[14]

One highly respected young photographer explained how he envisioned photographers would compete now that all images could move digitally: "Now in the industry there will be wire service images and there will be authors. I want to be an author." When I questioned him about what being an author meant, he spoke of creating images that have a certain personal voice, photos that you go to because you know it's so-and-so's work. "It's not just a matter of style. I've now worked out my style. I'm searching for a language for myself." Soberly, he acknowledged that there would be only a handful of authors.

I began to understand the ramifications of photojournalists with personal vision as I walked around the Couvent des Minimes, the sixteenth-century nunnery where most of the festival's exhibitions are displayed. Many of the photographer biographies in 2004 explicitly commended a photographer's personal vision or mentioned that this was the photographer's particular vision of the subject being photographed. In one room off the long corridor was Ami Vitale's exhibition on Kashmir. Vitale received the 2003 Canon Female Photojournalist Award for this body of work, in which she tries to capture "the simultaneous apprehension of beauty and terror." Images of landscapes and conflict were interspersed with large portraits of women. Vitale herself was in the room giving an interview to a French journalist. The journalist stopped in front of one of the portraits and asked, "Now, this photograph here. It just doesn't seem like an Ami Vitale image to me." Vitale, who came across as a modest, mild-mannered photographer, explained at length to the journalist interviewing her how she had become enchanted with Kashmir in 2001 and had kept returning ever since. Her in-person narrative was as earnest as the text accompanying the images explaining her "desire to give justice to the beauty, strength, and suffering of Kashmir's people and to the unique richness of their history and culture."[15]

What struck me was not Vitale's answers but the journalist's question. Pointing to a photographic portrait exhibited as part of a story about a conflict zone and its population, she had remarked on whether the particular image was identifiable as "an Ami Vitale" photograph. The language of authorship, of a signature style, was being used in the context of photojournalistic images as if the journalist were looking at the image not to see a woman in Kashmir, but rather to detect traces of Vitale's style or what Vitale herself was referring to as her "vision" of Kashmir.[16]

Photographers and even photojournalists have styles, of course, and their photographs are certainly always also aesthetic objects. As visual theorist Ariella Azoulay argues, we must get rid of the distinction between the aesthetic and the political in evaluating documentary photography. Rather, Azoulay claims, "[c]ontrary to the presupposition that the 'political' is a trait of a certain image and absent from another, I say that the political is but a space of human relations exposed to each other in public, and that photography is one of the realizations of this space."[17] Yet, not only does the language of personal vision risk stripping the subjects in the photographs of any agency and turning them into a palette for the photographer's artistic choices, or at best, subjects to whom the photographer can give voice, but more important, it obscures the politics of the encounter between the subject and the photographer—and certainly the spectator at a distance, whether a gallery visitor or newspaper reader. The goal here is not to return to a vulgar identity politics and police who can take photographs of whom. Rather, I want to foreground the politics of which categories of people have mobility and which do not, both behind the camera and as subjects.

In 2004 Visa celebrated the personal visions of cosmopolitan storytellers, authors whose *écriture* was clearly legible and recognizable. Notably, local photographers—even when their work was being honored at the international festival of photojournalism, as in the case of Iraqi or Afghan photographers—could at best bear witness and provide documents. The term *documentary records* was precisely what Jean-François Leroy had used to articulate the value of the Abu Ghraib abuse photos. A few years later, Bangladeshi photographer Shahidul Alam, the founder of the Drik Picture Library photo agency, wrote about how aesthetic evaluations circumscribed the mobility of certain photographers while guaranteeing those of others accelerated circulation: "This represents a shift from the position of 20 years ago when we started asking why Majority World photographers were not being used by mainstream media and development agencies. The answer then had been: 'They don't exist.' Today our existence is difficult to deny. The internet; the fact that several Majority World agencies operate successfully; and that photographers belonging to such agencies regularly win international awards: all these things mean we are no longer invisible. Now it's a different set of rules. We have to prove we have the eye."[18] Indeed, over the years, Visa has included the work of many non-Western photographers. At issue is not whether or not they are exhibited, but rather at specific moments how praise is voiced for different categories of photographer and how different kinds of visual journalism are valued.

In 2015, Bülent Kılıç, a Turkish staff photographer for AFP, won the Visa d'Or prize for his coverage of Syrian refugees at the Turkish border. Turkey is a liminal borderland between center and periphery, and especially when viewed from within the European Union, always already almost European.[19] During the summer of 2015 Turkey was regularly in the news as a European frontier. On the one hand, with over two million registered Syrian refugees, the country became a de facto detention center for those who were fleeing conflict and seeking resettlement in Europe. On the other hand, Istanbul's Atatürk airport was the point of entry for citizens of Western countries seeking to join Islamist militants by traversing porous borders with Iraq and Syria. Summer news coverage was full of closed circuit television images of Western teens at passport control, accompanied by articles that they had been intercepted or reported missing by their families.

Should we read Kılıç's award as a sign that the ranks of cosmopolitan photojournalist have expanded to include some of the former periphery? Perhaps. As I will discuss in the conclusion, there are many more local photographers producing excellent work today, and drastically reduced budgets mean personal vision is less valued in journalism at large. Yet, as a longtime staff photographer for a French wire service, Kılıç is far from the Afghani and Iraqi photographers with limited mobility whose photographs had been praised as "very good documents" at Visa 2004. In fact, his coverage of the conflict in Ukraine was also featured in the exhibit of his photographs at Visa 2015. Kılıç won in the spot news category and what was praised were his powerful individual shots, not his storytelling or his personal vision. This is not a feature of Kılıç's identity, but rather the institution in which he works. Wire services have many more local photographers.

What seems much less likely to change is the vision of the world exhibited at the festival. The news photo that defined Visa 2015 was that of a three-year-old Syrian child's corpse that had washed up on a Turkish beach. The photograph of the little boy who had drowned as his family attempted to cross the Aegean Sea to Greece and traverse the borders of the European Union circulated widely as a global news image during the professional week at Perpignan. The photograph was a frequent topic of conversation, inescapable. It was shown with a slightly different discursive framing almost every night of the screenings. Moreover, at Visa, where the focus remains on photographs of atrocities and suffering, it illustrated how certain categories of people such as refugees are perpetually re-created as passive victims in the circulation of certain kinds of photographs. It was a stark reminder of the tragedy that some bodies have free rein in a globalized world, while the conditions of passage for others are horrifyingly precarious. Many of the celebrations of photojournalism like Visa Pour l'Image are also celebrations of mobility without adequately recognizing that this necessarily narrows the kinds of eyes and personal vision that can produce photographs that circulate.

World Press Photo

Developing World Photography

When a country changes its regime, it invites World Press Photo because it makes an impression on people that emphasizes the changes in structure that have been made. People say, "Now I think we really belong to the civilized world."

—Chairman of World Press Photo, 2005

"We exist to inspire understanding of the world through quality photojournalism," read World Press Photo's mission statement on its website.[1] Clicking on the tab promising more about the foundation, one was greeted by a clearly stated belief in the power of visual storytelling to "inform and shape" the world. If representations are central to worldmaking, as philosopher Nelson Goodman argues, because they contribute to both the understanding and the building of reality, then World Press Photo is the organization in photojournalism most explicit about its worldmaking project.

In October 2005, World Press Photo, an independent, nonprofit organization located in Amsterdam, commemorated its fiftieth anniversary by gathering many of the leading figures of the photojournalism industry together for a weekend. The chairman quoted above was discussing the world's largest photography exhibition; administered by World Press Photo, it travels to more than forty countries and is seen by more than 3.5 million people worldwide every year.[2] His comment implies that the very ability to host the World Press Photo exhibition had become a rung in the ladder of progress toward civilization, a sign that a country was now freer than it had been. The exhibition is the culmination of what is by many accounts, including the organization's self-description, the most prestigious photography competition in the world. Judged by an international jury that changes every year and is publicly announced, the competition results in a yearbook and an exhibition that then travels worldwide, including to Visa Pour l'Image.[3] The first exhibition is in Amsterdam, and all the winning photographers and many in the photojournalism world gather at the World Press Photo Awards Days every spring. Neutrality is often voiced as a core value by World Press Photo, along with the desire to be a platform for photojournalism rather than the vision of a single individual. Unlike Barnstorm and Visa Pour l'Image, World Press Photo is not the personal project of a single individual with whom people associate the organization. There is no equivalent of Eddie Adams or Jean-François Leroy. This is not to say that there aren't very charismatic people who work at World Press Photo but rather that there seems to be a concerted effort to prevent a single personality from dominating the institution.

At our first meeting in 2003, the director of World Press Photo emphasized to me that the organization was unique in the world of photojournalism because it was not a commercial organization producing, distributing, or publishing news. Rather, sponsored by the Dutch postcode lottery and Canon, it is an independent platform with a twofold mission: to generate wide public interest in and appreciation for the work of photographers and to support and advance high standards among professionals. He explained to me that it was by taking the annual exhibition on the road that World Press Photo had begun establishing connections with local photography organizations. Eventually it began receiving subsidies from the Dutch foreign ministry to subsidize the exhibition traveling to countries that could not fund it domestically, and as the exhibition and yearbook raised the profile of press photography, many more entries were sent in to the competition from more and more countries. In 1994 World Press Photo began organizing an annual "Masterclass," which brings together a few of the most respected individuals in photojournalism to share their knowledge and experience with a dozen young, promising photographers. As global photography networks were built, local organizations worldwide also asked for educational programs, and the idea for offering photojournalism seminars in developing countries was born. World Press Photo began offering a series of seminars specifically aimed at photojournalists in developing countries in an attempt to increase the expression of "democratic values" in the press. By 2005, seminars had been hosted by India, Macedonia, Mali, China, Sri Lanka, Uganda, Turkey, and Vietnam.[4]

In the same interview in which the director of World Press Photo emphasized to me the organization's unique status as a noncommercial entity and boasted of its competition's international entries and presence, he also specified, "We operate worldwide, but we are not an international organization in that we are all Dutch and I think it is important that we be so." On the day when he made this comment I had joined the staff for a typical Dutch lunch in the Amsterdam office: everyone sat around the kitchen table making simple sandwiches with the cheese and coldcuts on the table, coming and going as their schedules demanded. The director had explained his comment on the quintessential Dutchness of the organization by underlining that it made it easier to work in a casual environment in which everyone spoke the same language and sense of easy collegial understanding prevailed. As this chapter will make clear, this movement between national specificity and internationalism, even universalism, recurred again and again in World Press Photo's activities and the telling of its history.

By the time I joined the festivities for World Press Photo's fiftieth anniversary in 2005, I had attended the Annual Awards Days in Amsterdam (2004), seen the annual exhibit in several different countries, and participated in both the 2004 Masterclass and the seminar for photojournalists in Turkey that took place over the course of two years. In addition I had conducted interviews at World Press Photo's office in Amsterdam and had had many opportunities to spend time with World Press Photo staff at other events such as Visa Pour l'Image and the photojournalism panel at the 2004 World Association of Newspapers Forum. This chapter focuses on debates about aesthetics and ethics generated by World Press Photo activities of various scales. Specifically, I draw attention to the binaries that structure so many of these events: local/global, developing/developed, national/universal. What do appeals to universality and humanity make visible, and what do they obscure? What kind of a worldmaking project is World Press Photo?

HALF A CENTURY OF BALANCING WORLD VIEWS

Anniversaries are of course a time of amplified rhetoric making and ritualized performances. They are also a time to emphasize publicly an organization's values. The anniversary weekend comprised two different types of activities. The first was a series of symposia titled "Trends in the Industry," geared mainly to the industry professionals. The other activities were aimed at larger audiences served by photojournalism:

Things As They Are: Photojournalism in Context since 1955, a commissioned book and exhibition that opened at Foam, Amsterdam's International Photography Museum; and a gala celebration to which many dignitaries from the world of politics, diplomacy, and journalism at large had also been invited. These activities corresponded elegantly to World Press Photo's twofold mission of generating public appreciation for photography and supporting professional photojournalism.

The proceedings of World Press Photo's fiftieth-anniversary celebrations began with a cordial welcome address by its chairman, pitched at industry professionals. He emphasized that World Press Photo was about more than just photography and highlighted its connection to larger ideals such as the freedom of information: "I think that one of the most important decisions ever made in the existence of World Press Photo was in the nineties to invest in the future of our profession. To speak not only to the contests, to not only look at what already was there, but invest for example in countries that were lagging behind and teaching photographers. How to help many of you to be photographers who could just say a word and the world leapt. And I think that because some of these people, and I saw how their self-confidence grew, how they got their own opinions to stimulate the local newspapers and the local media they work for, and so I sincerely believe that we had some, some little contribution to their worlds. And that is what a free press is for I suppose." The chairman spoke also of the significance of the exhibition of award-winning photographs from the competition in countries from China to South Africa. It was in this context that he made the statement that opens this chapter, about moments when World Press Photo had been invited to countries following regime changes. He had spoken to viewers brought to tears by the mere possibility of hosting the exhibition. "It's more than photography," he said. It's also a contribution to freedom of speech, and I'm proud of that." Developing photographers, developing the press, and developing the world were thus articulated as joint projects.

He then reminded those in the industry about the organization's own development: "Fifty years ago three Dutch photographers had the idea to invite photographers from abroad to enter their pictures in a Dutch contest and they did and fifty years later it flourished, it became professional, it became international. What started in the cradle as an Amsterdam initiative to invite people from abroad is now a flourishing international organization based in Amsterdam, and you could ask, 'Why the Netherlands in 1955?' Maybe because those days in the middle of the cold war the Netherlands were seen as something in between." This in-between identity, something in the middle occupying in a neutral position, was central to how World Press Photo presented itself.

Alan Fare, a founder of an important photography agency, has been involved with World Press Photo since 1979, and he put the bridging function of the organization into historical perspective for me.

> It was developed in the mid-1950s at the height of the cold war. There were very little relations between capitalist and noncapitalist countries. The Dutch photographers who started it quickly realized they could do more and that as a small country they'd be perceived as neutral or at least less ideological. The initial jury members came from different nationalities—Russian, American, German, French, Dutch—all countries where there were strong traditions of photojournalism, but World Press Photo became the rare news organization that allowed content from both sides of the iron curtain. It was mainly the powers behind World War II who played a central role, as World Press Photo was meant to be a link between the socialist and capitalist worlds. The idea was to give this competition the status of the Nobel Prize in photography and give photojournalism status. Holland was perceived as another Switzerland.

When I inquired about World Press Photo's role today, Alan suggested that it had perhaps less geopolitical and human rights weight than it had had from the mid-1950s to the fall of the Berlin Wall. The organization had moved from being a bridge between divided worlds to being a central node of worldwide networks.

> It used to be extraordinary to attend the competition as a judge. This was the Olympics of the media, nothing like this existed in TV journalism or the written press. Today the world is a smaller place, but back then there was an essential component of bridging several political ideologies. Today the organization allows for a lot of networking, and perhaps that is what they see as a continuation of their work—to get people in difficult situations to connect with those who are better off. And to help those in America, Europe, and Japan to realize it is difficult to be a photographer in different parts of the world.

Both the chairman's address at the anniversary and Alan's comments stress the perceived neutrality of the Netherlands in 1955. By the 1950s the power of photography had been widely acknowledged in Western journalism and broader public culture. In 1955, the same year in which World Press Photo was founded, just a decade after the founding of the United Nations, Edward Steichen curated the *Family of Man* exhibition at MOMA. This exhibition, organized around humanity's supposedly universal experiences such as birth, childhood, love, the arts, and war, traveled the world until 1964. It was seen by over nine million people and remains one of the most successful photo exhibitions of all time. In other words, this was a time when there was both a significance to speaking about the world as a category of investigation and an emerging belief that how one visualized the world could itself be a political project.[5] At the time, the World Press Photo competition brought together jury members and images from different political ideologies, mainly those from the two sides of the cold war. Hence, Alan Fare's recollection of the competition as being "an Olympics of the media" underscores that judging it provided not only an occasion to celebrate the best photographic accomplishments but also an opportunity to encounter people coming from countries with very different political ideologies. In the introduction to a volume published in 1987 by the World Press Photo foundation, then director Joop Swart described the competition's international jury as the "United Nations of Press Photography."[6]

The fall of the Berlin wall and increased globalization in the 1990s complicated such a neat east–west geographical and political division, if that had ever been an accurate representation of lived experiences. World Press Photo's efforts seem to have turned more toward bridging not only ideological but also economic differences and significantly expanding the "world" it hoped to include in its competition and activities. By the time I began attending World Press Photo events in 2003, many in the organization were using the language of *north/south* and *global south* as well as *developed* and *developing* when describing their efforts as an institution.[7] I draw attention to these terms to highlight that World Press Photo from its inception not only has been a platform supporting photojournalism but has been enmeshed in the logics of development narratives. The idea of the photojournalist as an empathetic, noble, and brave observer, a lone figure who aids simply by shedding light on certain dark corners of the world, is a common trope in the photojournalism world and ever present at Barnstorm and Visa Pour l'Image. Whereas a development paradigm more familiar in institutions such as the UNDP or World Bank is much more apparent at World Press Photo events. The world in World Press Photo is not one that is given but one that can be developed through photography.

When I asked the director in 2003 about the current selection process for the jury, he explained the lengths they went to in order to have a jury representative of international photojournalism: "If we have a female photographer from North America, then we would try to balance that with a male photographer from Asia. . . . Editors and distributors, we try to reflect the various different aspects of the photography business." Yet, while he acknowledged that there was at times some confusion about what was and was not allowed among photographers, he emphasized that the jury members rely on the assumed integrity of photography: "The jury members take this integrity for granted. It is assumed that the photographers will respect the code within the profession." Hence, in the selection of jury members, as in many other activities that will be detailed in this chapter, there is a clear and intentional acknowledgment of significant diversity within the photojournalism community depending on a person's origins, gender, or role in the industry. Yet at the same time there is not only confidence that differences can be balanced and neutrality achieved by bringing together the right combination, but also a belief that there exists an unarticulated universal code of ethics that guides the profession. The various activities of World Press Photo provide an ideal site to interrogate this code because, depending on the activity, World Press Photo is involved in acknowledging, celebrating, and also teaching this code that it also presumes already exists everywhere.[8]

Whereas diverse government ideologies are perhaps somewhat easier to bridge by having representatives with different nationalities, there are inherent challenges in trying to bridge economic inequalities. Moreover, this challenge to having a balanced jury is also harder in an organization that regularly emphasizes universality. It is as if there were simultaneously a recognition of the importance of political ideology and the effects of the press, and yet a belief that somehow photographers and viewers around the world can all share in a universal ethics of photojournalism, separate from the specific press institutions and social, political, and economic realities of particular places in the world. I want to turn now to examples from two different World Press Photo workshops to look at ways in which these frictions became apparent: the two-year seminar offered to a group of photojournalists in Turkey; and the 2004 Masterclass held in Amsterdam

DEVELOPING PHOTOJOURNALISM IN ISTANBUL

Anna was exasperated with the young Turkish photojournalists whose photo assignments on the topic of the environment she had not found particularly impressive. "A big part of the assignment is connecting with people," she told them. "Ask questions. When you feel you've made a connection, that's when you start shooting, because that's when you can show me or anyone why this is important." It was the first day of session 2 of the World Press Photo Seminar organized by World Press Photo in Istanbul. The seminar comprised three sessions of a week each, roughy six months apart from one another. Around the table that day were a dozen photographers; Marijke, the Dutch World Press Photo coordinator; two Turkish mentors; and Anna and Eitan, the two non-Turkish "masters." Between sessions photographers had had several months to work on projects that they had submitted to the masters before the next session began. Anna, the disappointed master, was a highly respected photo editor in the photojournalism world and had most recently been a regional director for one of the major wire services' photography department. She was being courted by a visual content provider to head its news and editorial group. Everyone acknowledged that the environment projects had not been particularly successful. Anna tried to get the students engaged: "What do you want to attack now while we are here? What can we do for you, what can we show you?"

One female photographer confessed to having a hard time choosing opening shots in her layouts, and a male photographer who worked for a daily paper asked if they could go over how to present a story if it wasn't specifically shot on assignment for a particular client. Anna was clearly not getting the response she wanted. These were not the large issues she was sure must be on the photographers' minds. "Come on! You all have questions, you need to ask more questions. . . . My personal goal is to drag out of you your own very personal feelings and thoughts about what you're doing and how you wish your story would develop. Where do you want to go in your photographic life? So it's about making a personal connection with you. This goes beyond taking pictures. My goal is much deeper than that. We have to make the connection with you that we want you to make with your subjects." In other words, Anna was drawing a parallel between what she found lacking in the photographers' work—connection with the subjects— and a lack she felt in the seminar: the photographers were not sufficiently connecting with her and the other master.

The seminar was in English, but several of the photographers did not have adequate English language skills to follow the conversations, so others started translating. When Marijke expressed concern that one of the photographers was spending too much energy translating for the others, I took on the task of simultaneously translating the seminar.[9] However, the challenges to comprehension were not only linguistic. As the examples below will highlight, there were difference in how individuals understood the concepts of representations and representativeness. The Turkish mentors had chosen the participating photographers from applicants who had responded to ads in national newspapers. Over lunch at a small cafeteria-style restaurant nearby, one of the Turkish mentors conveyed to me his dismay that Marijke, the World Press Photo coordinator, had asked him why there weren't any Kurdish photographers in the group. "She tells me that she's heard that soldiers in the Southeast treat photographers very badly," he said. In fact, the mentor told me, he didn't know if any of the photographers were Kurdish and thought it would be awkward to ask. This same photographer has long been active politically in advocating for Kurdish rights, and he has since become part of a photography collective that has several Kurdish members. The issue here, then, is not whether this photographer recognized the Kurdish plight in Turkey but rather his not understanding how explicitly selecting Kurdish photographers for the World Press Photo seminars would address the issues. He did not understand why the selection process for the World Press Photo seminars should have included affirmative action based on certain identities. However, given how the jury for the World Press Photo competition is chosen, where there is an attempt to achieve neutrality through balancing representatives of different kinds, it makes sense that Marijke was looking for a similar logic in the selection of photographers in Turkey.

The Turkish mentor continued our conversation by broadening the scope of his comment on Marijke's criteria: "So those are the eyes through which she sees Turkey. So we see through the spectacles they give us. Every now and then we swap spectacles, but ultimately what is in conflict here are the spectacles." Indeed, over the course of the seminar, much of what the masters showed the young Turkish photographers was how to look through different spectacles. However, while exercises were presented as instructions in photojournalism, they were often perceived both by the Turkish mentors and some of the students as not only aesthetic recommendations but also ideological framings. There was often slippage between aesthetics and ethics in conversation. A key issue became how to understand the specific frame in which a particular debate occurred.

The television was on in the corner at the cafeteria where the group was eating lunch on the first day of the second session. Eitan, the Israeli photographer attending the seminar as one of the masters, had never before been to Turkey. During lunch he watched the music videos being shown on TV with great interest. Pointing to the screen where a female singer was grinding in suggestive garb in the music video of a chart-topping hit, he expressed surprise to the students around him: "Wow, how modern for a Muslim country." He was coding the singer's attire and dance moves as modern and contrasting them with his concept of Muslim. However, given that the artist in question was one of the country's most popular, the students did not understand what was remarkable about the video. I was reminded of Jock Sturges telling the photographers at Barnstorm, "In foreign countries, people often photograph what is different not significant." Yet since Eitan was the master photographer in Istanbul, what he saw as significant came to shape what he taught the students.

After lunch Marijke told the photographers they would be going on a walk with the masters: "They will show you some nice pictures in Istanbul. What they see in Istanbul." And so the group followed Anna and Eitan through the backstreets of Beyoğlu, a bustling downtown neighborhood. Some of the Turkish photographers were from out of town, others had never been down these alleyways, and still others knew them very well. As noted above, Anna had been to Istanbul before, but it was Eitan's first visit. He got quite excited when through his viewfinder he spotted a man selling brooms approaching in the street. He stopped and addressed the students while composing his frame. "This is a great picture. Now I wait until something very specific walks into my frame." Eitan had been telling the photographers about the importance of a human presence in any shot. Once he found what he wanted to photograph, he told them, he would frame the shot and then wait for something to move into the frame that would make it interesting. Unlike a setup where he would have asked someone to take a certain pose or behave in a certain manner for the camera, Eitan explained that framing the shot and waiting for the perfect moment was not in any way problematic. Eitan's secret to a good photograph was to look for a good frame, compose it well, and then wait for a moment.

Eitan was also trying to get the students to think about how they might later pitch these photographs and therefore encouraging them to think about what topics might sell. On a main street crowded with people Eitan instructed the students to "look for Islamic content stories." Alternately he offered, "The European Union. Just go with an idea." He was anticipating what anthropologist Ulf Hannerz calls "story lines" that would make international editors interested in particular images from Istanbul.[10] Moreover, he was trying to capture visual contrasts that would be easy to pitch as visualizations of "story lines." Eitan stopped in front of a lingerie store and framed his shot. He waited once again, explaining his strategy to the group: "Let's wait to see someone come by. Maybe a religious man will walk by and think this is ridiculous." Eventually a woman covered from head to toe in a black chador passed, and Eitan got the contrast he was looking for, untroubled by the fact that the woman was somewhat incongruous with the swarms of people buzzing by in this neighborhood. Some of the Turkish photographers were smiling at the fact that there were signs in the lingerie store's window wishing customers a happy Mother's Day, suggesting that racy lingerie might make a good gift for mom, but this detail was lost on the non-Turkish speakers. In other words, the Turkish students had also caught what they perceived to be a contrast—motherhood versus sexy femininity—but it did not translate into a visual binary and required Turkish language skills. Eitan's contrast trumped that noticed by the Turkish photographers.

The group left the main street and headed down the alleys. Anna marveled at the intricate webs of laundry hung to dry between the buildings. A man pushing a wooden cart piled high with cucumbers for sale passed the photographers, and Eitan, gathering all of them together, said, "The whole group just walked in front of a very interesting photo without stopping." Peering back at the cucumber salesman, he continued, "There it is: old world/new world. Small hand/big hand of economy." While some of the photographers had not been down these particular side streets or perhaps others like them, neither the layers of laundry nor the cucumber seller had caught their attention. It wasn't merely that these were familiar sights in certain neighborhoods, but also that the photographers were not seeing through the binaries in which Eitan was narrating the potential frames. As the Turkish mentor had suggested, it was a negotiation of spectacles. Eitan and Anna were showing the students what to see, how to visualize modernity or development versus tradition. Given the conversations among image brokers at *Newsworld* highlighted in chapter 4, the masters were also anticipating how the text editors might make sense of the images.

These contrasts and binaries work in different ways, but not all were being observed by the photographers. For instance, Eitan took a photo of an older woman; caught unawares, she was visibly upset to have her picture snapped. She began grumbling. To appease her, the Turkish mentor apologized and said she was justified in her irritation. Eitan and the young photographers moved on, but the Turkish mentor stayed with the woman a few minutes longer, apologizing all the while. The woman continued in anger, "Are you not at all civilized? Why take photographs without asking permission?" The irony here, of course, is the different actors' use of a presumably universal notion of civilization. Eitan had photographed her as a traditional older woman in a part of town where laundry is still strung between buildings, implying a distance between her and a more modern civilization elsewhere, whereas the subject herself was questioning the civility of taking photographs without permission: a clash of civilizations.

The issue of old and new worlds, centers and peripheries of civilization, and photographs of progress narratives emerged again the following day when Nico, an Albanian photographer, shared his portfolio with the group as a PowerPoint slideshow. Nico had taken part in the World Press Photo seminar in the Balkans and had been invited to Istanbul by the Turkish mentors based on his work. During introductions the day before Nico had explained his work as mostly feature stories and a lot of fashion photography. "Everything for money, everything for art," he'd said. Eitan had jovially responded, "That's called [being] a photo whore."[11] Nico's portfolio reflected the diversity of his work—from color fashion photography to black-and-white images of rural life in Albania complete with folk festivals and weddings.

Both Anna and Eitan had quite strong reactions to the portfolio. Eitan jumped in first:

> You have a big opportunity here. You are a good photographer with a good eye and you have the ability to document change in Albania. This is perhaps not a politically correct way to say it, but turn the disadvantage of living in a small country, a developing country, into an advantage for yourself. You have the opportunity to document Albania as it changes. Don't try to compete with fashion week in Paris. Albania will someday come to the level of Europe and there will be time for that. But for now document that which will change in the next ten years. If you document Albania over the next ten years I promise you in ten years you will have an amazing book and a book that no one can compete with because I don't think Albania is being documented by many good photographers. Take advantage of the fact that you live there and speak the language and can get to know the people. Because other photographers may just fly in for a few days and shoot a war and then leave.

Anna also steered Nico in the direction of his black-and-white work, insisting it was far superior to his color fashion photography: "You have a great eye for details in ordinary life. . . . Even though you like it a lot, your fashion photos do not have the same sense of irony that your black and whites have. I am guessing you are distracted by the young women." Then she connected Nico's work with the walk exercise from the afternoon before: "This is exactly the type of thing we were trying to show you yesterday. I know many of you didn't understand what we were pointing out to you yesterday and said, 'But this is the type of thing that we see all the time.' But that is exactly what we want you to do: document that which is everyday and ordinary."

Anna encouraged the students to capture the everyday and ordinary, but she was framing their everyday in relation to a global modernity that had not yet quite arrived.[12] The everyday of fashion photographs was deemed not interesting. While both masters were drawn to the black-and-white images of a timeless Albanian village, the implicit agreement appeared to be that fashion shows could not possibly capture a changing Albania. These conversations recalled the comments I had heard at *Newsworld* and elsewhere appreciating photographs that looked as if they were out of a historical film, photographs that seemed almost "pre modern," to use text editor Joel's term.[13]

The following day I asked Eitan why he had seemed hesitant while making his comments. "The hesitation came from referring to Albania as a third-world country," he answered, "because I was there in '94 and for sure it was a third-world country then. OK, 'developing country' sounds better. . . . I'm not sure it's appropriate to tell someone that he is from a third-world country. But I'm sure [Nico] knows; he's an intelligent guy." In other words, any hesitation on Eitan's part concerned how to characterize Albania in a politically correct manner—not the ramifications of suggesting the equivalent of a salvage ethnography project in the early twenty-first century.[14] What is being valued here is visual contrast, documenting difference from "a pictorial view." Eitan is encouraging Nico to capture photographically time out of joint with a European center.[15]

Like Ilan, the photographer originally intended for the embed position that launched Alex Levy's career as described in chapter 2, Eitan knew firsthand the challenges of being a photographer whose travel is restricted:

I must say that there is nothing more depressing than being a photojournalist with an Israeli passport because in most cases the politics today has a lot to do with Muslims and I can't enter any Muslim country at all. You know all my friends are on their way to Baghdad and I sit at home sulking. . . . I can't go to Afghanistan either, same problem. It's very depressing. . . . I have great feelings for covering conflict and I have one in my backyard, which is very hard for me to cover. . . . I don't see myself living anywhere else. . . . This is why I travel once or twice a year to New York. I see the magazines, have lunch with the editors, visit the agencies. I discuss what I want to do with my editors for next year, brainstorm ideas, and so on. . . .

Because Israel is very isolated I think that photography is not really developed . . . and I don't want to be good compared to the Israeli photographer, I want to be good, period. I want to be inspired by things happening outside of Israel. I go to magazine shops once a week to see who did what, who was where, who got one of the best pictures out of something, whatever. I learn photography from magazines and photography books. . . .

This is what I told some of the guys that I spoke to yesterday. Don't put everything you have on your website, because when a photo editor wants to assign you, he has to know exactly what kind of photographer you are. Don't show him that you can do fashion and portraits and et cetera, because when he gets to the end of the website, he doesn't know what to give you. . . . I have reached the point where editors think about Israel and my name pops up. I pay the price that they don't think about sending me all over the world for a lot of reasons probably, especially the fact that I can hardly travel anywhere with my Israeli passport. But at least I know that in my backyard, there is no doubt that my name will come up."

Because Eitan has limited mobility as a combat photographer who wants to cover conflicts that concern the mainstream Western media, he himself regularly goes to New York, a center of photojournalism, to keep editors interested in his work. He tries to turn his immobility into a strength by marketing himself as a photographer who automatically comes to mind if an editor is looking for a photographer to cover an event in Israel. The advice he gave Turkish photographers and Nico was that similarly they should focus on gaining a reputation as local photographers, experts on their home country. He boasted about the fact that when anything happens in Israel he knows before anybody else because he has long-standing relationships with ambulance drivers who call him while rushing to the site of an incident. He has a motorcycle and is often the first on the scene. Yet Eitan spoke openly about the importance of his getting recognition in New York. His work was represented and distributed by an agency in New York, and they helped him maintain connections with image brokers in New York.[16]

Eitan was not simply a local photographer, then, but a local photographer who understood the needs of image brokers at the center of the photojournalism world. Hence, he followed publications, such as *Newsworld,* that inspired him every week and kept him abreast of trends in the industry. Moreover, his readership of these magazines clearly influenced the advice he gave the young photographers. The images in *Newsworld* serve as powerful formative fictions, not only influencing whatever Eitan might think about specific topics but, moreover, influencing how he visualizes news events and, as was the case in Istanbul, how he teaches other photographers. Marijke had brought with her several World Press Photo yearbooks from past years, and the Turkish photographers were very appreciative of these. "We look through them for ideas on how to shoot," one of them told me afterward.

What Eitan did not acknowledge to the Turkish photographers is that Albania or Turkey rarely gets the journalistic attention regularly given to Israel in the North American and European press. Moreover, while many of the Turkish photographers also followed North American and European newsmagazines carefully to educate their eye and stay abreast of industry trends, they rarely had the connections or funds to be able to make personal connections with editors and visit them to show their portfolios in person. During the World Press Photo seminars they were being trained by masters used to working for, if not at, the centers of the photojournalism industry. There was little acknowledgment that they would likely have local careers. Moreover, there were no senior journalists from the Turkish press who might actually provide information about work opportunities at home, and indeed there weren't many. In conversations I had with the photographers it was clear that they were unsure as to whether they should be trying to launch global careers and aim to get international assignments from magazines in the centers of photojournalism, or whether they should be focusing on becoming the photographer that comes to mind when any editor thinks of covering an event or feature in Turkey. Furthermore, with news publications forced to reduce their budgets and reluctant to fly photographers to the other side of the world, there was a growing trend of Western photographers basing themselves abroad. Istanbul in particular was beginning to be a top choice as a foreign base for several such photographers. Were the Turkish photographers supposed to compete with them?

Coincidentally, the third and final session of the World Press Photo seminar offered in Istanbul took place in November 2003 just a week after Turkey made headlines in the international news: a bombing at the British consulate and HSBC bank's headquarters killed forty people and wounded four hundred. Even though most of the casualties were

Turkish citizens, some claimed that the British targets indicated that the attacks had been planned to coincide with President George W. Bush's visit to England. The local photography foundation where the group had met for the first two sessions was located directly across from the British consulate. The bomb had exploded just a few meters from the front room in which Eitan had encouraged Nico to focus his photography on Albania, and was one of many buildings severely damaged by the explosion. In fact, had the workshop dates not been moved at the last moment, the photographers, World Press staff, and I could have found ourselves victims of the attack rather than in the position of evaluating the coverage of it a week afterward.

At the third session of the seminar, a few of the photographers who had covered the bombings shared their work with the others. However, the person whose work had gotten the most play was Lyndsey Addario, a photographer then based in Istanbul and frequently on assignment for the *New York Times* and *Newsworld*.[17] Many of the photographers at the seminar admired Addario's work, including her coverage of the bombings. Moreover, although several of the photographers had been in the neighborhood, they talked about not feeling comfortable taking photographs of the carnage and the immediate aftermath of the bombings. Their images focused more on shopkeepers' efforts to clean up later in the day.[18] It was precisely their personal connections with the site of the incident and those in the neighborhood that they claimed proved an obstacle to their producing images they could sell to the international press.

Furthermore, they were exceptionally slow. I was still doing fieldwork at GVI at the time of the attacks and immediately called to see if any in the group had photographs. Instructed to do so by Ed, I had asked them to send via FTP any photographs shot that day. Years later they confessed it had taken then much effort just to figure out what FTP was (File Transfer Protocol), let alone how to send images by using it. They had not asked, fearing that this might make them look unprofessional and ill equipped for the digital age. Some of their images might have gotten picked up for showing a different view of the events, but it took more than a day for them to arrive. There were Turkish photographers working for wire services who did cover the bombings extensively. However, for the group at the World Press Photo seminar, their local connection to the events prevented them from being able to visualize it as a global media event, at least not quickly enough for global newstime.

Anna was once again present as a master at the last Istanbul seminar. She was joined by Alan Fare, the head of one of the long-standing photo agencies that had not been bought up in the acquisition frenzy of the industry's digitalization. As mentioned at the beginning of the chapter, Alan had been involved with World Press Photo activities for decades. The third master was a Malian photographer and director of the Bamako Photo Festival. This time, when not editing student work on the topic of gender, the masters presented a wide range of other photographers' work: among their selections, a Chinese newspaper photographer's work during the Cultural Revolution, an Argentinian photographer's portrait of Buenos Aires, and a New York photographer's long-term project about prostitution and drugs that had required her to have very close relations with her subjects. Many of the conversations during the final World Press Photo seminar in Istanbul centered on the type of relations with subjects demanded by different stories, and the ethics of these relations. Students were being told never to edit for a particular magazine but instead always to edit for the story.[19] The implication seemed to be that a photographer's responsibility toward his or her subject was clear and was independent of the context in which the images might be published.

One master, Alan Fare, also emphasized that the key was never to mislead the reader. If for the purpose of a story they needed to ask a subject to pose, that was fine as long as they indicated this to the reader. This of course requires shooting for a particular reader and having significant contact with the image brokers who will use the images rather than the practice that was common among the Turkish photographers at the workshop of either putting their work on a collective's website and hoping it might get picked up now or in the future or sending material to a foreign agency and every now and then getting a check for the rare sale, often to magazines unknown to them. Fare also pointed out that in the case of the Chinese photographer whose work was now being presented as critical and dissident images, his own newspaper had used his images at the time they were taken as propaganda for the regime. He underscored that the ethical choices available to a photographer did not fully determine the ends to which his images might be used. One of the challenges to ethical photography is time itself. The photographer's decision to photograph an event can be significantly separated both temporally and institutionally from an image broker's decision to publish it, and yet the discussions of ethics during the seminars mostly focused on the decisions made by the individual photographers as they were shooting.[20] Fare's presentation allowed the students to differentiate between ethics within a particular frame and the ethics of a particular geopolitical framing itself.

The group was particularly interested in the issue of ethics because there had been much debate after the Israeli master Eitan's presentation at the second seminar. Eitan had presented a very intimate portrayal of a nineteen-year-old Israeli soldier's rehabilitation after losing both of his legs. Eitan had insisted he had taken an objective approach to the story, and presented his project as a balanced reportage. Whereas the students felt that by the very nature of the conflict in which this soldier had lost his limbs, Eitan's position as an Israeli photographer and the fact that the project centered on just one individual meant that the story was a subjective piece. Rather than critiquing this bias, however, the Turkish photographers had merely been surprised that Eitan insisted on maintaining that his position was neutral whereas they interpreted his work as politically engaged photography to be commended precisely for being clear about its politics. In this moment of friction the spectacles that were in conflict with one another had to do with what objectivity might mean. Eitan was presenting a version of objectivity that had to do with whether he was being truthful and avoiding set-up images. In other words, he felt he had been ethical in his relationship with the subject and truthful toward his reader, whereas the students were asking questions about ethics in a larger context and couldn't understand how anyone could make intimate portraits of a wounded soldier in the context of contemporary Israel and claim objectivity. For Eitan, Anna, and some of the staff from World Press Photo, the dispute about objectivity was interpreted partly as an issue of the Turkish students' assumed opposition to Israel and sympathy with the Palestinian cause. In my discussions with the photographers after the seminar ended, some of them did express general opinions about Israel–Palestine relations. However, their more nuanced questioning of the very possibility or desirability of an objective approach to such a subject was eclipsed by their assumed sympathy for Palestinians. In other words, the Turkish students were arguing that nationality and geopolitics inevitably structured the conditions of Eitan's project and its reception. That their critique was dismissed as inevitably a reflection of their assumed sympathy for Palestine proves their point.

By the time of the last seminar, this memory of Eitan's presentation had spurred the Turkish photographers to differentiate between honesty and objectivity. Alan Fare gave the example of a photograph taken by Ken Jarecke, an American photographer active during the first Gulf war, of a dead Iraqi soldier charred at the wheel of his vehicle. The UK's *Observer* had been the only publication to print it, with other publications claiming that it was not in "good taste."[21] Fare emphasized that even when a photographer took certain images with ethical considerations in mind, the politics of editing could keep certain images out of the press. In other words, Alan was making clear to the students that image brokers other than photographers also make decisions based on beliefs and ethics and that these considerations often determine the circulation of news images. Once again, Fare differentiated between the ethics framing a particular context and the ethical choices made by a photograph in constructing a particular photographic frame.

Many of the Turkish photographers understood all too well that they did not have full control over their images. One of the Turkish mentors had told the story of how, several decades earlier, his collection of photographs of union rallies had been confiscated by the police for purposes of identifying individuals. Hence, while there was genuine disagreement in the group about what constituted staging in photography, they were all aware that their photographs could be used for purposes very different from their intentions when taking them. The Turkish students did not believe that photographs spoke for themselves, and certainly didn't believe that their own personal intentions as photographers adhered to the images. After all, their mentor had given an example of powerful images of collective action doubling as visual arrest warrants. The myth of the universally legible image that shed light in and of itself did not seem to hold much sway for them.

The seminar closed with conversations about how the photographers might build their careers. The seminar attendees were very interested in how to approach foreign markets and were given lots of advice: "Attending workshops is a good start. Go to festivals like Perpignan [i.e., Visa Pour l'Image, described in chapter 6] and build a network." They were also encouraged to sell their images through agencies that had international reach and to develop an understanding of what gets published in which publications. Again and again the importance of contacts was underscored. Alan stressed, "People prefer to work with people they know, because they want to trust them and know that they have mutual understanding and good communication. Recommendations help."[22] In other words, the suggestion was that even in a digital age when their photographs might circulate, the photographers also had to find the means to go to certain centers of photojournalism to build their networks. Despite its global reach, photojournalism as presented at the World Press Photo seminars was a personal business, and face-to-face meetings mattered. Hence, photography, at least in terms of getting assignments, was clearly not beyond translation, nor were opportunities universal. Language was a key factor, as were connections. Yet at the same time the attendees were being reminded that publications had smaller and smaller budgets and fewer pages to dedicate to photography, and that they ought to seek out other ways of publishing their work, whether through exhibitions or books.

INSIDE/OUTSIGHT

The seminar in Turkey culminated in an exhibition that opened during World Press Photo Awards Days in Amsterdam in April 2004. The exhibition was titled *Inside/Outsight,* as were the accompanying two volumes, and combined the work from the seminars in the Balkans, Mali, Uganda, Turkey, China, Sri Lanka, and India.[23] The work from the seminars was exhibited at the same weekend celebrating the winners of the prestigious annual photojournalism festival, a peripheral event for the main Awards Days. While not technically a binary, the title *Inside/Outsight* certainly suggested that the work of the seminar participants be seen as photography by local insiders and recalled the Turkish mentor's comment about conflicting spectacles. What was left out of sight, and who was showing whom what to see? In his introduction to the volumes, the director of World Press Photo emphasized visual storytelling: "Some exercises such as producing a picture story were mandatory for all groups. . . . The photo stories presented in these two books show how different photographers with very diverse cultural references interpreted the two themes [i.e., gender and environment]. Together these essays afford fascinating insights into the way in which issues of gender and environment fit into the worlds of these local journalists. While the books do not offer an exhaustive treatment of the issues addressed, they do provide perspectives rarely available to international audiences." Yet, just like the Iraqi photographer's work featured in Visa Pour l'Image that was described in chapter 6, the images of the photographers from these seminars were not presented as stories; rather, they were single images grouped into various themes chosen by an editor. The seminars had taught all the photographers how to shoot and layout photo essays. Why, then, the absence of a story format in the final publication?

One answer might be found in the second introduction to the books, penned by the Dutch Minister for Development Cooperation, Agnes van Ardenne. The seminars in the developing world were, after all, funded by her ministry, and her focus seems to be entirely on single images: "A powerful image can mobilize public opinion and influence political decision-making. The harrowing images of starving Ethiopian children in the early 1980s speeded up food aid to the country. The famous photograph of a Vietnamese girl caught in a napalm attack influenced world opinion on the Vietnam war."[24] Furthermore, she concludes that the power of images is stronger in developing countries with millions who are illiterate and poorly educated. So perhaps forgoing the presentation of individual photographers' stories as photo essays that might have hinted at their personal styles or approaches to the material is the compromise World Press Photo itself had to agree to in order to finance the project. The minister's introduction also tells us, "Gender and environment also happen to be two priorities of Dutch development policy." It was the funding agency rather than the photographers or World Press Photo that determined the topics to be explored. [25]

The minster's note ends on a hopeful progress narrative: "I am sure that World Press Photo will manage to build as strong a name for itself in the developing world as it has in Europe and North America. Perhaps one day, the winning photograph will not be just about Africa, South Asia or Latin America but will also come from there." The irony, of course, is that the napalm girl photograph so celebrated by the minister did come "from there," if by that she means taken by a Vietnamese photographer. Or is the Vietnamese photographer's "from there"-ness trumped by his working for Associated Press, an American wire service, or his image's alleged impact on American viewers? What determines a photograph's provenance? The nationality of the photographer? The residence of the photographer? Its means of circulation? Perhaps we ought to ask what photographs "from there" would show that photographs "from here" don't and whether the very paradigm of development might be preventing the circulation of different points of view. Of course it is important not to conflate the minister's words with World Press Photo's values as a photography platform, yet as the spokesperson for the financing of World Press Photo's activities in developing countries, by her comments she give us a sense of the conditions of possibility for World Press Photo's work, the frame in which the organization could function.

Two of the Turkish photographers attended the weekend awards ceremonies in Amsterdam, and while they enjoyed the presentations by the prize-winning photographers of World Press Photo competition 2004, they were much less comfortable around the *Inside/Outsight* exhibition or at the dinner organized for seminar participants and masters. As they commented to me later, they were uncomfortable being engaged with not as individual photographers with particular styles or particular portfolios but as photographers of a particular developing nation. Unlike the award winners, they did not have an opportunity to show a portfolio or talk about their work. Professionally they were represented only by the single photographs they had in the show. Although grateful for the opportunity to attend Award Days, they told me repeatedly that they were not comfortable being ambassadors of Turkish photography. Thus, they brought to my attention the frictions of developing the world through photography.

GROOMING A MASTERCLASS

The issue of ethics and questions about considering alternative markets for one's work were also central topics in the 2004 World Press Photo Joop Swart Masterclass held in Amsterdam for one dozen young photographers chosen by an international jury. Every year the photographers in the Masterclass are asked to arrive having prepared an assignment on a given theme ("pride" was the 2004 theme) that forms the basis of the final catalogue and exhibition. The invited masters give presentations on their own work or, if they are editors or art historians, lecture about some element of the industry or photography. In 2004 the participant photographers and masters worked together to come up with edits of each photographer's project. The focus of the Masterclass was on the individual career trajectories of each photographer: over the course of six days photographers met individually for forty minutes with each of the masters, showing their portfolios and often discussing how they might further develop their personal vision.[26]

The head of the developing-country seminar programs at World Press Photo had explained to me that "the whole idea of the seminars [in developing countries] came out of the idea of the fact that there were no photographers from the south in the Masterclass so the seminars in other countries were designed to increase photographers from the south." His use of the language of north/south here reflects the development paradigm of World Press Photo described earlier. If the seminars in developing countries were about developing each country's national press by developing its photographers, the Masterclass was about developing individual talents. Whereas during the seminars in Istanbul the framework of Turkey had been impossible to escape, partly because a national focus had been central to everything from securing funding to choosing photographers, the Masterclass was clearly celebrated for being global; the focus was on the personal vision of the photographers rather than on what they communicated about their home countries.

Attending Masterclass that year were three prominent photographers, two photo editors, and a historian of photography. A renowned curator had been asked to curate the exhibition of photographs submitted by the young photographers without having met them or heard them contextualize their work. Marijke, who had managed the Istanbul seminars and was in charge of running the 2004 Masterclass, expressed some trepidation about this experiment: "It could be controversial to do an edit for an art exhibition based purely on hard news images. Some will like it, others not."[27] Moreover, while the goal of the Masterclass is to give students from different parts of the world the unique opportunity to discuss various ethical, technical, journalistic, and emotional aspects of their photojournalistic work, several of the photographers had projects more easily classified as art photography. Then again, as Stewart, one of the master photographers, put it, "Interesting photographs often resist easy categorization."

The young photographers were all under thirty-five and had garnered significant accolades, from prizes to publication in prestigious magazines and newspapers. The photographers chosen for the Masterclass are nominated by a number of independent international committees and invited to submit a portfolio for review. Hence, they must already have some level of professional contacts just to get nominated. In 2004, most of the photographers had about four or five years of professional experience. One photographer—Alex Levy, whose break into professional photography is described in chapter 2—had been working for major publications only since 2003. His rapid success had gained much attention. Of the twelve photographers chosen, four were American, and the others came from Denmark, Sweden, Canada, Hungary, England, Slovakia, France, and Latvia. Yet these national identities were somewhat misleading since so many of the photographers had complex national ties, such as the Peruvian-born, Spanish-educated American or the Russian-born Hungarian. The British photographer with a Norwegian parent had spent the first twenty-four years of his life in Norway, and he had discovered photography while doing his military service there. The very international makeup of both nominations and those selected was constantly underscored; collectively Masterclass participants were representative of a world. This desire for worldwide representation means that nationality is never entirely absent in World Press Photo activities. In fact, during initial introductions, the very first photographer to speak during the 2004 Masterclass subtly underlined the arbitrariness of being identified as a photographer from a particular place: "I am from a small country near the Baltic Sea, though I don't know if that says much about me or my country."

One of the honors of attending the Masterclass was getting personalized attention from illustrious editors and photographers whom many of the young photographers revered. One young photographer had been applying to join Magnum, the prestigious photography agency, and found herself showing her portfolio to a Magnum photographer who had seen her application during deliberations at Magnum and could assure her that she was getting as far as the finals but not quite making it yet. The photographers also enjoyed seeing one another's work. One photographer told me, "It's stimulating to see the images of other people of my generation. I've been educated by people of an older generation." In fact, while the young photographers were thrilled to get feedback from the highly regarded masters, the radically different conditions facing this new generation of photographer were a major topic throughout the week. How much of the advice they had gotten was still valid? many of the young photographers asked.

Susan, the highly respected managing photo editor at *Newsworld,* acknowledged the group directly as "a new generation of photographer," and continued, "You've never shot film. There is a revolution in the industry." For Susan on whose desk one could still find a loupe, this revolution had to do with how much editorial control now lay in the hands of the photographer. Addressing the photographers, she continued:

> In the digital world, I have a lot less understanding of the photographer.
> I used to edit film. They would send me raw film, you know. I would have twenty-five rolls one day, and twenty-five rolls the next day and twenty-five rolls the next day, so I'd sit at my table and follow the photographer around everything they shot. The first time I ever went to Havana, Cuba, I was with a group of people who had been there before and we were lost. . . . I had never been there before. . . . I said, "Just trust me," and so I took the four people and we went down this road, down this alley, and we came out exactly where we were supposed to be, and they said, "How the hell did you do that?" I'd walked down this street with four or five photographers. I'd never been there, but I recognized that landmark and that corner and I have déjà vu like nobody's business and I've never been somewhere and I've been there

many times, so I feel like that's how I lived my life as a picture editor in the beginning of my career. It was very vicarious, because I felt like I was with the photographers all the time. That doesn't exist anymore, now you're shooting digital. . . . So my relationship with photographers now is entirely different. I don't know what else they were shooting, I only know what twelve pictures they decided to send me from their edit so you have a lot more control over it, but I have a lot less understanding of the photographer.

Lamenting the fact that most young photographers sent in only twelve to twenty frames, Susan told them, "The photographer is making those decisions, so it's very important that you learn to be very disciplined about editing." She encouraged them to send more images to their editors to give the editors more opportunity to see what they were like as photographers, and she encouraged them to return to their material once they had returned from an assignment. "I have a huge amount of distance," she said. "That's what's useful as a picture editor." She feared that many important images were being lost as photographers stayed up late after working all day, making editorial choices that they then never reconsidered. In a sense, then, what Masterclass was providing this small group of young photographers was a weeklong exposure to the type of relationship with editors that an older generation shooting film might have taken for granted. The young photographers were hungry for precisely the kind of editorial probing and conversation that the best image brokers can provide.

Other masters discussed dramatic changes in the business of photography. Daphne had been in the business for well over two decades, first at a small but highly successful photo agency in the days when "pictures were really decisive in the press," then at Magnum, and finally at a major wire service. Or as she put it, after spending ten years basically producing what the market needed and wanted, she spent the next decade trying to impose upon the market what top photographers wanted. Now at a wire service she worked with hundreds of photographers, many of whom are from the place that they photograph. She acknowledged right from the beginning that all of them would need to think about their own particular situation and then gave a history of the development of agencies in broad brushstrokes:

Any agency is always linked to the marketplace. Whatever an agency presents itself like, whatever they say about themselves, if they exist it's because they are making money somewhere. It's always a compromise. It is a constant balance between risk and profit, and if it's an ambitious agency, it's basically a balance between ambition and survival within the photography industry. . . . When you wonder about an agency, the first question is, Where does the money come from? If you answer that question it will tell you a lot about where your agency is heading, how long it will last, and what ultimately it can do for you.[28]

In the earliest days of photojournalism, Daphne emphasized, photographers were not identified with agencies but rather with the publications they worked with, where they were intimately linked to the writing staff. Eventually there was more of a differentiation between text and photo. *Newsworld* had remained an exception, because the magazine was identified by its photographers. However, as Susan pointed out to the students, even *Newsworld* had no staff photographers anymore. It had a few contract photographers who were guaranteed a certain amount of work (say, twenty days a year or one hundred days a year), but all of them were freelancers. Echoing what I had learned from the sales team at GVI, Daphne also pointed out that across publications there had been a shift in content: "Now a lot of it is lifestyle and entertainment: food and clothing are getting a lot of play."

The themes raised by Daphne and Susan echoed what I had learned at several other sites in the photojournalism industry—the rule of text, the balance between commercial pragmatism and idealism, or between journalistic and artistic freedom and compromise, and the need for timeless lifestyle photographs that could provide worldwide visual content—and came up repeatedly throughout the week. However, this time the emphasis was on how these particular photographers might best negotiate current industry conditions in the interest of their personal goals. Let me turn to some specific conversations to illustrate the types of dilemmas these young professionals, the first generation of digital photographers, were grappling with at this moment of radical change in the industry. In them you will hear the challenges brought by digitalization analyzed throughout this book. Because the uncertainty of the industry's future was as unsettling for the masters as for the students, these conversations moved between mentoring and often sounded more like collective brainstorming sessions. The past was a lot easier to talk about than the future.

Johan, an established Swedish photographer and one of the masters, structured his talk as a retrospective of his work, highlighting his own career shifts:

I'm going to talk to you about working at a newspaper because twenty-five years ago I wanted to become a staff photographer because the staffers got all the good assignments. Today I'm better off as a freelancer. I began in sports because I had this idea that a good sports photographer would be great at shooting anything. I got used to working fast. At the end of two days I had all the photos I needed then I had a turning point and got to spend two weeks at a refugee camp. At a newspaper it's very hard to get time to do a good story. When you work in a newspaper you almost drown in daily projects. I get depressed if I don't have something of my own going on [an outside project that can have a different timeline than daily staff assignments for the paper]. I worked for a wealthy Swedish paper; they sent their own photographers and reporters to almost every big world event. They had three staff photographers at the first Gulf war. I was in Saudi Arabia but there was no chance I could get in the pool [the small group of journalists chosen to cover a limited-access event who, in exchange for their access, have to share their images with all others] or on a trip to the border because I worked for this Swedish newspaper that none of the US press officers had heard of. In the late nineties many newspapers had to cut their budgets due to falling circulation and falling advertising budgets. I quit and became a freelancer. I ended up covering the Iraq war for the same newspaper, but I had to make my own preparations and get insurance. I could also work for other newspapers. I traveled with a Norwegian journalist and shot for her magazine as well. This year I worked on the Bam earthquake.[29] There were several newspapers sending reporters but not photographers, so I got freelance assignments for three different papers. If I compare my time as a freelancer to my time as staff. I miss the monthly paycheck, but otherwise I like the control and freedom I have to do these projects. For example, in Iraq when Swedish newspapers were calling their reporters back to Sweden [out of safety concerns], I had the freedom to stay.

Daphne contextualized Johan's golden years at a newspaper by pointing out that the per capita newspaper circulation in Scandinavia was still one of the world's highest, making it a region very privileged in terms of the kinds of opportunities for staffers. Another master, Bruce, a well-known conflict photographer, underscored the importance of relations with writers: "Newspapers are run by word people. So are the magazines, even if they have photo editors. So the thing to do is form good relations with some of the best writers, because they will listen to them." Many of the young photographers' experiences confirmed this. When one student asked if photographers could still pursue their own ideas when working with a writer, Michael, a student working for an American newspaper, answered, "It helps if the writer is behind it as well. Especially with a foreign trip, they won't go with it if it's just a photo essay, so it really helps to have a writer behind it. So a lot of times you go with a writer to a place and then do your own work as well." Johan's narrative also pointed out how freelance photographers could take advantage of publications or news organizations prioritizing sending writers over photographers by teaming up with those writers once in the field.

Later it became clear that Johan's presentation had resonated with the Michael, the young staff photographer working for an American newspaper, because he was trying to make a key career decision; he was thinking about leaving his paper. Daphne discovered this when she asked him what the purpose of his portfolio was, since he was already on staff at a paper and hence did not need to constantly show his work in order to generate more assignments. Turning from images of Gaza to those of Iraq and Afghanistan, Daphne advised him about how the portfolio could be arranged to make him more competitive: "You have a very difficult portfolio. You've shot some of the most difficult and most shot issues in photojournalism. Editors have seen too much of this. . . . Try to find a line, and don't sort them by news story; mix them photographically just to catch people's interest. Present it differently. Show your more enigmatic images so that people wonder what is happening." Michael had been with his paper for over three years. His main concern was not having editorial guidance: "Most of these images have never been published. I'm on my own. I have no direction. I'm a bit confused about what I should do next. . . . It's a weird balance I'm trying to keep between the types of pictures I'd like to take versus those the paper expects."

Daphne said she could see the dilemma: "My feeling is that you are in between a magazine and a newspaper photographer: you're not always shooting a story but you're also not exclusively a single-image photographer." Michael liked shooting abroad, documenting conflict and social issues. Daphne offered some advice: "Create a more determined style. In each isolated image try to get at something bigger. . . . Right now this is a generic portfolio; you don't yet have a style. That's not a problem, it's natural. . . . If you propose this portfolio to a magazine they'd say it's too generic. What you need is some creative editing." Moreover, she offered one way of thinking of his work as more than just generic newspaper conflict coverage: "You have a nice feeling of land, sky, birds—something larger than the people. It's a very nice thing to build upon." Turning to me, Daphne concluded, "He has some very nice images—more about territory than conflict." In this assessment she was offering Michael one direction for creative editing. Territory was a completely different way to organize his photographs, which were now sorted chronologically by conflict.[30]

Despite being the youngest attendee, Alex was no longer the rookie he had been when I observed his entry into the industry from the vantage point of his editor Ed at GVI, detailed in chapter 2. In fact, among the student photographers at Masterclass 2004, Alex was the one whose work had been most visible in the past year. GVI had continually gotten him assignments at *Newsworld* and at other prominent publications. Moreover, since GVI's sales team had also sold Levy's photographs extensively through second sales, they had circulated extensively, bringing him young celebrity status in the industry. During one break, six of the other students gathered around Alex's laptop to view his slide show on Iraq. As his speaking at Barnstorm 2003 (chapter 5) had foreshadowed a year earlier, Alex had emerged as one of the digital generation's most prominent conflict photographers.

One of the most poignant portfolio conversations I observed was between Alex Levy, the youngest of the photographers present, and the master conflict photographer Bruce. Bruce had begun covering conflict during the 1982 war in Lebanon and had introduced himself to the group by stating, "I've been a photographer for thirty-three years, and I've had a fantastic time nearly every day except when I got hit by a mortar in Sarajevo." Their conversation was clearly one where an older-generation conflict photographer was mentoring one of the next generation, and yet there was an implicit acknowledgment that the industry itself had changed significantly, putting them into direct competition with one another, since there were fewer assignments and more of their work required digital expertise.

Their conversation began with Bruce asking Alex, "Who are you as a photographer?" Alex gave him a list of the conflicts he'd covered. Bruce then asked, "In five years where are you going to be?" The normally brash Alex grew more timid as he answered other, similar questions that pertained less to a specific image he had shot than to his larger identity as a photographer. "Who do you admire?" "Why are you there?" Finally Bruce asked a question that seemed to restore Alex's self-esteem a bit by allowing him to talk about his style and technical mastery: "How much work do you do on Photoshop?" "I underexpose two-thirds of a stop and I meter off the color I want to saturate," Alex answered. It was acknowledged by many that one of the striking elements of Alex's photography was his color management. By underexposing while shooting, Alex allows himself the latitude to create greater contrasts in Photoshop afterward.

On the first day of the Masterclass another student had bluntly asked him, "Are you ever aware of your files looking overworked?" Alex had replied, "I don't want them to look fake, but there is the style I'm going for," with a confidence that suggested he'd encountered the question before. "I'm not changing reality, I'm just bringing up the colors. I want to move the reader. Anything you wouldn't do in the darkroom, I would never do." There is a tension here between aesthetics and ethics. When fellow photographers inquire about the ethics of Alex's aesthetics, he replies by speaking about the technical ways in which he creates greater contrast in the form of heightened colors. For Alex then there seems to be a clear distinction between creating aesthetic contrast and journalistic bias. At another moment during the week, when the group was collectively editing Michael's images from Iraq, Alex emphasized, "We in the West have these ethical concerns. The Iraqi stringers don't have any of the same concerns." Hence, it is not that Alex sees himself as an art photographer less concerned with journalistic ethics, but rather that he separates out stylistic contrasts in the images he sends to publications—part of his personal vision—from his ethics of reporting and getting into position to take the photographs in the first place.

In their one-on-one portfolio review, Bruce didn't challenge Alex but instead recognized his style: "You're absolutely about colors and shapes. I see you in *Geo* and *National Geographic* much more than newsmagazines." He then touched on the issue Alex seemed preoccupied with throughout the Masterclass: "Do you have a personal project?" "I've mostly done assignment work," Alex confessed. In other words, despite the attention and praise he was receiving for his photography, Alex had very little experience crafting his own stories; he had mostly executed assignments he'd been given. Bruce asked Alex who was syndicating his images and learned that Alex was represented by GVI. Earlier in the Masterclass Bruce had made clear that he didn't think highly of the new visual content providers because he believed they had changed the model established between photographers and agencies. Bruce had worked at a time when agencies shared the risk of assignments by investing their money in a photographer's project and then putting all their efforts into selling it so they could make a profit. Bruce criticized GVI and other visual content providers for profiting from distributing and selling work they had not necessarily invested money in producing. Such disdain for GVI, particularly in European publications, was by now familiar to Alex, who was considering leaving GVI but admitted that the syndication of his work through them alone was bringing in three thousand dollars a month. Yet despite his own negative opinion of GVI, Bruce reassured Alex, "Look, if it ain't broke, don't fix it."

Rather, his main concern was getting Alex to think about his future. With humble generosity he once again acknowledged Alex's talent: "What can I say? You're a brilliant photographer. You've found your style. Your photography is excellent, distinctive, stylish. There is a real sense of space. Your sense of color is great. I wish I could shoot like this. Where are you going and where do you want to see yourself? . . . Now you have the tools, what are you going to do with it? You're very good. . . . If I had any criticism I'd say I feel your work is a little too remote. I'd like to see more of a sense of rawness. The temptation is to get so wrapped up in how good you are as a photographer that you forget why you're there."

"Do I need to know what I want to do?"

"No. But it looks easy for you, and it might get boring unless you have a sense of purpose or accomplishment. . . . To be honest, there's not much I can do for you. You're lucky. You don't have the problem of becoming a better photographer. It will come."

"That's my problem: I want to find a project that makes my heart jump. . . . A lot of the others have personal projects, but I didn't do a lot on my own."

"Searching from the heart is what no one can help you with. You've got plenty of time. . . . Be thankful you have a real gift."

Comparing this conversation with Bruce's portfolio review with Armin, another young photographer, highlights the value Bruce places on personal work. This photographer was Danish and had spent six weeks shooting at a large psychiatric facility in Denmark where 550 staff members cared for 220 residents in what they called "the village." "A lot of Danish photographers are going abroad to take photographs, putting themselves in danger. I wanted to spend six weeks making pictures," Armin explained. Bruce concurred that this was wise: "If you go somewhere foreign, it takes you two weeks to figure out where you are." Once again he was very complimentary of the young photographer: "This is fantastic work." But Armin had had trouble getting it published and was discouraged. Bruce insisted he shouldn't be: "It took me too long to focus on personal work. This is great work. You're a very good photographer, very personal. That's your strength. You're a thinker, keep shooting." As for taking the rejections from publications too personally, Bruce insisted:

We can't just work for these guys [i.e., the magazines]. Their time is coming to an end. Lifestyle is so powerful as content that it is all people pay attention to anymore. . . . [Your photographs will be published eventually] and you are going to be a successful photographer. But it might take ten years. You're not shooting only on assignment, it's a way of existing for you. . . . The hot young guys I used to run around with are all out of the business; conflict guys are going to have to find more elements to photograph. It's a struggle for them. Alex has only been in the business eighteen months and he's already having that problem, he's confused about what to do next. You're not going to have that problem. You have to believe that what you're saying is important and get joy out of it. . . . You've got to be schizophrenic in some way: you've got to make a living as well, but you can't make a living off these images, you have to go out. One job a year with advertising will pay for all your other jobs; this is the compromise you have to make. You're very, very good at it but you have to be global. It's an international business we're in. There is another market: there are the charities. Christian Aid, Greenpeace—they all have photo editors now. Next week I'm off to Tanzania for Oxfam.

Bruce wasn't concerned about Alex making a living or finding new revenue streams, but with Armin much of his advice had to do with helping him think of alternate markets, whether advertising or charities, that might allow him to continue working on the types of personal projects he's passionate about. As Daphne had soberly told the photographers, "It's hard to be totally pure as a photographer unless you are independently wealthy."

The third master photographer, Stewart, also emphasized the theme of compromise, though what this meant for him was quite different. Although he was very well known, particularly as a color photographer, and gave workshops around the world, he told me he was not entirely embraced by what he called the photojournalistic mafia. Though he lived in New York, he had never been asked to teach at the Eddie Adams workshop described in chapter 5. He believed this was because he tended to emphasize personal photojournalism, exploring one's own vision, and his workshops as well as his own photographs incorporated elements of art photography as well as traditional photojournalism.[31] At the same time he was not primarily an art photographer. "I often choose to work in places that people more often associate with traditional photojournalism," Stewart explained to me, meaning places where there is some kind of conflict. His preferred vehicles for his work were exhibitions and books.

Whereas Johan, the Swedish master, had discussed the compromises involved in working for daily newspapers as opposed to being a freelancer doing work for magazines, Stewart, like Bruce, perceived even working for magazines as a compromise because you had to accept their edits. Bruce and Susan presented work they had done on assignment for *Newsworld* together, and both showed different edits of the same work, highlighting what the photographer had chosen versus what the photo editor had been able to publish in the magazine. "I realize that magazines have different agendas than mine," Stewart said. He was very sensitive to the fact that magazines were run by text people, who had diverging concerns: "Writing and photography are very different. Photographers affirm reality, they don't explain it." Yet he emphasized to the students that throughout his career he had used all kinds of methods to finance the work he wanted to do: "I've used magazines at different times to help me do parts of a project, sometimes I've had friends, sometimes I've done a little commercial work . . . sometimes I've gone into debt."

As the senior photo editor at *Newsworld*, Susan also encouraged the young photographers to see magazines as vehicles for their work. As we saw in chapter 4, Susan and the other image brokers at *Newsworld* took great pride in getting photo essays published, not only because they thought the work would bring a new perspective to their readers but partly because they knew that in so doing they helped photographers finance larger projects or projects that might be harder to publish. Reflecting on the Masterclass a few months later, Stewart told me he'd been intrigued by where the various photographers were going: "It was interesting—the variety of work that existed in the context of a World Press Masterclass—in that I think that just a few years ago it really would have been much more what we consider traditional photojournalism. I thought there was a great range, and I was pleasantly surprised by that." Indeed, the curator was the last master to address the group, and her advice primarily concerned how they might target galleries and museums. "The same body of work can be assembled in many ways," she reminded them and encouraged the photographers to look for people who would make "personal, emotional, aesthetic commitments and investments" in them. Although many of the photographers, particularly those used to seeing their images in the context of news, did not entirely appreciate how she had curated their images, she insisted that "[p]hotojournalism is entitled to look as good and as stylish as art photography."

Perhaps the issue that was harder to address was the question of in what ways this was an international business or what it meant to be global. As all the World Press Photo staff continually emphasized and the director of the photography museum echoed, the Masterclass brought together an *international* group of photographers. Yet perhaps even more than whether they might be embraced by the art world or journalism circles, the photographers were marked by the differences between them in terms of their approach to particular localities. In one of his closing remarks, Stewart reminded the students, "You have to believe in yourself, you have to believe in your work, you have to feel that you have to do it; the process of doing it itself has to ultimately be what motivates you." For several of the photographers this motivation itself had to do with a particular locality. This might have been more apparent in 2004 precisely because the theme assigned to the photographers had been pride—a theme that is often perceived differently in different places and for many is tied to a particular place. The Latvian photographer's work stood out from that of the others because he had chosen to photograph old industrial factories. He had produced a collection of stark black-and-white images of now-empty buildings "because before the regime change, factories were a part of pride and a part of ideology." He had tried to document the disappearance of the meaning of factories. Unlike several of the other photographers who worked as freelancers, he had a permanent teaching job in a department of photography in Latvia, and much of his funding came from the Latvian ministry of culture. In effect he had photographed former Soviet factories as places that had also manufactured pride, places that now stood empty, decaying as the new country struggled economically.

Similarly the Slovakian woman had chosen to present a small segment of her much larger body of work on how women interacted with Communism. Specifically she told Johan during their portfolio review, "I am looking at the boom generation, the generation who were in kindergarten with Communist ideology. Ours is the first generation that changed, now waiting for something new. . . . I want to continue this work in Ukraine, Poland, Hungary—the differences are interesting to me." When Johan asked if she knew the women in her photographs, she replied, "Yes, I started with women I knew." In fact, she had included a portrait of herself "because I, too, am a Slovak woman."

Daphne, the master now working at a wire service, had addressed the issue of photographers working in their own countries during her presentation: "Local photographers don't shoot the same things. There is always an element of pride. The content changes a lot, and there are less misery stories than when photographing a foreign place. There is an urge to show emerging realities." When Stewart emphasized the idea of an "individual vision" in his presentation, a way of seeing unique to each photographer, the Slovak photographer asked him politely about the portability of this vision: "If you find this visual language, can you use it everywhere, or does everywhere have a different energy and therefore require you to change your visual language?" At issue was in what ways place matters once a photographer has found his or her personal vision. In the terms set out in chapter 6, her question highlighted a tension between striving to visualize an event or a place and expressing one's own personal vision.

What was significantly less a part of the conversation during the Masterclass, at least explicitly, was the photographer's connection with people or places—a topic that had been central to conversations in Istanbul. In contrast, remember Anna's admonition that the students in Istanbul needed to connect to both her and their own subjects much better. Yet in at least two discussions of how a photographer's story was to be edited, it became abundantly clear that regardless of the photographer's own personal vision or relationship to the subjects, how other image brokers perceive the subjects in the photographs and imagine how readers will perceive them becomes critical to whether it will circulate or how it can be framed for publication.

One photographer had produced a story on teenage parents in Britain, a group who he thought were often criticized. "I wanted to show that they can have pride as well," he said. "I wanted to represent them as they wanted to be represented." Susan, the *Newsworld* editor, immediately objected to how he had laid out the story: "In a magazine you have to be incredibly sensitive about opening on a black teen parent. If you open on a black teen parent the implication is [that] there are more black teenage parents. . . . You have to be sensitive to that. It's a huge issue, and the readership will take issue with it." Regardless of what the photographer intended for the images to convey or where they were shot, in order to be published they would need to be arranged according to the political concerns of the publication. Here what was determining how this story might be laid out was the anticipated backlash from readers based on their imagined reaction to the particular layout rather than anything within the frame of the photograph itself. Even if the topic for the photographer had been the pride felt by teenage parents, Susan was explaining how her magazine would inevitably lay out the piece according to racial binaries: opening on a black teen couple would make the story about the problem of black teen pregnancy, whereas opening on a white couple would somehow be unmarked, possibly allowing the piece to retain its focus on pride.[32]

This exchange also made clear the impact of editing decisions at *Newsworld*. Even though its readership may mostly be American, precisely because so many of the photographers talked about looking through the magazine to understand trends in photography and editing, and because Susan was regularly invited all over the world to share her expertise in workshops, the context-specific concerns about racial representation were discussed as if they were universally applicable.

Similarly when Susan was helping Armin, the Danish photographer, edit his work on Inuit hunters in Greenland, she asked if drinking was a problem among the hunters. "Yes, but every time I see a story from Greenland, it's all about drugs and alcohol," Armin responded. He had wanted to illustrate the hunters' pride in their land even though currently social security rather than fishing and hunting were their main sources of income. Armin wasn't satisfied with the group's edit of his work, and Daphne pointed out that editing was highly culturally specific. Pointing at the images showing the hunters and their reindeer against a barren landscape, or Inuit families eating raw meat off their knives or sitting in front of shacks with their hunting equipment, she commented, "In Denmark no magazine would accept this. They're close to this story, so it's not just a visual story. They'd want to know what's happening specifically in these images." Hence, Daphne drew attention to the fact that although an editor elsewhere may be drawn to this story for its exotic visuals or ability to capture difference "from a pictorial view," editors familiar with Greenland might find the work superficial. The art historian master chimed in to underline that "any editing is cultural," and yet the discussion didn't continue much further. Perhaps one reason for this is because this was a group gathered together as an international group of photographers, young talent from around the world working in what was repeatedly emphasized to be a global industry. That framing, so dependent on celebrating internationalism, leaves little room to address the frictions and inequalities in how various photographs circulate and come to acquire value—not only commercial value, but also journalistic credibility and aesthetic praise from a professional community.

There was certainly no sense that the ambitions of the photographers who worked closer to home were any narrower than those for whom shooting meant traveling to far-flung corners of the earth, or at least those that had temporarily become hot spots for the news. After all, they had all been chosen for the World Press Masterclass. Echoing what Eitan, the Israeli master, had shared with me in Istanbul, the Slovak photographer clearly told Johan, "I don't want to be just good in Slovakia, I don't want to just be best in Slovakia, there are only four million people in Slovakia." There were, however, differences in the types of financial compromises considered by different photographers and the fetishization of mobility or complaints about immobility. A Canadian photographer brought in all the ticket stubs for her flights over the last few months, bemoaning the fact that she had spent just five days at home, and many of the more news-oriented photographers spoke of going abroad as a central part of their photography. Whereas the Slovak photographer said she had made the choice not to go to Perpignan to attend Visa Pour l'Image the summer before, because she was able to work for two months on the money she would have spent on the trip: "If I can do two or three stories somewhere else, I can keep funding my work. I sleep in my car. I just spend money on gas and materials." Yet she also acknowledged that because she did not attend festivals she did not know key players in the industry who might provide her with more opportunities. Johan informed her she should go to Arles, a more artistic festival, where her images might get more attention. Everyone acknowledged the importance of going to festivals in order to show work and meet individuals who might support their work. For the Hungarian photographer attending Masterclass, Visa Pour l'Image had also being very influential in terms of the presentations he saw and had inspired him to want to tell stories through images rather than shoot impressive single pictures.

In addition to exposing the photographers to the latest trends and the work being talked about in the industry, festivals were also perceived as a way for the photographers to circulate. Daphne warned them, "This is a tiny, tiny world. If you get a reputation as annoying, obnoxious, aggressive, lazy, it will hurt you. Picture editors talk, journalists talk, curators talk—you have no idea how much word of mouth spreads." Of course, positive reviews also circulate widely. The Masterclass itself was an excellent networking opportunity. I heard Roger tell the Slovak photographer that he would show her book to contacts he had at the Hasselblad Foundation in Sweden; another master promised to put a photographer in contact with a publisher of photography books who he thought would like her work. These were not just vague promises; these connections often resulted in a photographer getting more assignments. In fact, the first time I met Susan was at a staff meeting at *Newsworld* a year earlier when she had just returned from the 2003 Masterclass and had spoken enthusiastically to her staff of photo editors about the young talent she had just met. She had passed around the CD with the photographers' portfolios and encouraged the editors to consider them for assignments. Not surprisingly, the 2004 crop of photographers have all gone on to build strong careers in photography, though not all in journalism, and no matter how many awards they have received since, all of them mention being a part of the Masterclass as part of their professional biography. Attending the Masterclass remains a significant mark of prestige in the international photo world.

BLACK AND WHITE: BACK BY POPULAR DEMAND

A Belgian photographer got quite a few chuckles during Awards Days 2004 with a black T-shirt he wore bearing the message "Black and White: Back by Popular Demand" in white lettering. At a moment when many photographers were discussing their own personal transitions to digital photography, including sharing tips on the best labs that would still develop film or how best to transform color digital files into black-and-white images, the ambiguous message of the T-shirt resonated with many. I encountered it during the World Press Photo Awards Days when the *Inside/Outsight* exhibition was making me consider the function of binaries in photojournalism. The buzzwords of the moment were the *international* nature of the contest, the *universal* legibility of the winning images, and *the humanity* of certain prominent photographers. Therefore, I read the T-shirt as a comment on the state of ethics rather than aesthetics in photojournalism.

A conversation with Stewart, the photographer I had met as a master in the Masterclass, who comfortably occupies a space between photojournalism and art photography, several months later reminded me of the T-shirt. Stewart articulated a discomfort many photographers echoed: the ambiguity of photographic interpretation and the fear that work intended to spearhead political action could in fact instead merely confirm that certain situations were hopeless or certain conditions inevitable in certain geographies.

> My sense of what in fact happens with photographs in the world in general is that the responses to photographs can be very, very complicated and it's not, it's really very, very hard to predict how people are going to respond. I mean if we look at the history of photography of black Africa, crises in black Africa for the last forty years or something, my suspicion is that the first

pictures truly horrified people. People were truly overwhelmed they hadn't seen anything like that, and as we sort of go into the famine in Ethiopia and ultimately Rwanda, people seem—my sense is that people have become increasingly inured to it and there's much less of a sense of shock and there's sort of like, "That's Africa." And my suspicion is also that there are those out there that say, "Well yeah, that's what blacks do in Africa." And sort of the whole intention that one might have in terms of showing the world how terrible the situation in Rwanda is—it's totally subverted by someone who says, "Oh yeah, blacks, that's what they do." So I think it's very, very complicated, very hard to predict how people are going to respond to photographs. . . . Pictures are really malleable according to their context. And the other thing is, interesting photographs, photographs that really deal with ambiguity with subtly and so forth—it's so hard to predict what different people are going to find in them. If they're really simplistic and heavy-handed pictures, they become a kind of propaganda.

Scholars and photographers alike give examples of how the same image can be put to serve completely contrary ideological purposes. Moreover, Stewart echoed an argument made by many others about compassion fatigue, or the idea that overexposure has somehow dulled viewers' sensitivities.[33] Yet, just a few years after digitalization had completely shaken up the industry, in the context of World Press Photo as well as other settings in which photojournalism was being taught, evaluated, or celebrated, such as Barnstorm and Visa Pour l'Image, the ability of an image to convey a clear message and the potential for it to move people to political action was continually underlined. Professional ethics were assumed even while technological changes, changes in journalism, and new configurations in contexts where photographers work were constantly raising new questions that required a reconsideration of these ethics. At this moment when photojournalism had been deeply unsettled, it seemed all the more important to present an image of the profession as one that always contributed to free speech and democracy and hence, in and of itself, was always a positive force in the world. Ethical ambiguity was rarely discussed publicly at seminars and workshops. Yet, privately, image brokers talked to me about doubting their effectiveness in the world or questioning the ethics of their work. Stewart addressed this issue as well:

At times it's tough to face some of the incredible complexities of what it is that motivates people to photograph. It's a lot easier to say you're going to Rwanda to show the world how horrible it is than to look at oneself and say, "Yeah I'm doing that," but I'm also really intrigued by violence. I get off on the chaos of war. I have to say—a few times—I'm not a war photographer, but the few times that I've been in extreme situations, the adrenaline rush is incredibly exciting and you just feel intensely alive. And nothing else in the world seems to matter: wow all this stuff's going on. And I don't think it's bad for people to accept that. I don't think there's anything wrong with that, but I think that a lot of people in the photojournalistic community have difficulty dealing with that and dealing with . . . I mean there are a lot of moral questions about doing this kind of work. . . . I just think there are lots and lots of very, very complicated moral questions that are perhaps ultimately unanswerable about this work. And I'm very uncomfortable putting any photographer up on the pedestal about their moral purity. That doesn't mean I don't think there are wonderful photographers that have done something incredibly valuable, but it's complicated. I think in the US people want to see things in this black and white, it's good or bad. But it's not just good or bad, it's complicated. Everything lies in between.

BUILDING TRUST IN THE DIGITAL AGE

Perhaps no one presented photojournalism in terms as black and white as the CEO and cofounder of Getty Images, Jonathan Klein, who opened a series of sessions titled "Trends in the Industry" at the fiftieth anniversary of World Press Photo, an event aptly titled "The Picture of Truth: Building Trust in the Age of On-Demand Journalism." Eager to build rapport with the audience of industry professionals, some of whom were still skeptical of Getty, Klein immediately addressed Getty's position in the industry: "I think it goes without saying, but it's an enormous honor to be invited to speak to you today. We've been supporting photojournalism for just five years now, and we still very much feel like the new kid on the block. So when the new kid on the block is invited into the inner sanctum, we often have to question our credentials. . . . I'm delighted and honored to be here." He continued with uncomplicated admiration for photographers:

> I am very fortunate to work with many photographers who will live through just about anything to capture the essence of a story in a perfect shot. You continue to show us all the world in ways most of us would never experience. Because of World Press Photo we're all able to be here today to acknowledge your dedication to a profession that many times causes you to put your very lives in jeopardy. My belief in the power of imagery and my respect and awe for what each of you accomplish is the reason and the only reason that I go to work each day. I'm honored, I'm humbled, and I'm privileged to work with the many men and women with more talent, more commitment, and more courage than I will ever have. . . . [The values that] are at the heart of the World Press Photo mission also inspire photojournalism at Getty Images. Over the last several years many World Press Photo award recipients have taken their decision to join us. It is a great honor, and we do not take it lightly.

Klein's speech reminds us of another important function of awards: by conferring prestige on a photographer, they increase the value of her photo agency. When photographers who had won World Press Photo prizes joined Getty, they also brought esteem to Getty as an organization that supported visual journalism. Klein continued by voicing absolute faith in photography's universality, power to bring about change, and undeniable connection to truth:

> We all know in this group that throughout history, imagery has proved to be a universal language that transcends political and social boundaries to communicate the shared human condition. Images have been used . . . sometimes to promote peace, often to incite war—simply put, images mark the times, showing the best, testifying to the worst, and often providing hope that the very best is still ahead. . . . Every time people see powerful, polished images they react. Why? Perhaps it is because imagery reveals truth and today people don't run from what they see—they don't trust what they read, but they trust what they see.

Directly addressing the tension between word and image people that I had seen at multiple sites, Klein reminded all those present that Michelle McNally, a photo editor, had been promoted to assistant managing editor at the *New York Times* a few months earlier and that the executive editor of the paper had signaled the promotion as "an overdue acknowledgement of the status photojournalism has earned." Klein insisted, "For us, photographers are the journalists. Period. . . . We believe in the ability of a photograph to tell a story. We don't mean to say anything negative about people who use words, we just don't need them. Our photographers are the reporters. Our phtoographers are not in service to text journalism providing the story or running the organization. . . . We tell the story just by the pictures, thank you very much."

The intense celebration of the profession and defensive tone need to be understood of course not only within the context of the anniversary at which the speech was delivered but also within the context of the speaker's desire to ingratiate himself and Getty Images within an industry at a moment when visual content providers such as Getty Images and Corbis were still seen by many to have forever changed the industry and corrupted it with corporate commercial interests. Nonetheless, it was only the most bombastic version of praise for photojournalism that I heard repeated over and over again at industry events. This public insistence on universality and truthfulness was surprising, because over the years, usually in private conversations, I had heard many image brokers and photographers, like Stewart, express far more nuanced and ambivalent evaluations of their profession. Perhaps it was precisely because World Press Photo's fiftieth anniversary corresponded to the moment of transition analyzed throughout this book, full of complex compromises and a pervasive sense of being threatened by amateurs, that the celebrations were also a public defense of photojournalism.

The ostentatious ceremony's most sober moment was when Dr. Jan Pronk, UN Special Representative to the Sudan, addressed the photographers during the closing ceremony claiming that militia had for years carried out acts of genocide in the Darfur region without international outcry because there had been no photographers there. "Objectivity," Pronk said, "is indifference. Please come to Sudan. Please come from abroad, because, despite the lifting of censorship before a text or photo goes to press, Sudanese journalists fear arrests after publication. Moreover, they lack the means to go to the field. Please come and document Darfur, burn the images in the minds of the world's public and their leaders."

Pronk's comments were an invaluable endorsement of press photography's value, especially since he affirmed that he could be moved by photographs not only as a private viewer but also as a politician and policy leader. Inadvertently perhaps, he was also drawing attention to precisely that which the insistence on universality obscures: the significant power asymmetries inherent in international journalism, photography included. Photographs still accrue political value by circulating among certain specific, mostly Western news centers. Moreover, as we have seen throughout this chapter, the ability of foreign photographers to circulate, to leave once they have taken certain images, and not face the repercussions of being local is precisely why the structures that create the inequalities and conflicts that photographers so heroically document also structure world press photography.

Conclusion

Waiting for the Dust to Settle

I have waited several years for the dust to settle so that I could provide an overview of where photojournalism has come and what its futures might be.[1] Yet the world of visual journalism is as much in flux as when I began this project, if not more.[2] The gap in time between my fieldwork and today not only allows us the opportunity to discuss two moments in history. It also provides the luxury of comparing the unfolding present with the way the present was imagined and anticipated as the futurepast a decade ago. Therefore, rather than offer a soon-to-be-out-of-date status of photojournalism today, I want to conclude by considering a paradox that I watched as it evolved.[3] Despite an intense demand for images, visual journalists have been hard hit by layoffs, and freelancers find it increasingly difficult if not impossible to earn a living through editorial work. The increasing demand for and even appreciation of imagery has, rather than enhancing the value of photojournalists and the professionals who broker their work, significantly diminished it.

Much has changed in the world of journalism since Jackie, a photo editor at GVI, pushed aside an established photographer's rolls of film because they were out of pace with a war that was to be covered digitally. Alex Levy and many of the other young photographers I met during fieldwork have produced a lot of stunning photography, garnered many awards, and been widely published. Many now work in multiple media; some have been very successful in documentary film production. As the first editors, all of them now spend several hours editing on a computer screen at the end of already long working days. In this way all photojournalists have also become brokers of their own work. Most of the photographers are no longer represented by the agencies they were with when I met them. Some of them, and other photographers I did not get a chance to interview, have been kidnapped or killed while working. Many tell me there's never been as dangerous a time to be a photojournalist.

Nonetheless, the competition is fiercer than ever, and many insist there has never been a richer time for photojournalism. Already in 2004, Pierre Martin, director of photo at AFP, had told me, "There is no single eye behind the camera today. There is not an AFP eye. It is a multicultural eye, and there are more photographers than ever working for us." This is true not only of wire services but of documentary photography at large today: it is being done by more people in more places than ever. When I returned to Visa Pour l'Image in 2015, I found a far more diverse group of photographers than had been there a decade earlier. Many were willing to wait in line four or five hours for the opportunity to have their portfolio reviewed. Jean-François Leroy, the director of Visa Pour l'Image, frequently insists that it is not photography but rather the press that is in crisis, and the crowds of young photographers at Perpignan seem to validate his point. At least, if there is a crisis, it has not resulted in a lack of passion or enthusiasm. Alan Fare, a founder of a photo agency that has so far survived the turbulence of the last several decades, enthusiastically points out, "You don't send people to China anymore because there are excellent photographers in Shanghai and Guangzhou. . . . There are very qualified people in many places—Bangladesh, Turkey, China, Australia, Brazil, Mexico." But, he cautions, "[t]he financial side of things is an impossible equation." It seems that the industry's budgets ran dry just when the dream for the democratization of vision with which digitalization had arrived might have been realized.

Compared to a decade ago, much more news is consumed online, where news stories are frequently updated throughout the day, often with changing photographs. Many of the publications mentioned in this book are either exclusively or predominantly digital—or have ceased to exist all together. Online there is a lot more "real estate," to recall the term used by *Newsworld* editors for space in the magazine, and many articles are linked to multiple images in the form of online galleries or slide shows. The rise and spread of social media means that many readers' initial encounter with a news story is through an image—often quite small and on a mobile screen. Photography blogs have flourished and present stellar work from around the world.[4] In some parts of the world, such as India, print newspapers are flourishing. Elsewhere, new kinds of entities such as the home- and apartment-renting startup Airbnb are publishing print magazines. The status of journalism is not uniform worldwide.

Global pundits regularly tell us that we live in an age of images. Regardless of whether the end product is digital or print, decisions need to be made and images posted at ever-greater speeds. Almost none of the image brokers I've written about in this book have the jobs they once did, and in many cases their position has been eliminated. In many parts of the world, journalism has seen drastic losses in revenue, and photojournalist's positions and certainly those of other image brokers have become increasingly precarious. There are so few researchers and editors that photographers have had to take on many new roles on ever-shorter assignments and sometimes transmit their photographs directly to designers in art departments. As for those archives that everyone was feverishly buying up, digitizing, and filling for the future, very few professionals have the time to search through them and take advantage of their richness, let alone dream up innovative uses for this visual history. Their financial value has plummeted. Visual content providers have radically cut image-licensing prices. In 2014, Getty Images made thirty-five million images free for noncommercial usage.[5]

I began this investigation at the beginning of the War on Terror by noting that the work of image brokers was mostly invisible. The digital environment has given rise to news kinds of image brokers. We've seen many more governments, nongovernmental organizations, corporations, and terrorists, among others, circulate their own images, bypassing the traditional press. Moreover, the networked world of social media has made image brokering a common practice for many. The widespread nature of everyday image brokering has devalued the already invisible work of professionals. The perception is that anyone can move images. This chapter will show how news images continue to be critical to visual worldmaking. Four recent news events—the 2013 Gezi protests in Turkey, the January 2015 attacks on the French satirical magazine *Charlie Hebdo,* World Press Photo's decision to revoke a prize in its 2015 Contemporary Issues category, and the earthquake in Nepal in April 2015—illustrate how formative fictions operate in visual worldmaking practices today despite ongoing shifts in infrastructures of representation. I have stayed in touch with many informants throughout the years, and this conclusion draws heavily on conversations with them. The horizon of my writing has changed because I have spent most of the last decade teaching and my students have taught me much about a born-digital generation's news consumption and their relationship to different genres of photography.[6] There is only one thing of which I am absolutely certain which is that the future of journalism is visual. Which is not to say that it is only visual, but that it is impossible to discuss the future of news without explicitly addressing news images, whether moving or still. News in the twenty-first century cannot move without images.

OBLIGATORY IMAGES

Not everything has changed: Think back to the discussion about how AFP should cover absenteeism for the 2004 European Parliamentary elections in which ten new European Union member states had elected representatives to the European Parliament for the first time. At the time, Marie, the director of AFP's international photo desk in Paris, had noted with chagrin that the most popular photograph used to illustrate the elections was a Reuters image of "little Hungarians with their little skirts."[7] Marie lamented that, despite the availability of many alternative photographs, publications around the world had chosen to circulate a frame she considered a visual stereotype as a news image. The dominant that day was that many voters in countries formerly considered Eastern Europe had now joined the European Union. The particular frame was not representative of the electorate but was a powerful formative fiction: the indexed Hungarian women in their colorful traditional outfits represented the bodies politic of newly Europeanizing nations on the brink of joining their modern Western partners.

Ten years later, many publications used very similar photographs to illustrate the 2014 European parliamentary elections. In fact, one news image published widely was taken by the same photographer who had taken the 2004 image referred to by Marie. Figure 8 shows how the image was used as the online image of the day for *Paris Match,* a popular French newsmagazine. What is surprising is not that the same photographer—Laszlo Balogh, a Hungarian who has long been working for Reuters—took similar images to represent European elections in Hungary ten years apart but that similar photographs that reify comically stereotypical portrayals of Hungarians circulated as news images in the pages and on the cover of reputable newspapers and journals.

FIGURE 8. Hungarian women at the ballot box for European Parliamentary elections. Published in *Paris Match* and many other publications on April 6, 2014. Photograph by Laszlo Balogh/Reuters.

Why, when so many talented photographers, Mr. Balogh included, are taking sophisticated photographs around the world do such stereotypical frames keep getting published? One reason is in what Igor Vobič and Iliya Tomanić Trivundža calls "the Tyranny of the Empty Frame." The transition to online journalism has meant that much news is now assembled using content management systems (CMS), "computer interfaces used for assembling, editing and publishing online which require a minimum of one still or moving image per news item." The result is "the tyranny of the empty frame," defined as "a hard-coded technological requirement that 'news must be visual.'"[8] As more publications have cut photo editors from their staff, the work of attaching an image to a story falls increasingly to an already harried writer or to online journalists sometimes referred to as new kinds of news workers or a "special breed of journalist."[9] Vobič and Tomanić Trivundža studied online journalists at two leading Slovenian newspapers and found that many were frustrated by the mandate to find images that they perceived as slowing down news production, and in desperation would often fill the frame with "'a symbolic photograph'—a generic image that is not directly linked to the specific reported event—from their archives or from agency feeds." For the moment, the tyranny of the empty frame might not be dictating the selection of images in every newsroom using CMS, but it is nonetheless very widespread. The logics of increased productivity mandate that everything happen faster with fewer people. Image brokering has become something many news workers do as part of their job, with very few professionals dedicated to it. Replaying familiar images takes much less work and time than innovating or researching the best way to visualize a particular story.

Many journalistically important stories, especially those about legal, economic, or complex political issues, are on some level abstract and hard to visualize, especially if an image has to be shot the day of the story. Such stories produce a crisis in visualization: a moment when routine visualization itself is challenged or disturbed. Hence, although elections and economic sanctions certainly have substantial concrete effects, we end up seeing lots of photographs of ballot boxes "with Hungarians in their little skirts" and officials giving press briefings. These news images illustrate the time of the news story as dominant rather than visualize the forces influencing the vote or the effects of trade barriers being addressed at the press briefing—issues that unfold over time. In the past, part of the work of image brokers was anticipating the futurepast and helping photographers conceive of ways to best visualize world news. Today there is much less time for visual journalism in news publications. As sociologist Eric Klinenberg noted in his analysis of convergence in news production in 2005, news cycles have spun into news cyclones.[10] The cyclones have only grown stronger since.

Reflecting back on the old differentiation between fast and good photographs, one photo editor told me that the greatest changes in photojournalism over the last decade were in fact not changes in photography: "Workflows at publications have changed. We've seen the rise of content-management systems in all big groups of newspapers. . . . The journalist has to put in the image with the story, and the wires are what get used [since publications usually pay an annual subscription rate rather than per image] or whatever imagery they can get for free." The image is necessary to the story, obligatory for it to be filed, but merely an afterthought to the actual journalism in the absence of resources in terms of time, talent, and skill to visualize news meaningfully. Ironically, the technical and aesthetic quality of photography worldwide is much higher overall than it has ever been. All of my informants agree that wire services are producing excellent photography. Therefore, the tyranny of the empty frame has not necessarily produced "bad" photography. However, we are back to "fast photos" in the news not because they are the only ones that can move in time but because they are often the only ones that can be easily searched online and embedded into the story in the time available to the journalist. Very few publications have the luxury to ask which images will best visually express this news and engage the imagination of the reader rather than which will illustrate this topic that I can I find immediately and will cost as little as possible. The result is a lot of "good" photographs moving fast, but little time for good visual journalism.

THE DISAPPEARING NEWS PHOTOGRAPHER IN THE DIGITAL AGE

Digitalization—not merely digitization but the institutional changes such as the rise of visual content providers with their new business models—disrupted photojournalism a few years before the full force of journalism's migration online was felt. The year 2006 marked the first time that print advertisement revenue began to fall at American newspapers and resulted in the closure of many metro dailies and magazines.[11] In the years leading up to this, while I was doing fieldwork, I watched photo editors pay for physical space according to the size an image was run on a page, or pay day rates (which had not changed in over twenty years), but the amounts negotiated for online use of images were negligible. Even at digital giant GVI, the news and editorial team often didn't bother making the sales for online usage and saw those as crumbs they could leave for the sales team. The industry complained of a revenue squeeze, but the common belief was that it came from monopolization and the rise of the visual content providers. In other words, for a few brief years it seemed that photojournalism could move from analog to digital without massive losses in revenue because photojournalism was digitalized before most news publications migrated online. People paid less attention to the incredibly low cost of licensing images for online use while there was still some physical real estate in the form of actual pages. Slowly, advertising began going online and then, during the financial crisis of 2008, seemed to disappear from print entirely.

As a senior executive at a visual content provider told me, "The whole news industry went through a major shift. When it happened in photojournalism, no one was thinking about what was going to happen. Once you put up your information for free, there is no going back. We can't change that. Those models are gone." When news images were being put online for free or for negligible sums, few were making the argument that information or journalism was being given away for free. Chroniclers of the rise of digital journalism almost always discuss the popularity of online photo galleries, and the role of visuals in bringing readers online.[12] It may be that photography departments, long used to the rule of text, were too flattered by the visibility they got online to demand that their work be financially valued. Photographers and other image brokers represent the category of newsroom staffers hit hardest by the constant layoffs over the last decade in the United States.

In May 2013 the *Chicago Sun-Times* laid off its entire photography department, including Pulitzer Prize winner John White, a regular speaker at the Eddie Adams workshop, who had inspired many in the 2003 audience with his speech about his camera making him a visual servant. Subscription numbers at the newspaper had fallen 23 percent since 2006.[13] The decision was explained as an effort to "evolve with [their] digitally savvy customers," who were "consistently seeking more video content with their news." The newspaper would still use images but would source them from freelancers and text journalists equipped with iPhones. Other publications have seen similar layoffs. Even *Sports Illustrated,* despite its name, laid off all of its remaining staff photographers while reiterating its commitment to creating original content.[14] The wording of the *Sun-Times* statement is telling: the news audience no longer comprises readers but customers, and allegedly not only prefers video but also does not perceive visuals as part of the news. Rather, the customers are reported to want "more video content with their news," the way I might ask for fries with a hamburger.[15]

Though photojournalism prides itself on having brought visibility to many issues, the work behind producing and circulating news images has remained mostly invisible. Most narratives about photojournalism, including reports on the *Chicago Sun-Times* layoff, focus exclusively on photographers, whereas photographers are only part of a network of image brokers who make complex decisions about how to visualize the world. Keeping the focus narrowly on the critical moment when a shutter button is pressed effectively renders invisible all the other framing that goes into the production and circulation of a news image. Yet photojournalists as well as the relatively few scholars writing about photojournalism rarely discuss the research and complex decision making that take place both before and after a photograph is "taken." This much less glamorous work is often collaborative and the site where much of the knowledge that then frames the photograph happens. The myth of the intrepid and committed photographer single-handedly shining light on world affairs has cost the profession at large. With the work behind news images reduced to a mere moment of button pressing, it is much easier to argue that the work can be performed readily by drones or reporters equipped with iPhones. In fact, in fall 2013 Apple's iPhone5 promised "a better photographer built in."[16] "Instead of teaching people to take better photos, why not teach the camera?" Apple asked.

Supporters of visual journalism respond by highlighting the "craft" of professional photojournalists. Yet often what is lamented is a loss of aesthetic rather than journalistic excellence. Typical statements conclude that employers are not willing to pay for *excellence in photography*. Others bemoan that photographs will be less *artfully* framed or that those not trained in photography won't know how to handle challenging lighting. All this is true, but these arguments also obscure much of the labor behind insightful investigative visual journalism. Good reporting by photojournalists, like such reporting by all journalists, takes time. A narrow focus on aesthetics makes it seem as if audiences are merely being offered less artfully shot video *with their news,* as if the news simply happens or exists in the world waiting for the next iPhone camera to cross its path.

As I've pointed out, not all photographs are news images. News images are made with the help of image brokers. For all the criticism one can make about image brokers reproducing worldviews while brokering representations, repeatedly during fieldwork I saw how the best image brokers contribute to the production of richer knowledge about world events. They do this not merely by choosing the better photo but by working with photographers, helping them get into place, asking them questions, discussing their shoots, sharing information, fact-checking, and advocating for images to tell stories and not merely illustrate text. What is at stake is not merely better photos, but better journalism. Staged events such as splashy presidential moments will always get covered, whether by amateurs or by reporters who have iPhone photography basics training. What will suffer is investigative visual journalism: the production of news images that prompt audiences to ask better questions as citizens and enable different ways of understanding a community. "Ordinary, everyday people, these are the treasures, that's what's important," former *Chicago Sun-Times* photographer John White stressed in an NPR interview.

THE NAR PHOTOS NEWS HOUR

One person wrote that he'd figured out that we tended to post the day's images in the wee hours of the morning and said he looked forward to the Nar Photo hour as if our daily slideshow were his nightly news.

—member of the Nar Photos Collective

The Nar Photos Collective is an independent agency with offices in Istanbul and Diyarbakır, Turkey. Many of the photographers who established the collective in 2003 met at the World Press Photo seminar organized for Turkish photographers described in chapter 7, and I have witnessed the evolution of the collective over the ensuing years, during which Turkey has received more attention from global media than anyone suspected a decade ago. They specialize in social documentary photography: most of their stories feature narratives about changing landscapes—both social and physical—in Turkey. One hot night in June 2013 I spoke with seven members of the Nar Photos Collective about their coverage of the protests in Gezi Park against the Turkish prime minister at the time, Tayyip Erdoğan, and the government-sanctioned use of excessive police force.[17] The photographers were exhausted and relieved at having survived without major injury. They had inhaled a lot of tear gas and had a few encounters with rubber bullets and tear-gas canisters thrown by the police. After occupying the park for over two weeks, the protesters and their encampments had been forcibly cleared by police forces earlier in the day, and it was the first night the photographers were not working. There was a sense of political disappointment, yet remarkably absent was any sense of cynicism. Over the course of our discussions late into the night, I watched as they grew cautiously hopeful as individuals got tweets or saw Facebook updates on their cell phones about groups of citizens gathering in parks around the city to hold open forums.

Since the days when some of them had taken photographs following the 2003 terrorist bombings in Istanbul but hadn't been able to get the images to GVI in New York all day, they had figured out the technicalities of digital image distribution. They now had agreements with several foreign agencies that occasionally sold their images to clients, but they weren't on any assignment to cover the protest. "As soon as we began posting daily photographic summaries of the protests via Facebook there was an explosion in visitor numbers," one member of the collective told me. Another hadn't been able to get to the office on the first day of the protests. When she called in to ask how she could help, she was told to approve friends on Facebook:

> Don't laugh! Prior to the Gezi protests, we used to get fifty or one hundred visitors a day and we didn't even know about the five-thousand-friend limit, nor that there was a difference between a Facebook profile and a page. One other member logged on to our Facebook page and both of us spent the next two hours literally just hitting the return button over and over again, accepting new friends who wanted to be able to see our photographs. Then Amnesty International asked us for our photographs. So did a few environmental organizations and academics. We let people use the images for their personal blogs as well.

Mainstream Turkish media didn't cover the protests at first, and there was backlash against this censorship during the protests. "Telling people we weren't shooting for a Turkish mainstream media calmed people down," thereby securing the photographers' access. "Everyone was furious . . . it was a real shock for people to see their own media completely silent." The protestors not only did not feel politically represented by their government but were also initially denied media representation. Eventually, the protests got extensive global coverage; there were many foreign and domestic photojournalists, both freelancers and wire service photographers, at the events. Many of the foreigners were well-equipped combat photographers—unlike the Nar photographers, who couldn't afford a gas mask till several days into the protests.

> We'd give the best mask to the person working up front, and the others would hang back and work in the crowd. We began to see that the story is not all on the front line. You really begin to see things farther back in the crowd. After a few hours of inhaling tear gas it's hard to work, so we'd come back here and recover. Going out a second time was very difficult. You'd be completely worn out by the gas and the water cannons, but we'd encourage each other and go back out. We were also motivated by those looking at our images and leaving us supportive comments.

When I asked if they'd been able to sell their coverage, one of the photographers who had attended the World Press Photo seminars and been in the collective from the start replied, "I work for shares." Confused, I asked what he meant. "He works for shares. You know 'shares' and 'likes'," another explained, teasing me for being so slow to catch on. That

September a selection of Nar Photos' coverage of the Gezi protests was shown during the Saturday evening slide show at Visa Pour l'Image. None of them could afford going to Perpignan for the festival; a few years earlier they had sent a member of the group but had not found the investment worthwhile because it did not bring them many new assignments or sales and had been a heavy financial burden for the group. I wondered if they thought the World Press Photo seminar had been a waste, getting them to think about the international market though they had found that there were many barriers to entry. Their quick response surprised me. "Not at all!" stressed one of the founders of Nar Photos with whom I'd gone to the *Inside/Outsight* exhibition. He insisted, "We learned how to tell stories visually, how to develop a story."

In the two years since the protests they've collectively made less than two thousand dollars on their coverage of the Gezi protests, but the images have been widely used by civil society organizations. The collective has always struggled financially, it rarely covers its expenses, and all of the photographers work other jobs. Nonetheless, during a watershed political moment in Turkish history they had a diverse audience—around twenty thousand "friends" on Facebook—from those occupying the park to others all around Turkey and on the other side of the world who were anticipating their nightly posting of images to help them make sense of the extraordinary events taking place. In 2014, the Istanbul Modern Art Museum mounted a ten-year retrospective of the collective's work showing profound shifts in Turkey in the twenty-first century. At a time when there was tremendous disillusionment with mainstream media, the nightly Nar Photo Hour was producing highly valued visual journalism. They weren't providing visual "content," because it wasn't filling space in any preexisting print or online news publications. Moreover, this was visual journalism, not just a slide show of images, since they were reporting on many different aspects of the protests.

They respected the coverage of some of the foreigners whose work they'd seen, and they also saw the value of their own work: "We're personally implicated. We are not just witnesses here. As citizens, we are ourselves victims of this state violence." They felt a great responsibility not to incriminate individuals and not to allow their cameras to be coopted by the government's dramaturgy by producing images of violent protestors engaged in vandalism that could then be used to justify the police crackdown. Every night they discussed which images to post and argued about how not to reinforce nationalist framings of the events, a visual challenge because of the hyperpresence of flags. Precisely because they were local photographers who had been documenting increasing social consciousness about urban issues for many years, they saw the political significance of the peaceful gathering of very diverse groups. While much of the foreign press framed the Gezi protests as violent clashes between protestors and police, the Nar Photos collective visualized the tremendous gathering of a wide spectrum of citizens. Nar Photos documented that ideologically very different groups in Turkey could gather as citizens in peaceful protest, and that the prime minister was not the only person who could draw large crowds. They were brokering their own photographs, undertaking investigative visual journalism, and becoming a trusted source of information.

At the end of the interview, the youngest member of the collective told me: "You know there is a moment which I will never forget. Early on I was sitting at the computer, editing my images and loading them into the archive. Other people's images were also up on the screen. Looking at them out of the corner of my eye, I found myself wondering: where in the world are these images of protest from? Where are people standing up for their rights? I simply couldn't imagine that images of such mass protests were from my country. I would not have thought it possible just a few days ago."

What surprised him was how many people had come together to take a stand. Even though he had produced some of them, the images on his screen were formative: they showed him that this could be what defending democracy looked like—not somewhere else in the world, but in his own country. Formative fictions can produce hope as well as reinforce stereotypes. Nar Photos' images inspired him, and thousands of others, to imagine that their world could be different.

CIRCULATION AS NEWS

Digital obliges us to think much more about the image in terms of production.
—Michèle Léridon, global news director, AFP

On January 8, 2015, the Kouachi brothers stormed into the weekly editorial meeting at the offices of French satirical magazine *Charlie Hebdo* and killed twelve people in retaliation for the magazine's depictions of Muslims—specifically, the prophet Mohammed. The magazine had also run the controversial 2005 cartoons initially published in the Danish paper *Jyllands-Posten*. Across town another man killed five people, and at the end of a three-day manhunt all three assassins were also killed. Cherif Kouachi, the younger of the two brothers, had served time in prison for ties to terrorism. In the transcript of his 2007 trial Kouachi states that he got the idea of joining a terror group when he saw images of the torture and humiliation of Muslims at the hands of American soldiers in Abu Ghraib prison in Iraq.

What was true during my fieldwork—that images in the press, from photographs to cartoons, were not just illustrating current events but were often factors in causing events, thereby playing a critical and highly controversial part in political and military action—is even truer now. The war of images intensified because of the seismic changes in the infrastructures of representation. Elsewhere I've analyzed the complex military calculations around circulating photographs of corpses during the Iraq war, especially the larger-than-life framed close-up of Jordanian terrorist Zarqawi's face after his death.[18] When Osama bin Laden was finally killed in 2011, President Obama did not allow for any photographs to be released in fear that there might be a backlash. A few years later he announced a decision to increase air strikes against ISIS in Syria shortly after the circulation of a video showing photojournalist James Foley's beheading. Images do not just matter politically; their circulation or censorship is a political act in and of itself.

The unity rally called for by French President François Holland following the *Charlie Hebdo* attacks was a spectacle staged by the state to produce images of unity after an act of terror allegedly caused by injurious visuals. The photograph that circulated worldwide and showed "[m]ore than a million people [surging] through the boulevards of Paris behind dozens of world leaders walking arm-in-arm Sunday"[19] was a laboriously constructed and highly symbolic news image.

At the turn of the twenty-first century, new digital technologies promised instantaneous dissemination and global reach, but they regularly do not deliver on that promise. Paul Blec, a veteran photo editor at AFP, emphasized that a major challenge in AFP's coverage of the unity rally had been the circulation of images: "I don't even remember how many photographers we had working. We even managed to get a photographer who was working from an airplane who could provide aerial views. . . . There were lots of photographers who worked for an hour or two but then they left because it was impossible." Given the extraordinary number of people on the streets, "they couldn't really circulate," Paul stressed, conflating the circulation of the photographer with the circulation of the image. "They could practically only photograph what was right in front of them, so they found ways to leave or to transmit."

Earlier Paul had described to me how photographers worked in tandem with an editor back at the desk in central Paris during big events such as the unity rally. Once the photographers transmitted their selected images, which they could do directly from their camera (either through a Wi-Fi connection or over a 3G or 4G network), the editor at the desk in the AFP office could see the photographer's output on a designated channel right on his or her computer monitor. In theory this could happen practically instantaneously once the photographer had released the shutter button. So why had transmission been a problem the morning of the rally? "There was practically no network because there were approximately a million people on the street and everyone was photographing themselves and sending selfies to their friends. And all those people were making calls from a single spot so there was absolutely no network functioning, making it impossible to transmit photographs [to the desk]."

The saturated networks meant the photographers were obliged to physically leave the event. Even once they could get to their motorcycles they had to negotiate blocked roadways due to traffic. In other words, the principal challenge in photographing the crowd amassed in Paris was the size of the networked crowd itself. Perhaps the actual democratization of photography is not just a matter of whose images get published or made available to publics, but rather one of network neutrality, a result of using the same networks to circulate images. The sheer volume of new media production—photographs taken on cell phones circulated over wireless telephone networks—and bodies in the streets forced the professional photographers not shooting aerial views back onto their motorcycles as in the days prior to on-site digital transmission. They had physically to take their memory cards to the AFP office or at least find a spot far enough from the crowds that they could connect to the Internet and transmit their images. This time it was the selfies that grounded the circulation of professional photographs. Whether or not the professional photographs had to compete with amateur images for real estate or payments, they were competing with them for the means of circulation, the infrastructures of representation.

Referring to the widespread use by news outlets of the video of the Kouachi brothers gunning down Ahmed Merabet, the French policeman they encountered outside *Charlie Hebdo*'s offices, Paul explained, "If a video like that is circulating online you have to decide whether or not to circulate it on the wire. This decision depends not only on whether or not the video itself is journalistically important but whether its circulation itself is news. So the news might not be what's in the video but that this video is in wide circulation. . . . There is a distinction between using the video or image as a document itself and saying that this photo or video is circulating on social networks."

Paul reminded me that he had in fact not spent the whole day on coverage of the rally: "There were sports and wars elsewhere." Specifically, reports had emerged of a massacre in Baga, Nigeria, on the border with Chad. Terrorist group Boko Haram had allegedly killed up to two thousand civilians. Paul had to validate aerial shots showing the regions of destruction, but neither AFP nor any of its competitors had anyone in northern Nigeria. "It was simply too dangerous," Paul explained. The 2014 AFP annual report stated that AFP not only would not send any of its own reporters to parts of Syria, Iraq, and northern Nigeria, but also that they would not use work produced by freelancers who went to these regions on their own. Global news director Michèle Léridon observed that AFP was confronted with "the unprecedented use of images intended to terrorise." AFP's decision not to send reporters into such risky areas "means that propaganda photos and videos released by IS are often our only sources of information about what is happening inside the self-declared 'caliphate.'"[20] Which is to say, there are now procedures in place to verify and find the source of images released by terrorist groups, but AFP and news organizations have decided that the circulation of images that terrorists produce is news that needs to be covered. So AFP brokers their images—adding captions and pushing the images out to news clients.

"ISIS doesn't need anybody to tell its side of the story. They should be holding workshops on social media use for us," one veteran photographer explained when I asked why he was so much more wary now than in prior conflicts. "Photojournalists are no longer viewed as neutral players . . . but rather as protagonists. There is less a sense that certain players, particularly in the Islamic world, need us." Digital technologies transformed the infrastructures of representation that enabled terrorist organizations, militaries, governments, and NGOs to all broker images in new ways. As I had already begun to see during my fieldwork at AFP, they could now produce and circulate photographs independently and had many more online publications of their own. Meanwhile, the increasing demand for visual content and the tyranny of the empty frame meant that their production was circulating ever more widely in the mainstream media.

AFP now has a social media editor, who was responsible for, among other things, launching AFP's Instagram account in 2014. AFP also continues to supply news directly to online news portals. Its relationship to the French state might be changing, though it is too early to tell to what extent, but the annual report gives a picture of an organization that is overtly more client and profit focused than the AFP of my fieldwork. This is revealed in such comments in the report as "[S]trategically, video and sport will continue to be our absolute priorities in order to guarantee the internationalisation of revenue." Last year AFP took advantage of its global reach by putting together "lifestyle packages." At the time of my fieldwork, a Getty Images senior executive explained the strength of a visual content provider as the ability to address the diverse picture needs of the newspaper world: "We can supply travel pictures, lifestyle pictures, celebrity, sports, and news pictures. I don't think the traditional wires offer anything close to that."[21] A decade later, they are certainly making an effort to catch up.

What is the greatest change at AFP Photo? Paul chuckled when I ask this question: "It's quiet. If you walk in to the editing room now you'd think you were at a bank. The desks resemble a bank: there's a lot less movement in the room, and there is little noise other than the tapping of fingers on keyboards." The number of meetings has been reduced, the little café is gone, everything in the office is electronic, and there are many more processes in place to handle the significantly increased volume of images—three thousand new photos a day. "There is no Desk France, there is no Desk Inter anymore. They've been fused." Now there's one desk. Fifteen editors in Paris all do the same job, and all supposedly do it in English. All images must now be captioned in English despite the fact that AFP still has a significant percentage of Francophone clients, because it was decided that translating the caption was slowing down circulation of the images and creating a disadvantage for AFP in comparison to its competition. The stakes are also higher since many of the editors at the publications, who would have fact-checked the wire caption, have been laid off.[22]

"If I edit four hundred images a day now, one hundred of them are of football," Paul told me. When photographers shoot at soccer matches, they have assigned spots and plug their cameras right into the network of the agency. The images then appear instantly as a channel on the editor's desk. To maximize the number of images they can work on and to keep track of photographers' channels, editors now work on two or three screens before them at once. The cost of such coverage is, however, high, since event organizers in sports and in cultural events increasingly try to control their public image by charging high fees for credentials, thereby framing the photographs to be taken long before the photographer arrives on site.

Meanwhile, Maggie, a photo editor at *Newsworld,* told me about receiving a breaking news story text notifying her of the *Charlie Hebdo* attack. "Cost concerns determine everything now," she said. Her first thought was not who to assign to cover the story, though a decade ago she may have had three or four photographers covering multiple aspects of the story. She assumed she'd have to rely instead on the wire services for the images. Given that the event was still in flux, "you can't have a photographer on assignment," she explained. "You don't know where to put him." The photographer must be *put* somewhere, for there is no time for investigation. As the event grew in magnitude, she decided to assign a photographer to the story: "So I went online and spent hours on Facebook, Twitter, and Instagram looking at who was sending pictures out. . . . It's not like before where there was a person at the agency feeding me ideas and pitching me their photographers"

The photographer she reached out to covered the rally. She also asked him to photograph the mosque the Kouachi brothers had attended. The news publication's reporter had interviewed the chief imam of the mosque earlier. The photographer sent Maggie the first photos by WeTransfer, an online file-transferring platform, within two hours of their initial conversation. He ended up working an additional day or two in order to cover stories about the suburbs of Paris, anti-Semitism, and Muslims in Paris. Maggie explained to me, "You need someone who can edit, who is fast and who has an eye. So you're watching on Facebook to see who is posting pictures soon after an event. Are they moving in the digital realm? His images stood out to me on the agency's website, but you always take a chance and have to assume that he can not just shoot but transmit really, really fast. . . . Speed and reach have replaced exclusivity as the key value of news images."

IMAGE ETHICS: A SIGN OF THE TIMES

Every February news publications around the world run the story of the World Press Photo contest awards being announced. At the 2015 awards, Mads Nissen, a staff photographer for the Danish paper *Politiken,* received first prize for an intimate photograph of a gay couple in St Petersburg, Russia, and there was much celebration of the photograph's not being one of conflict—a subject that has been perceived to dominate World Press Photo winners in the past.[23] However, the attention paid to the winners in the press report was somewhat overshadowed by the announcement by Lars Boering, World Press Photo's new managing director, that 22 percent of the entries that made it to the final round had been disqualified for postprocessing deemed inappropriate for journalism. The message being sent by the new leader of World Press Photo was that the 2015 winners had not only impressed the international jury of experts but also passed the scrutiny of two technicians—working separately—checking the original files (RAW files) for significant alterations to the content of the image.[24]

A few weeks later the organization revoked the award for the winner in the Contemporary Issues category. Italian photographer Giovanni Troilo had won with a gritty ten-image series titled *The Dark Heart of Europe,* about Charleroi, Belgium, a city he claimed symbolized the whole of Europe: "the collapse of industrial manufacturing, rising unemployment, increasing immigration and outbreak of micro-criminality."[25] The series included ominous scenes of nudity, from a shirtless tattooed man with a gun to a naked woman in a cage. Intentionally or not, the images suggest a connection between sexual deviance and postindustrial blight. The mayor of Charleroi wrote a complaint letter addressing not only the negative light cast on his community but also the allegations that some of the photographs had been staged, including one showing the photographer's cousin having sex in the back of a car. The lighting of the photograph—apparently the photographer had placed a flashlight inside the car to light the couple from below—drew criticism from many photographers. At issue was whether there was any place in photojournalism for staging—defined by the contest's rules as something that would not have happened without the photographer's presence. Jean-François Leroy, director of Visa Pour l'Image, announced that it was canceling World Press Photo's exhibit for the 2015 festival.

In the end, Troilo's award was revoked—not because of any allegations of staging, but because one particular image had been captioned by the photographer as taken in Charleroi but in fact had been taken in Molenbeek, some sixty kilometers away. The particular image is as bizarre as it is visually striking, showing a powdered male body stretched out on a table surrounded by several nude female bodies and men (clothed) who seem to be at a lascivious feast. The image apparently showed the re-enacting of a painting in the studio of the well-known Belgian artist Vadim Vosters. This proved to be the crucial detail. At issue was not the ambiguous relationship between this restaging of a painting and postindustrial urban Europe, but rather the actual postal code of Vosters's studio, since that had been given as the location of the shot. The managing editor of World Press photo could now claim, "We now have a clear case of misleading information, and this changes the way the story is perceived. A rule has now been broken, and a line has been crossed." In an article for the *Columbia Journalism Review,* photographer Nina Berman described this as "an Al Capone–style solution: if we can't get him on murder let's get him for tax evasion."[26]

Boering concluded that the whole matter had been a sign of the times, in which photojournalism and documentary photography are changing rapidly. The issue was simply that *The Dark Heart of Europe* belonged to a category of personal storytelling that was somewhere in between art and photojournalism. Would this change photojournalism in the digital age? one interviewer asked him. He answered, "I think photojournalism will become more and more part of the visual industry, the creative visual industry, and the communication through images is going to be massive. It already is. I think we should talk about visual communication in the future, and photojournalism will be a part of that."[27] As this book has shown, photojournalism has been a part of the creative visual industry at least since the rise of visual content providers. What is unclear is how this might contribute to better journalism.

These debates are not new. Think back to Alex Levy's comments to his peers during the 2004 Masterclass insisting that he was "not changing reality . . . just bringing up the colors" to move the reader.[28] Boering notes, "We always know it will be processed. There is no such thing as a negative these days. It's a file that's been processed."[29] Of course photography historians have rightly underscored that the potential to enhance images long predates pixels, but the question has shifted from "Has this image been manipulated?" to "In what specific ways has this image been manipulated?" One of the roles of the World Press Photo jury these days is apparently to judge postprocessing by applicable industry standards.

If we compare Troilo's transgression with Michael Finkel's, described in the introduction, there are some similarities: Finkel misidentified a particular individual; Troilo misidentified a specific location. However, there are also differences. Finkel argued that he had extrapolated facts "from what he learned was *typical* of boys on such journeys," and the newspaper issued a second editor's note some months later claiming that, with a couple of minor corrections, Finkel's reporting had held up to scrutiny.[30] Troilo told the *Guardian* that "some of his images were staged to recreate issues or scenes he says typify Charleroi, but he argues this does not affect the journalistic integrity of his work." His defense partly rests on the fact that he was, he says, "telling a story based on things that happened in Charleroi and during that year I always checked these in the press."[31] Whose journalistic integrity was Troilo relying on? In other words, Troilo seems to have taken his task as precisely what some of the text editors I encountered thought appropriate for photography: illustrating the news that was constructed in words, providing cutting-edge photography or avant-garde visual content for those who might want it "with their news." That Troilo always checked events in the press implies that he does not see himself as part of the press itself. On his webpage Troilo diligently provides links to several articles about Charleroi on which he based his images.

Moreover, as was evident in the number of stories Maggie needed the freelance photographer to cover in just a few days, budgets prevent even those within the press from doing more in-depth coverage. Nina Berman, an experienced documentary photographer, sums up the complexity and interconnection of the changes well:

> Before the great media disruption, photographers were sent out on a story for weeks, sometimes months. The purpose was for the photographer to watch. Quietly, patiently, carefully observing subtle changes in mood, emotion, light, shadow, and through framing and positioning, and trusted relationships with subjects, we were to bring back images that reflected an uncompromised, closely seen reality.
>
> Then budgets shrank, three months turned into three weeks, three weeks into three days, three days into three hours and what's left to shoot? A portrait where posing, lighting, sometimes propping, is now the norm.
>
> Digital cameras, and the ease of moving pictures from laptops and phones, created a wave of overnight photographers from diverse backgrounds—art, journalism, fashion—all vying for the same publications. Major media players like the *New York Times* and *Time* now routinely publish a variety of photographic styles from staged portraits, some of them heavily post-processed, to traditional reportage to app-laced iPhone images, making it difficult to know what constitutes photojournalism today.[32]

JOURNALISTIC CONTENT

World Press Photo's new managing director, Lars Boering—in great contrast to many voices who over the years have declared photojournalism to be under threat, ailing, or dead—declared, "People are always surprised when I say that I'm very optimistic when I look at the opportunities and chances photographers and visual storytellers have these days."[33] I want to argue that Boering's optimism makes perfect sense for photographers and visual storytellers. We need to be asking about the future of journalism as well. Perhaps the director of Visa Pour l'Image, Jean-François Leroy, is right; maybe it is the press and not photography that is in crisis. But if the news must be accompanied by obligatory images due to content-management systems, a press in crisis nonetheless shapes public perceptions of the possibilities for photography. What is lost if photojournalists are merely visual storytellers? I ask this question not to reify an outdated and never attainable ideal of truth, but rather to suggest that we are losing some anchoring of the value of images to knowledge about the world. This anchoring is central to the political power of news images.

I heard similar optimism from a senior executive responsible for editorial assignments at a prominent visual content provider: "Imagery has never been as important as it is now. This is a time of opportunity." Part of his enthusiasm came from a conviction that today's youth have a different relationship to imagery and that everyone's being a photographer in a digital age of social media platforms is a positive development for professional photography because more people appreciate images. When I inquired about the shrinking budgets for editorial work and archival sales, he replied:

> There is a new church. It is no longer [established media outlets]. They don't have those budgets anymore. But Merrill Lynch [the investment banking division of Bank of America] does. There are lots of foundations that are being set up by blue-chip companies such as the Hewlett Foundation, and they do good things. Nothing to do with the corporation. We're doing good things like empowering women around the world through microcredit.
>
> For the photographer this is a great opportunity because they get to do ethical work and tell stories they would have told anyway but they just have to go to a different church. My job is to help them find different outlets.
>
> You need to think about it as the church paying for it. As noblemen used to pay for art, this is about artists finding revenue. Personal vision is of course still important. If you look hard enough and are smart enough you can survive. You need to be looking at different ways of making money.

The executive repeatedly referred to photographers as artists in search of revenue. In his telling, news is just another art form for which one can find a wealthy donor. What the analogy to papal patronage runs counter to is the very ideal of a free press that serves public interests. Who will have access to these images? At the fiftieth-anniversary events for World Press Photo in 2005, when most of the attendees were bemoaning citizen

journalism, Drik Picture Library founder Shahidul Alam had underscored the importance of independent websites, especially for "stories
mainstream media is afraid to publish": stories critical of advertisers and
sponsors, of the media itself, or, in developing countries like Bangladesh,
of nongovernmental aid organizations. "No one likes to bite the hands
that feeds you," says Alam.[34] Moreover, a patronage model is hardly
democratic in terms of who will get support. Which church will support
those whom Alam calls "photographers in the majority world"? When I
asked about this uneven playing field, the executive mentioned a young
Latin American photographer who had applied for the visual content
provider's grant for a photographic project: "That's how we discovered
him. Now he will be shown at Perpignan."

Contests are perhaps more important than ever because not only do
they get a photographer recognized in the journalism world, but an
agent can then approach a corporation and suggest using a Pulitzer
Prize–winning or World Press Photo Award–winning photographer for
their commercial work. "The public is far more discerning, and they are
looking for reality," the executive told me. "Journalistic content is what
marketing wants. That's the kind of marketing people believe." The
executive's optimism stems from his belief in a claim, made by many in
marketing, that the public is moved by journalistic imagery. My question is how this might translate into better institutional support for
visual journalism, not just commercial work for prize-winning photojournalists. So if one is thinking of photographers, there do seem to be
many opportunities, most of which revolve around corporations, either
directly through commercial work or indirectly through work for cor-
porate-sponsored philanthropic foundations. The question remains,
however, of what happens to journalism itself when what photographers can get paid for is producing "journalistic content" for marketing.
If the public are looking for reality, can we not find ways to get them to
pay for quality visual journalism rather than paying for goods marketed
with journalistic imagery?

VISIBILITY, NOT MONEY

As the chapters of this book have demonstrated, the pressure for photographers to earn their living partly through commercial work or
through celebrity photographs is not new—the financial equation has
always been a difficult one—nor is the sense among photojournalists
that there is something dirty about profits. Yet because both the volume

of and budgets for editorial work have dropped drastically, photographers have to do more commercial work to stay afloat. In this context, the enthusiasm about work for foundations and nongovernmental organizations becomes even more comprehensible. For example, a veteran photographer explained that, compared with commercial work, editorial work for NGOs "is closer to my heart—still what I want to do." Moreover, the work was often fulfilling because he knew photographers could not affect change on their own but could have an impact by "working with the change makers." And, once produced, journalistic content, or what Boering calls "genuine images," might then appear in traditional news publications, whether digital or print. The above photographer told me that every now and then he might still get a project commissioned by *National Geographic* or the *New Yorker,* but "more often I get the work supported through alternative means and then go to more traditional outlets so that they can publish the work once I have created it through other means."

The critical question is, Where does journalism happen? Does a photograph become a news image just by appearing in a news publication, or do the processes of production matter as well? Is there actually anything being lost if photographers find creative ways of producing work that is important to them by working for foundations and NGOs? For starters, the potential depth of reporting generated by writers and photographers collaborating on a story together is lost. Might we not see this as creative adaptation at a time of great transition and uncertainty? After all, photographers are then able to accept the low payments offered by news publications or their blogs that want to show their work or can even agree to let it be used for free because the bulk of their income is not generated through editorial sales. If you recall the news and editorial division at GVI, they made first sales to news publications; then the sales team could sell the image for commercial purposes or to other kinds of publications. Here it has been reversed: an NGO assumes the cost of production; the second sale is to the press, which is offered a finished product to whose production it did not have to contribute resources.

David Campbell draws a distinction between modes of information, photojournalism being his principal concern, and modes of distribution, such as the traditional press. He argues that photojournalism can not only survive but thrive if it moves beyond the fortunes of newspapers and magazines.[35] Approached not from the perspective of how photographers can make a living, but how publics can be served by quality visual journalism, the question again is, Where does journalism happen? While I do not believe that the solution lies only in existing magazines and newspapers, I believe that photographs are shaped by the institutional contexts in which they are produced and brokered. When photographers are willing to let their images be put online for free or paltry sums, they at least get visibility. The real cost may be the invisibility of the work of professional image brokers and their disappearance altogether.

"Visibility is in the 2000s what money was in the 1990s," Daphne, the industry veteran, explained to me. The photo blogs of traditional media are important because no one will hire you if you're not visible.[36] It is easy to see why all kinds of photographers—from the young, naive idealists to the war-weary veterans—might jump at the opportunity to work with organizations perceived as change makers: this is a way to skip over all the self-doubt confessed to me over the years about whether news images actually have impact. And yet what is also short-circuited is a core function of journalism in democracy: the contribution to a vibrant public sphere. If a photo essay is appearing in a news publication only after it has been produced by an NGO, can it possibly offer information that might challenge the solutions proposed or pursued by that organization? Who will produce the work about issues that foundations might not yet have tackled? What about work that isn't necessarily geared to highlight a problem or offer a solution?[37] How do these image brokers and those at traditional news outlets share information when a project is chosen for publication in the latter? It is imperative for us to investigate how philanthropic foundations and NGOs are funding the production of news images and to better understand whether this is a new form of journalism or the production of journalistic content as marketing.

LOOKING AT THE WORLD PICTURE AFTER ANOTHER EARTHQUAKE

In the beginning of this book about the seismic changes in the landscape of the photojournalism industry, I analyzed a photograph of a villager looking through the window of a helicopter as he was being evacuated following the devastating 2005 earthquake in Pakistan. On April 25, 2015, a massive earthquake struck Nepal, resulting in almost nine thousand deaths—one of the largest and most tragic news stories of the year. Yet there was no influx of cosmopolitan photojournalists.[38] Perhaps we should celebrate this. Daphne told me that she always reminded those looking back to the glory days of news photography that it was a time when practically all of the photographers came from the Western world and worked for Western media: "It was a small profession, mostly of foreign observers, for a relatively small audience. . . . Information is now created locally. This is a big change. It's not just about not sending people [because there aren't any travel budgets anymore]; this is a change in perspective. A local photographer is talking about his or her own country. They are interested in development and growth, and people in photojournalism have not traditionally been interested in growth."[39] Presumably there have been many people, not just the mayor of Charleroi, Belgium, who have felt misrepresented by photojournalism. And some of the most respected work in photojournalism certainly ired the officials in the part of the world being represented. Which is to say, image brokering is always a situated and political activity. Daphne assured me that, thanks to online journalism, blogs, and social media, "[t]he world population who saw quality photojournalism before was small. Now a very big part of the world sees quality photojournalism."

Just a few hours after the magnitude 7.8 earthquake, Nepalese professional photographer Sumit Dayal and New Delhi–based freelance writer Tara Bedi—along with several others who ran Photo.Circle, a platform for emerging photographers in Kathmandu—launched an Instagram feed titled "Nepal Photo Project." Instagram, owned by Facebook, is an online mobile photo- and video-sharing service that enables users to share visual material through social-networking sites like Twitter, Tumblr, and Flickr. The Nepal Photo Project, set out "to collectively put out useful and credible information from people that we know and trust on the ground, all under one banner," Bedi explained to *Time* magazine's *Lightbox* blog.[40] They gathered images from thirty-five photographers from Nepal, India, and Bangladesh. "The group chose Instagram and Facebook because "it is becoming evident that people tend to consume news and information through images," wrote Dayal for the *Lightbox* blog. "Nepal Photo Project is our way of attempting to make sure that the visuals become more functional and personal in nature as opposed to just devastation porn." In addition to the images shared on Instagram, all of which have extensive captions, the group's Facebook page has links to fund-raising campaigns, photographs of missing people, volunteer opportunities, and other pertinent resources. Bedi added, "We've been thinking a lot about what Nepal

Photo Project is doing and if it's making a significant contribution—or any contribution at all—and what we're beginning to realize is that it is not the strength of the images that get responses, it is the stories they communicate and the captions. It sets us apart from regular reportage and our followers have really appreciated the photographers' putting such a personal face on this tragedy."

Bedi is voicing what many other image brokers in the preceding chapters have also emphasized: that news images are a way to put a human face on a map. Ironically, what she is describing—stories that communicate, with excellent captions—is what my informants described as good reportage. It is not the kind of reportage that can be done quickly while searching for a photo to illustrate a story so it can be filed. I found out about the Nepal Photo Project because as soon as the group began to establish themselves, Sumit Dayal invited several key image brokers at various news publications and blogs to a private group that the photographers involved had formed. This allowed photo editors at news publications to see exactly how these photographers were being instructed to write captions or guided in terms of how to post their photography. For example, Dayal encouraged everyone to link their Instagram account to Facebook and Twitter and then post everything to Instagram so that it could immediately find three outlets. Moreover, he reassured photographers stranded in places with little or no Internet connectivity that an advantage of Instagram was that you could post even with very slow connections. Dayal's tips were directly about the infrastructures of representation. Watching their production as she searched for ways to visualize the earthquake story for *Newsworld,* photo editor Maggie was impressed: "They were taking control of the story. Local photographers were being their own news service."

In November 2015, the Nepal Photo Project had sixty thousand followers. Like the Nar Photo Collective's Facebook page, it appealed to diverse audiences. The Nepal Photo Project's images are accompanied by extensive comments and detailed information. Figure 9, a photograph taken by Indian photographer Ritesh Uttamchandani, shows a boy and his father aboard an Indian Air Force rescue helicopter. Or rather, it shows the photograph as it appeared on the Nepal Photo Project's Instagram feed. There is no pretense of seeing through anyone's eyes. The photographer tells us the context of his encounter with nine-year-old Suresh Tamang, and the boy stares at us. It is a photograph about being looked at. The frame is almost that of a selfie. Next to the image one can see comments by viewers, a certain audience's

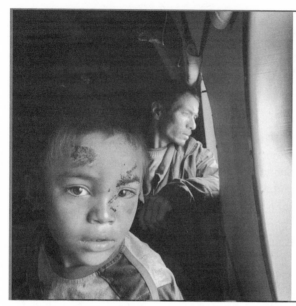

FIGURE 9. Child and father in a helicopter as they are being evacuated after the April 25, 2015, Nepal earthquake. Photograph taken with an iPhone 5s and posted on Instagram as part of the Nepal Photo Project. © Ritesh Uttamchandani/ www.riteshuttamchandani.com. Used by the kind permission of the photographer.

reception becoming part of one's view of the image. Facebook purchased Instagram in 2012. The time is ripe for more research on what kinds of journalism are possible on commercial social media platforms as new infrastructures of representation.

VISUAL WORLDMAKING TOMORROW

By the time this book is published it is likely that former Associated Press photographer David Guttenfelder will have a million followers on Instagram. Photographers emphasize to me that the potential readership on social media is far beyond that of traditional news outlets. Michael Strong, who no longer works at GVI, couldn't be more excited about the future of photojournalism: "I think it's an epic moment. Everybody's taking pictures, consuming pictures. Pictures have become absolutely critical. Look at Instagram. People are browsing other people's photographs. It is a beautiful moment in terms of engagement. . . . People love pictures. Now when they see truly great photographs they appreciate the craft in a new way." He admits that "[t]he business side is a mess." But when I ask about the future of visual journalism he's exuberant: "The new currency is Instagram followers. Right now social media creates a lift, but we haven't monetized it. . . . But you know that's coming. . . . Right now if you are an independent storyteller you can communicate directly with your audience. If you have something to say, you can say it and find your audience." Strong believes we will soon be asked to pay to see certain Instagram feeds or other venues for visual journalism.

I have focused this book on image brokers and their invisible labor because I want to push back against the myth of the solo visual storyteller. David Guttenfelder's Instagram feed might have many followers, but he also had Associated Press and *National Geographic* behind him, both institutions with considerable resources devoted to knowledge production. This is not to take anything away from his or any other photographer's talent or identity as a journalist, but rather to argue that the visual knowledge a photojournalist shares with others, whether they are newspaper readers or Instagram followers, is not his or hers alone. Guttenfelder himself points to people who have contributed to his photography.[41] News images are fundamentally shaped by the infrastructures of representation in which they are produced and circulated. Professional image brokers committed to journalism are key to ensuring that it is not merely commercial interests that shape the ways in which world news is visualized. Visual journalism can be strong only if it is more than just a part of the visual content industry.

Even World Press Photo these days is more modest about its mission. Its website tells us that the world, press, and photography are all being interrogated at this moment.[42] We cannot return to a predigital moment. Nor should we desire to do so. As Daphne repeatedly told me, "It was a time when practically all of the photographers came from the Western world and worked for Western media." Yet I do share Michael Strong's optimism. This is moment of great potential—a moment when a new kind of journalism could emerge. Michael Schudson claims, "Everything we thought we knew about journalism needs to be rethought in the digital age."[43] The time is now to harness the explosion of interest in photographic imagery and promote forms of journalism in which images are not merely illustrative but generate new kinds of investigations. Moreover, because of the ways in which photographs can potentially circulate, visual journalism can provide possibilities for more global collaborations and platforms, providing opportunities not only for infinitely mobile cosmopolitan photographers, but also for photographers worldwide who want to share their visions. From selfies to satellite images, photographs are integral parts of our daily practices of worldmaking on many scales. News images are central to our understandings of places in the world—both our own and that of others—and shape our ability to imagine the global political possibilities before us. The best news images are the ones that spark conversations and provoke questions. The best image brokers ask critical questions before, during, and after the shutter button has been released. Understanding the work of image brokers, and the ways that images and worldviews are jointly produced and circulated, is a first step to discovering new ways of seeing.

Acknowledgments

In spite of a persistent fiction, we never write on a blank
page, but always on one that has already been written on.
—Michel de Certeau, *The Practice of Everyday Life*

Edward Said, Susan Sontag, José Saramago, Allan Sekula, Stuart Hall,
and Harun Farocki all passed away during the years it took to complete
this research. I never met any of these individuals, but their work is in
the fiber of the pages on which this book was written. These intellectuals profoundly shaped the way I think about many of the core themes of
this book: representations, visuality, photography, and their complex
relationship to political and social possibilities. I have attempted to note
specific intellectual debts throughout the text, no doubt with some
unintentional omissions, yet I want to begin my acknowledgments by
paying my respects to these individuals, whose clarity of thought and
provocative questions I miss when trying to make sense of images today.

I learned to read and write in Athens, Greece, where my father, Mustafa Rasim Gürsel, was the correspondent for a prominent Turkish
daily newspaper. Over the course of three decades, he worked as a
writer and producer in radio, print, and television. That journalism
matters deeply is a value I absorbed too long ago to remember. I prac-
ticed my alphabet on the perforated telex paper that seemed to grow in
mounds in the office every night, which is to say I learned to write on
strips of day-old breaking news. Because the newspaper's Athens bureau
was a room in our family's apartment, the background noise to my
childhood was the sound of my father forming his ideas, and crafting
his words, whether via telex, click-clacking in his rapid-fire two-fin-
gered style on his typewriter, or in his booming voice over the phone

during an interview. For me, the newspaper was the most magical of gifts that arrived every day and provided, above all, the chance to ask many questions. My father and I crafted an unusual father–daughter bond out of discussions about how stories were constructed, whether in newspapers, novels, or films, in images or text. These conversations anchored my peripatetic childhood, and over the years, many of them centered on front-page photographs.

As an anthropologist, I have learned about the photojournalism industry from a group of extraordinarily talented, passionate, and intelligent people whether behind the lens, at an agency, at a wire service, at a workshop, or at news publications. The twenty-first century has brought many challenges and changes, and almost all of my informants and their institutions were grappling with how to adapt to constant upheaval. Partly I believe my informants entrusted me with their thoughts and allowed me into their lives because we share a passion: telling better stories, stories that matter politically, stories that can move people. Like them, I am convinced that news images matter profoundly in this endeavor. Moreover, based on watching how my students learn, I have no doubt that photography will continue to play an important role in capturing the imaginations of others.

I wish I could acknowledge by name the many people in the photojournalism world, particularly at GVI, AFP, *Newsworld,* and World Press Photo, who shared with me their thoughts, passions, and frustrations. In accordance with the guidelines of the Committee for the Protection of Human Subjects of the University of California, Berkeley, I had to promise all of my informants anonymity, which is why I have used pseudonyms throughout. To a certain extent I think that this is helpful because it kept the focus on the types of decisions made by many different image brokers rather than on particular personalities. However, I am saddened that I cannot express my gratitude by name to individuals who put up with me for hours, days, weeks, and, for a few unlucky ones, months or years on end. Access is critical to covering any story: *you* made this project possible.

I was tremendously fortunate to be allowed to attend the 2003 Eddie Adams Workshop (thanks to Jessica Stuart and especially to Alyssa Adams, who generously provided me with video and audio recordings of earlier workshops). Visa Pour L'Image (2003, 2004 and 2015) and the 2004 World Association of Newspapers meeting (thanks to Bertrand Pecquirie) were central to my education in photojournalism and its role in world news. All the World Press Photo events I participated in constituted critical parts of my fieldwork. Special thanks to all those at World Press Photo at the time and the masters and photographers in their workshops, both in Amsterdam and in Istanbul, for trusting me with their aspirations, successes, and disappointments over many years.

This book began as a dissertation written in the Department of Anthropology at UC Berkeley. Or perhaps it began when Nejat Dinç gave me a copy of Catherine Lutz and Jane Lou Collins's *Reading National Geographic* before classes had even begun. Nelson Graburn is the dissertation advisor everyone wishes they had. His enthusiasm, curiosity, and productivity set an impossible example. Donald Moore helped me find a place within the discipline, took my writing on documentary photography seriously, and saw a project where I had seen only a paper for his class. I remain humbled by his ethics of care. Paul Rabinow fundamentally shaped how I think about subjects in many senses and taught me that discomfort is a condition of thinking hard. Alexei Yurchak, Lawrence Cohen, and Charles Hirschkind also contributed to my development as an anthropologist. Ulf Hannerz, William Mazzarella, and Mark Pedelty offered encouragement and suggestions early in the formation of this project. Paul Frosh kindly shared the manuscript of his book *The Image Factory* at a moment when it was very helpful in shaping my fieldwork and has been an inspiring interlocutor ever since. I benefited tremendously from discussions with fellow anthropology students Ivan Arenas, Cristiana Giordano, Saida Hodžić, Kevin Karpiak, Liz Roberts, Dar Rudnyckyj, Sholeh Shahrokhi, and Maria Stoilkova. Leo Hsu, a photographer and anthropologist, became an invaluable advisor and friend. Ekin Kocabaş and Tom Christensen helped me understand the technology behind wire photo transmission. Gretchen Case was a stellar writing partner and perfected an impression of Bela Karolyi's "You can do it!"

The Designated Emphasis in Film Studies at UC Berkeley led me to Linda Williams's "Film Theory" and Mark Sandberg's "Film Historiography" seminars and the extraordinary group of students with whom I was introduced to diverse ways of thinking about images. It was in Linda's class that I undertook my initial fieldwork on the uses of 9/11 imagery, from which the idea to do fieldwork on decisions behind the circulation of images grew. It was from working with her on *Screening Sex* that I learned what it takes to finish a book. Irina Leimbacher lovingly introduced me to Dziga Vertov—specifically, the scene in *Kino Eye* where the magic of reverse motion gives the slaughtered cow his entrails back—and got me thinking about the radical potential in illustrating production processes.

The fieldwork for this project was made possible by a Social Science Research Council International Dissertation Research Fellowship, a Dissertation Fieldwork Grant from the Wenner-Gren Foundation, and a UC Berkeley Chancellor's Opportunity Award. Volunteer Lawyers for the Arts in New York helped me negotiate a nondisclosure agreement that allowed me to keep working. A Doreen B. Townsend Center for the Humanities writing fellowship, and a Dan David Prize Scholarship (Journalists in Print Media) funded the early stages of writing.

Professor Haluk Şahin and Niyazi Dalyancı are my guiding voices of old-school journalism and have talked to me about the news (quite literally) all my life. They led me to key interlocutors Gökşin Sipahioğlu, the legendary founder of the Sipa Press agency; and Sinan Fişek, who opened the way for fieldwork at AFP. Ayperi Karabuda Ecer shared her experiences in many domains of photojournalism and contributed her wisdom to the project from beginning to end. I am indebted to Professor Michael Watts for suggesting I contact photographer Ed Kashi, who became an important interlocutor. At a critical juncture, over breakfast, Ed called a friend and cajoled him to finally answer my emails, and only then did my fieldwork actually get rolling. Melek Ulagay shared her home with me and at critical times gave me the liberty to make choices I would not otherwise have dared. I learned much about Paris, French photojournalism, life, and love from Magdalena Herrera, Elodie Perreau, and Michel Rubinel, each of whom was essential to my research. I am honored to have a photograph by Michel on the cover. Melissa and Mitch Scott kindly hosted me during my stay in Washington, D.C. Photographers Kerem Uzel and especially Tolga Sezgin taught me not just about ways of seeing but also about ways of living. Özcan Yurdalan modeled the importance of documenting photographic processes during politically tumultuous times. I am honored to have seen the birth of the Nar Photos collective and watched it develop into its unique role in Turkish civic life today. *Tüm Nar Photos ekibine canı gönülden teşekkür ederim.*

This book took shape while I was part of the Michigan Society of Fellows. Miranda Johnson contributed insights and good cheer regularly. Krisztina Fehervary sharpened my anthropological lens and made writing a book a much less lonely journey. Over the years the book benefited from conversations with Elif Babül, Liz Bird, Amahl Bishara, Craig Campbell, Feride Çiçekoğlu, Ed Clark, Gabriella Coleman, Elizabeth Edwards, Tejaswini Ganti, Bishnupriya Ghosh, Faye Ginsburg, Sherine Hamdy, Mark Haxthausen, Heiko Henkel, Matthew Hull, Kajri Jain, Webb

Keane, Tom Keenan, Chris Kelty, Stuart Kirsch, Charlotte Klonk, Brian Larkin, Don Lopez, Tina Lupton, Nomusa Makhubu, Fred Myers, Marline Otte, Alejandro Paz, Rima Praspaliauskiene, Aswin Punathambekar, Fred Ritchin, Robert Samet, Oksana Sarkisova, Naomi Schiller, Chris Skeaff, Patsy Spyer, Janelle Taylor, Jennifer Terry, Halide Velioğlu, and Patsy Yaeger. The chapter on Barnstorm owes much to Christina Schwenkel's generous and provocative comments on an earlier draft. I am grateful to audiences at several universities and conferences who thought through the material with me, and particularly to the organizers and participants of the following events, which significantly contributed to the shape of the argument and my thinking on photography and media in general: the 2002 "From Art History to Visual Culture: Studying the Visual after the Cultural Turn" course at Central European University; the 2006 Getty Summer Institute "Constructing the Past in the Middle East"; the 2010 "Visible Presence: Memory, Photography and the Historical Imagination" workshop at Williams College; the 2011 University of Cincinnati "Look Better: The Critical Visions Symposium"; the 2013 "Semiha Es Women Photographers International Symposium"; the 2014 "Image Operations" conference at ICI Berlin; and the 2015 "Wenner Gren New Media, New Publics" symposium.

I specialize in short forms and hence am particularly grateful to those who encouraged me when I struggled to see the next steps in such a long project. The Visual Culture Writing Group and the Race and Gender Visual Group, both at UC Berkeley, provided valuable feedback, and Elizabeth Abel and Leigh Raiford gave me the opportunity to publish "Reflecting on Daguerreotypes in the Digital Age" at a key juncture. The Social Science Research Council Book Fellowship spurred my thinking about the project as a book. Peggy McCracken became an inspiring intellectual mentor and cherished friend, and had the kindness to tell me when the book wasn't ready. The book would surely not exist at all if Kathryn Babayan had not insisted on hosting a manuscript workshop for me and inviting interlocutors whose work I admire. I remain humbled by the thoughtful engagement and significant contributions of Gillian Feeley-Harnik, Alaina Lemon, Joanne Leonard, Alex Potts, Paddy Scannell, and Andrew Shryock. *Kathryn-can, dünya bir yana, sen bir yana.*

This book is being published at a time when scholarship on photography is flourishing. I am fortunate to count some particularly astute interlocutors on visual culture among my friends: Kelly Askew, Jenny Chio, Lucia Nimcova, Meg McLagan, Rosalind Morris, Ben

O'Loughlin, Stephanie Sadre-Orafai, Olga Shevchenko, and Ruti Talmor. I met Rebecca Stein at the beginning of my academic career. It was a felicitous meeting. One of the pleasures of working on photography has been conversing with her as her own research has turned increasingly toward politics at the level of the pixel. In 2010 I read *Refracted Visions: Popular Photography and National Modernity in Java* almost as soon as it was published and could not sleep till I had finished it. In awe, I wrote to the author with a few questions, and one of the greatest gifts of this project has been my ensuing friendship with Karen Strassler. Karen read the entire manuscript and helped me see it as part of many larger conversations. Finally, Kathryn Mathers was always there: she welcomed me to anthropology, fundamentally shaped how I think about representations and places in the world, guided me in my fieldwork, and brainstormed subtitles for the book. For almost two decades now, Kathryn was always willing to talk and read, and through many storms of research and life was a model of integrity and resilience. Through her own scholarship, Kathryn taught me to take anthropology as seriously as I'd always taken journalism and also showed me the generative ways in which the two fields could be put into conversation. These three women in particular clarified my thinking with hard questions and engaged critique, and for all its flaws, this is no doubt a better book than it would have been without them.

Some portions of the book have been published in earlier versions: A portion of chapter 1 appears in "A Short History of Wire Service Photography," in *Getting the Picture: The Visual Culture of the News,* edited by Vanessa Schwartz and Jason Hill (Bloomsbury Publishers, 2015). A version of chapter 3 was published as "The Politics of Wire Service Photography: Infrastructures of Representation in a Digital Newsroom" in *American Ethnologist* 39, no. 1. A much earlier version of chapter 4 appeared as "The Rule of Text: Everyday Practices of Editing the World," in *The Anthropology of News and Journalism: Global Perspectives,* edited by S. Elizabeth Bird (Indiana University Press, 2010). Portions of chapters 4 and 7 appear in "Worldmaking, Frame by Frame," in *Image Operations: Visual Media and Political Conflict,* edited by Jens Eder and Charlotte Klonk (Manchester University Press, 2016). And a kernel of chapter 6 appeared as "Visa Pour L'Image: Negotiating the Network World-Making of Photojournalism" in *Anthropology News* 47, no. 6.

In the end, I needed to find a home to finish this book, and my classroom in the Department of International Studies at Macalester College provided me with one. All of my students, especially those who took my photography seminars, made working on an overdue project exciting again with their contagious curiosity. I am convinced that this generation appreciates the potential of visual journalism more than any before it, and I hope to learn from their engagements with documentary visuals for many years to come. Madeline Gerrard, Liz Hallgren, and Molly Starks Ragsdale and librarian Ginny Moran provided valuable research assistance and help preparing the final manuscript. Clay Steinman generously read the entire manuscript and pointed me to key texts in communication studies. I am grateful for the collegiality of all the faculty and staff of the Departments of International Studies, Media and Cultural Studies, and Anthropology. I appreciate the careful and thoughtful comments I received from three reviewers for the University of California Press and wish to thank Dore Brown, Stacy Eisenstark, and Reed Malcolm for guiding the book through production. Carl Walesa provided expert copyediting.

Throughout the many moves and transitions that shaped my life while I worked on this project, I was sustained by an incredible family and community of friends who ground me: Zeynep Atikkan and Bülent Gültekin, Karen Barkey, Sina Baydur, Gretchen Case, Niyazi Dalyancı, Lee Ann Denley, Andrea Goulet and Jed Esty, Amanda Hammar, Pam and David Leeming, Deirdre Mackey, Diana Matteson, Tony and Marilyn Mociun, Ferhunde Öktem, Rima Praspaliauskiene, Bengü and Whit Shepard, Meltem Sönmez, and Ami Walsh.

In the end, this book was completed thanks to the love and support of the people who are my home, wherever in the world I may be. I could not have wished for a better or more erudite mind to think with than Sean Silver's. He has read this manuscript too many times and repeatedly made it better. Our daughter, Ada, is my island of joy where I begin and end each day. I lived with my sister, Umut Gürsel, during my fieldwork in New York, filling her living room with unwieldy stacks of newspapers and magazines. Fittingly, it is in her home that I have edited the final draft. I lean on her in all I do—*kapı gibi hep arkamdasın*. This book was written in memory of my father, Mustafa Rasim Gürsel, with whom I still have daily conversations, often about news images, though it has been almost twenty years since he died. This book is dedicated to my mother, Nuran Gürsel, the most selfless person I know, whose commitment to this project surpassed even mine, and who makes everything possible.

Cast of Characters

Character	Title or Position	Appearance (chapter)
Agence France-Presse (AFP)		
Pierre Martin	Director of the photo department	1, 3, conclusion
Olivier Valery	Senior manager of the photo department	1, 3
Marie	Director of the Desk Inter	3
Christophe	Codirector of the Desk Inter	3
Paul Blec	Experienced photo editor	conclusion
Janet	American working the Third Desk	3
Magda	Polish photo editor of Desk Inter	3
Patrick	Head of sales representatives	1
Manoli	Sales representative	1, 3
Global Views Inc. (GVI)		
Portia Friedman	Vice president of global marketing	introduction, 1
Michael Strong	Vice president of news and editorial	introduction, 1, 2, conclusion
Henry Smith	Director of news	2
Edith	Director of global research	2
Ed	Senior photo editor	2, 6
Robert	Senior photo editor, Paris	2
Alain	Senior photo editor, Paris	2
Jackie	Assistant photo editor	introduction, 2
Liz	Assistant photo editor	2
Paul	Temp photo editor also responsible for correspondence with military and officials to get access for photographers	2
Sophie	Temp responsible for captioning	2

Character	Title or Position	Appearance (chapter)
Photographers represented by GVI		
Alex Levy	New photographer, embedded	2, 5, 7
Ilan	Relatively new Israeli photographer	2
Jacques	Senior combat photographer, unilateral[1]	1, 2
Lydia	Experienced photographer, unilateral	2
Philippe	Experienced photographer, unilateral	2
Sean	Experienced photographer, unilateral	2
Suzanne	Photographer covering Afghanistan	2
Freelance photographers		
Ahmed	Negotiating own assignments, holds passport from an Arab country	2
Kelly	Trying to get behind the scenes with General Tommy Franks	2
Yoshi	Being courted by GVI	2
Newsworld		
Joel	Senior text editor	4
Sarah	Senior text editor, World section	4
Susan	Managing photo editor	4, 7
Eric	Senior photo editor	4
Maggie	Photo editor, World section	4, conclusion
Simon	Photo editor, World section	4
Mary	Art director	4
World Press Photo		
Marijke	Staff, managed Istanbul seminars and Masterclass	7
Alan Fare	Founder of photo agency, master at Istanbul seminar	7, conclusion
Anna	Veteran photo editor, master at Istanbul seminar	7
Eitan	Israeli photographer, master at Istanbul seminar	7
Nico	Albanian photographer, Istanbul seminar participant	7, conclusion
Daphne	Veteran photo editor, Masterclass speaker	7
Johan	Swedish freelance photographer, Masterclass speaker	7
Bruce	Well-known conflict photographer, Masterclass speaker	7
Stewart	Established documentary photographer, Masterclass speaker	7
Armin	Danish photographer, Masterclass participant	7
Michael	Newspaper staff photographer considering becoming freelance, Masterclass participant	7

NOTE: All names are pseudonyms

[1]Position during the first few months of the American war in Iraq.

Timeline of the "War on Terror"

Throughout *Image Brokers* I have discussed the War on Terror not as a single military campaign but rather as a news story, a discursive construct that, as an umbrella term, provided semantic coherence for a whole range of activities both within the United States and internationally. There are many possible timelines that could be provided for the War on Terror, ranging from its historical precedents to the September 11 attacks to the surveillance laws enacted afterward. One could include violent acts in many geographies—from terrorist bombings in Bali, Madrid, London, or Paris to US drone strikes in Pakistan, Yemen, and Somalia. Below is a timeline that highlights the intertwining of the War on Terror and the digital circulation of news images.

Date	Event
September 11, 2001	Al Qaeda attacks the World Trade Center and the Pentagon.
October 7, 2001	US and British forces begin air and ground attacks, "Operation Enduring Freedom," against Al Qaeda and Taliban targets in Afghanistan. Coalition forces take Kabul on November 13, 2001.
January 11, 2002	Detainees begin to arrive in Camp X-Ray, located in Guantánamo Bay, Cuba.
February 21, 2002	*Wall Street Journal* reporter Daniel Pearl, kidnapped in Pakistan, is confirmed dead based on a video showing his beheading. The video is soon posted on several websites.

Date	Event
Feburary 5, 2003	US Secretary of State Colin Powell addresses the UN Security Council and gives a detailed description of Iraq's weapons of mass destruction and a deadly terrorist network headed by Abu Musab al-Zarqawi, who is claimed to be a collaborator of Osama bin Laden. The weapons of mass destruction turned out not to exist.
March 19, 2003	US and coalition forces launch an attack on command and control structures in Iraq. "Operation Iraqi Freedom" begins.
March 20, 2003	US and British ground troops enter Iraq from the south.
March 21, 2003	The United States launches its "Shock and Awe" campaign.
April 9, 2003	A statue of Saddam Hussein is pulled down by a US tank in Al Firdos Square, Baghdad.
May 1, 2003	Forty-three days after announcing the start of the war in Iraq, President George W. Bush lands on the deck of USS *Abraham Lincoln* and tells the nation that "major combat operations in Iraq have ended." Behind him, a banner declares "Mission Accomplished." In Kabul, Secretary of Defense Donald Rumsfeld declares an end to "major combat" and the beginning of "a period of stability and stabilization and reconstruction and activities."
Jul 22, 2003	Saddam's sons Uday and Qusay are killed in gun battle in Mosul, Iraq. Photographs of their corpses are released to the press.
December 14, 2003	Saddam Hussein is captured in Tikrit, Iraq.
March 31, 2004	Four US contractors are killed, burned, and hung from a bridge in Fallujah, Iraq. Images circulate worldwide.
April 28, 2004	*60 Minutes II* broadcasts a story that reveals photographic evidence of abuse of Iraqi prisoners by US troops at Abu Ghraib.
May 11, 2004	A video of the beheading of contractor Nicholas Berg becomes public. More beheadings—including that of American engineer Paul Marshall Johnson (June 18) in Saudi Arabia and Korean missionary Kim Sun-il (June 22) in Iraq—follow.
June 28, 2004	Sovereignty of Iraq is transferred to an Iraqi interim government headed by Prime Minister Ayad Allawi. Saddam Hussein is transferred to Iraqi legal custody.
July 1, 2004	Saddam Hussein goes on trial on charges of crimes against humanity.
June 7, 2006	Abu Musab al-Zarqawi, said to be responsible for many beheadings of foreigners, including Nicholas Berg, is killed in an air strike. Large, framed, close–up photographs of his corpse are presented to the press.
December 30, 2006	Saddam Hussein is executed by hanging.
Early 2009	The official use of the term "War on Terror" is phased out, with Pentagon officials receiving an email suggesting the use of "overseas contingency operations" instead.[1]

May 1, 2011	Osama bin Laden, founder and head of Al Qaeda, is killed in a raid in Pakistan. Photographs of his corpse and burial at sea are not released for fear of violent backlash. The White House hands out a photograph, titled *The Situation Room*, showing top government staff watching the raid.
December 18, 2011	The last US troops pull out of Iraq. Approximate cost: 165,00 Iraqi civilians, 4,500 American soldiers (32,000 wounded), and 300 coalition casualties.
May 27, 2014	President Barack Obama announces a timetable for withdrawing most US forces from Afghanistan by the end of 2016.
August 7, 2014	President Obama authorizes targeted airstrikes against Islamist militants in Iraq.
August 19, 2014	A video released by Islamic State in Iraq and Syria shows the beheading of American photojournalist James Foley and threatens to kill other journalists if President Obama does not end military operations in Iraq. Similar beheading videos of American journalist Steven Sotloff (September 2) and British aid worker David Haines (September 13) follow in quick succession.
December 28, 2014	NATO formally ends its war in Afghanistan.
October 15, 2015	President Obama halts the withdrawal of US military forces from Afghanistan.
	Total economic cost of War on Terror through fiscal year 2014: $1.6 trillion.

SOURCES: Watson Institute, Brown University, "Costs of War," http://watson.brown.edu/costsofwar/costs; Amy Belasco, "The Cost of Iraq, Afghanistan, and Other Global War on Terror Operations Since 9/11" (Congressional Research Service, 2014), http://www.fas.org/sgp/crs/natsec/RL33110.pdf.

[1]Washington, "Obama Administration to End Use of Term 'War on Terror.'"

Notes

1. Berger, *Ways of Seeing*. My very approach to photography and the kinds of questions I ask of and with photographs is deeply influenced by John Berger. This project also parallels long-standing findings in journalism scholarship. Building on Gans's 1972 research, Harvey Molotch and Marilyn Lester in 1974 concluded, "We see media as reflecting not a world out there, but the practices of those having the power to determine the experience of others." Molotch and Lester, "News as Purposive Behavior," 111.

2. This is a book about tranformations in photojournalism. However, naturally, these cannot be entirely separated from the disruptions in journalism at large. Nonetheless, they will not be my focus here, partly because they have been so well documented by others. Exemplary of this work is Boyer, *The Life Informatic;* Klinenberg, *Fighting for Air;* Domingo and Paterson, *Making Online News;* McChesney and Nichols, *The Death and Life of American Journalism;* McChesney and Pickard, *Will the Last Reporter Please Turn Out the Lights;* Henry *American Carnival;* Meyer *The Vanishing Newspaper;* and Boczkowski, *Digitizing the News.*

3. A photo editor at a major American newsmagazine informed me that the magazine had begun using digital images during the war of Kosovo in 1998 and 1999. Once they had received a digital image that, though it was merely two megabytes, was journalistically so important that they used it despite trepidations that it would look awful. However, just a few years later, by the time Jackie was sitting at her desk on the first day of the 2003 Iraq war, developing film to cover current events seemed unthinkable to her, a member of the youngest generation of image brokers.

4. In photography the term *nodal point* signifies the point at which all rays of light that enter a lens converge. (Strictly speaking, a more accurate term

might be *entrance pupil*.) Building on Jacques Lacan's notion of *point de capiton* (literally, "quilting point"), this term has also been used by political theorists Ernesto Laclau and Chantal Mouffe to mean master-signifiers or "privileged signifiers that fix the meaning of a signifying chain." Laclau and Mouffe, *Hegemony and Socialist Strategy*, 117. Laclau and Mouffe investigate nodal points to understand how hegemony is constructed. In the context of studying the manner in which world news gets visualized, I use *nodal point* to signify a site where choices have to be made and where one can track how certain images circulate and become dominant images while others do not.

5. Adams shot perhaps his best-known photograph while covering the Vietnam War for the Associated Press. The photograph shows police chief General Nguyen Ngoc Loan executing a prisoner, Nguyen Van Lem, at point-blank range on a Saigon street, on February 1, 1968, during the opening stages of the Tet Offensive. Adams's complex relationship to this photograph is addressed in chapter 5.

6. Michel Foucault explains that "[i]n order for a domain of action to enter into the field of thought, it is necessary that a certain number of factors have made it uncertain, have made it lose its familiarity, or have produced around it a certain number of difficulties." Cited in Rabinow, *Anthropos Today*, 47. For more on how technological innovations raise especially heated debates around the very essence of media and the work they perform, see Gitelman and Pingree, *New Media, 1740–1915*; and Larkin, *Signal and Noise*.

7. See J. S. Brennen and Kreiss, "Digitization and Digitalization," for a concise clarification of these terms and an overview of how they have been used by scholars to date.

8. Some examples that will get taken up later in this book are the photographs of Iraqi prisoner abuse in Abu Ghraib prison, the video of American Nick Berg being beheaded, and the cartoons depicting prophet Mohammed in the Danish newspaper *Jyllands-Posten*.

9. For a rich discussion of how digital media have transformed understandings of journalistic expertise, see Boyer, *The Life Informatic*.

10. Taking a cue from Zelizer's research on American journalists, we might consider image brokers as part of an interpretive community (Zelizer, "Journalists as Interpretive Communities"). One way I learned about them was by listening to them interpret both world news and professional news. This was a time when there was much to discuss in both domains. For a more recent discussion of journalists as an interpretive community, see Cotter, *News Talk*.

11. The last decade has been a time when it is unusually clear that, as Timothy Mitchell reminds us, "the distinction between the material world and its representation is not something we can take as a starting point." Mitchell, *Rule of Experts*, 6. On the War on Terror and the digital dissemination of the war of images specifically, see W. J. T. Mitchell's *Cloning Terror*. In *Frames of War*, Judith Butler explicitly states that "the frames of war are part of what makes the materiality of war." Butler, *Frames of War*, 29. While the War on Terror is highly mediated and packaged, as the Gulf war had been in 1991 when Baudrillard famously declared it did not take place, its digital nature led to the emergence of new infrastructures of representation and news kinds of image brokers.

Baudrillard, *The Gulf War Did Not Take Place*. The Gulf War in 1991 was a moment of transition for the representation of war with cameras. It was during this war against Iraq that precision guided munitions (PGMs) received much attention. Cameras mounted on these PGMs, also known as smart bombs, transmitted "a bomb's-eye" view of a war in which representations of collateral damage were minimal. The inherently violent images of 1991 that conflated any separation between the production of an image and a violent act were important backdrops to the 2003 war in Iraq. These camera-equipped bombs had already fused representations and acts of violence. On the inseparability of the War on Terror and its representations, see also Andrew Hoskins and Ben O'Loughlin, *War and Media*, and Roger, *Image Warfare in the War on Terror*. See Kennedy, "Seeing and Believing," for a thought-provoking essay on emergent visual repertoires of perpetual war.

12. For more on the impact of spectacular terrorism based on interviews with American news viewers, see Gürsel, "Spectacular Terrorism."

13. I am borrowing the term *visual economy* from anthropologist Deborah Poole, who uses the term instead of *visual culture* to think about "visual images as part of a comprehensive organization of people, ideas and object." By *visual economy* Poole means the organization of production (both individuals and technologies that produce the images), the circulation of images and image-objects, and "the cultural and discursive systems through which graphic images are appraised, interpreted and assigned historical, scientific, and aesthetic worth." Poole, *Vision, Race and Modernity*, 8–10. I do not use the term *visual economy* more extensively in this book because I feel it is a term that becomes less generative when used to discuss an actual visual industry—specifically, the international photojournalism industry. Poole's object of analysis is the visual economy of the Andean image world. Without using Poole's terminology explicitly, I have written elsewhere about what might be called a visual economy of certain key images from the War on Terror—specifically, head shots of Abu Musab Al-Zarqawi, leader of Al Qaeda in Iraq from 2004 to 2006. Gürsel, "Framing Zarqawi."

14. I build on scholarship such as Azoulay, *The Civil Contract of Photography*; Butler, *Frames of War*; Sontag, *Regarding the Pain of Others*; Batchen et al., *Picturing Atrocity*; Kennedy and Patrick, *The Violence and the Image*; Kozol, *Distant Wars Visible*; Zelizer, *About to Die*; Zelizer, "When War Is Reduced to a Photograph"; Campbell, "Representing Contemporary War"; Griffin, "The Great War Photographs; and Brothers, *War and Photography*.

15. Ironically, I set out to write an account of photojournalism that would intentionally *not* center on combat photography, the most studied genre in the medium. However, because of that peculiar time lag between when a project is conceived and when fieldwork can officially begin, my "field" as an anthropologist became the visual landscape of the War on Terror because it dominated so much of my informants' time and energies.

16. Michael Schudson claims that "when the media offer the public an item of news, they confer on it public legitimacy." Schudson, *The Sociology of News*, 21.

17. Although my focus is on what happens when a private photograph gets made public by being circulated as news, see Sarkisova and Shevchenko, "Soviet

Past in Domestic Photography," for an example of family photographs being used for public history making about the Soviet era, or Strassler, *Refracted Visions,* for a discussion of how photographic genres need to be understood in relation to each other.

18. In a similar vein, Dona Schwartz turns to the role played by publishers to investigate "the establishment of photojournalism as an objective reportorial strategy." Schwartz, "Objective Representation," 161.

19. News images are a form of situated knowledge. "Vision is always a question of the power to see." Haraway, "Situated Knowledges," 585.

20. Geertz, *The Interpretation of Cultures,* 452.

21. Crapanzano, "Hermes' Dilemma," 74.

22. For many anthropologists working in the late twentieth century, radical difference often resulting in culture shock gave way to anthropology "at home," anthropology that was "exotic no more," and fieldwork in places a subway ride away. In parallel there has been much discussion of the very compositions of "natives" and anthropologists. In other words, this shift was partly a result of anthropologists looking at their own Western culture and partly connected to more anthropologists from diverse backgrounds entering the discipline. Already in 1988 Arjun Appadurai had asserted, "Natives, thus, are creatures of the anthropological imagination." Appadurai, "Putting Hierarchy in Its Place," 39. See Passaro, " 'You Can't Take the Subway to the Field!' "; MacClancy, *Exotic No More;* Ortner, *New Jersey Dreaming;* di Leonardo, *Exotics at Home;* and Gupta and Ferguson, *Anthropological Locations.*

23. The word *stereotype* comes from the Greek words *stereos* and *typos,* meaning "firm, solid, substantial" and "impression," respectively. The French term "stereotype plate" as used in printing originated in the early nineteenth century. Within two decades of the invention of the daguerreotype one finds the term *stereotype* used to mean "an *image* perpetuated without change."

24. Mitchell, *What Do Pictures Want?,* 337.

25. Mitchell, *What Do Pictures Want?,* 353.

26. Dona Schwartz also claims, "Photojournalism is distinctive for its dual rhetoric, which simultaneously asserts the objectivity of news photographs, while praising the skill and artistry of its best practitioners." Schwartz, "Objective Representation," 160.

27. Photography functions not only as a "vehicle of truth or meaning, but equally . . . a technology used to construct certain kinds of truth about certain categories of persons." King and Lidchi, *Imaging the Arctic,* 13. Another way to think about the particularity of news images is through Ian Hacking's categorization of things that might be socially constructed: objects, ideas, and "elevator terms." By "elevator terms" he means words such as *facts, truth, reality,* and *knowledge,* "words [that] are used to say something about the world, or about what we say or think about the world," words that when used in philosophical discussion raise the level of discourse (Hacking, *The Social Construction of What?,* 21). Hacking himself points out the blurred boundaries between these categories. News images are curious because they fit all three categories but are irreducible to a single one. They are at once objects, ideas, and visual facts.

28. *Oxford English Dictionary*, s.v. "fact."

29. Sontag, *On Photography*, 3.

30. Heidegger, *The Question concerning Technology and Other Essays*, 129–30.

31. This research was published in Gürsel, "Spectacular Terrorism."

32. Sontag makes a similar point when she emphasizes, "The more remote or exotic the place, the more likely we are to have full frontal views of the dead and dying." Using postcolonial Africa as an example she concludes, " These sights carry a double message. They show a suffering that is outrageous, unjust, and should be repaired. They confirm that this is the sort of thing which happens in that place. The ubiquity of those photographs, and those horrors, cannot help but nourish belief in the inevitability of tragedy in the benighted or backward—that is, poor—parts of the world." Sontag, *Regarding the Pain of Others*, 70. Hence, certain places become the kind of place in the world where certain kinds of violence, injustice, or tragedy can take place.

33. Goodman, *Ways of Worldmaking*. Michael Warner also emphasizes that public address is ultimately "poetic world-making." Warner, *Publics and Counterpublics*. 114.

34. Boczkowski, *Digitizing the News*, 11. Moreover, my focus on news images—specifically, images that were used to convey world news at the time of this study (the launch and early years of the War on Terror)—also made the ideological structures involved more apparent.

35. In general, visual knowledge production has not been a focus in classic newsroom ethnographies, and when it has been addressed, it has most often been in the form of television broadcasts. See Tuchman, *Making News;* Gans, *Deciding What's News;* Fishman, *Manufacturing the News;* White, "The Gate Keeper"; Breed, "Social Control in the Newsroom"; and Usher, *Making News at* The New York Times. The notable exception to this is Barbie Zelizer's long-standing investigation into news images, the labor behind them, and their impact. Zelizer, *About to Die;* Zelizer, "Journalism through the Camera's Eye"; Zelizer, "When War Is Reduced to a Photograph"; Zelizer, "Words against Images." Even when there has been attention given to the work of news images in the world, there has been far less given to the work behind images in newsrooms. See Machin and Niblock, *News Production,* for a similar critique of studies of visual journalism. For an excellent overview of news ethnographies see Cottle, "Ethnography and News Production." A few very recent articles that seem to bring a more ethnographic approach to the work of producing and distributing news images include Pogliano, "Iconic Photographs in the Newsroom"; and Pantti and Sirén, "The Fragility of Photo-Truth."

36. In discussing digital photography, a senior photo editor at a newsmagazine told me the field had changed dramatically. "One of the key elements of a good photo editor used to be having a great visual memory. Basically we all have images in our heads ... When you edit film you remember the whole take. So you have a reference in your head not just for what the magazine ran but also for all that you saw." Now the digital photographer does the first edit and editors get sent a small selection. "When you edit film you might remember an image later that was not significant at the time, or didn't fit what you were

editing for then but has significance at a later time. Now I wouldn't even know that frame existed."

37. This approach has been generative for scholars working on representations of particular groups such as Inuit, Indians, and African Americans or specific groups affected by an event. Exemplary of the kind of work I have in mind are Smith *American Archives;* Linfield, *The Cruel Radiance;* Pinney, "The Parallel Histories of Anthropology and Photography"; Ryan, *Picturing Empire;* Landau and Kaspin, *Images and Empires;* and Lydon, *Eye Contact.*

38. Here we can think of any number of biographies, memoirs and scholarly studies of individual photographers. There are also a number of books that bring together interviews with several photographers. Light, *Witness in Our Time;* Jaeger, *Image Makers, Image Takers.*

39. Hariman and Lucaites, *No Caption Needed;* Sliwinski, *Human Rights in Camera;* Raiford, *Imprisoned in a Luminous Glare;* Kratz, *The Ones That Are Wanted;* Zelizer, *About to Die.*

40. Many of the works I've just named in fact combine more than one approach. For example, Raiford analyzes lynching photographs and describes how African-American activists during the civil rights movement reframed the same images for antilynching campaigns. Lutz and Collins, *Reading National Geographic,* is structured around three distinct research phases on the process of producing images, the structure and content of images, and how readers view the photographs.

41. Azoulay, *The Civil Contract of Photography,* 23.

42. Gross, Katz, and Ruby, *Image Ethics,* 4.

43. Similarly, Michael Schudson states, "Journalists not only report reality but also create it. . . . To say that journalists construct the world is not to say they conjure the world." Schudson, *The Sociology of News,* xiv. As he puts it squarely, "[F]aking is not the point." Schudson, *The Sociology of News,* xvi. Rather than using Schudson's term *making news,* I find it generative to employ the term *fiction,* as defined by Raymond Williams, partly as a way to explicitly push against ideas of photographs as indexical representations showing the world as it is. In other words, I hope that my use of the term *fiction* might eclipse the possibility of thinking that one way news is made by inserting photographs taken in the world out there. Moreover, unlike news articles, photographs that become news images can be unmade and used in commercial contexts or remade as other news.

44. Benedict Anderson's classic *Imagined Communities* also explores "the two forms of imagining which first flowered in Europe in the eighteenth century: the novel and the newspaper." His purpose is not an etymological but rather a historical analysis to illustrate how these particular forms were critical to the formation of the nation—the particular imagined community he is investigating. Nonetheless, Anderson specifically emphasizes the "profound fictiveness" of the newspaper as a cultural product. Anderson, *Imagined Communities,* 30–31.

45. Williams, *Keywords,* 134–135.

46. For two other tellings of this event, see the memoir by Michael Finkel (Finkel, *True Story*) and the 2015 film based on the memoir, *True Story.*

47. In 2003 Jayson Blair, a promising reporter at the *New York Times,* was discovered to have plagiarized and fabricated dozens of stories, often about places he'd never visited and events that never took place. This subgenre of news article escalated from focusing on the journalistic misdemeanors of individuals to introspections on newspapers' shortcomings in their coverage of an event, perhaps best exemplified by the multipage article "The Times and Iraq," published on May 26, 2004. We might think of this as news paradigm repair at different scales. Bennett, Gressett, and Haltom, "Repairing the News"; Berkowitz, "Doing Double Duty"; and Hindman, "Jayson Blair, the *New York Times,* and Paradigm Repair."

48. *New York Times,* February 21, 2002. www.nytimes.com/2002/02/21 /nyregion/editors-note-731463.html. (Emphasis mine.) Note how the newspaper tries to minimize its institutional responsibility in the matter by emphasizing that the writer was a mere freelancer, not a staff member. Similarly, the editorial mentions that the photograph was uncaptioned. This could be interpreted to mean that there is no text that specifically claims that the young man in this photo *is* Youssouf Malé—that the falsification is in the potential visual interpretation rather than in a verbally explicit false identification. Or it could mean that because the photograph was taken by the writer and not the professional photographer with whom he was traveling, it was submitted to the editor without a caption. Hence, the newspaper intimates that only the writer and no one else was aware that this young man was not Youssouf Malé, and the trespass is his alone and not an institutional wrongdoing. This was the only photograph taken by the writer that was published. Of course, neither what size the image should be when published nor whether it should have a caption is a decision that either the writer or the photographer typically make. Rather, those are decisions that would have been made by image brokers working for the magazine. Which is to say, that there were moments where others in the publication might have asked further questions.

49. Sontag, *Regarding the Pain of Others,* 46.

50. On similar modes of reading photographs, see Sekula, "On the Invention of Photographic Meaning"; and Hall, "The Determinations of News Photographs."

51. The magazine article itself, both in print and online, includes other images showing Gula's face or showing her with her family. Yet the decision was made to feature her on the cover in a burqa. In discussing similar images of Afghan women in burqas and the supposed feminist call to war, Judith Butler enjoins us to investigate the narrative function in which images are mobilized. Butler, *Precarious Life,* 143. For discussions of the politics of images of the burqa in the context of the US war in Afghanistan, see Abu-Lughod, "Do Muslim Women Really Need Saving?"; and Kozol, *Distant Wars Visible.* Jessica Winegar makes a forceful argument that a few years later, the anonymous repetition of unnamed women in veils in Iraq became "signifiers of the beneficence of the Americans and the necessity and validation of military intervention." Winegar, "Of Chadors and Purple Fingers," 392.

52. Afghanistan was not featured on the cover of *National Geographic* between "Afghan Girl" 1985 and "Afghan Girl" 2002. Moreover, there have

been no covers featuring Afghanistan since. Edwards, "Cover to Cover," provides an overview of the lifecycle of Gula's cover image.

53. Photographs are not utterances. As I elaborate on below, they have a very particular temporality, which is why I do not think it appropriate to speak of performativity in photography in a strictly Austinian sense. Nonetheless, my thinking on formative fictions builds on J. L. Austin's ideas of performativity, particularly his emphasis on felicitous conditions. As Austin argued, to understand what an utterance does as action, it is necessary to see how it is performative in context. Similarly, it is important to analyze how certain photographs become news images and yield a certain force by circulating in specific journalistic publications. They also interpolate different audiences in different ways. My thinking on this draws from both Bourdieu and Butler. Specifically, Bourdieu draws attention to the power of certain words coming from the spokesperson delegated to speak them. Butler complicates the notion of agency by underscoring that Austin assumed a sovereign speaker rather than one more likely to exist in reality, who might be untethered from a speech act. Ultimately, however, my research here is not about the impact of news images on readers but rather about how professional image brokers receive, edit, and circulate these images. See Austin, *How to Do Things with Words;* Bourdieu, *Language and Symbolic Power;* and Butler, *Excitable Speech.*

54. The last few years have yielded many examples of photographs that were manipulated and yet made it into a news publication or garnered prestigious awards. Two prominent examples: Photographer Adnan Hajj's use of the Adobe Photoshop cloning stamp in 2006 to enhance plumes of smoke in a photograph showing the aftermath of Israeli shelling in Lebanon. Hajj had worked as a freelancer for Reuters for several years, and Reuters had circulated the image. All of his images were removed from the wire service's archive, and a photo editor was fired. *Los Angeles Times* staff photographer Brian Walski's picture of a British soldier addressing a crowd of Iraqis in Basra was published on March 30, 2003, in both the *Times* and several other papers owned by the same parent company. Walski "improved the composition" of the photograph by combining two images taken moments apart. Walski was fired. Holmes, "Reuters Toughens Rules after Altered Photo Affair"; Van Riper, "Manipulating Truth, Losing Credibility"; Irby, "L.A. Times Photographer Fired over Altered Image." For an excellent discussion of how the US journalism community reacted to the Walski case, see Carlson, "The Reality of a Fake Image." David Campbell deftly points out that "the more significant ways in which pictures structure reality through exclusions are themselves excluded from the discussion so long as the professional responsibility not to alter what the shutter secures is maintained" (Campbell, "Representing Contemporary War," 107).

55. For classic pronouncements on the temporality of photographs, see Barthes, *Camera Lucida;* Sontag, *On Photography;* Bazin, *What Is Cinema?;* Rosen, *Change Mummified.*

56. In part, it was precisely this methodological challenge that caused me not to undertake an audience ethnography, though I think that such work, particularly if conducted as a large collaboration, could be very valuable. Hariman and Lucaites's *No Caption Needed* captures uptake by studying how images get

reused, embedded, or alluded to in later images as a way of analyzing the impact of certain iconic images. My experience of audience interviews was that, short of a significant visual event such as the September 11 attacks, and possibly even then, interviews captured what the interviewees thought the researcher wanted to hear. It is very difficult to be in place as an ethnographer when people happen to be talking about news images. Unless, that is, you are studying image brokers and their consumption practices within their everyday work of producing and distributing images.

57. In *Modernity at Large: Cultural Dimensions of Globalization,* Arjun Appadurai underscored "the image, the imagined, the imaginary" as terms that directed us to something critical and new in global cultural processes: "the imagination as a social practice." Before assuming the newness of this form of imagination, however, it makes sense to explore what connections there are between images and imaginations. One of the motivations for *Image Brokers* was to go beyond their mere etymological kinship as terms in romance languages and render visible actual practices that forge relationships between images and imaginations.

58. The similarities and historical entanglements between these ways of worldmaking have of course been noted by others, such as Chris Pinney and Elizabeth Edwards in the case of photography and Ulf Hannerz in the case of journalism, who goes so far as to say, "Foreign correspondents are a sort of anthropologists . . . to the extent that they engage in reporting from one part of the world to another." Hannerz, *Foreign News,* 4.

59. Appadurai, "Theory in Anthropology."

60. It is still relatively recently that there has been any negotiation of the ethnographic field site. See Clifford, *Routes,* for a still-relevant discussion of this anxiety around "the field" at the moment when the notion of culture is no longer exclusively the domain of the discipline of anthropology.

61. Gupta and Ferguson, *Culture, Power, Place,* 36.

62. Gupta and Ferguson, *Culture, Power, Place,* 47.

63. Askew and Wilk, *The Anthropology of Media;* Ginsburg, Abu-Lughod, and Larkin, *Media Worlds.*

64. There were, however, already a few key texts, such as Pedelty, *War Stories;* Hannerz, *Foreign News;* Hasty, *The Press and Political Culture in Ghana;* and Boyer, *Spirit and System.* The last decade has seen a modest swell in anthropological scholarship on journalism, exemplified by the 2010 publication of Elizabeth Bird's edited volume *The Anthropology of News and Journalism: Global Perspectives.* And by recent volumes such as Boyer, *The Life Informatic;* and Bishara, *Back Stories.*

65. Ferguson, *Global Shadows,* 5.

66. Ferguson, "Novelty and Method," 199.

67. Ferguson, *Global Shadows,* 6.

68. Mitchell, "Interdisciplinarity and Visual Culture." Some exemplary texts exploring the cultural turn in visual studies include Bal, "Visual Essentialism and the Object of Visual Culture"; Mitchell, *Picture Theory;* Bryson, Holly, and Moxey, *Visual Culture;* Alpers, "Visual Culture Questionnaire"; Mirzoeff, *An Introduction to Visual Culture.*; and Dikovitskaya, *Visual Culture.*

69. Tagg, *The Burden of Representation,* 211.

70. Hasty, "Journalism as Fieldwork," 193. Similarly, Zelizer explains that journalism has proven to be a challenging topic for cultural studies because journalism's legitimacy depends on its ability to provde "facts, truth, and reality," whereas how such knowledge is constructed is typically the starting point of a cultural inquiry. Zelizer, "When Facts, Truth, and Reality Are God-Terms."

71. Tagg promises, "Only in this way will we come to understand how ideologies are produced in real representational practices in material apparatuses; how these representations are disseminated, consumed, elaborated, modified, and sustained; how are they meaningful, how they affect and are affected by other productive activities within the same social complex. And all this is to be done by studying actual material entities and processes, entirely without the need for pregiven mental or spiritual phenomena. This then would be the beginnings of a materialist account." Tagg, *The Burden of Representation,* 211.

72. Similarly, in studying Hollywood as "an entity that is spread discontinuously across and beyond the city of Los Angeles," Sherry Ortner reminds us that Hollywood's "spatially discontinuous nature should not be confused with the question of whether there is in fact a 'community,' and in this case the answer would very definitely be yes." Ortner, "Access," 213.

73. Marcus, *Ethnography through Thick and Thin,* 90.

74. For a complementary view of the photojournalism world from outside these centers, see the finely researched work of D. J. Clark on majority world photographers. Clark, "Representing the Majority World."

75. Nader, "Up the Anthropologist," 292. See Hannerz for a discussion of fieldwork among foreign correspondents as an example of studying sideways.

76. Nader even underscored that anthropologists might need to forgo participant observation in order to study up successfully, and yet Hugh Gusterson in 1997 was still writing of the trepidation of abandoning or subordinating "the research technique that has defined anthropology as a discipline and served as our own parochial rite of passage into maturity since Malinowski." Gusterson, "Studying Up Revisited," 116.

77. IRB approval was initially designed for biomedical research and behavioral science such as psychology experiments. Many have discussed the ill-suitedness of IRB processes to anthropological fieldwork, especially in situations where asking people to sign an informed consent form itself might subject the subject to danger. See Shryock, *Off Stage/On Display,* 8, for a persuasive claim that IRB forms reduce reflexivity to methodological transparency.

78. Another recent account of an anthropologist negotiating nondisclosure is Shankar, "Creating Model Consumers."

79. When I heard James Ferguson speak at a conference about the importance of not being too enamored by the novelty factor of global ethnographies at sites that anthropologists had not studied before, I chuckled at the thought that it was precisely the lack of novelty value for GVI that had enabled me to conduct fieldwork in a way that was best suited for this project.

80. Zelizer, "Journalism's 'Last' Stand."

81. I turn to the ramifications of this erasure of labor in the conclusion. See also Gürsel, "A Challenge for Visual Journalism."

82. This second question places me in conversation with a wide range of scholars whose work on a particular visual form also pays attention to the nonvisual elements produced. Some examples are Janelle Taylor's work in medical anthropology on the production of contemporary motherhood through sonograms, Barry Saunders's explanation of the production of diagnoses through CT scans, Joseph Dumit's investigations of the use of objectified brain imagery in the construction of personhood, Brian Larkin's work on media technologies and their mode of hailing new sorts of political subjects, Esra Ozyürek's attention to the production of particular Turkish nationalist ideologies through the circulation of specific sets of historical photographs, William Mazzarella's work on Indian advertising linking moving products with the birth and development of a nation, and Joseph Masco's work on cold war images of nuclear explosions and the microregulation of a nation on an emotional level—to mention the work of just a few anthropologists. However, this approach to visual forms is certainly not limited to anthropology. For instance, both film scholar Linda Williams's work on the production and reception of cinematic sex acts and medical historian Joel Howell's writing on early hospital technologies investigate ways in which gender and ideas of sexual norms are produced in the process of consuming particular types of images.

83. See Robert Hariman and John Louis Lucaites's *No Caption Needed: Iconic Photographs, Public Culture, and Liberal Democracy* for accounts of how images gained significance through their continued circulation as part of public culture long after publication.

PART ONE. IMAGE-MAKING

1. On thick description, see Geertz, *The Interpretation of Cultures.*

2. For a particularly cogent description of how "labor processes are processes of cultural interpretation through everyday practice," see Lisa Rofel's research on Chinese silk factories. Rofel, "Rethinking Modernity," 96.

3. See Foster, "Tracking Globalization," for an excellent overview of the ways in which researchers trace the movement of commodities including "the social relations and material linkages that this movement creates and within which the value of commodities emerges" (285). Foster claims that tracking commodities and value in motion becomes a means for apprehending the "'global consciousness' (Robertson 1992) and 'work of the imagination' (Appadurai 1990) often associated with globalization" (286). This is especially true when the commodity being tracked is a news image, both a product of global consciousness and raw material for it. My thinking on the production of news images has also been shaped by philosopher Ian Hacking, who states, "Production itself can mean the process of producing or in other circumstances, the result of producing" and asks, "Is the production of a play process or product?" Hacking, *The Social Construction of What?*, 36. The production and circulation of news images is a form of visual worldmaking.

4. Hall, "Signification, Representation, Ideology," 103.

5. Anderson, *Imagined Communities.* Cultural production has increasingly been framed within a system of relations among agents and institutions engaged

in producing, distributing, and valuing works while creating cultural capital for themselves. See Bourdieu, *The Field of Cultural Production;* Hall, *Representation;* Hesmondhalgh, *The Culture Industries,* and Hesmondhalgh and Baker, *Creative Labour.* There is also a growing body of scholarly work that focuses on producers and distributors in the culture industry—what, borrowing from Andrew Shryock, we might term the professional "off-stage" of the production of public culture. Examples include Shryock, *Off Stage/On Display;* Boyer, *Spirit and System;* Caldwell, *Production Culture;* Dornfeld, *Producing Public Television, Producing Public Culture;* Hasty, *The Press and Political Culture in Ghana;* Mayer, Banks, and Caldwell, *Production Studies;* Mazzarella, *Shoveling Smoke;* Mahon, "The Visible Evidence of Cultural Producers"; Ganti, *Producing Bollywood;* Deuze, *Media Work;* Punathambekar, *From Bombay to Bollywood;* and Tinic, *On Location.*

6. Several scholars have undertaken visual framing analyses of the news stories that dominated during my fieldwork. Some examples include Fahmy and Kim, "Picturing the Iraq War"; Griffin, "Picturing America's 'War on Terrorism' in Afghanistan and Iraq"; Schwalbe, "Visually Framing the Invasion and Occupation of Iraq in *Time, Newsweek,* and *US News & World Report*"; and Parry, "Images of Liberation?" For a similar image-focused approach from an international relations perspective, see Van Veeren, "Captured by the Camera's Eye."

CHAPTER 1. WHAT PRECEDES THE DIGITAL NEWS IMAGE?

1. This book looks at the conditions under which certain photographs as objects circulate in different "regimes of value." Appadurai, "The Social Life of Things," 4. News images accrue and risk losing value through their circulation. Moreover, precisely with the rise of visual content providers and new possible biographies for images, photographs can move in and out of the commodity state. Appadurai, "The Social Life of Things," 13.

2. My inquiry is inspired by Jessica Dubow's work in "Rethinking Sight, Space and the Colonial Subject," where she builds on Jean Baudrillard's claim: "[T]he map precedes the territory." Dubow's purpose is to ask "What precedes the map?" so that she can address the position of the viewing body that orients space at a particular viewpoint, upon which the map is contingent. See Dubow, "'From a View on the World to a Point of View in It,'" 89. I'm also thinking about what makes a photographic form of news possible. See Barnhurst and Nerone, *The Form of News.*

3. For more on the history of photography, see Newhall, *The History of Photography;* also see Marien, *Photography.* On press photography specifically, see Brennen, "Photojournalism: Historical Dimensions to Contemporary Debates, "Chapnik, *Truth Needs No Ally;* Freund, *Photography and Society;* Hicks, *Words and Pictures,* Morris, *Get the Picture;* Newton, *The Burden of Visual Truth;* and Panzer and Caujolle, *Things As They Are.* Hill and Schwartz, *Getting the Picture,* contains an excellent list of further resources.

4. For parallel tensions between commerce and creativity in the culture industries, see Hesmondhalgh, *The Cultural Industries;* and Hesmondhalgh and Baker, *Creative Labour.*

5. Daguerre's invention continues to be perceived as an invention of global rather than national interest: On November, 18, 2011, the Internet search engine Google commemorated physicist and artist Louis Daguerre on his 224th birthday with a Google doodle, a playful rendition of the Google logo, on the company's home page. It depicted a daguerreotype of a family portrait. Periodic Google doodles mark important events and figures whose work has had great impact. This doodle served as a reminder to web-surfing shutterbugs, Flickr stream feeders, and YouTube fans to acknowledge the man most often credited with the invention of photography, or at least the first commercially successful form of photography. Unlike some doodles intended only for certain specific national or regional audiences, Daguerre's doodle was deemed to be of global interest.

6. Azoulay, *The Civil Contract of Photography*, 121. For important alternative framings of the invention of photography, see Batchen, *Burning with Desire;* and Sheehan and Zervigón, *Photography and Its Origins.*

7. Arago, "Report," 24. For a compelling history of Daguerre and his time, see Pinson, *Speculating Daguerre.*

8. Solnit, *River of Shadows,* 22.

9. Prominent examples are Newhall, *The History of Photography;* Jeffrey, *Photography;* Rosenblum, *A World History of Photography;* Dickie, *Photography;* Lavoie, *Photojournalismes;* and Gustavson, *Camera.*

10. Halftone pictures first appeared in the 1880s. Before then many newspapers and magazines used woodcuts. See Zervigón, "Rotogravure and the Modern Aesthetics of News Reporting."

11. Hopkinson, Hunt, and Knight, *Scoop, Scandal, and Strife.*

12. Hopkinson, Hunt, and Knight, *Scoop, Scandal, and Strife.*

13. The technology that transmitted images by cable is the same as common fax technology. The technology was patented in 1843; however, it was not put to commercial use until the 1860s, and did not take off in the consumer market until the mid-1980s when the Japanese economy boomed. Fax technologies were particularly useful for languages, like Japanese and Chinese, whose characters did not adapt easily to Western telegraph and telex systems. My knowledge of the rich and illustrative story of fax technology's initial commercial failure and eventual success comes from historian Jonathan Coopersmith. His extensive research on fax technology has been collected in *Faxed.*

14. For more on these organizations and their contributions to photojournalism, see Light, *Witness in Our Time;* Dejardin, "The Photo League"; and Evans and Klein, *The Radical Camera.*

15. Zelizer, "Journalism's 'Last' Stand," 78.

16. Coopersmith, "The Failure of Fax," 275.

17. Zelizer, "Journalism's 'Last' Stand," 81.

18. Zelizer, "Journalism's 'Last' Stand," 87. See also Newton, *The Burden of Visual Truth;* Hardt, "The Site of Reality"; and Schudson, *Discovering the News.*

19. Sontag, "Looking at War," 49. See Gervais, "Witness to War," for a description of the entangled early history of military conflict and photography. Zelizer argues that "it is to images that journalism turns in times of war."

Zelizer, "When War Is Reduced to a Photograph," 118. For a recent condemnation of the anesthetization of combat, see Shields, *War Is Beautiful.*

20. Miller, *Magnum.*

21. In his detailed account of the founding of Magnum, Russell Miller makes note of a reference to the agency as "The Time Inc. Stink Club" in the earliest correspondence about Magnum. He interprets this insult as a reflection on Time-Life's reaction to the news that the photographers of the new agency intended to keep the copyrights to the images they supplied. Miller, *Magnum,* 52.

22. Edey, *Great Photographic Essays from Life.* More recently, exemplary essays on the death knell for photojournalism include Campbell, "Dead or Alive?"; Kraus, "Rest in Peace"; Guerrin, "Photographiez sans entraves"; Burgess, "Editorial Photographers UK"; Murabayashi, "How the Internet Killed Photojournalism"; Howe, "Photojournalism at a Crossroads"; Roussel, "Photojournaliste, un métier rongé par la précarité"; Halstead, "The End of History and Photojournalism"; Halstead, "Revisiting the Death of Photojournalism, Part II"; Halstead, "Revisiting the Death of Photojournalism, Ten Years Later"; and Jolly, "Lament for a Dying Field." In 2015, Scam, a French civil society organization concerned with copyrights for multimedia authors, put out an extensive report on the state of photojournalism by Béatrice de Mondenard titled *Photojournaliste: Une profession sacrifiée* (Photojournalist: A sacrificed profession), but referred to as "the black book" of photojournalism.

23. Rabinow, *French DNA,* 180. Rabinow borrows the term *assemblage* from Bruno Latour's description of a late-model car to emphasize that "[i]t is a disparate aggregate of scientific and technical solutions dating from different periods. . . . The ensemble is only contemporary by assemblage." Rabinow, *French DNA,* 45.

24. This focus on infrastructures both contributes to and expands the very productive debates around the "politics of representation" both within and outside of the discipline of anthropology. See Clifford and Marcus, *Writing Culture;* Hall, *Representation;* Lutz and Collins, *Reading National Geographic;* Marcus and Fischer, *Anthropology as Cultural Critique;* and Said, *Orientalism.* However, rather than focusing only on the politics of representation, I add to scholarship that pays closer attention to the politics of the infrastructures behind visual representations. See Ganti, *Producing Bollywood;* Jain, *Gods in the Bazaar;* Larkin, *Signal and Noise;* Mazzarella, *Shoveling Smoke;* Marcus and Myers, *The Traffic in Culture;* Pinney, *Camera Indica;* Schwenkel, *The American War in Contemporary Vietnam;* and Strassler, *Refracted Visions.* For a similar attention to infrastructure in a nonvisual medium see Kunreuther, *Voicing Subjects;* and Spitulnik-Vidali, "'A House of Wires upon Wires.'"

25. Larkin, *Signal and Noise,* 47. A similar call for more attention to materiality has been made more recently in journalism studies. See Anderson and De Maeyer, "Objects of Journalism."

26. This is a Western-centric version of the history of news agencies and also one that privileges the largest wire services because the focus is on those that could afford to be early adaptors of the expensive technologies behind picture transmission. Oliver Boyd-Barrett's introduction in *News Agencies in the*

Turbulent Era of the Internet provides extensive histories of international news agencies, and the volume gives many examples of smaller and more geographically diverse wire services. Though outside of the scope of this book, Russia's TASS (founded in 1904 as the St. Petersburg Telegraph Agency) and China's Xinhua News Service (founded in 1931 as the Red China News Agency) are both state-run news agencies with significant size and reach.

27. For more on the history of the news agencies, see Alleyne, *News Revolution;* Boyd-Barrett, *International News Agencies;* Boyd-Barrett, *News Agencies in the Turbulent Era of the Internet;* Hachten, *World News Prism;* Laville, *Les transformations du journalisme de 1945 à 2010;* Pigeat, *Le nouveau désordre mondial de l'information;* Read, *The Power of News;* Read, "Don't Blame the Messengers"; and Winseck and Pike, *Communication and Empire.*

28. "Associated Press." Accessed January 1, 2004. www.ap.org.

29. "Reuters: La Rolls de l'info." For an excellent, detailed history of Reuters's picture service, see Ilan, "The Best of Both Worlds. " Canadian Thompson Corporation acquired Reuters in 2008, creating Thompson-Reuters.

30. I heard many stories of the old days of wire photo transmission. The details of how long transmission took varied depending on the decade the person was referencing, whether the photograph was black and white or color, the quality of the telephone line being used, and whether the image was being sent internationally. See "Spot News," an industrial film by Jam Handy, for a visual explanation of the technology behind the transmission of photographs over communication networks. https://archive.org/details/SpotNews1937. For a written account of the challenges of wire-photo transmission in the 1990s, see Wilkins, "Photojournalist or Pack Mule?"

31. One measure of this is the percentage of images entered in the annual World Press Photo competition, the most prestigious in the field. In 2000 only 17 percent of the images entered from around the world were digital, whereas by 2006, 98 percent of entries were digital.

32. See the introduction for an explanation of why I use the term *digitalization* rather than *digitization.*

33. After underperforming financially for several years, Groupe Hachette Filipacchi Photos was sold in December 2006 to Green Recovery, an industrial group known for taking over companies in difficulty. Faced with the threat of liquidation, in 2010 the company was relaunched as Gamma-Rapho again, and in a poignant turn of events for the industry, one of Gamma's own photographers managed to gain control of it, though many in the industry remain skeptical about whether it can survive. Gamma now focuses on its archive of twenty million images. The defensive tone on its website is notable and a sign of their tumultuous history: "Do you know our images? The whole world knows them. It's us. Gamma Rapho. Still here!" www.gamma-rapho.com/fr/who/page/1. In the United States Gamma's collection is distributed by Getty Images. For an overview of the Gamma Rapho agency's latest reincarnation, see Guillot, "L'avenir incertain du groupe d'agences Eyedea met en péril le troisième fonds de photographies au monde"; Guillot, "Les agences photo Gamma et Rapho (Eyedea) reprises par François Lochon"; Puech, "François Lochon, un patron-photographe à l'agence Gamma-Rapho"; and Puech, "Keystone, Gamma,

Rapho: Scandale ou miracle?" Similarly, after many financial difficulties SIPA Press was reclaimed by journalists in 2013.

34. Thomas Edison's first technological invention, long before the kineto-scope and early movies, was a hybrid telegraph–stock ticker in the 1870s. Jonathan Crary argues, "This is paradigmatic for what it foreshadows in subse-quent technological arrangements, including those of the late twentieth century: the indistinction between information and visual images, and the making of quantifiable and abstract flow into the object of abject consumption." Crary, *Suspensions of Perception,* 33.

35. For more on the rise of visual content providers, see Frosh, *The Image Factory;* Machin, "Building the World's Visual Language"; and Clark, "Repre-senting the Majority World."

36. "Getty Images." Accessed January 1, 2004. www.gettyimages.com.

37. For now, all of these agencies still exist.

38. "VII: A Group of Engaged and Committed Photographers Concerned with the World and the Lives of Others." Accessed January 1, 2004. www .viiphoto.com.

39. Because they were formed September 7, 2001, in Perpignan at the Visa Pour l'Image festival, and James Nachtwey, a megastar even within this group of star photographers, quite coincidentally happened to return to New York the evening of September 10, 2001, VII was able to immediately get attention through the sale of September 11 photography. Furthermore, Ron Haviv, another of the VII photographers, had already worked extensively in Afghani-stan. Very fortunately for VII, specific circumstances allowed their first year to be very profitable, but it was certainly not the type of year that one can use as a measure. James Nachtwey has since left the group and represents himself.

40. For a discussion of the conflicting opinions about this move—visual his-tory locked up in a tomb or a philanthropic act of conservation—see Sarah Boxer's article "A Century's Photo History Destined for Life in a Mine" (*New York Times,* April 15, 2001). See part 1, *Underground,* of *The Invisible Photo-graph,* a documentary series produced by the Hilman Photography Initiative and the Carnegie Museum of Art. One of the ontological questions raised by the digitization of historical images is that we can now speak of photographs that could potentially last forever, as long as they are continually transitioned to digital formats that are not obsolete. The very possibility of a historical photo-graph being immune to decay invites us to rethink the ontology of the historical image and how the relationship between history, photography, and memory have been theorized.

41. For a humorous and provocative look at requests made of photographic archivists, see filmmaker Laurie Hill's short film *Photograph of Jesus,* made as part of a challenge set by Getty Images to filmmakers to create a piece using images from their Hulton Archive. Of course, few independent filmmakers would ever be able to afford licensing fees for this kind of project were it not for sponsorship by firms such as Getty Images.

42. Some of these sources of revenue have changed considerably. For exam-ple, archival sales have plummeted. See the conclusion for a discussion of recent changes in the industry.

43. There was much debate over whether a photographer had to share his income if he got the assignment on his own, with no help from the agency. But if the photographer then submitted these images to the agency and they were resold, there seemed to be agreement that he would share that profit.

44. The average day rate while I was doing fieldwork was five hundred dollars. Sometimes double day rates were given in conflict zones. That day rates had not changed in well over a decade was a source of great consternation for photographers.

45. In the case of commercial use, other factors that would be considered are how frequently the image might appear and in what markets it might be used.

46. This makes it more fruitful now to compare the circulation of these images to that of images in the art world. See Myers, *The Empire of Things*. One of the early ideas behind Corbis was that individual consumers would want to license digital copies of art images for private use. This consumer trend had not yet taken off in 2003 (and still hasn't) but was always anticipated, such as in the design of websites on which a news image could be put in a client's shopping cart or a "buy this image" button would be visible next to each of the week's top photos.

47. Kleinman and Kleinman, "The Appeal of Experience," 1.

48. Fred Ritchin's *In Our Own Image: The Coming Revolution in Photography* addresses the journalistic and ethical implication of digital production and editing in a very prescient manner. Here, however, I focus more on the structures that render the distribution and publication of digital news photography possible rather than on the important issue of the changing ontology of the image and the serious ethical dilemmas digitization poses for photography. Although we focus on different parts of the production cycle, we arrive at very similar questions. Ritchin ends his chapter titled "Authoring the Image" by drawing our attention to the questions that remain to be asked about the economics of digitization: "Perhaps the greatest question is whether there will be a diversity of news and other information available or whether it will be controlled by a few large corporations. Also, will the individual voices of the journalists and others be allowed to come through, or will information be pooled and homogenized?" Ritchin, *In Our Own Image,* 115.

49. Frosh, *The Image Factory,* 9.

50. Frosh, *The Image Factory,* 197.

51. Commissions can be significant. One account executive explained that he got 1.5 percent of total monthly sales as commission if he met his goal but 2.25 percent for 110 percent of goal, 3.25 percent for 125 percent of goal, 4.25 percent for 150 percent of goal, and so on, and that there was no ceiling. On a good month, if he managed to achieve 150 percent of his goal, he could make five thousand dollars in commissions, in addition to his salary.

52. Walter Benjamin might have found the analogy delightfully appropriate, since he saw the arcades of the same Paris neighborhood as central to the transformation of visuality by modernity.

53. Later in the presentation another executive emphasized, "We're providing raw material for their [i.e., the editors'] creativity."

54. I have used italics for this word to emphasize that it was always used in English.

55. As if to emphasize this point, a few weeks later, when Greece won the 2004 European cup, Manoli, a French sales rep of Greek origin, blasted the tune to *sirtaki,* a popular Greek dance, at random intervals throughout the day.

56. Hartley, "Documenting Kate Moss," 558. Christian Caujolle, the founder and photo editor of the French newspaper *Libération,* had in the late 1980s already addressed the problem of photographs being produced with the intent of appearing in multiple publications. Which is to say, the desire for a universal image was not invented with the rise of the visual content industry but was significantly amplified. Frustrated that too many newsmagazines were publishing similar images, Caujolle states, "It is also the result of certain developments in photographic agencies, which have become large industrial machines distributing their products in more than fifty countries and which, to get their pictures published, must supply material fitting the most common characteristics of the entire world. In these circumstances, the best picture is also the most neutral picture which can be used for the most purposes. It is no longer a matter of photography, but markets, economies, demands and profits." Caujolle, "Photography and its Uses," 67.

CHAPTER 2. GLOBAL VIEWS INC.

The chapter epigraph is the text of the multimedia ad that greeted visitors to GVI's website. "QRS" is a pseudonym for a wire service that partnered with GVI. (For details of this type of arrangement, see chapter 1). GVI distributes QRS's images through its website and gets a share of the revenues generated. QRS's content supplements GVI's own production.

1. The American war in Iraq officially lasted from March 20, 2003, to December 18, 2011, when US troops pulled out of the country. However, the insurgency and civil conflict continued after this date, and the United States still maintained a significant staff in Iraq at the time of publication.

2. "Public Affairs Guidance (PAG) on Embedding Media during Possible Future Operations/Deployments in the U.S." I have used approximate numbers provided in Vaina, "The Vanishing Embedded Reporter in Iraq"; and Wright, "Assessment of the DoD Embedded Media Program." This chapter focuses on how a newsroom back in the United States supported an embedded photographer and how image brokers evaluated embedded reporting while actively working to visualize the beginning of the war in Iraq. Most of the embedded journalists had disembedded within a month of US military entering Baghdad in April 2003. There is now an extensive literature that focuses on the US military program of embedding media. For scholarly treatment of the issue, see Tumber and Palmer, *The Media at War;* Seib, *Beyond the Front Lines;* and Pfau et al., "Embedding Journalists in Military Combat Units." See Katovsky and Carlson, *Embedded,* for an oral history of embedding. For an assessment of embedded media from the perspective of the military, see Paul and Kim, *Reporters on the Battlefield;* and Wright, "Assessment of the DoD Embedded Media Program."

3. As described in the introduction, my access was jeopardized briefly as I negotiated a nondisclosure agreement, but I remained on-site almost daily for most of eight months.

4. See Maas, "The Toppling."

5. Susan Sontag draws attention to the fact that since the Vietnam War, "it is virtually certain that none of the best-known photographs were set-ups." Her explanation for this is that due to the proliferation of television crews, "the witnessing of war is now hardly ever a solitary venture." She concludes, "Technically the possibilities for doctoring or electronically manipulating pictures are greater than ever—almost unlimited. But the practice of inventing dramatic news pictures, staging them for the camera, seems on its way to becoming a lost art." Sontag, *Regarding the Pain of Others,* 57–58. Yet by analyzing the US Department of Defense's and various news media's preparations for the war, well in advance of its actual declaration, one might ask if the intrepid lone photographer's actions are the only place we need look for set-ups or invention of political drama. Put provocatively, why stage a war photograph if you can stage a war? See Gürsel, "Framing Zarqawi," for a discussion of the use of very unspectacular head shots in the run up to the Iraq war.

6. Herbert Gans and Jeremy Tunstall make this practice very clear in their studies of newsrooms.

7. I conducted some amount of research at all three of the main US news weeklies—*Time, Newsweek,* and *U.S. News & World Report*—and watched weekly news cycles closely at two of them. By using the aggregate pseudonym *Newsworld,* I refer to them collectively for the purpose of anonymity and also because I am focusing on what was common rather than dissimilar about their methods as important news publications in which world news is visualized.

8. GVI would get 30 percent of this assignment rate.

9. Second rights are the rights to publish the images after they have been initially published in the magazine. See chapter 1 for a discussion of the sales team's concerns about when they should get credited with second sales.

10. The newspaper editor wanted to have guaranteed profits from these photos for the duration of the war, which he imagined would be over in a matter of weeks. Ed, on the other hand, wanted the option to sell the images but wanted to make a minimal commitment so as not to find himself sinking money into images that might not sell, especially should the war continue longer than expected.

11. Emphasis mine. For a further discussion of Rumsfeld's claims of appropriate and proportionate targets and images, see Gürsel, "Framing Zarqawi."

12. Rumsfeld, "DoD News Briefing—Secretary Rumsfeld and Gen. Myers." Emphasis mine.

13. "Press Briefing by Ari Fleischer."

14. This Jacques is the same photographer who, during the sales meeting described in chapter 1, suggested that the sales team might stop in Fez to shoot a Four Seasons hotel en route to covering the war in Monrovia.

15. *Stern* is a German newsmagazine, highly reputable in the photojournalism world.

16. Magazines will often grant syndication permission once the weekly news cycle has passed.

17. First drafted in 1929 and revised in 1949, the Geneva Convention Relative to the Treatment of Prisoners of War (POW) is one of four Geneva

Conventions that, along with Additional Protocols, are the core foundations for International Humanitarian Law. These treaties exist to regulate the treatment of civilians, prisoners of war, and soldiers who are considered incapable of fighting. www.icrc.org/applic/ihl/ihl.nsf/vwTreaties1949.xsp. In 2003, the British Red Cross and British government put forth a pledge to create an up-to-date version of Article 13, which states that "prisoners of war must at all times be protected, particularly against acts of violence or intimidation and against insults and public curiosity." In *The Media at War,* Howard Tumber and Jerry Palmer discuss the International Committee of the Red Cross's criticism of the broadcasting of images of American and Iraqi POWs as a violation of the Geneva Conventions. How the conventions should apply to photographs and news images is still widely debated. More recently these debates resurfaced in relation to the US government's decision not to release photographs of Osama bin Laden's body after he was killed during a May 2011 attack in Pakistan.

18. The Public Affairs Guidance on embedding media states that members of the press will be given access to prisoners of war only within the provisions of the Geneva Conventions. (Article 3.S) 4.G.18 further specifies that no photographs or other visual media showing an enemy POW's face, name tag, or other identifying feature may be taken. My focus here is not on the actual wording of the guidelines but rather on what photographers and image brokers back in the United States seemed to know and the extent to which guidelines were implemented.

19. Many seemed to be coming to the same conclusion that Sontag had about the practice of inventing dramatic news pictures becoming a lost art. Yet the many instances of staged photographs that have circulated and hurt the reputations of photojournalism and news publications more broadly during the war in Iraq suggest that, on this point at least, Sontag was mistaken.

20. Among the journalism community at the time, Kuwait was seen as a safe backstage to the war in Iraq, a place for journalists to go to recuperate.

21. I heard a senior photo editor for the *New York Times* claim, "We see hiring a staff photographer as a Supreme Court appointment. . . . Once in with us, they're not likely to leave."

22. General Tommy Franks was a four-star army general and commander-in-chief of Central Command near Doha, Qatar. He led the attack on the Taliban in Afghanistan in October 2001.

23. This could happen for myriad reasons. For example, a more important story "dominates" the coverage, or the image gets stale by appearing in many daily publications that the readers may have already seen by the time they get their weekly magazine.

24. For a lengthier discussion of the friction between the sales and editorial teams, see Chapter 1.

25. Hannerz, *Foreign News,* 103.

26. This debate about merely being an unbiased conduit, a wholesaler supplying publications with images, will return in chapter 3 in regards to Agence France-Presse's changing politics in a digital world.

27. With these epic stories, which Strong envisioned having global reach and generating interest beyond a single news peg, he was actually anticipating the

demands of the sales team mentioned in chapter 1 but making a journalistic rather than commercial argument for why the team ought to pursue this type of coverage.

28. Copies of publications where a photographer's work has been published are often included as part of a portfolio to demonstrate the type of publications in which a photographer has gotten his work placed.

29. This is an example of where I think Tuchman and Schudson's analytic language of "making news" is not specific enough to capture how photographs become news images. Many of the elements that make these photographs formative fictions are similar to issues these scholars underline when talking about news being made. However here is a moment when Ed is brokering photographs for journalistic purposes but explicitly saying he is not making news. Yet, Ed's choices structure the conditions of possibility for the news that can be made from these images by image brokers at news publications. In other words, because Ed works at a visual content provider, Ed doesn't see his job as making news. However, in the process of making sales for photographers, he is by default part of the process of making news.

30. On April 8, 2003, Al Jazeera's bureau in Baghdad was hit by US missiles, killing a reporter and wounding a cameraman. Three hours later a US tank fired at the Palestine Hotel, where almost all foreign journalists who had not left after the Pentagon advised press to evacuate were based. A Reuters photographer and a Spanish television cameraman were killed, and many others were wounded. US forces also opened fire on the offices of Abu Dhabi television. The Pentagon had been notified that all three were media locations.

31. It turned out that Levy was doing some translating but had minimal Arabic language skills.

32. It is precisely because photographers are always supposed to send in captions that it was noteworthy that the 2002 editor's note, discussed in the introduction, disclosing Michael Finkel's inappropriate journalistic techniques mentioned that the photograph in question had been sent in uncaptioned. Had the professional photographer taken the shot, he should have captioned it. Because there was allegedly no caption attached to the image, it was conceivable for the newspaper to argue that no one other than Finkel knew that the photograph was not of Youssouf Malé.

33. Her story and the media's portrayal of it was later challenged, and Lynch herself testified before Congress in April 2007, claiming that her weapon had jammed like those of everyone in her unit and therefore she had never fired a single shot.

34. This is an example of a situation where it does not make sense to separate news production and consumption or distribution and reception.

35. A few months later Rumsfeld, too, conflated Iraq and Romania when asked about the appropriateness of how Saddam's sons' bodies were allowed to be depicted. For an extended discussion of appropriate depictions of corpses and the political ramifications of Rumsfeld's evoking the specter of Ceaușescu, see Gürsel, "Framing Zarqawi."

36. A May 2, 2015, op-ed piece in the *New York Times* begins: "It should come as no surprise that the United States and its coalition partners are

discussing widening the war against the Islamic State beyond the borders of Iraq and Syria." New York Times Editorial Board, "Stumbling into a Wider War."

CHAPTER 3. AGENCE FRANCE-PRESSE

1. Most of the interviews and fieldwork that this chapter draws on occurred in French. I have translated all speech into English. However, I have left this particular expression, "the dominant," in its French usage because the concept of having a "dominant"—a noun that is awkward in English—is central to my concerns here. For a discussion of the significance of certain words being used only in English at AFP, see chap. 1.

2. Of course, evaluations of importance are never universal. A local fluctuation in rice prices might have far greater significance to millions in Asia than a high-level meeting between two European leaders. Furthermore, the location of headquarters and bureaus might, to some extent, predetermine which regions get more attention. Nonetheless, what I want to underscore here is that, at the level of daily planning meetings, the dominant is discussed as if it were knowledge production of a universally significant kind. I never heard anyone in the meetings actually debate whether a particular story really had global rather than merely regional significance, although this may have happened in meetings I did not attend. For an example of national framings specifically of the war in Iraq, see Ravi, "Looking beyond Flawed Journalism."

3. In "The Political Field, the Social Science Field, and the Journalistic Field," sociologist Pierre Bourdieu draws attention to how negotiation between specific publications shapes each one's coverage. Wire services, too, are very aware of their competition. They all cover daily worldwide news, so speed—who has the story on the wire first—is a major basis for comparison.

4. Lina Khatib gives a compelling genealogy of what one might call a visual turn in politics in her book *Image Politics in the Middle East: The Role of the Visual in Political Struggle*. I concur entirely that "to understand political dynamics in the Middle East, one needs to take into account the role of the image in those dynamics" (Khatib, *Image Politics in the Middle East*, 3). Although she begins her account from the visual legacy of the Cedar Revolution in 2005, the image brokering from September 11 on, and particularly during the beginning of the war in Iraq, was an important prehistory to that genealogy. I believe this emergence of the circulation of certain images as news events had visual and political repercussions in other regions as well.

5. This argument is built on the persuasive literature on representational worldmaking (Goodman, *Ways of Worldmaking*; Mitchell, *Picture Theory*) and the constructed nature of facts (Hacking, *The Social Construction of What?*; Latour, *On the Modern Cult of the Factish Gods*; Poovey, *A History of the Modern Fact*), but also seeks to go beyond it. In this chapter I investigate moments in the production and circulation of certain photographs as news images as events in themselves.

6. For more on amateur photographs and how they can become news images, see Andén-Papadopoulos and Pantti, "Re-Imagining Crisis Reporting"; Mortensen, *Journalism and Eyewitness Images*; and Allan *Citizen Witnessing*.

Andén-Papadopoulos and Pantti, *Amateur Images and Global News,* provides an excellent multifaceted introduction to the subject.

7. For an extensive discussion of how the War on Terror is inseparable from its visual representations, see Butler, *Frames of War;* Mitchell, *Cloning Terror;* and Gürsel, "Spectacular Terrorism." See also Rumsfeld's comments on visual representations of the war in chapter 2.

8. This aspect of journalism, perhaps best captured by Tuchman's phrase "routinizing the unexpected," has been well documented in Born, *Uncertain Vision;* Fishman, *Manufacturing the News;* Gans, *Deciding What's News;* Schlesinger, *Putting "Reality" Together;* Tuchman, *Making News;* and Tunstall, *Journalists at Work,* among others.

9. Clifford and Marcus, *Writing Culture;* Hall, *Representation;* Lutz and Collins, *Reading National Geographic;* Marcus and Fischer, *Anthropology as Cultural Critique;* Said, *Orientalism.*

10. I am thinking of work that treats diverse forms of visual representations, such as Ganti, *Producing Bollywood;* Jain, *Gods in the Bazaar;* Larkin, *Signal and Noise;* Mazzarella, *Shoveling Smoke;* Marcus and Myers, *The Traffic in Culture;* Pinney, *Camera Indica;* Schwenkel, *The American War in Contemporary Vietnam;* and Strassler, *Refracted Visions.*

11. The legendary elite photo agency Magnum is believed by many to be the home of the world's most esteemed photographers.

12. For a discussion of the dominance of wire agencies within German news, see Boyer, "Digital Expertise in Online Journalism (and Anthropology)."

13. "Rumsfeld Testifies before House Armed Services Committee." www .washingtonpost.com/wp-dyn/articles/A9251–2004May7_2.html.

14. For discussions of journalists' attempts to grapple with the digital journalistic regime, see Boyer, *The Life Informatic;* and Vesperi, "When Common Sense No Longer Holds." Also, see Russell, "Salon.com and New-Media Professional Journalism Culture," for a discussion of how, in 2006, its management of a large number of Abu Ghraib images became a way for Salon.com, an online news publication employing journalists mostly trained in traditional newsrooms, to demonstrate what it could contribute to news followers. See also Perlmutter and Hamilton, *From Pigeons to News Portals,* for a collection of mass communication scholarship specifically on new challenges in foreign reporting brought on by new technologies.

15. Since my research, the European Commission regulators have been investigating AFP's state subsidy and commercial activities. In recent years, the 1957 statute has been much debated, since it prohibits AFP from having outside investors. Many—including, most recently, trade unions—oppose such investors as a step in the privatization of the news agency. In April 2015 the French parliament approved changes to the 1957 statutes that some perceive as a threat to AFP's structural independence. For the reaction from the media union, see "Parliament Squeezes AFP into EU Straitjacket."

16. See Azoulay, *The Civil Contract of Photography,* for a provocative reading of early photography history in conjunction with the Declaration of the Rights of Man and of the Citizen. Article 11, about press freedom as an inalienable right, is somewhat of a national touchstone in France. It was immediately

invoked by the French prime minister in his condemnation of the November 2011 bombing of the satirical paper *Charlie Hebdo* following its publishing an issue with the prophet Muhammed featured on the cover serving as guest editor ("Condamnation unanime de 'l'attentat' contre les locaux de 'Charlie Hebdo'").

17. Only significant events got mentioned in the play reports, and there was no way of knowing which specific images had been used or in what dailies they had been published, because the bureaus gathered the information from the major dailies of their regions and then sent in the aggregated results.

18. This is a material manifestation of what Boczkowski calls emerging media. Ethnographies of newsrooms in transition are sure to capture seemingly anachronistic practices that highlight rapid change. An organizational example of this from Boczkowksi is the detail that producers in the *New York Times*'s CyberTimes desk needed to yell out "Anyone publishing?" before moving a file from the mirror server to the public server because the publishing tool could not deal with two requests simultaneously. Boczkowski, *Digitizing the News*, 85. Even when technical innovation is rapid, then, it is never immediate, and it is often in seemingly insignificant material artifacts or mundane practices that the pace and complexity of innovation can be grasped best.

19. Janet's comment also points to what was perceived to be an important distinction between wire services and photo agencies in terms of those to whom they provided images—strictly editorial versus editorial and commercial clients—and the resulting differences in terms of revenues and resources. For further discussion, see chap. 1.

20. That he used the expression "*il faut pas laisser la place*," which literally translates to "we must not *leave space*" (for our competitors), highlights the interesting and constant conflation of space and time at a wire service. Marc continued, "We must not let those who aren't a part of us open the fields" (literal translation). By this he meant that, for a wire service, what is critical is initial coverage of an event. Because many clients subscribe to multiple wire services, his belief was that what determined whether a publication used an AFP photo depended on the wire service's ability to provide the first image of the event. So, not leaving an opening for a competitor, although it means a race in time, translates into a contest over space in a publication.

21. Wire services are particularly well positioned to provide coverage of phenomena experienced worldwide because they can coordinate across many bureaus. The 2004 Venus transit received global media coverage because it was the first such transit to take place after the invention of broadcast media. The previous Venus transit took place on December 6, 1882.

22. A small sales team within the photo department at AFP sells individual images to publications that do not subscribe to the wire. This commercial section of the department is the cause of much controversy, since the editors on the desks like to see themselves as journalists who have no financial interest in the images but instead serve only the nobler cause of informing the public. See chapter 1 for more on the AFP Retail Sales Service.

23. UNRWA (United Nations Relief and Works Agency), "Where We Work." www.unrwa.org/where-we-work. There are 455,000 refugees registered with

the UNRWA in Lebanon. Many live in one of the twelve camps in the country. Several of the camps were established in 1948. Although I could not read his mind, I observed Valery handling Palestine-related news events on other occasions and do not think this comment was in any way an attempt to avoid reporting on Palestinians. What is interesting to me here is the specifically visual rationale he gave for his decision.

24. For more on how news audiences are imagined by media producers, see Dornfeld, *Producing Public Television, Producing Public Culture.* Donna Schwartz, "To Tell the Truth," analyzes photojournalism textbooks and states that whereas the needs and desires of the reader of often invoked, rarely is any explicit evidence provided. Anthropologists have addressed this role of the imagined viewer in popular media as well. See Abu-Lughod, *Dramas of Nationhood;* Mandel, "A Marshall Plan of the Mind"; and Mankekar, *Screening Culture, Viewing Politics.*

25. For an excellent and complementary discussion of nonvisual modes of marking difference, see anthropologist Kira Kosnick's investigation of Radio Multi Kulti, a German radio station with the slogan "we speak with an accent." Kosnick, "'Foreign Voices.'"

26. Rantanen, "European News Agencies and Their Sources in the Iraq War Coverage," provides a pertinent discussion of the issue of trust in sources according to nationality in coverage of outbreak of the Iraq war.

27. Throughout my fieldwork, I observed constant tension between word and image people. For an extensive discussion, see chapter 4.

28. Mass communication scholars Brooke Barnett and Amy Reynolds argue that the media is central to terrorist activity, adding, "Breaking news is the new vehicle to transport the terrorist message." Barnett and Reynolds, *Terrorism and the Press,* 1. For an extensive analysis of the uneasy and controversial yet key relationship between the media and terrorism, see Liebes and Kampf, "The PR of Terror"; and Nacos, *Mass-Mediated Terrorism.*

29. See Pantti and Sirén, "The Fragility of Photo-Truth," for a description of how amateur images are evaluated in newsrooms and the role assigned to wire services by their subscribers.

30. See Barnett and Reynolds, *Terrorism and the Press,* 82, for a discussion of how the editor of the *Pittsburgh Tribute-Review* justified his decision to publish some of the less graphic images.

31. Interpreter, Christian missionary, and South Korean hostage Kim Sun-il was decapitated on June 22, 2004, by the group who took him hostage, allegedly led by Abu Musab al-Zarqawi. The video of his decapitation was sent to Al Jazeera television. "Pentagon: South Korean Hostage Beheaded."

32. For a discussion of the common practice of indexing bodies but representing bodies politic in photography, see the introduction. The same logics are at work in the news image showing the Hungarian women in folk costume or in Marie's concerns about how the images of the sangomas watching Venus's passing would be interpreted.

33. For a fascinating analysis of how wire service feeds on the Internet play into the planning processes and imaginations of local activists, see Amahl Bishara's analysis of multiple interpretations of the appearance of an image

produced in Bethlehem on Yahoo News. Bishara, "Covering the Barrier in Bethlehem." See Kuntsman and Stein, "Another War Zone," for a discussion of the Israeli state's use of social media during the May 2010 flotilla crisis and of how state forces and activists both use live online feeds—often the same ones—to frame events for audiences. In an interesting twist, in an attempt to differentiate themselves in the 24/7 Internet news landscape, Yahoo, Politico, MSNBC, and others began competing for the best feature stories with original assigned photography. In 2015, Yahoo News boasted photo galleries "hand-curated" by Yahoo News photo editors.

34. On this point, the photograph on the cover of this book is typical of what comes across a wire service editor's screens.

35. There are differing views on whether who the image broker is makes a difference. One journalist wrote, of the release of the video of *Wall Street News* journalist Daniel Pearl's beheading, "[The fact that] the video was produced by terrorists rather than journalists is a mere detail. After all it depicts what happened, which is the most elemental definition of news." Kennedy, "The Daniel Pearl Video," 81.

36. For an extended discussion of head shots and body politics in the digital age, see Gürsel, "Framing Zarqawi."

37. Boczkowski, *Digitizing the News;* Henry, *American Carnival;* Meyer, *The Vanishing Newspaper.*

38. Images from the military are also designated as "handout" photographs.

39. According to French law there are many restrictions against showing someone in handcuffs, so standard practice is to pixelate these sections of the photo, which causes a blurring effect.

40. One day, Valery shared with me his business plan to create a company that would just take screen grabs of television coverage of events. He joked with his colleagues on the desk about how he was going to make a mint editing at a distance with no staff, few costs, and no photographers.

41. CNN, "Transcript of Saddam Proceeding." The only other report from the courtroom immediately makes it apparent that even the most mundane description is constructed and open to interpretation: "After six months' imprisonment, [Saddam's] hair was unkempt, his beard gray and straggly, and his favored Italian hand-stitched suits replaced by cheap store-bought jacket and pants provided by the Americans for the occasion." Burns, "The Reach of War," 1.

42. CNN, "Amanpour: Saddam's 'Bizarre Rant.'"

43. CNN, "Paula Zahn Transcript."

44. CNN, "Transcript of Saddam Proceeding."

45. Peter Jennings, also present in the courtroom, confirmed the order to unplug mikes. Some reporters disobeyed this order, and the censors managed to delete only some of the sound, so the crews were able to get some audio to their headquarters.

46. CNN, "Amanpour: Saddam Story among Career's Top Ten."

47. See Zelizer, "Journalism's 'Last' Stand," for a compelling historical account of how, from the beginning of the widespread use of photography in news publications, photojournalism was seen as merely an "adjunct to word-journalism" (87).

48. The peculiar staging of this event and the inchoate and highly interdependent nature of Iraqi sovereignty were also apparent in the setting of the trial in a building that had been part of Saddam Hussein's palace. According to CNN's report, the US military had had the courtroom renovated, and in fact, just a week earlier, the space had been used for a hearing related to the Abu Ghraib prisoner-abuse scandal. According to CNN, the Iraqi judge had asked that there be no symbols of Iraq's new sovereignty, such as flags, visible in the courtroom. Saddam's legal custody had been handed over to the Iraqis, but coalition forces were still responsible for his physical security. CNN, "Saddam's Hearing on Grounds of Former Palace."

49. Many of the same tensions I saw being negotiated in the Photo Department are discussed by Michael Palmer in relation to the news at large in news agencies. Palmer, "International News from Paris- and London-Based Newsrooms." For an excellent history of shifts in journalism seen through the lens of foreign correspondents at AFP, see Laville, *Les transformations du journalisme de 1945 à 2010.*

50. In 2007 AFP acquired 34 percent of *Citizenside,* an amateur journalism website. Photographs uploaded to the site are licensed to worldwide media outlets via AFP's archive.

CHAPTER 4. *NEWSWORLD*

1. At the time of my fieldwork *Newsworld* had a minimal but growing online presence. Today online readership is significant, and many news publications have online-only blogs or sections focusing on photography.

2. Although I am using Anderson's term, I am discussing not only how image brokers imagine their own communities but also those communities to which they and their imagined readers do not belong. Anderson, *Imagined Communities.* Even within *Newsworld,* the imagined reader is not always Euro-American. There is an Asian edition of the magazine as well as a European edition, and at one point there had even been a Canadian edition. Stories and images are tweaked for these different editions, though a significant amount of content remains the same. All of these acts of everyday worldmaking are part of producing and representing publics. However, more research is needed on how stories produced by image brokers are actually taken up by readers. Here I focus on how certain categories of people are represented with the imagined needs, desires, and limitations of the imagined reader in mind. For an excellent overview of how publics have been conceptualized and researched, see Cody, "Publics and Politics."

3. Circulation data from the Pew Research Center.

4. Before, photographers would send in their film without having seen it themselves and the photo editors would be the first to edit the images. Now, as Ed mentioned in chapter 2, photographers are the first editors. One veteran photo editor lamented, "We'll never see what a photographer doesn't want to show. . . . Before I could see someone thinking [as I edited], I would see how they felt and [I would] go through the emotional process [with them while looking through their film]. It's less intimate now." Another pointed out, "Before I

felt like I knew how a photographer was thinking—for example, how controlled or frustrated or manipulated someone felt."

5. For a visual framing analysis of images that ran at the time of my research, see Schwalbe, "Visually Framing the Invasion and Occupation of Iraq in *Time, Newsweek,* and *US News & World Report.*" For a visual content analysis of coverage of the Gulf war in these same magazines, see Griffin and Lee, "Picturing the Gulf War: Constructing Images of War."

6. Walter Benjamin famously claimed, "Every day the urge grows stronger to get hold of an object at very close range by way of its likeness, its reproduction" (Benjamin, "The Work of Art in the Age of Mechanical Reproduction," 223). This claim has been richly elaborate on in Taussing, *Mimesis and Alterity.*

7. Hariman and Lucaites go further and argue that compelling photographs, particularly images with shock value, compel readers to engage with the story differently: "Strong images can activate strong reading." Hariman and Lucaites, *No Caption Needed,* 293.

8. Mitchell, *Picture Theory,* 5.

9. A senior photo editor told me about important breaking news events in the past where she had been sent to the field with the photographers: "They trusted me to actually pick the image. I was on the phone with the director of photography and the art director and described the original edit I had made of five and then we picked one. That's the one I transmitted." As described in chapter 2, today the photographs that are sold unseen are the ones that have yet to be taken. Since images could be transmitted back to the office with relative ease, she no longer was sent to the field to edit—something reserved only for highly time-sensitive major news stories even in the past. On any given story, there was less editing to do in general. The editorial role has shifted to the photographer in the digital era. "I used to look at eighty rolls on a topic at more than thirty frames each. Now I might get eight to ten frames from any shoot." See also note 33 of the introduction and note 4 of this chapter.

10. Clay Aiken is an American pop singer who rose to fame in 2003 on the television show *American Idol.*

11. *Newsworld* had conducted focus groups with readers to better understand what they appreciated in the magazine. Mary, the art director, had been frustrated by them: "The reader's understanding of a predominance of war photography is that it's not fun to look at, it's necessary. The groups were fairly discriminatory and they picked out good images, but I had problems with the moderator because she didn't express that photographs in and of themselves could be newsworthy; she kept asking them to evaluate based on 'visual attractiveness.'" Mary emphasized that of course no reader was going to suggest that any image of the battlefield, no matter how significant it may be journalistically, was "visually attractive."

12. I am aware of the political ramifications inherent in referring to this structure as a wall rather than a security fence or separation barrier or any number of other labels. I have repeated the terms used by my informants, who often used these terms interchangeably, sometimes depending on whose opinion they were mediating.

13. Good captions are critical for photo editors. Maggie often felt embarrassed in front of a text editor because she didn't have enough caption information. Clear captions allow her and other image brokers to better advocate for a

photograph because captions represent journalism in a medium more familiar to the text editors: words.

14. Maggie often mentioned visual similarities to other historical moments when pointing out the strengths of an image, such as "This has a Somalia feel of general discontent to it" or "I love this one, it is totally Vietnam looking." Yet she was hesitant to showcase work that was too similar to another photographer's. Evocative work was powerful, but Maggie was always wary of derivative photography, or images that might look too familiar to the reader.

15. In the wall example she was interested in a photograph in which the subjects were all clustered in the middle of the image.

16. How many options are worked on simultaneously also has to do with a magazine's budget. Two-tracking—preparing two alternative cover stories and slightly different magazines—might be typical at a magazine with a large production budget, whereas another magazine might be able to afford only a 10 percent "kill rate" (the percentage of material prepared for publication but not used).

17. In Amahl Bishara's terms, this is an example of one category of person being *unmade* in the process of making another category. In other words, the category of working Palestinian woman is reinforced with the selection of the photograph of the supposedly working woman crossing the wall, but the category of modern Palestinian woman is unmade by the image of the blonde being left out of the selection.

18. Watching teams at newsmagazines work on visualizing world news often seemed to me like a debate about whether a news image should be denotative or connotative. Though I cannot generalize about all instances I observed, photo editors often appreciated the connotative register of an image more but had to make an argument in the language of what was being accurately denoted to get text editors to validate their selection. Barthes, "The Rhetoric of the Image."

19. The manner in which image brokers make use of aesthetic conflict, often in the form of binaries, directly shapes the production of categories of people—categories that are central to how political conflict is imaginable even before it is actionable. For further discussion of aesthetic conflict as a principle of visual worldmaking, see Gürsel, "Worldmaking, Frame by Frame."

20. In a chapter titled "A World Brightly Different: Photographic Conventions, 1950–1986," Lutz and Collins provide a cogent analysis of how tradition and modernity were illustrated in *National Geographic* during a historical period focused on modernization and progress narratives. Some of these visual conventions are still in use. The very photograph they chose to illustrate these conventions used by *National Geographic,* titled *Traditional and Modern Worlds Contrasted,* shows "a traditional woman," naked from the waist up, seated at a classroom table looking through a microscope. Lutz and Collins, *Reading National Geographic,* 112.

PART TWO. WORLDMAKING

1. These event-based field sites can be thought of as temporary sites such as refugee camps, athletic events, and tourist destinations. See Malkki, "News and Culture."

CHAPTER 5. BARNSTORM

1. Today students departing for Barnstorm meet at the Event Space in the giant B&H Superstore on 9th Avenue. Established in 1973, B&H is the largest independent photo and video equipment store in the United States. Its motto is "The Professional's Source."

2. www.eddieadamsworkshop.com.

3. Following Arnold Van Gennep, anthropologist Victor Turner defined a rite of passage as a transition between states characterized by three stages: separation, transition (liminality), and aggregation. Turner encouraged researchers to pay particular attention to the liminal phase: the processes of midtransition, he claimed, "expose the basic building blocks of culture." Turner, *The Forest of Symbols,* 110. See La Fontaine, *Initiation,* on initiation ceremonies. Reflecting on the workshop years later, photographers have described it variously as "formative," "a game changer," and an event that "charted my destiny in some ways." One photographer recalls returning home and feeling "like a new person; like I had an awakening." Garcia, "The Impact of the Eddie Adams Workshop—20 Years Later." A more recent alum comments, "You leave the Eddie Adams Workshop as part of a family." Hansen, "Insights and Experiences from the 2011 Eddie Adams Workshop."

4. Students pay a minimal fee for meals and lodging. The workshop is committed to being tuition-free and financially accessible to all chosen students. Whereas in the past the workshop was sponsored by Kodak and Nikon, it is now mainly sustained by Nikon.

5. Barnstorm: The Eddie Adams Workshop, NYC: *Life Going On.*

6. How I think about experts and expertise is informed by T. Mitchell, *Rule of Experts.*

7. Keith Bedford, a freelance photographer who initially went to Barnstorm as a student and then returned for many years as a team producer, mentions "toys" as one of the many reasons aspiring photographers should go to the Eddie Adams Workshop: "If any photographer tells you he is not into his gear he is lying. Nikon cameras, Profoto lights, Manfrotto tripods, and PocketWizards are all there for you to play with. By play with I mean make photos right then and there. Want to mount a camera onto a hang glider with a 6 millimeter lens? Bam!! Done! Need a 400 Millimeter? Team Nikon will give you one. Done! Want to light a barn? Hell, how about an entire football field? Cliff Hausner with Profoto will help make your dreams come true. Never use any of this stuff? The good folks at these companies will help you learn it and even be your personal assistant. They are all there for you. They want you to succeed." Bedford, "Why You Should Go to the Eddie Adams Workshop." In recent years all teams also have a dedicated tech person.

8. I thought back on this young female photographer's vow not to let her competitive streak interfere with her ability to be a part of the photojournalism community some time later when listening to a very prominent American male photojournalist discuss the status of women in the business. He was speaking to a group of young Turkish photographers, male and female admirers of his work. In an attempt to encourage them to pursue photography, he reminded them of the many great female photographers in the past and assured them that

he thought very highly of his female colleagues. What he disapproved of, he told them, was the kind of fierce competitiveness he had recently witnessed while on assignment in Iraq. A young female photographer's elbows had gotten in his way as he tried to take a photo, and she jockeyed for a spot in an area crowded with photographers.

In an admiring tone, the photographer told the Turkish photographers about Dickey Chapelle, the accomplished photojournalist who had brazenly covered many wars before she was killed on the battlefield in Vietnam in 1965. He emphasized her petite physique and her signature pearl earrings, commenting that the latter were visible even in the photo taken of her by photographer Henri Huet as a chaplain administered her last rites before she passed away. I couldn't help but think back to the young woman at Barnstorm. Given that this award-winning photographer had chosen the image of Dickey Chapelle, however well accessorized, dying in the mud as the portrait of a successful female photojournalist, I wondered if perhaps a competitive streak and sturdy elbows might not be just what the student would need to succeed in the field.

The issue of gender in photojournalism is a very important one and deserves much greater attention than I can give it here. For starters, one of the first women I spoke to at Barnstorm was a student riding up on the bus who told me she was divorced with kids. "It makes everything more complicated," she told me. " There is a project I want to shoot in Africa. . . . I just wish it wasn't so far away." There are many extremely talented female photojournalists working around the world today, some of whom also have children or other family responsibilities. Many aspects of the topic of gender in photojournalism merit careful ethnographic study since female photographers in different parts of the world (as well as of different ages, classes, ethnicities, marital status, etc.) face different kinds of obstacles. In the United States at least, the disparity is less noticeable in the early stages of photographers' careers. From 1988 to 2003, when I attended Barnstorm, female photographers made up roughly 35 to 40 percent of each workshop.

However, photojournalism remains a male-dominated field. The reasons for this are multiple and complex, as are the consequences for photographers, image brokers, and news audiences. Too often the topic has been raised only to be treated superficially. One cannot reduce the question of whether the gender of the photographer or image broker matters to an impossible yes-or-no question. Should we assume that the number of female photographers is necessarily an indication of whether the culture of photojournalism is male-dominated? In other words, simply counting more women doesn't indicate a change of culture. I have chosen not to write on gender in photojournalism explicitly because I think it is too important a subject to address tangentially.

9. In recent years, each team has had its own technology expert attached to it as well.

10. Multimedia presentations put together by various teams since 2009 can be seen on the workshop's website at www.eddieadamsworkshop.com /multimedia.

11. Photographer Denny Simons recalls a time when, working with his team leader, Bill Frakes, he lost track of time shooting at a racetrack. First Frakes

read him the riot act for missing the van pickup and the first presentations, and then he rewarded Simons with powdered doughnuts because he had missed breakfast. Garcia, "Impact of the Eddie Adams Workshop."

12. I recognize that this was a judgment call and that differentiating between public and private speech is complex. For example, presentations tend to be more prepared than comments made during a panel discussion. In this chapter I credit comments to individuals if they were made publicly to all those in the barn. I do not do so if an idea was shared with me privately, even if this was done by an individual I have named elsewhere. For more on pseudonyms, see the introduction.

13. Buell, *Moments;* Goldberg, *The Power of Photography;* Griffin, "The Great War Photographs"; Hariman and Lucaites, *No Caption Needed;* Stepan, *Photos That Changed the World;* Lacayo and Russell, *Eyewitness;* Seels, Good, and Berry, "Recognition and Interpretation of Historically Significant News Photographs"; C. Sullivan, *Great Photographic Essays from Life.* The study of iconic images has tended to be centered on Western, especially American, audiences. There is less work on the cross-cultural reception of such images or on how they function in non-Western public spheres. For a notable exception, see Ghosh, *Global Icons.*

14. Many of the heavies return year after year, often repeating key stories, and so this chapter draws not only on my own observations and extensive field notes from Barnstorm in 2003 but also on articles about and recordings of Barnstorm in other years as published on blogs or on the Eddie Adams Workshop's website. I am thankful to Alyssa Adams for lending me a video recording of the 1995 workshop, the first attended by Kim Phuc during her first visit to the United States. Since I was interested in Barnstorm as a site where professional lore is passed on to new generations, I was eager to see which stories are repeated annually and which elements remain unchanged in the tellings.

15. For a detailed historical look at the myth of neutrality when it comes to combat journalism, see Knightley, *The First Casualty.*

16. Henri Huet, forty-three, of the Associated Press; Larry Burrows, forty-four, of *Life* magazine; Kent Potter, twenty-three, of United Press International; and Keisaburo Shimamoto, thirty-four, of *Newsweek,* all died when their helicopter was shot down over Laos in February 1971.

17. There is a rich literature on representations of the Vietnam War, exemplified by Griffin, "Media Images of War," Hallin, *The "Uncensored War";* L. Kennedy, "'Follow the Americans'"; Sturken, *Tangled Memories;* Moeller, *Shooting War;* and Kinney, *Friendly Fire,* and the relevant sections of Perlmutter, *Photojournalism and Foreign Policy;* Hariman and Lucaites, *No Caption Needed;* Zelizer, *About to Die.* Schwenkel, *The American War in Contemporary Vietnam,* provides a much-needed perspective from contemporary Vietnam.

18. Timothy McVeigh was the US Army veteran and former security guard convicted of and executed for detonating a truck bomb in front of the Alfred P. Murrah Building in Oklahoma City on April 19, 1995, killing 168 people.

19. For a recent discussion of photographers deciding not to take certain photographs for fear of political repurcussions for subjects or because they suspect that they are being made to validate a staged event as authentic, see my

interview with the Nar Photos Collective about their coverage of the 2013 Gezi protests. Gürsel, "Covering Gezi."

20. From a presentation made by Adams at Barnstorm 1991. www .eddieadamsworkshop.com/presentations/.

21. Adams would have preferred to get a Pulitzer Prize for his 1979 photograph *Boat of No Smiles*, an image showing fifty refugees on a thirty-foot fishing boat off the coast of Vietnam heading to Thailand that allegedly helped convince President Carter to accept two hundred thousand refugees from Vietnam. When *Eddie Adams: Vietnam* was published posthumously in 2008 by Alyssa Adams, Eddie's wife, she explained that he would never have allowed for the photograph of General Loan to appear on the cover of the book had the book appeared while he was alive. For one possible explanation of Adams's discomfort with the *Saigon Execution* photograph, see Winslow, "The Pulitzer Eddie Adams Didn't Want."

22. Adams, Eddie. "Eulogy: General Nguyen Ngoc Loan." *Time,* July 27, 1998. http://content.time.com/time/magazine/article/0,9171,988783,00.html.

23. The 2002 Barnstorm was held early to coincide with the first anniversary of the September 11 attacks. Students spent the day of the anniversary photographing life going on in all five boroughs of New York. Adams published the result as a book: *NYC: Life Going On; A Dedication of Love by the Photographers of Barnstorm, the Eddie Adams Workshop and Their Subjects; The Men, Women and Children of New York City on 9/11/02.*

24. Twelve Pulitzer Prize–winning photographers, many of them former students at the workshop, gathered at Barnstorm 2015.

25. Schwenkel claims that, "[f]or the US press, Vietnam ceased to be a newsworthy country when it ceased to exist as a war." Schwenkel, *The American War in Contemporary Vietnam,* 52.

26. See note 54 of the introduction.

27. This hierarchy is not universal. To give the obvious example, photographers often get much higher fees to shoot celebrity portraits or corporate headquarters than battlefields. Even at festivals and workshops, the focus on war photography may be less; it is especially revered at Barnstorm and Visa Pour l'Image.

28. Adams's opinion is shared by many in the profession, at least those of a certain generation: the 1945 Iwo Jima image was voted "the greatest news photograph of all time" in a 1990 poll of the National Press Photographers Association. Griffin, "The Great War Photographs." 153. See Hariman and Lucaites, *No Caption Needed,* for a discussion of the many ways in which the Iwo Jima flag-raising image has circulated in US public culture.

29. The workshop no longer allows students to submit captions with their application portfolios, arguing that the images need to be strong enough visually to not require them.

30. Even articles that do not accuse Rosenthal of fraud often dwell at length on the rumors of the photograph being staged. Landsberg, "Negatives Aside, Photographer of Iwo Jima Fame Feels Worthwhile." The allegations of fraud were mentioned in almost all the obituaries of Rosenthal when he died in 2006.

31. For a provocative discussion of the comparative thinking encouraged by boiling military campaigns down to an image, see Zelizer, "When War Is Reduced to a Photograph."

32. Schwenkel, *The American War in Contemporary Vietnam*, 55.

33. Schwenkel, *The American War in Contemporary Vietnam*, 57.

34. In fact, due to the difficulty of traveling after the war, only very recently have Vietnamese photojournalists been able to imagine and realize reunions with some of the people they photographed during wartime. See Schwenkel, *The American War in Contemporary Vietnam*.

35. Schwenkel, *The American War in Contemporary Vietnam*, 57.

36. "Alex Levy" is a pseudonym. See the introduction for my discussion of pseudonyms.

37. Yang, "Interview with Hal Buell."

38. For more on travel restrictions, see Schwenkel, *The American War in Contemporary Vietnam*. As mentioned in earlier chapters, certain Israeli photographers had to sit out the War on Terror's early years for lack of visas; "local photographers" may not be able to travel because they lack the resources to do so.

39. Azoulay, *The Civil Contract of Photography*, 14.

40. Azoulay, *The Civil Contract of Photography*, 342.

41. Azoulay, *The Civil Contract of Photography*, 20.

42. Azoulay, *The Civil Contract of Photography*, 342.

43. This point was tragically underscored when Iraqi photojournalist Namir Noor-Eldeen and camera assistant Saeed Chmagh, both working for Reuters, were killed along with a group of civilians by fire from a US helicopter in 2007. Apart from the important question of whether this was a deliberate targeting of journalists and civilians or a mistake, Mr. Noor-Eldeen's camera was mistaken for a weapon and targeted by the helicopter pilots. For a provocative discussion of the Wikileaks video "Collateral Murder," whose circulation drew public attention to this attack, see Christian Christensen, "Uses of YouTube during the Iraq War."

44. Ray Evans Harrell, Didahnvwisgi (medicine priest) for the Nuyagi Keetoowah Society, telephone interview with the author, November 29, 2015.

45. Denise Chong begins her book *The Girl in the Picture: The Story of Kim Phuc, the Photograph, and the Vietnam War* by noting that Esper told her that the photo of Kim Phuc helped stop the war.

46. Schwenkel, *The American War in Contemporary Vietnam*, 84.

47. See the introduction for a discussion of countries and their "place in the world."

48. For a compelling discussion of *Requiem: By the Photographers Who Died in Vietnam and Indochina*, see Schwenkel, *The American War in Contemporary Vietnam*, chap. 2.

49. Schwenkel, *The American War in Contemporary Vietnam*, 9. See Hagopian, "Vietnam War Photography as a Locus of Memory," for a discussion of how the meanings of war images shift according to new interpretations of the past.

50. Mary Ann Vecchio, the fourteen-year-old runaway whose horror at the 1970 Kent State shooting of unarmed students was captured in a Pulitzer Prize-winning photograph, also attended Barnstorm 1995. Vecchio spoke openly about how the news image had brought her much trouble; she had received

threats and verbal abuse once its publication made her a symbol of the antiwar movement. She did not meet the photographer, John Filo, until May 1995, a few months before the workshop. As Vecchio explained to the students, she struggled for many years with the repercussions of unknowingly having been the subject of Filo's photograph. Vecchio has not returned to the workshop.

51. Chong, *The Girl in the Picture.*

52. Chong, *The Girl in the Picture.*

53. For a compelling discussion of photographs of Kim Phuc, including Nick Ut's photograph and its many remediations, and their relationship to collective memory and political reconciliation, see Hariman and Lucaites, *No Caption Needed,* chap. 6.

54. In May 2013, his Pulitzer Prize and thirty-five years of service not with-standing, John White was fired when the *Chicago Sun-Times* laid off its entire full-time photography staff due to rapidly changing business demands. Specifically, the publication claimed that audiences desired "more video content with their news." See Gürsel, "A Challenge for Visual Journalism," for an extensive discussion of these layoffs.

CHAPTER 6. VISA POUR L'IMAGE

1. Morris, *Get the Picture,* 313. Born in 1916, John Morris is one of photo-journalism's living legends. A photo editor for Life during World War II, he went on to work at the *Washington Post* and the *New York Times.* He was also the first executive editor of Magnum Photos. He moved to Paris as *National Geographic*'s European correspondent in 1983 and has lived there since.

2. In 2015 almost 240,00 visitors saw the exhibitions at Visa, and 3,000 professionals attended. Festivals average about 1,000 accredited photographers from fifty countries. Jaeger, "25 Years of Visa Pour L'Image: A Tribute to Jean-François Leroy."

3. Visa 2015 included an exhibition of the work of Mohamed Abdiwahab, a Somalian photographer who works freelance for AFP. The exhibition contained powerful and graphic images of daily violence in Somalia, many the aftermath of suicide bombs. Though ongoing conflict in Somalia has been a big news story for years, Abdiwahab was the first Somalian photographer exhibited at Visa. It was his first trip outside of Africa. When the Minister of Culture and Communication, Fleur Pellerin, visited the festival, Abdiwahab was one of the photographers chosen to show her his work. Hence, he appeared in many of the photographs in newspapers the next day illustrating the French government's support of photojournalism. When I asked if he'd like to work outside of Somalia or be a staff photographer for AFP, Abdiwahab underscored his immobility to me: "There are very few embassies in Mogadishu. If I need a visa, I need to go to Kenya. I have done so in the past, but it's always hard to know how long it will take." In other words, even if AFP wanted to make Abdiwahab a staff photographer, enabling his mobility would be challenging. blogs.afp.com /correspondent/?post/from-streets-of-fear-in-mogadishu-to-paradise-in-paris.

4. For a discussion of why the World Press Photo exhibition was canceled for 2015, see the conclusion.

5. "Visa Pour L'Image | A Guide to Portfolio Reviews | InFocus."

6. What is at stake here is how the assignment fee is shared, because the percentage an agent gets from an assignment or sale of an image from the photographer's archive is supposed to be for the agent's work in promoting the photographer and getting him or her work so that he or she can focus on photographing. Some contracts explicitly stipulate that a photographer will not share the profits from an assignment that he or she secured independently.

7. Olivier Laurent is the editor for *Lightbox, Time*'s photography blog. In a guide he wrote for first-timers at Visa, he stresses, "Agence France-Presse, Getty Images, National Geographic, Canon, Paris Match and many other organizations will be organizing private parties during professional week. The keyword here is 'private.' Unless you've been formally invited or are someone's +1, you will not be allowed in." Laurent, "A Guide to Visa Pour l'Image and Perpignan—2013 Edition."

8. See chapter 1 for a distinction between fast images and good images and the kinds of photographers taking each.

9. See Glaser, "Photojournalism Gets Boost Online."

10. See chapter 5 for a discussion of how geographic place-names serve as shorthand for coverage of an event. *Haiti* becomes coverage of the political crisis following the 2004 coup d'état, and *Hebron* becomes the tension over settlements.

11. See chapter 1 for a discussion of the historical hierarchy between multi-image stories and single shots that sum up an event.

12. Anzenberger Gallery, "Paolo Woods."

13. See chapter 7 for a discussion of the costs of not being able to circulate.

14. Historically, of course, there are many examples of the ontology of the photographic image being thought of in terms of an automatic writing or a trace of the real. Bazin, *What Is Cinema?*; Berger, *About Looking*; Sontag, *Regarding the Pain of Others*; Talbot, *The Pencil of Nature*. These citations are but a sample of a tradition of focusing on the indexicality of photography. For an interesting rereading of Talbot's *The Pencil of Nature*, see Azoulay, *Civil Imagination*.

15. For more on Vitale's description of her work, see Vitale and Katyal, "A Conversation with Ami Vitale."

16. I have since had the opportunity to interview Ami Vitale and share the story of the interview I overheard. It troubled her: "There is so much emphasis on you as an artist. . . . It starts early in your training. So much emphasis on style. We need to refocus. It's not about us. We're there to be this medium that tells stories, to give those people voices." Vitale tied the focus on personal vision to what she perceived as an awards culture in the industry where your work circulates and you get work because you've gotten an award, but the award draws attention to your style. Vitale said the conversation I had overheard with the journalist made her deeply uncomfortable and she worried about the messages being sent to the next generation of photographers.

17. Azoulay, "Getting Rid of the Distinction between the Aesthetic and the Political," 251.

18. Alam, "The Majority World Looks Back."

19. Turkey has the distinction of being the country with the longest candidacy for European Union membership. Turkey officially applied for membership in the European Economic Commission (EEC) on July 31, 1959. The EEC then became the European Community (EC). Turkey applied for membership in the EC in 1987. The EC evolved into the European Union (EU). Turkey's EU candidacy was accepted in 1999. Official membership negotiations began in 2005. They continue today. As of November 2015, there are over two million Syrians registered in Turkey, their numbers having tripled over the last two years.

CHAPTER 7. WORLD PRESS PHOTO

1. This tagline has been changed to: "We inspire understanding of the world through visual journalism." www.worldpressphoto.org.

2. The annual World Press Photo yearbook is perhaps the most literal version of what Susan Sontag describes as the most grandiose result of the photographic enterprise—the world held in one's head as an anthology of images. Sontag, *On Photography*, 3.

3. In the conclusion I will discuss the events that led to the 2015 World Press Photo exhibition not being shown at Visa Pour l'Image and the contemporary state of World Press Photo.

4. The seminars for developing countries were later changed to regional workshops rather than ones focused solely on individual countries. For example, a series of seminars were offered in Algeria, Morocco, and Tunisia for photographers from those countries as well as Egypt, Iraq, Lebanon Palestine, and Syria. Another brought together photographers from Mali, Ivory Coast, Congo, Cameroon, Madagascar, and Gabon, and another seminar trained students from the Balkans.

5. For more on the context of the production of the *Family of Man* exhibition, see Sandeen, *Picturing an Exhibition;* and Sandeen, "The Family of Man in Guatemala." Turner, "The Family of Man and the Politics of Attention," offers a compelling historical analysis of the politics of its design and circulation. Berlier, "Readings of an Exhibition" offers a thorough summary of critical responses to the exhibition. For notable examples of the way these images have been problematized, see Barthes, *Mythologies;* Hirsch, *Family Frames;* and especially Sekula, "The Traffic in Photographs."

6. Emile Meijer and Joop Swart, *The Photographic Memory*, 9.

7. In this way World Press Photo seems to have incorporated changing world geographic divisions that were used to talk about political and economic divisions. The United Nation Development Program initiative of 2003, "Forging a Global South," was important to the spread of the concept among both governments and organizations such as World Press Photo. For some the global South is just the latest version of terms such as *Third World, developing World, non-Western world,* and so on. See Rigg, *An Everyday Geography of the Global South.* For a provocative discussion of the term *global south* in relation to its antecedents, see Dirlik, "Global South." For a discussion of the term as one based on the recognition of globalization's failure as a master narrative, see Lopez, "Introduction."

8. In 2013, World Press Photo commissioned a report on worldwide understandings of ethics titled *The Image Integrity Report.*

9. I have no formal training but do have significant experience in simultaneous translation. I am fluent in Turkish and therefore was able to understand all side comments and conversations among the photographers at the seminars. Moreover, several of the photographers asked me to translate individual questions for the masters during breaks. After each session, I interviewed all the masters, World Press Photo staff and photographers involved in the Istanbul seminars individually. I followed the careers of the photographers over the following decade. I attended World Press Awards Days in 2004 with two of the Turkish photographers from the seminar.

10. Hannerz, *Foreign News,* 103.

11. Recall that this same metaphor of photographer as prostitute was used by a veteran photographer to describe the changes in the photojournalism industry after digitalization in chapter I.

12. Anthropologist Johannes Fabian's by now classic, incisive critique of how anthropologists construct their subjects in a bounded time apart from that inhabited by the anthropologist could just as easily be applied to photography. Fabian, *Time and the Other.*

13. See chapter 4.

14. In 1977 anthropologist Margaret Mead argued for the value of salvage visual ethnography when she wrote, "Nevertheless, the time will come when the illumination of genuine culture shock will be harder to attain, when the cultural diversity will be far more finely calibrated, and when greater and subtler educative experience will be required to perceive it and make constructive use of it. How then, in the future, will we be able to provide materials as contrastive as those from Europe, Asia, Africa and the Americas today and as comprehensive and comprehensible as the entire culture of an isolated Eskimo or Bushman group? It is by exposure to such differences that we have trained our students to gather the materials on which we have then developed our body of theory. The emerging technologies of film, tape, video, and we hope, the 360 camera, will make it possible to preserve materials (of a few selected cultures at least) for training students long after the last isolated valley in the world is receiving images by satellite." Mead, "Visual Anthropology in a Discipline of Words," 9.

Her mentor, anthropologist Franz Boas, had expressed this same sentiment in a letter to Will Hays, president of the Motion Picture Producers and Distributors of America, in 1933: "May I point out at the same time that most of the material of this kind has to be collected *now* because each year sees native cultures breaking down and disappearing under the onslaught of White civilization. It is not saying too much if I state that in many cases it may be a question of one, two, or perhaps five years until everything is gone that could possibly be obtained. Only today I received reports of the complete breakdown, *from a pictorial point of view*, of native life in Western Uganda in Africa and of Santa Catarina in Brazil." From Ruby, *Picturing Culture,* 84. Boas was writing this in the context of a funding request, so perhaps he is exaggerating the complete breakdown from a pictorial view. Nonetheless, he expresses the same logic Eitan did in 2003 for why Nico's black-and-white village photography will be valuable once Albania becomes developed. For an excellent discussion of coevalness in media, see Wilk, "Television, Time and the National Imaginary in Belize."

15. By now there has been significant critique of salvage ethnography, both within the discipline of anthropology and outside. See Rony, *The Third Eye*, for a visually focused example. However, salvage ethnography projects still flourish in photography at large. In *Reading National Geographic*, Lutz and Collins discuss the controversial ways in which modernity and tradition are visualized and juxtaposed. Eitan and Anna were encouraging Nico to pursue a salvage ethnography project. Moreover, Eitan's emphasis was not that it was culturally important to document certain ways of living before the past disappeared, but rather that this was a way that Nico could turn living in a third-world country to his advantage as a photographer without much mobility.

16. This is part of how an agency can support a photographer's career. On one occasion, I watched Ed and Liz at GVI set up meetings at nine different publications over the course of three days in New York and Washington, DC, for a photographer represented by their Paris office.

17. For Addario's own description of covering the bombings in Istanbul, see Addario, *It's What I Do*.

18. There were several Turkish photographers, most of whom work for the wire services, who did shoot the aftermath of the bombings, but the participants in the World Press Photo seminar were explicit about having felt ill at ease taking photos in the immediate impact of the attacks. While this was a single attack rather than a war zone, the photographers' comments recalled Christina Schwenkel's research on the subject matter captured by North Vietnamese photographers and draws attention to the fact that in contrast to the Western photographers in Vietnam covering the war, they covered survival and included far more images of perseverance in everyday life.

19. See chapter 4 for a discussion of conflicting responsibilities in which a text editor argues that her responsibility is to the reader, not the story, whereas she expects the photo editors' responsibility to be to the photos and the photographer.

20. This is understandable given that the workshops are aimed at photographers, not editors. However, that there are ethical choices that remain long after an image has been shot or even published was often not addressed. So there was no space, for example, to address a situation like the three unrelated images from Germany getting grouped together to illustrate the dispatch about a new immigration bill, discussed in chapter 3. As photographic archives become larger and more easily searchable, we may see images being used long after they have been shot.

21. See DeGhett, "The War Photo No One Would Publish."

22. This recalls the veteran photo agency owner in chapter 1 who compared a publication's desire to work with a trusted photo agency to a customer who happily relies on the same butcher for all his meat needs.

23. This list of countries makes clear how complex choosing countries "in the developing world" to target for photojournalism seminars was for World Press Photo. This is a highly varied set of countries in terms of former political

alignments, current regimes, economic strength, freedom of the press, and traditions of photojournalism. However, one of the requirements for the World Press Photo seminars was that there be a local institution to partner with, and these countries filled that requirement and presumably were acceptable to the Dutch funding agencies.

24. See chapter 5 for an extensive discussion of Nick Ut's photograph of Kim Phuc.

25. Gender as a topic was particularly difficult to explain in a manner that didn't reify stereotypical gender roles or assume that they were universal. In late 2003 the word was not yet common in public discourse in Turkish and in my role as translator, I struggled to explain it quickly at a session when the group was brainstorming possible stories to pursue. Marijke tried to encourage photographers to think of subjects they might then be able to publish. For example, the CEO of the Dutch oil company Shell in Turkey was a woman, she pointed out. In other words, the photographers were encouraged to find stories of gender that contrasted with expectations. The photographers were confused because it was unclear whose expectations to keep in mind when selecting a topic. Gender inequalities are different in different contexts. While women's participation in the workforce is low in Turkey relative to other comparable economies, there have been several women leaders both in business and politics. Which is to say, that the CEO of Shell in Turkey was a woman was not surprising to any of the students nor did it necessarily help them understand what a photo essay dealing with an aspect of gender might entail. Similar confusion seems to have existed elsewhere. The foreword to the exhibit catalogue contains this aside, "In Sri Lanka, a seminar participant told his group when he arrived one morning that he'd had a rough night. He'd spent the night photographing at Colombo Airport, which had been attacked by the Tamil Tigers. 'I was up shooting film all night,' he said, 'but that was not the problem. What gave me a headache was trying to figure out what gender means.'" World Press Photo Foundation, *90 Photojournalists Participated in the World Press Photo's Two-Year Workshop Program Organized in Seven Countries, 2001– 2003,* 13.

26. Back in New York, Susan, a photo editor from *Newsworld,* had pointed out to me, "[P]ersonal vision is such a World Press Photo concept!"

27. There have been many debates about the ethics of exhibiting news images in spaces traditionally reserved for art. One of the most salient of these in the photojournalism world centered on the work of French photographer Luc Delahaye. For an interview with Delahaye outlining some of the controversies involved, see B. Sullivan, "The Real Thing." In 2003 Delahaye was much discussed when his images not only were shown in large format in a gallery space but also commanded artwork prices.

28. Daphne's comment echoed what I heard from GVI's head of Creative Intelligence about the transition to digital technology shaping where the money came from for GVI, and that development in turn shaping their product. See chapter 1.

29. A powerful earthquake struck Bam, Iran on December 26, 2003, killing thirty thousand people.

30. Daphne was providing a way for Michael to escape being yet another photographer of the digital generation who had covered the usual places: Gaza, Haiti, Iraq, Afghanistan.

31. There were art photographers as well as fashion and sports photographers and even a celebrity portraitist at Barnstorm 2003. However, Stewart seemed to believe that he was kept out of the Barnstorm club because he worked in places associated with photojournalism but shot in ways that aesthetically blurred boundaries.

32. For more on layout logics at news publications, see chapter 4.

33. On compassion fatigue see Berger, *About Looking*; Moeller, *Compassion Fatigue*; Sontag, *On Photography*; Sontag, *Regarding the Pain of Others*.

CONCLUSION

The epigraph for the section titled "Circulation as News" is from the 2014 Agence France-Presse annual report, titled *The Whole World: The Whole Story*. www.afp.com/en/annual_report_2014.

1. I have waited so long, in fact, that Michael Finkel, the freelance writer mentioned in the introduction and fired for using a composite character in his article on child slavery in Africa, in the meantime published a mea culpa book on his transgression. Brad Pitt optioned the book, *True Story,* and has since produced a movie of the same name. Finkel is played by Jonah Hill, whom we no longer talk about as a young actor. Finkel has returned to magazine writing. He wrote a story on malaria, photographed by John Stanmayer, that was published in *National Geographic* and won the 2008 Magazine Award for Photojournalism.

2. Boyer, *The Life Informatic,* describes continued flux in journalism at large.

3. In September 2015 World Press Photo published a report, available on its website, that gives a detailed and data-rich overview of photojournalism worldwide: *The State of News Photography: The Lives and Livelihoods of Photojournalists in the Digital Age.*

4. Blogs are also online platforms for much debate about photojournalism. Some are attached to news publications, others are the work of individuals. A few such examples include: bjp-online.com, bagnewsnotes.com (now readingthepictures.org.) david-campbell.org, digitaljournalist.org, duckrabbit .info/blog, aphotoeditor.com, nocaptionneeded.com, politicstheoryphotography.blogspot.com, precise-moment.com.

5. Benton 2014, "Getty Images Blows the Web's Mind" describes how this free gift to the world is a way of ensuring that the Getty brand is even more ubiquitous. It will allow Getty to collect data on all of the websites where its images are embedded, and potentially to advertise in those spaces. See also Laurent, "Getty Images Makes 35 Million Images Free to Use."

6. An extremely sobering moment came in 2014, when my class studied the Abu Ghraib images of prisoner abuse by US soldiers ten years after their release. All through fieldwork and for years afterward, I had been told these were the defining images of the war in Iraq, these would be the iconic images that

endured. The majority of my American students were seeing the photos of prisoner abuse for the first time, and many did not know they existed. Even if they had encountered parodies of the images, they did not know the original referents. Most of my international students were aware of them and often visually familiar with them as well. Perhaps Hariman and Lucaites were right to declare, "In the United States, history lasts only one generation." Hariman and Lucaites *No Caption Needed,* 186. Perhaps many governments are happy to have shorter history cycles to match faster news cycles. By itself this anecdote is not significant, but it compelled me to rethink the assumed political impact of these photographs. Moreover, the time is ripe for more-nuanced research on how allegedly iconic images operate in different parts of the world. See Ghosh, *Global Icons.* My students' uneven historical recollection also suggests that more research is needed in how a particular media event is covered—not just initially, but as it unfolds over time or gains recognition as an important moment in a collective history. For how long is an image iconic? See "Global Iconic Events: How News Stories Travel through Time, Space and Media," Julia Sonnevend's analysis of the fall of the Berlin wall as a recurring media event.

7. See chapter 3 for a discussion of the visualization of the 2004 European Parliamentary elections and page 137 for an example of how the United Kingdom's *Guardian* ran the image in both its online and print editions. In 2014, photographs of the Hungarian women in "traditional dress" taken by Mr. Balogh and distributed by Reuters appeared in *Haaretz, El País,* the *New York Times,* the *Guardian, Die Welt,* the BBC website, at least one Russian independent Internet news portal, and the journal *Foreign Affairs,* among others.

8. Vobič and Tomanić Trivundža, "The Tyranny of the Empty Frame," 8.

9. Deuze, *Media Work;* Fortunati et al., "The Influence of the Internet on European Journalism."

10. See Klinenberg, "Convergence," 54.

11. See the report by the Newspaper Association of America.

12. See Boczkowski, *Digitizing the News,* for but one example.

13. Associated Press, "*Chicago Sun-Times* Lays Off All Its Full-Time Photographers." For my response to the layoffs, see Gürsel, "A Challenge for Visual Journalism."

14. In November 2015, just before this book went to press, *National Geographic* laid off 9 percent of its workforce months after announcing a partnership with Rupert Murdoch's 21st Century Fox. Many staff photographers, photo editors, and designers were among those laid off. In his staff memo, CEO Gary Knell assured employees, "Looking ahead, I am confident *National Geographic*'s mission will be fulfilled in powerful, new and impactful ways, as we continue to change the world through science, exploration, education and storytelling."

I chose not to do research at *National Geographic* because it is not a news publication. However, as Lutz and Collins have shown, it has produced extremely powerful formative fictions over the years. Many photojournalists publish some of their most important work in it, and as a publication in which images are not secondary, it has a very important place in documentary photography. However, had I done research at *National Geographc,* I could not generalize what I learned there to other news publications.

15. See Auletta, *Backstory: Inside the Business of News,* on how corporate management at news publications classified these institution's product as "content."

16. Once again photojournalists are being "denounced, disembodied and deflated" as they were in the 1930s, as discussed in chapter 1. Zelizer, "Words against Images."

17. See Gürsel, "Covering Gezi," for more of my interview with the Nar Photos Collective.

18. For an extensive discussion of the work being done by this anachronistically presented image, see Gürsel, "Framing Zarqawi."

19. Several news sites ran the Associated Press dispatch written by Angela Charlton and Thomas Adamson. Yahoo News, Al Jazeera, and Fox News, among others, used this first sentence verbatim.

20. From the 2014 AFP annual report.

21. Quoted in Frosh, "Beyond the Image Bank."

22. See Pantti and Sirén, "The Fragility of Photo-Truth," for a view from a newsroom of how the responsibility to verify images is seen as the role of news agencies.

23. See Zarzycka and Kleppe, "Awards, Archives and Affects," for more on the awards.

24. For a powerful discussion of "digital suspicion" as itself a sign of the times and an analysis of its political ramifications in Israel, see Kuntsman and Stein, *Digital Militarism.*

25. www.giovannitroilo.com/la-ville-noire/.

26. Berman, "The Problem with World Press Photo's Contest."

27. Crawford, "What Really Happened at the World Press Photo Contest?"

28. See chapter 7. For a compelling discussion of the ethics of conflict photojournalism using mobile photography apps, see Alper, "War on Instagram."

29. Crawford, "What Really Happened at the World Press Photo Contest?"

30. *New York Times,* April 14, 2002. http://www.nytimes.com/2002/04/14/magazine/editors-note-461911.html.

31. Chrisafis, "World Press Photo Award Withdrawn over Violation of Rules."

32. Berman, "The Problem with World Press Photo's Contest."

33. Laurent, "Learn How World Press Photo Plans to Evolve into a Think Tank."

34. Quoted in Hughes, "At 50 Years World Press Looks Back and Ahead."

35. Campbell, "Dead or Alive?'

36. Some examples include lens.blogs.nytimes.com, lightbox.time.com, http://www.theguardian.com/world/series/eyewitness, http://proof.nationalgeographic.com, http://pdnpulse.pdnonline.com.

37. These are questions my research will not allow me to answer, because what is called for is more research on the image brokers at philanthropic foundations and NGOs, as well as the evaluation processes behind grants for photographic projects.

38. Articles even appeared telling foreign photographers to stay away.

39. This is addressed poignantly by Shahidul Alam, founder of Drik Picture Library in Bangladesh. Alam documented the demonstrations to drive out military dictatorship the 1980s. The Bangladeshi media was controlled by the state, so photographers tried to get their photographs published abroad. No one was interested. "In 1991 we had a massive cyclone. Suddenly members of the Western media were all over us, their appetites insatiable. The image of the starving Bangladeshi with outstretched arms with the white man as their savior was the image they craved. My battle had just begun." Alam 2013, "Photography as My Guide," 135. See also Clark, "Representing the Majority World"; and Clark, "The Production of a Contemporary Famine Image."

40. Laurent, "How Photographers Are Using Instagram to Help Nepal."

41. Laurent, "David Guttenfelder: The Photographer as Explorer."

42. Whereas just a few years ago their website expounded on the power of visual storytelling to "inform and shape" the world and declared their mission to be "to inspire understanding of the world," nowadays they modestly claim, "We work to develop and promote quality visual journalism."

43. Schudson, *The Sociology of News*, 205.

Bibliography

Abu-Lughod, Lila. "Do Muslim Women Really Need Saving?" American Anthropologist 104, no. 3 (2002): 783–90.

———. *Dramas of Nationhood: The Politics of Television in Egypt*. Chicago: University of Chicago Press, 2004.

Adams, Alyssa. *Eddie Adams: Vietnam*. New York: Umbridge Editions, 2008.

Adams, Eddie. "Eulogy: General Nguyen Ngoc Loan." *Time*, July 27, 1998.

Addario, Lyndsey. *It's What I Do: A Photographer's Life of Love and War*. New York: Penguin Press, 2015.

Alam, Shahidul. "Photography as My Guide." *World Literature Today* 87, no. 2 (2013): 132–37.

———. "The Majority World Looks Back." *New Internationalist*, 2007. http://newint.org/features/2007/08/01/keynote-photography/.

Allan, Stuart. *Citizen Witnessing: Revisioning Journalism in Times of Crisis*. Cambridge: Polity, 2013.

Alleyne, Mark. *News Revolution: Political and Economic Decisions about Global Information*. New York: Palgrave MacMillan, 1996.

Alper, Meryl. "War on Instagram: Framing Conflict Journalism with Mobile Photography Apps." New Media and Society 16, no. 8 (2013): 1233–48.

Alpers, Svetlana. "Visual Culture Questionnaire." *October* 77 (1996): 25–70.

Andén-Papadopoulos, Kari, and Mervi Pantti, eds. *Amateur Images and Global News*. Chicago: University of Chicago Press, 2011.

———. "Re-Imagining Crisis Reporting: Professional Ideology of Journalists and Citizen Eyewitness Images." *Journalism* 14, no. 7 (2013): 960–77.

Anderson, Benedict. *Imagined Communities: Reflections on the Origin and Spread of Nationalism*. London: Verso, 1983.

Anderson, C.W., and Juliette De Maeyer. "Objects of Journalism: Media, Materiality and the News." *Journalism* 16, no. 1 (January 2015).

Anzenberger Gallery. "Paolo Woods." Accessed May 12, 2015. http://rmagalleryold.picturemaxx.com/en/article/18.html?showbiography = 1.

Appadurai, Arjun. *Modernity at Large: Cultural Dimensions of Globalization.* Minneapolis and London: University of Minnesota Press, 1996.

———. "Putting Hierarchy in Its Place." *Cultural Anthropology* 3, no. 1 (1988): 37–50.

———, ed. *The Social Life of Things: Commodities in Cultural Perspective.* Cambridge and New York: Cambridge University Press, 1986.

———. "Theory in Anthropology: Center and Periphery." *Comparative Studies in Society and History* 28, no. 2 (1986): 356–74.

Arago, François. "Report." In *Classic Essays on Photography,* edited by Alan Trachtenberg, 15–25. Sedgwick, ME: Leete's Island Books, 1980.

Askew, Kelly Michelle, and Richard R. Wilk. *The Anthropology of Media: A Reader.* Malden, MA: Blackwell Publishers, 2002.

Associated Press. "Chicago *Sun-Times* Lays Off All Its Full-Time Photographers." *New York Times,* May 31, 2013. www.nytimes.com/2013/06/01/business/media/chicago-sun-times-lays-off-all-its-full-time-photographers.html.

Auletta, Ken. *Backstory: Inside the Business of News.* London and New York: Penguin Books, 2004.

Austin, J.L. *How to Do Things with Words.* Oxford and New York: Oxford University Press, 1980.

Azoulay, Ariella. *The Civil Contract of Photography.* New York and Cambridge, MA: Zone Books, 2008.

———. *Civil Imagination: A Political Ontology of Photography.* London and New York: Verso, 2012.

———. "Getting Rid of the Distinction between the Aesthetic and the Political." *Theory, Culture, Society* 27, nos. 7–8 (2010): 239–62.

Bal, Mieke. "Visual Essentialism and the Object of Visual Culture." *Journal of Visual Culture,* no. 2 (2003): 5–32.

Barnett, Brooke, and Amy Reynolds. *Terrorism and the Press: An Uneasy Relationship.* New York: Peter Lang, 2009.

Barnhurst, Kevin G., and John Nerone. *The Form of News: A History.* New York and London: Guilford Press, 2001.

Barnstorm: The Eddie Adams Workshop. *NYC: Life Going On; A Dedication of Love by the Photographers of Barnstorm, the Eddie Adams Workshop and Their Subjects; The Men, Women and Children of New York City on 9/11/02.* Syracuse, NY: Syracuse University Press, 2003.

Barthes, Roland. *Camera Lucida: Reflections on Photography.* New York: Hill and Wang, 1981.

———. *Mythologies.* Collection Pierres Vives. Paris: Editions du Seuil, 1957.

———. "The Rhetoric of the Image." In *The Responsibility of Forms: Critical Essays on Music, Art, and Representation,* 1–17. Berkeley: University of California Press, 1991.

Batchen, Geoffrey. *Burning with Desire: The Conception of Photography.* Cambridge, MA: MIT Press, 1997.

Batchen, Geoffrey, Mick Gidley, Nancy K. Miller, and Jay Prosser, eds. *Picturing Atrocity: Photography in Crisis.* London: Reaktion Books, 2012.

Baudrillard, Jean. *The Gulf War Did Not Take Place*. Bloomington: Indiana University Press, 1995.

Bazin, André. *What Is Cinema?* Berkeley: University of California Press, 2005.

Becker, Karin E. "Photography and the Tabloid Press." In *The Photography Reader*, edited by Liz Wells, 291–308. New York: Routledge, 2003.

Bedford, Keith. "Why You Should Go to the Eddie Adams Workshop." *Photo Brigade*, May 14, 2012. http://thephotobrigade.com/2012/05/why-you-should-go-to-the-eddie-adams-workshop-by-keith-bedford/#sthash.KIoGe4Lg.dpuf.

Benjamin, Walter. "The Work of Art in the Age of Mechanical Reproduction." In *Illuminations: Essays and Reflection*, 217–51. New York: Schocken Books, 1986.

Bennett, Lance W., Lynne Gressett, and William Haltom. "Repairing the News: A Case Study of the News Paradigm." *Journal of Communication* 35, no. 1 (1985): 50–68.

Benton, Joshua. "Getty Images Blows the Web's Mind by Setting 35 Million Photos Free (with Conditions, of Course)." *Nieman Lab*, March 5, 2014. www.niemanlab.org/2014/03/getty-images-blows-the-webs-mind-by-setting-35-million-photos-free-with-conditions-of-course/.

Berger, John. *About Looking*. New York: Vintage International, 1991.

———. *Ways of Seeing*. London and New York: British Broadcasting Corporation; Penguin Books, 1972.

Berkowitz, Dan. "Doing Double Duty: Paradigm Repair and the Princess Diana What-a-Story." *Journalism* 1, no. 2 (2000): 125–43.

Berlier, Monique. "The Family of Man: Readings of an Exhibition." In *Picturing the Past: Media, History, and Photography*, edited by Bonnie Brennen and Hanno Hardt, 206–41. Urbana: University of Illinois Press, 1999.

Berman, Nina. "The Problem with World Press Photo's Contest." *Columbia Journalism Review*, March 9, 2015. www.cjr.org/analysis/nina_berman.php.

Bird, S. Elizabeth, ed. *The Anthropology of News and Journalism: Global Perspectives*. Bloomington and Indianapolis: Indiana University Press, 2010.

Bishara, Amahl. *Back Stories: U.S. News Production and Palestinian Politics*. Stanford, CA: Stanford University Press, 2013.

———. "Covering the Barrier in Bethlehem: The Production of Sympathy and the Reproduction of Difference." In *The Anthropology of News and Journalism: Global Perspectives*, edited by S. Elizabeth Bird, 54–70. Bloomington and Indianapolis: Indiana University Press, 2010.

Boczkowski, Pablo J. *Digitizing the News: Innovation in Online Newspapers*. Cambridge, MA: MIT Press, 2004.

Born, Georgina. *Uncertain Vision: Birt, Dyke and the Reinvention of the BBC*. New York: Vintage Books, 2005.

Bourdieu, Pierre. *The Field of Cultural Production: Essays on Art and Literature*. Translated by Randal Johnson. New York: Columbia University Press, 1993.

———. *Language and Symbolic Power*. Cambridge, MA: Harvard University Press, 1991.

————. "The Political Field, the Social Science Field, and the Journalistic Field." In *Bourdieu and the Journalistic Field,* edited by Rodney Benson and Eric Neveu, 29–47. Cambridge, UK, and Malden, MA: Polity Press, 2005.

Boyd-Barrett, Oliver. *The International News Agencies.* London: Sage, 1980.

————, ed. *News Agencies in the Turbulent Era of the Internet.* Barcelona: Government of Catalonia, Presidential Department, 2010.

Boyer, Dominic. "Digital Expertise in Online Journalism (and Anthropology)." *Anthropological Quarterly* 83, no. 1 (2010): 73–95.

————. *The Life Informatic: Newsmaking in the Digital Era.* Ithaca, NY: Cornell University Press, 2013.

————. *Spirit and System: Media, Intellectuals, and the Dialectic in Modern German Culture.* Chicago: University of Chicago Press, 2005.

Breed, Warren. "Social Control in the Newsroom: A Functional Analysis." *Social Forces* 33, no. 1 (1955): 326–36.

Brennen, Bonnie. "Photojournalism: Historical Dimensions to Contemporary Debates." In *The Routledge Companion to News and Journalism,* edited by Stuart Allan, 71–81. New York: Taylor & Francis (Routledge), 2010.

Brennen, J. Scott, and Daniel Kreiss. "Digitization and Digitalization." Edited by K.B. Jensen. *The International Encyclopedia of Communication Theory and Philosophy.* Malden, MA: Wiley-Blackwell., forthcoming.

Brothers, Caroline. *War and Photography.* London: Routledge, 1997.

Bryson, Norman, Michael Ann Holly, and Keith Moxey, eds. *Visual Culture: Images and Interpretations.* Middletown, CT: Wesleyan University Press, 1994.

Buell, Hall. *Moments: The Pulitzer Prize-Winning Photographs, a Visual Chronicle of Our Time.* New York: Black Dog and Leventhal, 1999.

Burgess, Neil. "For God's Sake, Somebody Call It!" *Editorial Photographers UK.* August 1, 2010. www.epuk.org/opinion/for-gods-sake-somebody-call-it.

Burns, John F. "The Reach of War: The Defendant; Defiant Hussein Rebukes Iraqi Court for Trying Him." *New York Times,* July 2, 2004, sec. A1.

Butler, Judith. *Excitable Speech: A Politics of the Performative.* New York and London: Routledge, 1997.

————. *Frames of War: When Is Life Grievable?* London and New York: Verso, 2009.

————. *Precarious Life: The Powers of Mourning and Violence.* London and New York: Verso, 2006.

Caldwell, John Thornton. *Production Culture: Industrial Reflexivity and Critical Practice in Film and Television.* Durham, NC: Duke University Press, 2008.

Campbell, David. "Dead or Alive? The State of Photojournalism," October 5, 2010. https://www.david-campbell.org/2010/10/05/dead-or-alive-the-state-of-photojournalism/.

————. "Representing Contemporary War." *Ethics and International Affairs* 17 (2): 99–108. 2003.

Caple, Helen, and John S. Knox. "Online News Galleries, Photojournalism and the Photo Essay." *Visual Communication* 11, no. 2 (2012): 207–36.

Carlson, Matt. "The Reality of a Fake Image: News Norms, Photojournalistic Craft, and Brian Walski's Fabricated Photograph." *Journalism Practice* 3, no. 2 (2009): 125–39.

Caujolle, Christian. "Photography and Its Uses." In *The Photographic Memory: Press Photography—Twelve Insights,* 55–71. London: Quiller Press, 1988.

Chapnick, Howard. *Truth Needs No Ally: Inside Photojournalism.* Columbia: University of Missouri Press, 1994.

Chong, Denise. *The Girl in the Picture: The Story of Kim Phuc, the Photograph, and the Vietnam War.* New York: Penguin Books, 2001.

Chrisafis, Angelique. "World Press Photo Award Withdrawn over Violation of Rules." *The Guardian*, March 5, 2015, sec. Media. www.theguardian.com /media/2015/mar/05/world-press-photo-award-withdrawn-over-violation-of-rules.

Christensen, Christian. "The Uses of YouTube during the Iraq War." In *Image Operations: Still and Moving Pictures in Political Conflicts,* edited by Jens Eder and Charlotte Klonk. Manchester, UK: Manchester University Press, forthcoming.

Clark, David James. "Representing the Majority World: Famine, Photojournalism and the Changing Visual Economy." PhD diss., Durham University, Durham, UK, 2009.

———. "The Production of a Contemporary Famine Image: The Image Economy, Indigenous Photographers and the Case of Mekanic Philipos." *Journal of International Development* 16 (2004): 693–704.

Clifford, James. *Routes: Travel and Translation in the Late Twentieth Century.* Cambridge, MA; and London: Harvard University Press, 1997.

Clifford, James, and George E. Marcus, eds. *Writing Culture: The Poetics and Politics of Ethnography.* Berkeley: University of California Press, 1986.

CNN. "Amanpour: Saddam's 'Bizarre Rant," 2004. http://edition.cnn/2004 /WORLD/meast/07/01/amanpour/index.html.

———. "Amanpour: Saddam Story among Career's Top Ten." 2004. http:// articles.cnn.com/2004–07–01/world/amanpour.scene-1-saddam-hussein-journalists-mustache?_s = PM:WORLD.

———. "Paula Zahn Transcript." 2004. http://premium.asia.cnn.com /TRANSCRIPTS/0407/01/pzn.00.html.

———. "Saddam's Hearing on Grounds of Former Palace." 2004. http:// edition.cnn.com/2004/WORLD/meast/07/01/saddam.palace/index.html.

———. "Transcript of Saddam Proceeding." 2004. http://edition.cnn.com /2004/meast/07/01/saddam.transcript/index.html.

Cody, Francis. "Publics and Politics." *Annual Review of Anthropology* 40, no. 3 (2011): 1–16.

Coleman, Simon, and Pauline von Hellermann, eds. *Multi-Sited Ethnography: Problems and Possibilities in the Translocation of Research Methods.* New York: Routledge, 2011.

"Condamnation unanime de 'l'attentat' contre les locaux de 'Charlie Hebdo.'" Le Monde.fr., November 2, 2011. www.lemonde.fr/actualite-medias/article /2011/11/02/condamnation-unanime-de-l-attentat-contre-les-locaux-de-charlie-hebdo_1597183_3236.html?xtmc=condamnation_unanime&xtcr =44.

Coopersmith, Jonathan. *Faxed: The Rise and Fall of the Fax Machine*. Baltimore: Johns Hopkins University Press, 2015.

———. "The Failure of Fax: When a Vision Is Not Enough." *Business and Economic History* 23, no. 1 (1994): 272–82.

Cotter, Colleen. *News Talk: Investigating the Language of Journalism*. New York: Cambridge University Press, 2010.

Cottle, Simon. "Ethnography and News Production: New(s) Developments in the Field." *Sociology Compass* 1, no. 1 (2007): 1–16.

Crapanzano, Vincent. "Hermes' Dilemma: The Masking of Subversion in Ethnographic Description." In *Writing Culture: The Poetics and Politics of Ethnography*, edited by James Clifford and George E. Marcus, 51–77. Berkeley: University of California Press, 1986.

Crary, Jonathan. *Suspensions of Perception: Attention, Spectacle, and Modern Culture*. Cambridge, MA: MIT Press, 1999.

Crawford, Adam. "What Really Happened At the World Press Photo Contest?" *Precise-Moment.com*, March 12, 2015. http://precise-moment.com/2015/03 /12/what-really-happened-at-the-world-press-photo-contest.

DeGhett, Torie Rose. "The War Photo No One Would Publish." *Atlantic*, August 8, 2014. www.theatlantic.com/international/archive/2014/08/the-war-photo-no-one-would-publish/375762/.

Dejardin, Fiona M. "The Photo League: Left-Wing Politics and the Popular Press." *History of Photography* 18, no. 2 (1994): 159–73.

de Mondenard, Béatrice. "Photojournaliste: Une profession sacrifiée." 2015. www.scam.fr/fr/ViewerArticle/tabid/363606/ArticleId/3539/Photojournaliste-une-profession-sacrifiee.aspx.

Deuze, Mark. *Media Work*. Cambridge, UK; and Malden, MA: Polity Press, 2007.

Dickie, Chris. *Photography: The 50 Most Influential Photographers of All Time*. Hauppauge, NY: Barron's, 2010.

Dikovitskaya, Margarita. *Visual Culture: The Study of the Visual after the Cultural Turn*. Cambridge, MA: MIT Press, 2005.

di Leonardo, Micaela. *Exotics at Home: Anthropologies, Others, American Modernity*. Chicago: University of Chicago Press, 1998.

Dirlik, Arif. "Global South: Predicament and Promise." *Global South* 1, no. 1 (2007): 12–23.

Domingo, David, and Chris Paterson, eds. *Making Online News*. Vol. 2, *Newsroom Ethnographies in the Second Decade of Internet Journalism*. New York: Peter Lang, 2011.

Dornfeld, Barry. *Producing Public Television, Producing Public Culture*. Princeton, NJ: Princeton University Press, 1998.

Dubow, Jessica. "'From a View on the World to a Point of View in It': Rethinking Sight, Space and the Colonial Subject." *Interventions* 2, no. 1 (2000): 87–102.

Dumit, Joseph. 2004. *Picturing Personhood: Brain Scans and Biomedical Identity*. Princeton, NJ: Princeton University Press.

Eder, Jens, and Charlotte Klonk, eds. *Image Operations: Still and Moving Pictures in Political Conflicts*. Manchester, UK: Manchester University Press, forthcoming.

Edey, Maitland A., ed. *Great Photographic Essays from Life*. Boston: New York Graphic Society, 1978.

Edwards, Holly. "Cover to Cover: The Life Cycle of an Image in Contemporary Visual Culture." In *Beautiful Suffering: Photography and the Traffic in Pain*, edited by Mark Reinhardt, Holly Edwards and Erina Duganne, 75–92. Chicago: University of Chicago Press, 2007.

Evans, Catherine, and Mason Klein. *The Radical Camera: New York's Photo League, 1936–1951*. New Haven, CT: Yale University Press, 2011.

Fabian, Johannes. *Time and the Other: How Anthropology Makes Its Object*. New York: Columbia University Press, 1983.

Fahmy, Shahira, and Daekyung Kim. "Picturing the Iraq War: Constructing the Image of War in the British and US Press." *International Communication Gazette* 70, no. 6 (2008): 443–62.

Ferguson, James. *Global Shadows: Africa in the Neoliberal World Order*. Durham, NC: Duke University Press, 2006.

———. "Novelty and Method: Reflections on Global Fieldwork." In *Multi-Sited Ethnography: Problems and Possibilities in the Translocation of Research Methods*, edited by Simon Coleman and Pauline von Hellermann, 194–208. New York: Routledge, 2011.

Finkel, Michael. *True Story: Murder, Mystery, Mea Culpa*. New York: Harper-Collins, 2005.

Fishman, Mark. *Manufacturing the News*. Austin: University of Texas Press, 1980.

Foster, Robert. "Tracking Globalization: Commodities and Value in Motion." In *Handbook of Material Culture*, edited by Chris Tilley, Webb Keane, Susanne Kuchler, Mike Rowlands, and Patricia Spyer, 285–302. London: Sage Publications, 2006.

Fortunati, Leopoldina, Mauro Sarrica, John O'Sullivan, Aukse Balcytiene, Halliki Harro-Loit, Phil Macgregor, Nayia Roussou, Ramón Salaverría, and Federico De Luca. "The Influence of the Internet on European Journalism." *Journal of Computer-Mediated Communication* 14, no. 4 (August 3, 2009): 928–63.

Freund, Gisèle. *Photography and Society*. Boston: Godine Press, 1980.

Frosh, Paul. "Beyond the Image Bank: Digital Commercial Photography." In *The Photographic Image in Digital Culture*, 131–48. London: Routledge, 2013.

———. *The Image Factory: Consumer Culture, Photography and the Visual Content Industry*. New Technologies/New Cultures Series. London and New York: Berg, 2003.

Gans, Herbert J. *Deciding What's News: A Study of "CBS Evening News," "NBC Nightly News," "Newsweek," and "Time."* Vintage Books, 1980.

Ganti, Tejaswini. *Producing Bollywood: Inside the Contemporary Hindi Film Industry*. Durham, NC: Duke University Press, 2012.

Garcia, Alex. "The Impact of the Eddie Adams Workshop—20 Years Later." *Chicago Tribune*, October 1, 2013. http://newsblogs.chicagotribune.com/assignment-chicago/2013/10/eddie-adams-workshop-the-impact-20-years-later.html.

Geertz, Clifford. *The Interpretation of Cultures: Selected Essays*. New York: Basic Books, 2000.

Gervais, Thierry. "Witness to War: The Uses of Photography in the Illustrated Press, 1855–1904." *Journal of Visual Culture* 9 (December 2010): 370–84.

Getty Images. "Getty Images." Accessed January 1, 2004. gettyimages.com.

Ghosh, Bishnupriya. *Global Icons: Apertures to the Popular*. Durham NC: Duke University Press, 2011.

Ginsburg, Faye D., Lila Abu-Lughod, and Brian Larkin. *Media Worlds: Anthropology on New Terrain*. Berkeley: University of California Press, 2002.

Gitelman, Lisa, and Geoffrey B. Pingree. *New Media, 1740–1915*. Cambridge, MA: MIT Press, 2003.

Goldberg, Vicki. *The Power of Photography: How Photographs Changed Our Lives*. New York: Abbeville Press, 1991.

Goodman, Nelson. *Ways of Worldmaking*. Harvester Studies in Philosophy. Hassocks, UK: Harvester Press, 1978.

Griffin, Michael. "The Great War Photographs: Constructing Myths of History and Photojournalism." In *Picturing the Past : Media, History, and Photography*, edited by Bonnie Brennen and Hanno Hardt, 122–57. Urbana: University of Illinois Press, 1999.

———. "Media Images of War." *Media, War and Conflict* 3, no. 1 (2010): 7–41.

———. "Picturing America's 'War on Terrorism' in Afghanistan and Iraq." *Journalism* 5, no. 4 (2004): 381–402.

Griffin, Michael, and Jongsoo Lee. "Picturing the Gulf War: Constructing Images of War of *Time, Newsweek*, and *U.S. News and World Report*." *Journalism and Mass Communication Quarterly* 72, no. 4 (1995): 813–25.

Gross, Larry, John Stewart Katz, and Jay Ruby, eds. *Image Ethics: The Moral Rights of Subjects in Photographs, Film and Television*. New York: Oxford University Press, 1988.

Guerrin, Michel. "Photographiez sans entraves." Le Monde.fr, August 28, 2015, sec. "Idées." www.lemonde.fr/idees/article/2015/08/28/photographiez-sans-entraves_4738857_3232.html.

Guillot, Claire. "Les agences photo Gamma et Rapho (Eyedea) reprises par François Lochon." Le Monde.fr, April 7, 2010, sec. "Économie." www.lemonde.fr/economie/article/2010/04/07/les-agences-photo-gamma-et-rapho-eyedea-reprises-par-francois-lochon_1330040_3234.html.

———. "L'avenir incertain du groupe d'agences Eyedea met en péril le troisième fonds de photographies au monde." Le Monde.fr, March 29, 2010. www.lemonde.fr/actualite-medias/article/2010/03/29/l-avenir-incertain-du-groupe-d-agences-eyedea-met-en-peril-le-troisieme-fonds-de-photographies-au-monde_1325810_3236.html.

Gupta, Akhil, and James Ferguson. *Culture, Power, Place: Explorations in Critical Anthropology*. Durham, NC; and London: Duke University Press, 1997.

———. *Anthropological Locations: Boundaries and Grounds of a Field Science*. Berkeley: University of California Press, 1997.

Gustavson, Todd. *Camera: A History of Photography from Daguerreotype to Digital*. New York: Sterling Publishing Company, 2009.

Gürsel, Zeynep Devrim. "A Challenge for Visual Journalism: Rendering the Labor behind News Images Visible." *Anthropology Now,* July 17, 2013.

———. "Covering Gezi: Reflecting on Photographing Daily Life during Extraordinary Events." *Jadaliyya,* June 24, 2013. http://photography.jadaliyya.com /pages/index/12390/covering-gezi_reflecting-on-photographing-daily-li.

———. "Framing Zarqawi: Afterimages, Headshots, and Body Politics in a Digital Age." In *Double Exposure: Memory & Photography,* edited by Olga Shevchenko, 65–89. New Brunswick, NJ; and London: Transaction, 2014.

———. "Spectacular Terrorism: Images on the Frontline of History." In *9/11 New York—Istanbul,* edited by Feride Çiçekoğlu, 152–93. Istanbul: Homer Kitabevi, 2003.

———. "Worldmaking, Frame by Frame." In *Image Operations: Still and Moving Pictures in Political Conflicts,* edited by Jens Eder and Charlotte Klonk. Manchester, UK: Manchester University Press, forthcoming.

Gusterson, Hugh. "Studying Up Revisited." *PoLAR: Political and Legal Anthropology Review* 20, no. 1 (1997): 114–19.

Hachten, William. *The World News Prism: Changing Media of International Communication.* Ames: Iowa State University Press, 1996.

Hacking, Ian. *The Social Construction of What?* Cambridge, MA: Harvard University Press, 2000.

Hagopian, Patrick. "Vietnam War Photography as a Locus of Memory." In *Locatin Memory: Photographic Acts,* edited by Annette Kuhn and Kirsten Emiko McAllister. Oxford and New York: Berghahn, 2006.

Hall, Stuart. "The Determinations of News Photographs." In *The Manufacture of News,* edited by Stanley Cohen and Young. London: Sage, 1974.

———. *Representation: Cultural Representations and Signifying Practices.* Culture, Media, and Identities. London and Thousand Oaks, CA: Sage, 1997.

———. "Signification, Representation, Ideology: Althusser and the Post-Structuralist Debates." *Critical Studies in Mass Communication* 2, no. 2 (June 1985): 91–114.

Hallin, Daniel. *The "Uncensored War": The Media and Vietnam.* New York: Oxford University Press, 1986.

Halstead, Dirck. "The End of History and Photojournalism." *Digital Journalist,* October 1999. http://digitaljournalist.org/issue9910/editorial.htm.

———. "Revisiting the Death of Photojournalism, Part II: The Wires." *Digital Journalist,* August 2009. http://digitaljournalist.org/issue0908/revisiting-the-death-of-photojournalism-part-2-the-wires.html.

———. "Revisiting the Death of Photojournalism, Ten Years Later." *Digital Journalist,* July 2009. http://digitaljournalist.org/issue0907/revisiting-the-death-of-photojournalism-ten-years-later.html.

Hannerz, Ulf. *Foreign News: Exploring the World of Foreign Correspondents.* The Lewis Henry Morgan Lectures. Chicago: University of Chicago Press, 2004.

Hansen, Bettina. "Insights and Experiences from the 2011 Eddie Adams Workshop." *NPPA: The Visual Student,* October 4, 2011. http://blogs.nppa.org /visualstudent/2011/10/14/insights-and-experiences-from-the-2011-eddie-adams-workshop/.

Haraway, Donna. "Situated Knowledges: The Science Question in Feminism and the Privilege of Partial Perspective." *Feminist Studies* 14, no. 3 (1988): 575–99.

Hardt, Hanno. "The Site of Reality: Constructing Photojournalism in Weimar Germany, 1928–1933." *Communication Review* 1, no. 3 (1986): 373–402.

Hariman, Robert, and John Louis Lucaites. *No Caption Needed: Iconic Photographs, Public Culture, and Liberal Democracy*. Chicago and London: University of Chicago Press, 2007.

Hartley, John. "Documenting Kate Moss: Fashion Photography and the Persistence of Photojournalism." *Journalism Studies* 8, no. 4 (2007): 555–65.

Hasty, Jennifer. "Journalism as Fieldwork: Propaganda, Complicity and the Ethics of Anthropology." In *The Anthropology of News and Journalism: Global Perspectives*, edited by S. Elizabeth Bird, 132–50. Bloomington and Indianapolis: Indiana University Press, 2010.

———. *The Press and Political Culture in Ghana*. Bloomington: Indiana University Press, 2005.

Heidegger, Martin. *The Question concerning Technology and Other Essays*. New York: Harper & Row, 1977.

Henry, Neil. *American Carnival: Journalism under Siege in an Age of New Media*. Berkeley: University of California Press, 2007.

Hesmondhalgh, David. *The Cultural Industries*. 3rd ed. London: Sage, 2012.

Hesmondhalgh, David, and Sarah Baker. *Creative Labour: Media Work in Three Cultural Industries*. London: Routledge, 2011.

Hicks, Wilson. *Words and Pictures: An Introduction to Photojournalism*. New York: Harper, 1952.

Hill, Jason, and Vanessa R. Schwartz, eds. *Getting the Picture: The Visual Culture of the News*. London and New York: Bloomsbury Academic, 2015.

Hindman, Elizabeth Banks. "Jayson Blair, the New York Times, and Paradigm Repair." *Journal of Communication*, 55, no. 2 (2005): 225–41.

Hirsch, Marianne. *Family Frames: Photography, Narrative and Postmemory*. Cambridge, MA: Harvard University Press, 1995.

Holmes, Paul. "Reuters Toughens Rules after Altered Photo Affair." *Reuters*, January 18, 2007. www.reuters.com/article/idUSL18678707.

Hopkinson, Tom, Allen Hunt, and Derrick Knight. *Scoop, Scandal, and Strife: A Study of Photography in Newspapers*. Edited by Ken Baynes. New York: Hastings House, 1971.

Hoskins, Andrew, and Ben O'Loughlin. *War and Media: The Emergence of Diffused War*. Cambridge: Polity, 2010.

Howe, Peter. "Photojournalism at a Crossroads." *Nieman Reports* 55, no. 3 (September 15, 2001): 25–26.

Howell, Joel D. *Technology in the Hospital: Transforming Patient Care in the Early Twentieth Century*. Baltimore: Johns Hopkins University Press, 1996.

Hughes, Holly Stuart. "At 50 Years, World Press Photo Looks Back and Ahead." *Editor & Publisher*, October 13, 2005.

Ilan, Jonathan. "The Best of Both Worlds." *Media History* 19, no. 1 (2013): 74–92.

Irby, Kenneth. "*L.A. Times* Photographer Fired over Altered Image." Poynter.org. April 2, 2003. www.poynter.org/how-tos/writing/9289/l-a-times-photographer-fired-over-altered-image/.

Jaeger, Anne-Celine. "25 Years of Visa Pour l'Image: A Tribute to Jean-François Leroy." Time.com, *Lightbox*, August 27, 2013. http://time.com/3801827 /25-years-of-visa-pour-limage-a-tribute-to-jean-francois-leroy/.

———. 2010. *Image Makers, Image Takers*. London: Thames & Hudson.

Jain, Kajri. *Gods in the Bazaar: The Economies of Indian Calendar Art*. Durham NC: Duke University Press Books, 2007.

Jeffrey, Ian. *Photography: A Concise History*. New York and Toronto: Oxford University Press, 1981.

Jolly, David. "Lament for a Dying Field: Photojournalism." *New York Times*, August 9, 2009. www.nytimes.com/2009/08/10/business/media/10photo .html.

Katovsky, Bill, and Timothy Carlson. 2003. *Embedded: The Media at War in Iraq*. Guilford, CT: Lyons Press.

Kennedy, Dan. "The Daniel Pearl Video." *Nieman Reports*, September 15, 2002.

Kennedy, Liam. "'Follow the Americans': Philip Jones Griffiths's Vietnam War Trilogy." In *The Violence of the Image: Photography and International Conflict*, edited by Liam Kennedy and Caitlin Patrick, 34–59. London: I.B. Tauris, 2014.

———. "Seeing and Believing: On Photography and the War on Terror." *Public Culture* 24, no. 2 (2015): 261–81.

Kennedy, Liam, and Caitlin Patrick, eds. *The Violence of the Image: Photography and International Conflict*. London: I.B. Tauris, 2014.

Khatib, Lina. 2013. *Image Politics in the Middle East: The Role of the Visual in Political Struggle*. London and New York: I.B. Tauris.

King, J.C.H., and Henrietta Lidchi. *Imaging the Arctic*. Vancouver, BC: UBC Press, 1998.

Kinney, Katherine. *Friendly Fire: American Images of the Vietnam War*. New York: Oxford University Press, 2000.

Kleinman, Arthur, and Joan Kleinman. "The Appeal of Experience; The Dismay of Images: Cultural Appropriations of Suffering in Our Times." *Daedalus* 125, no. 1 (January 1, 1996): 1–23.

Klinenberg, Eric. "Convergence: News Production in a Digital Age." *Annals of the American Academy of Political and Social Science* 597 (2005): 48–64.

———. *Fighting for Air: The Battle to Control America's Media*. New York: Metropolitan Books, 2007.

Knightley, Phillip. *The First Casualty: The War Correspondent as Hero and Myth-Maker from the Crimea to Iraq*. Baltimore: Prion Books, 2004.

Kosnick, Kira. "'Foreign Voices': Multicultural Broadcasting and Immigrant Representation in Germany's Radio Multi Kulti." In *Radio Fields: Anthropology and Wireless Sound in the 21st Century*, edited by Lucas Bessire and Daniel Fisher. New York: New York University Press, 2012.

Kozol, Wendy. *Distant Wars Visible: The Ambivalence of Witnessing*. Minneapolis: University of Minnesota Press, 2014.

Kratz, Corinne. *The Ones That Are Wanted: Communication and the Politics of Representation in a Photographic Exhibition.* Berkeley: University of California Press, 2001.

Kraus, Dick. "Rest in Peace: Photojournalism Is Dead." *Digital Journalist,* 1999.

Kunreuther, Laura. *Voicing Subjects: Public Intimacy and Mediation in Kathmandu.* Berkeley: University of California Press, 2014.

Kuntsman, Adi, and Rebecca L. Stein. "Another War Zone: New Media and the Israeli-Palestinian Conflict." *Middle East Research and Information Project,* September 2010. www.merip.org/mero/interventions/another-war-zone.

———. *Digital Militarism: Israel's Occupation in the Social Media Age.* Stanford, CA: Stanford University Press, 2015.

Lacayo, Richard, and George Russell. *Eyewitness: 150 Years of Photojournalism.* New York: Time Life/Oxmoor House, 1990.

Laclau, Ernesto, and Chantal Mouffe. *Hegemony and Socialist Strategy.* London: Verso, 1985.

La Fontaine, Jean S. *Initiation: Ritual Drama and Secret Knowledge across the World.* Manchester, UK: Manchester University Press, 1985.

Landau, Paul Stuart, and Deborah D. Kaspin. *Images and Empires: Visuality in Colonial and Postcolonial Africa.* Berkeley: University of California Press, 2002.

Landsberg, Mitchell. "Negatives Aside, Photographer of Iwo Jima Fame Feels Worthwhile." *Los Angeles Times,* February 12, 1995.

Larkin, Brian. *Signal and Noise: Media, Infrastructure, and Urban Culture in Nigeria.* Durham, NC: Duke University Press Books, 2008.

Latour, Bruno. *On the Modern Cult of the Factish Gods.* Durham, NC; and London: Duke University Press, 2010.

Laurent, Olivier C. "A Guide to Visa Pour l'Image and Perpignan—2013 Edition." Accessed May 16, 2015. http://olivierclaurent.tumblr.com/post/58687529720/a-guide-to-visa-pour-limage-and-perpignan-2013.

———. "David Guttenfelder: The Photographer as Explorer." *Time,* July 9, 2014. http://time.com/3810477/david-guttenfelder-the-photographer-as-explorer/.

———. "Getty Images Makes 35 Million Images Free to Use." *British Journal of Photography.* Accessed November 24, 2015. www.bjp-online.com/2014/03/getty-images-makes-35-million-images-free-in-fight-against-copyright-infringement/.

———. "How Photographers Are Using Instagram to Help Nepal." Time.com. Accessed June 28, 2015. http://time.com/3851836/nepal-instagram-project/.

———. "Learn How World Press Photo Plans to Evolve into a Think Tank." *Time,* February 3, 2015. http://time.com/3692479/world-press-photo-lars-boering-interview/.

Laville, Camille. *Les transformations du journalisme de 1945 à 2010: Le cas des correspondants étrangers de l'AFP.* Brussels: De Boeck, 2010.

Lavoie, Vincent. *Photojournalismes: Revoir les canons de L'image de presse.* Paris: Hazan, 2010.

Lebeck, Robert, and Bodo von Dewitz. *Kiosk: A History of Photojournalism.* Göttingen: Steidl, 2001.

Liebes, Tamar, and Zohar Kampf. "The PR of Terror: The Media's Response to the War on Terrorism." In *Reporting War: Journalism in War Time,* edited by Stuart Allan and Barbie Zelizer, 77–95. London and New York: Routledge, 2004.

Light, Ken. *Witness in Our Time: Working Lives of Documentary Photographers.* Washington: Smithsonian Institution Press, 2000.

Linfield, Susan. *The Cruel Radiance: Photography and Political Violence.* Chicago: University of Chicago Press, 2010.

Llewellen, Patrick. "Visa Pour l'Image: A Guide to Portfolio Reviews." *InFocus by Getty Images.* Accessed May 15, 2015. http://infocus.gettyimages.com /post/visa-pour-limage-a-guide-to-portfolio-reviews#.VVZFDofHJxu.

Lopez, Alfred J. "Introduction: The (Post) Global South." *Global South* 1, no. 1 (January 1, 2007): 1–11.

Lutz, Catherine, and Jane Lou Collins. *Reading National Geographic.* Chicago: University of Chicago Press, 1993.

Lydon, Jane. *Eye Contact: Photographing Indigenous Australians.* Durham, NC: Duke University Press, 2006.

Maas, Peter. "The Toppling." *New Yorker,* January 3, 2011. www.newyorker .com/magazine/2011/01/10/the-toppling.

MacClancy, Jeremy. *Exotic No More: Anthropology on the Front Lines.* Chicago: University of Chicago Press, 2002.

Machin, David. "Building the World's Visual Language: The Increasing Global Importance of Image Banks in Corporate Media." *Visual Communication* 3, no. 3 (2004): 316–36.

Machin, David, and Sarah Niblock. *News Production: Theory and Practice.* London: Routledge, 2006.

Mahon, Maureen. "The Visible Evidence of Cultural Producers." *Annual Review of Anthropology* 29 (2000): 467–92.

Malkki, Liisa H. "National Geographic: The Rooting of Peoples and the Territorialization of National Identity among Scholars and Refugees." *Cultural Anthropology* 7, no. 1 (February 1992): 24–44.

———. "News and Culture: Transitory Phenomena and the Fieldwork Tradition." In *Anthropological Locations: Boundaries and Grounds of a Field Science,* edited by Akhil Gupta and James Ferguson. Berkeley: University of California Press, 1997.

Mandel, Ruth. "A Marshall Plan of the Mind: The Political Economy of a Kazakh Soap Opera." In *Media Worlds: Anthropology on New Terrain,* edited by Faye D. Ginsburg, Lila Abu-Lughod, and Brian Larkin, 211–28. Berkeley: University of California Press, 2002.

Mankekar, Purnima. *Screening Culture, Viewing Politics: An Ethnography of Television, Womanhood, and Nation in Postcolonial India.* Durham, NC: Duke University Press, 1999.

Marcus, George E. *Ethnography through Thick and Thin.* Princeton, NJ: Princeton University Press, 1998.

Marcus, George E., and Michael M. J. Fischer. *Anthropology as Cultural Critique: An Experimental Moment in the Human Sciences.* Chicago: University of Chicago Press, 1986.

Marcus, George E., and Fred R. Myers. *The Traffic in Culture: Refiguring Art and Anthropology.* Berkeley: University of California Press, 1995.

Marien, Mary Warner. *Photography: A Cultural History.* Upper Saddle River, NJ: Pearson Prentice Hall, 2011.

Masco, Joseph. *The Nuclear Borderlands: The Manhattan Project in Post-Cold War New Mexico.* Princeton, NJ: Princeton University Press, 2006.

Mayer, Vicki, Miranda J. Banks, and John T. Caldwell, eds. *Production Studies: Cultural Studies of Media Industries.* New York: Routledge, 2009.

Mazzarella, William. *Shoveling Smoke: Advertising and Globalization in Contemporary India.* Durham, NC: Duke University Press, 2003.

McChesney, Robert, and John Nichols. *The Death and Life of American Journalism: The Media Revolution That Will Begin the World Again.* New York: Nation Books, 2010.

McChesney, Robert, and Victor Pickard, eds. *Will the Last Reporter Please Turn Out the Lights: The Collapse of Journalism and What Can Be Done To Fix It.* New York: New Press, 2011.

Mead, Margaret. "Visual Anthropology in a Discipline of Words." In *Principles of Visual Anthropology,* edited by Paul Hockings, 3–10. Berlin and New York: Mouton de Gruyter, 1995.

Meijer, Emile, and Joop Swart, eds. *The Photographic Memory—Twelve Insights.* London: Quiller Press, 1988.

Meyer, Philip. *The Vanishing Newspaper: Saving Journalism in the Information Age.* Columbia: University of Missouri Press, 2004.

Miller, Russell. *Magnum: Fifty Years at the Front Line of History.* New York: Grove Press, 1997.

Mirzoeff, Nicholas. *An Introduction to Visual Culture.* London: Routledge, 2000.

Mitchell, Timothy. *Rule of Experts: Egypt, Techno-Politics, Modernity.* Berkeley: University of California Press, 2002.

Mitchell, W. J. T. *Cloning Terror: The War of Images, 9/11 to the Present.* Chicago: University of Chicago Press, 2011.

———. "Interdisciplinarity and Visual Culture." *Art Bulletin* 77, no. 4 (1995): 540–44.

———. *Picture Theory: Essays on Verbal and Visual Representation.* Chicago: University of Chicago Press, 1994.

———. *What Do Pictures Want? The Lives and Loves of Images.* Chicago: University of Chicago Press, 2005.

Moeller, Susan D. *Compassion Fatigue: How the Media Sell Disease, Famine, War, and Death.* New York: Routledge, 1999.

———. *Shooting War: Photography and the American Experience of Combat.* New York: Basic Books, 1989.

Molotch, Harvey, and Marilyn Lester. "News as Purposive Behavior: On the Strategic Use of Routine Events, Accidents and Scandals." *American Sociological Review* 39, no. 1 (n.d.): 101–12.

Morris, John. *Get the Picture: A Personal History of Photojournalism.* Chicago: University of Chicago Press, 1998.

Mortensen, Mette. *Journalism and Eyewitness Images: Digital Media, Participation, and Conflict.* London: Routledge, 2014.

Murabayashi, Allen. "How the Internet Killed Photojournalism." *PhotoShelter Blog,* August 30, 2013. http://blog.photoshelter.com/2013/05/how-the-internet-killed-photojournalism/.

Myers, Fred R., ed. *The Empire of Things: Regimes of Value and Material Culture.* Santa Fe, NM: School of American Research Press; Oxford: James Currey, 2001.

Nacos, Brigitte L. *Mass-Mediated Terrorism: The Central Role of the Media in Terrorism and Counterterrorism.* Lanham, MD: Rowman & Littlefield, 2007.

Nader, Laura. "Up the Anthropologist: Perspectives Gained from Studying Up." In *Reinventing Anthropology,* edited by Dell Hymes, 284–311. New York: Pantheon Books, 1972.

Newhall, Beaumont. *The History of Photography: From 1839 to the Present.* New York and Boston: The Museum of Modern Art, 1982.

New York Times Editorial Board. "Stumbling Into a Wider War." *New York Times,* May 3, 2015, sec. SR.

Newton, Julianne Hickerson. *The Burden of Visual Truth: The Role of Photojournalism in Mediating Reality.* Mahwah, NJ: Routledge, 2001.

O'Neill, Claire. "Is Photojournalism Dead? We Almost Hate to Ask." NPR.org. Accessed November 18, 2015. www.npr.org/sections/pictureshow/2010/08/18/129284174/madagascar.

Ortner, Sherry. "Access: Reflections on Studying up in Hollywood." *Ethnography* 11, no. 2 (2010): 211–33.

———. *New Jersey Dreaming: Capital, Culture, and the Class of '58.* Durham, NC: Duke University Press, 2003.

Özyürek, Esra. 2004. "Miniaturizing Atatürk: Privatization of State Imagery and Ideology in Turkey." *American Ethnologist* 31, no. 3 (2004): 374–91.

Palmer, Michael. "International Stories from Paris- and London-Based Newsrooms." *Journalism Studies* 9, no. 5 (October 2008): 813–21.

Pantti, Mervi. "Seeing and Not Seeing the Syrian Crisis: New Visibility and the Visual Framing of the Syrian Conflict in Seven Newspapers and Their Online Editions." *JOMEC Journal: Journalism, Media and Cultural Studies,* no. 4 (November 2013): 1–22.

Pantti, Mervi, and Stefanie Sirén. "The Fragility of Photo-Truth: Verification of Amateur Images in Finnish Newsrooms." *Digital Journalism* 3, no. 4 (2015): 495–512.

Panzer, Mary, and Christian Caujolle. *Things As They Are: Photojournalism in Context since 1955.* New York: Aperture, 2006.

"Parliament Squeezes AFP into EU Straitjacket." SUD-AFP.org, April 2, 2015. Accessed November 14, 2015. www.sud-afp.org/spip.php?article344.

Parry, Katy. "Images of Liberation? Visual Framing, Humanitarianism and British Press Photography during the 2003 Iraq Invasion." *Media, Culture & Society* 33, no. 8 (2011): 1185–1201.

Passaro, Joanne. "'You Can't Take the Subway to the Field!': 'Village' Epistemologies in the Global Village." In *Anthropological Locations: Boundaries and Grounds of a Field Science,* edited by Akhil Gupta and James Ferguson, 147–62. Berkeley: University of California Press, 1997.

Paul, Christopher, and James J. Kim. *Reporters on the Battlefield: The Embedded Press System in Historical Context.* Santa Monica, CA: RAND, 2004.

Pedelty, Mark. *War Stories: The Culture of Foreign Correspondents.* New York: Routledge, 1995.

"Pentagon: South Korean Hostage Beheaded." CNN, June 23, 2004. www.cnn.com/2004/WORLD/meast/06/22/iraq.hostage/.

Perlmutter, David D. *Photojournalism and Foreign Policy: Icons of Outrage in International Crises.* New York: Praeger, 1998.

Perlmutter, David D., and John Maxwell Hamilton, eds. *From Pigeons to News Portals: Foreign Reporting and the Challenge of New Technology.* Baton Rouge: Louisiana State University Press, 2007.

Pfau, Michael, Michel Haigh, Mitchell Gettle, Michael Donnelly, Gregory Scott, Dana Warr, and Elaine Wittenberg. 2004. "Embedding Journalists in Military Combat Units: Impact on Newspaper Story Frames and Tone." *Journalism and Mass Communication Quarterly* 81, no. 1 (2004): 74–88.

Pigeat, Henri. *Le nouveau désordre mondial de l'information.* Paris: Hachette, 1987.

Pinney, Christopher. *Camera Indica: The Social Life of Indian Photographs.* Chicago: University of Chicago Press, 1998.

———. "The Parallel Histories of Anthropology and Photography." In *Anthropology and Photography, 1860–1920,* 1994.

Pinson, Stephen. *Speculating Daguerre: Art and Enterprise in the Work of L.J.M. Daguerre.* Chicago: University of Chicago Press, 2012.

Pogliano, Andrea. "Iconic Photographs in the Newsroom." *Sociologica* 2015, no. 1: 1–49.

Poole, Deborah. *Vision, Race and Modernity: A Visual Economy of the Andean Image World.* Princeton, NJ: Princeton University Press, 1997.

Poovey, Mary. *A History of the Modern Fact: Problems of Knowledge in the Sciences of Wealth and Society.* Chicago: University of Chicago Press, 1998.

"Press Briefing by Ari Fleischer." *White House Archives,* March 21, 2003. http://georgewbush-whitehouse.archives.gov/news/releases/2003/03/20030321-9.html.

Puech, Michel. "François Lochon, un patron-photographe à l'agence Gamma-Rapho." www.a-L-Oeil.info, April 25, 2010. www.a-l-oeil.info/blog/2010/04/25/un-patron-photographe-a-lagence-gamma-rapho/

———. "Keystone, Gamma, Rapho: Scandale ou miracle?" *Mediapart,* March 29, 2010. Accessed November 18, 2015. http://blogs.mediapart.fr/blog/michel-puech/290310/keystone-gamma-rapho-scandale-ou-miracle.

———. "Photojournalisme: Un Visa de combat?" Www.a-l-oeil.info, August 28, 2015. Accessed November 23, 2015. www.a-l-oeil.info/blog/2015/08/28/photojournalisme-un-visa-de-combat/.

———. "Photojournalisme: Un Visa entre grogne et espoir." www.a-l-oeil.info, September 8, 2015. Accessed November 23, 2015. www.a-l-oeil.info/blog/2015/09/08/photojournalisme-un-visa-entre-grogne-et-espoir/.

Punathambekar, Aswin. *From Bombay to Bollywood: The Making of a Global Media Industry.* New York: New York University Press, 2013.

Rabinow, Paul. *Anthropos Today: Reflections on Modern Equipment*. Princeton, NJ: Princeton University Press, 2003.

———. *French DNA: Trouble in Purgatory*. Chicago: University of Chicago Press, 1999.

Raiford, Leigh. *Imprisoned in a Luminous Glare: Photography and the African American Freedom Struggle*. Chapel Hill: University of North Carolina Press, 2013.

Rantanen, Terhi. "European News Agencies and Their Sources in the Iraq War Coverage." In *Reporting War: Journalism in War Time*, edited by Stuart Allan and Barbie Zelizer, 301–14. London and New York: Routledge, 2004.

Ravi, Narasimhan. "Looking beyond Flawed Journalism: How National Interests, Patriotism, and Cultural Values Shaped the Coverage of the Iraq War." *Harvard International Journal of Press/Politics* 10, no. 1 (January 1, 2005): 45–62.

Read, Donald. "Don't Blame the Messengers: News Agencies Past and Present." *Historian* 69 (Spring 2001): 9–15.

———. *The Power of News: The History of Reuters*. Oxford, 1999.

"Reuters: La Rolls de L'info." *Le Nouvel Observateur,* August 1995.

Rigg, Jonathan. *An Everyday Geography of the Global South*. London and New York: Routledge, 2007.

Ritchin, Fred. *In Our Own Image: The Coming Revolution in Photography*. New York: Aperture, 1999.

Roger, Nathan. *Image Warfare in the War on Terror*. London: Palgrave Mac-Millan, 2013.

Rony, Fatimah Tobing. *The Third Eye: Race, Cinema and Ethnographic Spectacle*. Durham, NC; and London: Duke University Press, 1996.

Rosen, Philip. *Change Mummified: Cinema, Historicity, Theory*. Minneapolis: University of Minnesota Press, 2001.

Rosenblum, Naomi. *A World History of Photography*. New York: Abbeville Press, 1984.

Roussel, Frédérique. "Photojournaliste, un métier rongé par la précarité." *Libération,* September 5, 2015. www.liberation.fr/ecrans/2015/09/05/photojournaliste-un-metier-ronge-par-la-precarite_1375629.

Ruby, Jay. *Picturing Culture: Explorations of Film and Anthropology*. Chicago: University of Chicago Press, 2000.

Rumsfeld, Donald H. "DoD News Briefing: Secretary Rumsfeld and Gen. Myers." News Briefing, March 21, 2003. www.defense.gov/transcripts/transcript.aspx?transcriptid = 2074.

Russell, Adrienne. "Salon.com and New-Media Professional Journalism Culture." In *The Anthropology of News and Journalism: Global Perspectives,* edited by S. Elizabeth Bird, 270–82. Bloomington and Indianapolis: Indiana University Press, 2010.

Ryan, James. *Picturing Empire: Photography and the Visualization of the British Empire*. Chicago: University of Chicago Press, 1997.

Said, Edward W. *Orientalism*. New York: Vintage Books, 1979.

Sandeen, Eric J. "The Family of Man in Guatemala." *Visual Studies* 30, no. 2 (2015): 123–30.

———. *Picturing an Exhibition: The Family of Man and 1950s America.* Albuquerque: University of New Mexico Press, 1995.

Sarkisova, Oksana, and Olga Shevchenko. "Soviet Past in Domestic Photography: Events, Evidence, Erasure." New Brunswick, NJ: Transaction, 2014.

Saunders, Barry F. *CT Suite: The Work of Diagnosis in the Age of Noninvasive Cutting.* Durham, NC: Duke University Press. 2008.

Schlesinger, Philip. *Putting "Reality" Together: BBC News.* London: Constable, 1991.

Schudson, Michael. *Discovering the News.* New York: Basic Books, 1978.

———. *The Sociology of News.* 2nd ed. New York and London: W.W. Norton and Company, 2011.

Schwalbe, Carol B. "Visually Framing the Invasion and Occupation of Iraq in *Time, Newsweek,* and *US News & World Report.*" *International Journal of Communication* 7 (2013): 239–62.

Schwartz, Dona. "Objective Representation: Photographs as Facts." In *Picturing the Past: Media, History, and Photography,* edited by Bonnie Brennen and Hanno Hardt, 158–81. Urbana: University of Illinois Press, 1999.

———. "To Tell the Truth: Codes of Objectivity in Photojournalism." *Communication* 13, no. 2 (1992): 95–109.

Schwenkel, Christina. *The American War in Contemporary Vietnam: Transnational Remembrance and Representation.* Bloomington: Indiana University Press, 2009.

Seels, Barbara, Barbara Good, and Louis Berry. "Recognition and Interpretation of Historically Significant News Photographs." *Journal of Visual Literacy* 19, no. 2 (October 1999): 125–38.

Seib, Philip. *Beyond the Front Lines: How the News Media Cover a World Shaped by War.* New York: Palgrave MacMillan, 2004.

Sekula, Allan. "On the Invention of Photographic Meaning." Halifax: Press of the Nova Scotia College of Arts and Design, 1984. 1

———. "The Traffic in Photographs." *Art Journal* 41, no. 1 (1981): 15–21.

Shankar, Shalini. "Creating Model Consumers: Producing Ethnicity, Race, and Class in Asian American Advertising." *American Ethnologist* 39, no. 3 (2012): 578–91.

Sheehan, Tanya, and Andrés Mario Zervigón. *Photography and Its Origins.* London and New York: Routledge, 2015.

Shields, David. *War Is Beautiful: The "New York Times" Pictorial Guide to the Glamour of Armed Conflict*.* New York: powerHouse Books, 2015.

Shryock, Andrew, ed. *Off Stage/On Display: Intimacy and Ethnography in the Age of Public Culture.* Stanford, CA: Stanford University Press, 2004.

"Significant Layoffs at *National Geographic* Magazine | NPPA." Accessed November 24, 2015. https://nppa.org/news/significant-layoffs-national-geographic-magazine.

Sliwinski, Sharon. *Human Rights in Camera.* Chicago: University of Chicago Press, 2011

Smith, Shawn Michelle. *American Archives: Gender, Race, and Class in Visual Culture.* Princeton, N.J.: Princeton University Press, 1999.

Solnit, Rebecca. *River of Shadows: Eadweard Muybridge and the Technological Wild West.* New York: Viking Adult, 2003.

Sonnevend, Julia. "Global Iconic Events: How News Stories Travel through Time, Space and Media," PhD diss., Columbia University, 2013.

Sontag, Susan. "Looking at War." *New Yorker,* December 9, 2002. www .newyorker.com/magazine/2002/12/09/looking-at-war.

———. *On Photography.* New York: Noonday Press, 1989.

———. *Regarding the Pain of Others.* New York: Farrar, Straus and Giroux, 2004.

Stepan, Peter. *Photos That Changed the World.* Munich and New York: Prestel, 2006.

Strassler, Karen. *Refracted Visions: Popular Photography and National Modernity in Java.* Durham, NC: Duke University Press, 2010.

Sturken, Marita. *Tangled Memories: The Vietnam War, the AIDS Epidemic, and the Politics of Remembering.* Berkeley: University of California Press, 1997.

Sullivan, Bill. "The Real Thing: Photographer Luc Delahaye." *Artnet,* April 10, 2003. www.artnet.com/magazine/features/sullivan/sullivan4-10-03.asp.

Tagg, John. *The Burden of Representation: Essays on Photographies and Histories.* Minneapolis: University of Minnesota Press, 1988.

Talbot, William Henry Fox. *The Pencil of Nature.* New York: H.P. Kraus, 1989.

Taussig, Michael T. *Mimesis and Alterity: A Particular History of the Senses.* New York: Routledge, 1993.

Taylor, Janelle S. *The Public Life of the Fetal Sonogram: Technology, Consumption and the Politics of Reproduction.* New Brunswick, NJ: Rutgers University Press, 2008.

Taylor, John. *Body Horror: Photojournalism, Catastrophe and War.* Manchester, UK: Manchester University Press, 1998.

Tinic, Serra. *On Location: Canada's Television Industry in a Global Market.* Toronto: University of Toronto Press, 2004.

Tuchman, Gaye. *Making News: A Study in the Construction of Reality.* New York: Free Press, 1978.

Tumber, Howard, and Jerry Palmer. *The Media at War: The Iraq Crisis.* London and Thousand Oaks, CA: Sage Publications, 2004.

Tunstall, Jeremy. *Journalists at Work: Specialist Correspondents; Their News Organizations, News Sources, and Competitor-Colleagues.* Beverly Hills, CA: Sage Publications, 1978.

Turner, Fred. "The Family of Man and the Politics of Attention in Cold War America." *Public Culture* 24, no. 1 (2012): 55–84.

Turner, Victor. *The Forest of Symbols: Aspects of Ndembu Ritual.* Ithaca, NY: Cornell University Press, 1967.

U.S. Department of Defense. "Public Affairs Guidance (PAG) on Embedding Media during Possible Future Operations/Deployments in the U.S." February 3, 2003. www.fas.org/sgp/othergov/dod/embed.html.

Usher, Nikki. *Making News at* The New York Times. Ann Arbor: University of Michigan Press, 2014.

Vaina, David. "The Vanishing Embedded Reporter in Iraq." *Pew Research Center: Journalism and Media,* October 26, 2006. *Journalism Project.* Accessed November 13. www.journalism.org/2006/10/26/the-vanishing-embedded-reporter-in-iraq/.

Van Riper, Frank. "Manipulating Truth, Losing Credibility." *Washingtonpost. com, Camera Works,* 2003. www.washingtonpost.com/wp-srv/photo /essays/vanRiper/030409.htm.

Van Veeren, Elspeth. "Captured by the Camera's Eye: Guantanamo and the Shifting Frame of the Global War on Terror." *Review of International Studies* 37, no. 4 (2010): 1721–49.

Vesperi, Maria D. "When Common Sense No Longer Holds: The Shifting Locus of News Production in the United States." In *The Anthropology of News and Journalism: Global Perspectives,* edited by S. Elizabeth Bird, 257–69. Bloomington and Indianapolis: Indiana University Press, 2009.

Vidali-Spitulnik, Debra. "'A House of Wires upon Wires': Sensuous and Linguistic Entanglements of Evidence and Epistemologies in the Study of Radio Culture." In *Radio Fields: Anthropology and Wireless Sound in the 21st Century,* edited by Lucas Bessire and Daniel Fisher, 250–67. New York: New York University Press, 2012.

Vitale, Ami, and Manik Katyal. "A Conversation with Ami Vitale." *World Literature Today* 87, no. 2 (2013): 88–93.

Vobič, Igor, and Ilija Tomanić Trivundža. "The Tyranny of the Empty Frame." *Journalism Practice,* April 20, 2015, 1–18.

Warner, Michael. *Publics and Counterpublics.* New York: Zone Books, 2005.

Washington, Oliver Burkeman. "Obama Administration to End Use of Term 'War on Terror.'" *Guardian.* Accessed January 21, 2015. www.theguardian.com /world/2009/mar/25/obama-war-terror-overseas-contingency-operations.

Wheeler, Thomas H. *Phototruth or Photofiction? Ethics and Media Imagery in the Digital Age.* Mahwah, NJ: Lawrence Erblaum Associates, 2002.

White, David Manning. "The Gate Keeper: A Case Study in the Selection of News." *Journalism Quarterly* 27, no. 4 (1950): 383–91.

Wilk, Richard R. "Television, Time and the National Imaginary in Belize." In *Media Worlds: Anthropology on New Terrain,* edited by Lila Abu-Lughod, Faye Ginsburg, and Brian Larkin, 171–87. Berkeley, CA: University of California Press, 2002.

Wilkins, Chris. "Photojournalist or Pack Mule? A Look Back at the Good Old Days of Wire Service Photography." *Dallas Morning News,* July 12, 2012. http://photographyblog.dallasnews.com/2012/07/photojournalist-or-pack-mule-a-look-back-at-the-good-old-days-of-wire-service-photography .html/.

Williams, Linda. *Screening Sex.* Durham, NC: Duke University Press, 2008.

Williams, Raymond. *Keywords: A Vocabulary of Culture and Society.* New York: Oxford University Press, 1976.

Winegar, Jessica. "Of Chadors and Purple Fingers: US Visual Media Coverage of the 2005 Iraqi Elections." *Feminist Media Studies* 5, no. 3 (2005): 391–95.

Winseck, Dwayne R., and Robert M. Pike. *Communication and Empire: Media, Markets, and Globalization, 1860–1930.* Durham, NC; and London: Duke University Press, 2007.

Winslow, Donald R. "The Pulitzer Eddie Adams Didn't Want." *Lens* (blog), April 19, 2011. Accessed May 13, 2015. http://lens.blogs.nytimes.com/2011/04/19/the-pulitzer-eddie-adams-didnt-want/.

World Press Photo Foundation, *90 Photojournalists Participated in the World Press Photo's Two-Year Workshop Program Organized in Seven Countries, 2001–2003.* Amsterdam, 2004.

Wright, Richard. 2004. "Assessment of the DoD Embedded Media Program." Alexandria, VA: Institute for Defense Analyses.

Yang, Wayne. "Interview with Hal Buell, Former Head of the Associated Press Photography Service," July 3, 2006. www.takegreatpictures.com/photo-tips/tgp-choice/interview-with-hal-buell-former-head-of-the-associated-press-photography-service-br-br-by-wayne-yang.

Zarzycka, Marta, and Martijn Kleppe. "Awards, Archives and Affects: Tropes in the World Press Photo Contest 2009–2011." *Media, Culture & Society* 35, no. 8 (2013): 977–95.

Zelizer, Barbie. *About to Die: How News Images Move the Public.* New York: Oxford University Press, 2010.

———. "Journalism through the Camera's Eye." In *Journalism: Critical Issues,* edited by Stuart Allan, 167–76. Milton Keynes, UK: Open University Press, 2005.

———. "Journalism's 'Last' Stand: Wirephoto and the Discourse of Resistance." *Journal of Communication* 45, no. 2 (1995): 78–92.

———. "Journalists as Interpretive Communities." *Critical Studies in Mass Communication* 10, no. 3 (1993): 219–37.

———. "When Facts, Truth, and Reality Are God-Terms: On Journalism's Uneasy Place in Cultural Studies." *Communication and Critical Cultural Studies* 1, no. 1 (2004): 100–119.

———. "When War Is Reduced to a Photograph." In *Reporting War: Journalism in Wartime,* edited by Stuart Allan and Barbie Zelizer, 115–35. London and New York: Routledge, 2004.

———. "Words against Images." In *Newsworkers,* edited by Bonnie Brennen and Hanno Hardt, 135–59. Minneapolis: University of Minnesota Press, 1995.

Zervigón, Andrés Mario. "Rotogravure and the Modern Aesthetic of News Reporting." In *Getting the Picture: The Visual Culture of the News,* edited by Jason Hill and Vanessa R. Schwartz, 197–205. London: Bloomsbury Academic, 2015.

Index